D0948932

THE EXPLORERS

FROM THE ANCIENT WORLD TO THE PRESENT

JG PRESS

Christopher Colombus

James Cook

"**B**y striving to do the impossible, man has always achieved what is possible. Those who have cautiously done no more than they believed possible have never taken a single step forward"

(Mikhail Bakunin)

Marco Polo

Ferdinand Magellan

Text by:
Paolo Novaresio

Editorial production:
Valeria Manferto De Fabianis
Laura Accomazzo

Graphic design:
Patrizia Balocco Lovisetti

Translation:
Neil Frazer Davenport

My thanks to Alberto Salza for having discussed and written the introduction and for his advice when planning the book; Prof. Oscar Norwich of Johannesburg (South Africa) for having sent me his research findings on expeditions by the Chinese; Enrico Goasco and Roberta Lanzone for their help in re-reading and correcting the texts. Without precious contributions from them and many others, too numerous to name, writing this book would have been more difficult and its contents less inspiring.

The Publisher would like to thank Maria Rosa Biason Accomazzo for her precious help. Special thanks to Liliana Ferraro Greppi. Thanks even to Gertrude Nobile; Jacques Piccard; Bob Moore, Jefferson National Expansion Memorial; Susan Seyl, Oregon Historical Society; Becky Fryday, Media Services Corporation, NASA.

Title page: This print is taken from a 1537 work by the geographer Giovanni da Sacrobosco who is represented on the left using a world map as a writing desk.

Opposite: A navigator observing the stars with a cross-staff, an instrument used for measuring the altitude of the stars over the horizon and thereby calculating latitude.

© 2002,2004 by White Star S.p.A.

Published by World Publications Group, Inc.
140 Laurel Street
East Bridgewater, MA 02333
www.wrldpub.net

ISBN-13: 978-1-57215-485-8
ISBN-10: 1-57215-485-3

Printed and bound in China

1 3 5 7 9 10 8 6 4 2

Color separation by Fotomec, Turin

4

CONTENTS

Tropicvs Capricornj~

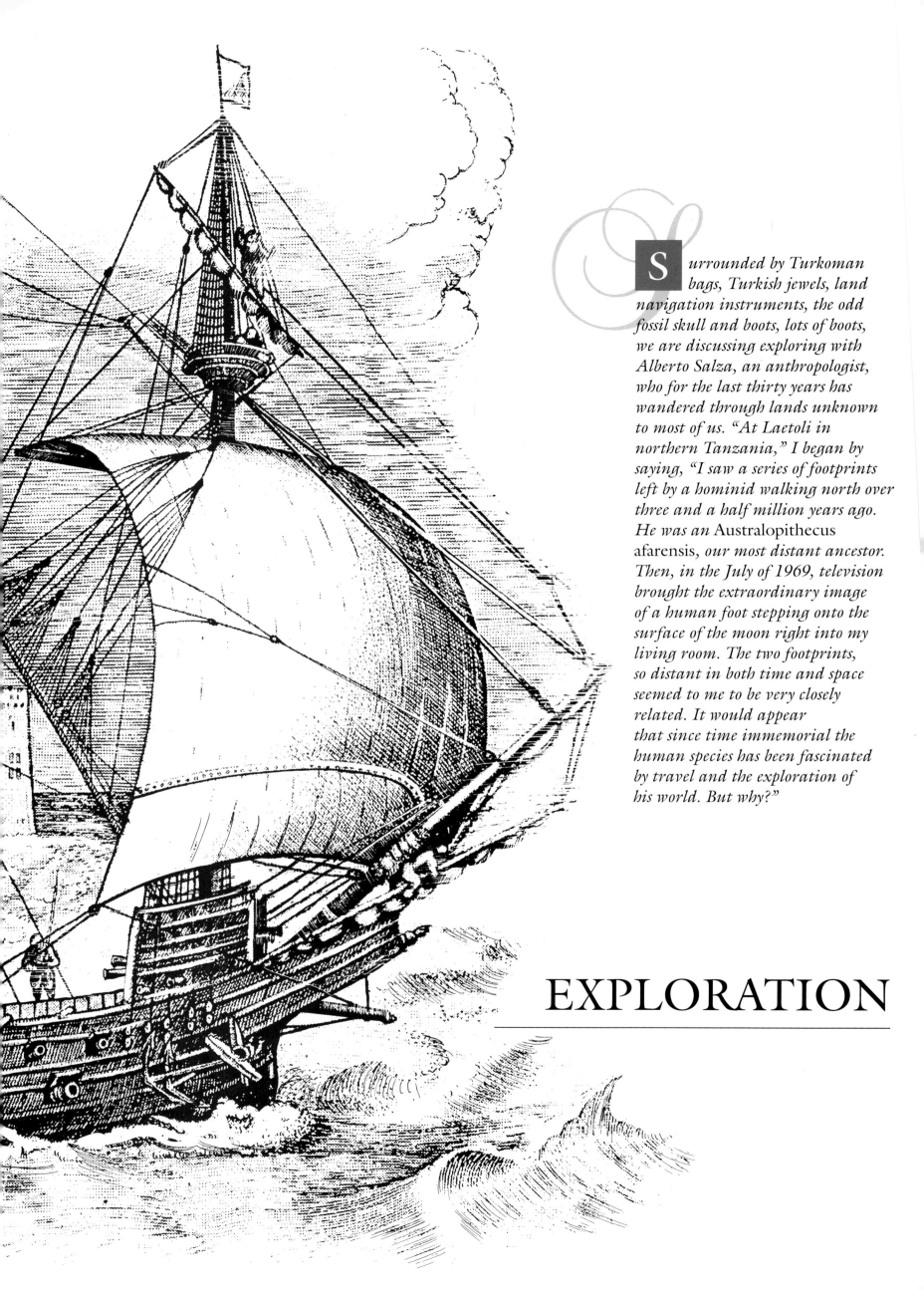

S urrounded by Turkoman bags, Turkish jewels, land navigation instruments, the odd fossil skull and boots, lots of boots, we are discussing exploring with Alberto Salza, an anthropologist, who for the last thirty years has wandered through lands unknown to most of us. "At Laetoli in northern Tanzania," I began by saying, "I saw a series of footprints left by a hominid walking north over three and a half million years ago. He was an Australopithecus afarensis, *our most distant ancestor. Then, in the July of 1969, television brought the extraordinary image of a human foot stepping onto the surface of the moon right into my living room. The two footprints, so distant in both time and space seemed to me to be very closely related. It would appear that since time immemorial the human species has been fascinated by travel and the exploration of his world. But why?"*

EXPLORATION

Above: The omphalos at Delphi, the sacred stone that marked the center of the Hellenic universe. All of the great civilizations of the past, the Greeks, the Egyptians, the Babylonians, and the Aztecs to name but a few, placed themselves in a central position in relation to their worlds. This "navel-gazing syndrome" and the consequent relationship with external space and its inhabitants pervades the history of the exploration of the Earth from the Egyptians' journeys to Punt to the discovery of the Antipodes (understood as sites diametrically opposed to Europe).

Center: The Laetoli "trail" in northern Tanzania. Two parallel rows of footprints stretching 89 feet that were made by our ancestor Australopithecus afarensis *over three and a half million years ago. The prints were made by three different individuals, one of whom placed his feet in the same marks left in the ashes by another of his species, almost as if it were a game.*

Bottom: The footprint left by Man's first step on the moon. Millions of people on the Earth were able to watch the historic event on television. "That's one small step for man, one giant leap for mankind" announced Neil Armstrong.

Picking up the plaster cast of the skull of a small *Australopithecus*, Salza replied: "It's the children's fault. We upright savannah apes required a larger brain to survive in a continuously mutating environment. Mutating and dangerous, moreover. However, given that we move on two legs (a form of locomotion rooted in catastrophe as we risk falling with each step), there is a structural limit to the width of our pelvis. The mothers of three million years ago, just like those of today, wanted very clever kids with large brains. But they risked their lives during labor due to their offspring's large cranium. Evolutionary adaptation thus led our ancestors to give birth to babies with immature skulls. What I am trying to say is that the first hominids of the genus *Homo* needed a couple of years following birth before their brains were fully developed. Just like our own babies. A child is a machine for exploring. Nowadays he is better protected, but until recently, anthropologically speaking, a child had to learn very quickly all that it needed for survival. Compared with its chimpanzee cousins, our baby's brain develops within the environment in which it lives, adapting in accordance with various experiences. A chimpanzee, whether born in the wild or in a zoo, has a preprogrammed brain (and therefore a basic behavioral pattern).

7

It is adapted to live in its natural environment. The human baby, on the other hand, immediately begins to modify itself and its behavior as it encounters the various environmental stimuli."

"It's not a difficult task for a baby," continued Salza, "yet everybody assumes that such a young creature should be protected from the environment rather than being left free to explore it."

"We are social and cultural animals. The transmission of culture through language mitigates the dangers: this is what we call 'education.' However, in an experiment carried out with mice (frequently used by behaviorists because of their 'human' behavioral patterns), it was observed that if manipulated and stimulated from an early age, the baby mice greatly increased their explorative habits. For example, they would cross a room diagonally rather than following the walls. Given a moderate degree of stimulation (avoiding exaggeration), the mice became explorers, overcoming their fear of open spaces that is also very common among humans."

"It would seem, then, that in the infantile phase we are all explorers," I said. "What is the mechanism that allows us to continue to explore as adults?"

"Play. Play is the only non-productive animal activity. That is to say, it represents a consumption of energy with no immediate return. Never mind within the ambit of macroeconomics and politics, this would also appear to be a mistake in day-to-day life. However, play has an exceptional characteristic: the activity not only prepares us for adult behavioral patterns (sexual roles, socialization and the procuring of food etc.), but also leads to an

Above: Ptolemy, a geographer and astronomer who lived in Egypt during the 2nd century AD, divided the world into 360 degrees, suggesting a method for establishing longitude and latitude, and projected the curved form of the Earth on a flat surface. Although in many cases his work was based on erroneous presuppositions, it marked the birth of scientific cartography and influenced geographers and astronomers for almost 1500 years.

Bottom: The map reproduced here was published in the 15th century and is now kept in the Marciana Library in Venice. Europe and the Mediterranean are represented with a reasonable degree of accuracy, while Africa appears as a stumpy, enlarged shape, and the Indian Ocean is drawn as an enclosed sea with the mysterious Terra Australis Incognita *to the south.*

experimentation with new, anomalous, and non-stereotypical patterns. It is through these innovations that we arrive at exploration and invention. Discovery is another matter: it signifies putting together or finding something that already exists. The exploration of the Earth leads to discoveries, whereas exploration within the ambit of play leads to invention."

"Explorers are therefore people somewhat out of the ordinary, but with less potential than a small child," I said.

"To a certain extent this is true. Although we take as given the fact that migratory behavior, and thus nomadism, is written into genetic code (true in part), not all individuals try to overcome the stereotype of the milieu in which they are born. The explorers have always been dislocated individuals (before they even depart), anomalous and outsiders. In some way they remain 'children,' with their minds free of the inhibitions of the society in which they live. They are essentially ignorant. They don't know what there is on the other side of the room, but it is there that they want to go, maybe as a result of escape anxiety. They are all babes in the woods, not abandoned (not always at least), but voluntary wanderers. An explorer is a creator of worlds: worlds that never existed before he found them (within the explorer's culture of course). In this sense explorations are crossed: the Arabs explored us while we went to see Jerusalem; the Egyptians went to the land of Punt, where there were men exploring their own borders; the Aztecs sent

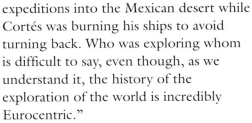

expeditions into the Mexican desert while Cortés was burning his ships to avoid turning back. Who was exploring whom is difficult to say, even though, as we understand it, the history of the exploration of the world is incredibly Eurocentric."

"In Latin *partire* means to divide," I said. "Leaving is akin to marking the passage from order into disorder. Goethe said 'leaving is a little like dying.' It would seem that exploring is a kind of personal catastrophe (that has frequently had environmental ramifications), that becomes an initiation into a higher level of humanity. Can exploration be a metaphor for the cognitive process?"

"There is more to it than that. It is something like the artistic process: exploration is creative. If we take quantum mechanics (bear with me here), we find that phenomena exist in an infinite number of possible states. It is only at the moment of observation that the universe assumes the physical state in which we know it. It is the explorer who creates the world, in the very moment in which he 'discovers' it and observes it. This is what God does in the Bible: Creation takes place on the seventh day when God 'contemplated' the world. Hardly a vacation (a word which, moreover, contains the concept of vacant or vacuum, an obsession with explorers). For an explorer the universe is polyvalent. As the quantum physician Finkelstein said: 'As well as a *Yes* and a *No*, the universe also contains a *Perhaps*. This is the explorers' planet Earth, and always has been."

Tabula orbis cum defcriptione ventorum.

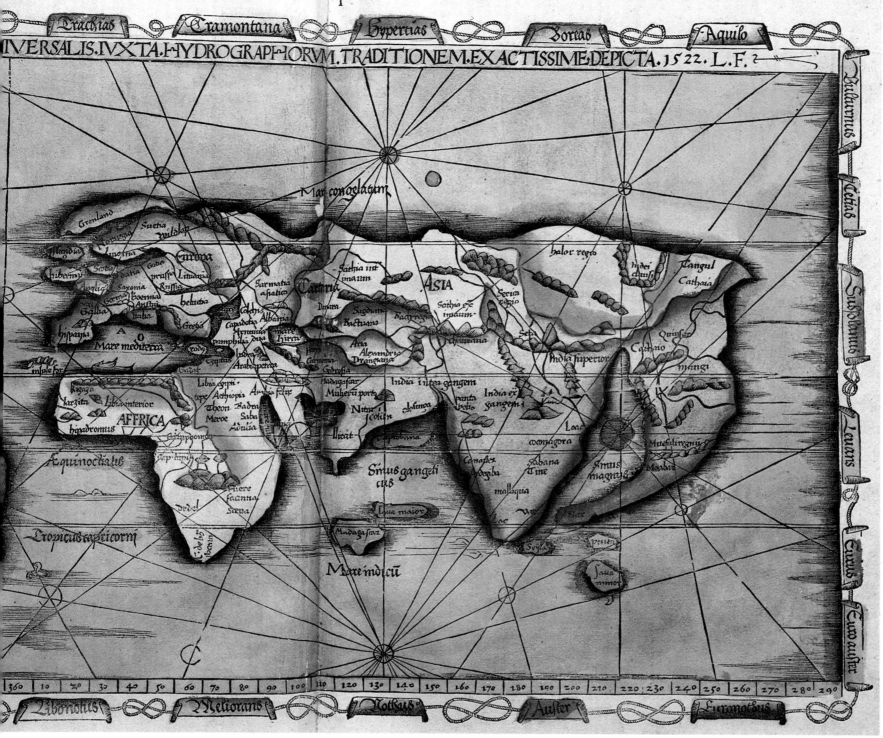

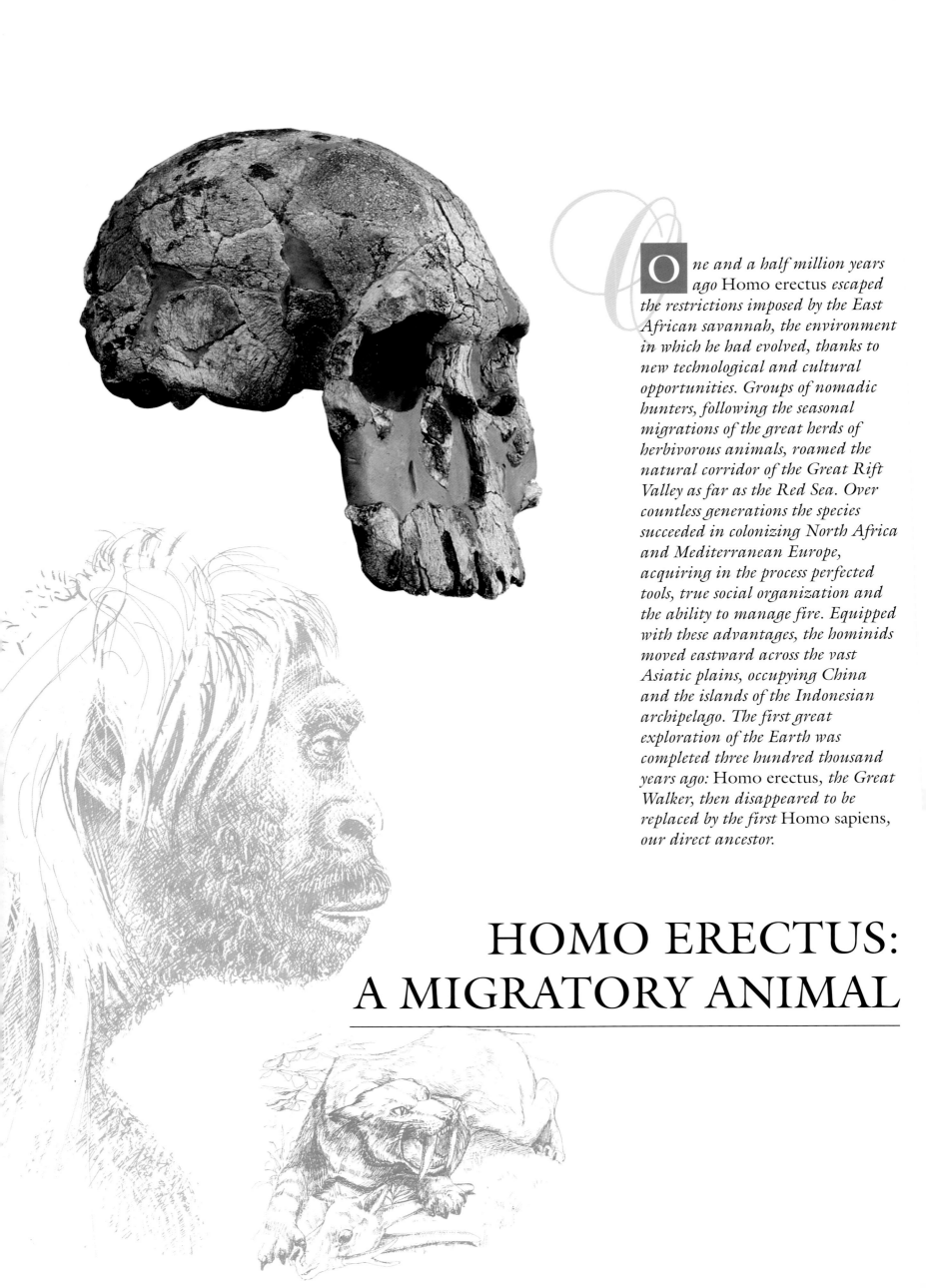

One and a half million years ago Homo erectus *escaped the restrictions imposed by the East African savannah, the environment in which he had evolved, thanks to new technological and cultural opportunities. Groups of nomadic hunters, following the seasonal migrations of the great herds of herbivorous animals, roamed the natural corridor of the Great Rift Valley as far as the Red Sea. Over countless generations the species succeeded in colonizing North Africa and Mediterranean Europe, acquiring in the process perfected tools, true social organization and the ability to manage fire. Equipped with these advantages, the hominids moved eastward across the vast Asiatic plains, occupying China and the islands of the Indonesian archipelago. The first great exploration of the Earth was completed three hundred thousand years ago:* Homo erectus, *the Great Walker, then disappeared to be replaced by the first* Homo sapiens, *our direct ancestor.*

HOMO ERECTUS: A MIGRATORY ANIMAL

A muscular body up to six feet tall, rather thickset, but not so different to our neighbor. And the face? Decidedly unattractive, according to the modern canons: a sloping forehead, a robust upper jaw, the merest hint of a chin and very protruberent eyebrows. The prototype of the person you would never want to share an elevator with. And yet this is none other than *Homo erectus*, the Great Walker, the species that colonized the world. Compared with his predecessors, the real novelty lay not in his physical features, but in his behavioral patterns. In contrast to *Homo habilis* from whom he descended, *Homo erectus* had a sophisticated brain: he hunted in groups, and shared the results; he regularly used stone, bone, and wooden tools and he knew how to use fire. He was no longer at the mercy of the environment, but was able to dominate it. In short, *Homo erectus*, inaugurated a new way of life. The story of hominization (the evolutionary process which led to the development of human beings) is frequently obscure. Anthropologists have taken on a thankless

Opposite: This fossil cranium of Homo habilis *KNM-Er 1470 (Kenya National Museum, East Rudolph, followed by the item number), was found on the eastern shore of Lake Turkana, rightly recognized as the "cradle of humanity." The fossil dates back over two and a half million years:* Homo habilis *was the inventor of flaked-stone technology that* Homo erectus *was to export throughout the world.*

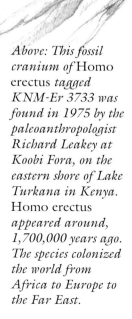

Above: This fossil cranium of Homo erectus *tagged KNM-Er 3733 was found in 1975 by the paleoanthropologist Richard Leakey at Koobi Fora, on the eastern shore of Lake Turkana in Kenya.* Homo erectus *appeared around, 1,700,000 years ago. The species colonized the world from Africa to Europe to the Far East.*

task: it is up to them to reconstruct the remote past of the human species on the basis of few, slender clues. Hominid fossils are rare. If those found so far were collected together in one place, they would barely fill a single museum display case. With such tenuous elements, the anthropologists can formulate hypotheses and put forward reliable models, but they have very little concrete information to work with. In paleoanthropology, phrases conditioned by "perhaps" or "might be" are the order of the day. *Homo erectus* appeared on the scene a little over 1,500,000 years ago and was to remain center stage until 300,000 years ago when he was replaced by *Homo sapiens*. During this vast period of time, *Homo erectus* gradually spread throughout the world, leaving traces from Spain to China. Once again, the story commenced in Africa, on the savannah of the Great Rift Valley, the immense break that divides the continent from the Red Sea to Mozambique. It was there that with the help of increasingly sophisticated technology,

13

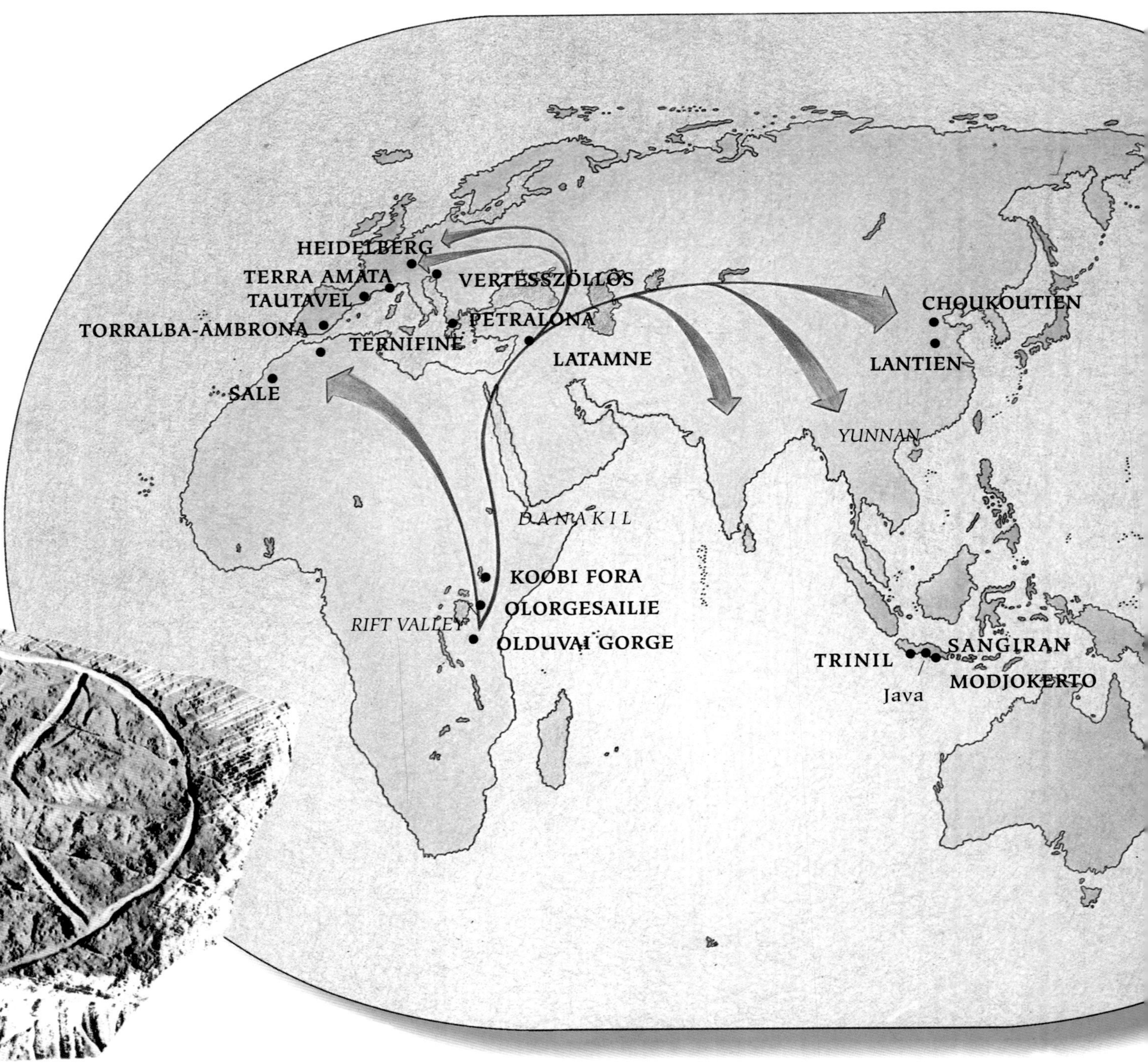
HEIDELBERG
TERRA AMATA
TAUTAVEL
TORRALBA-AMBRONA
TERNIFINE
SALE
VERTESSZÖLLÖS
PETRALONA
LATAMNE
CHOUKOUTIEN
LANTIEN
YUNNAN
DANAKIL
KOOBI FORA
OLORGESAILIE
RIFT VALLEY
OLDUVAI GORGE
TRINIL
SANGIRAN
MODJOKERTO
Java

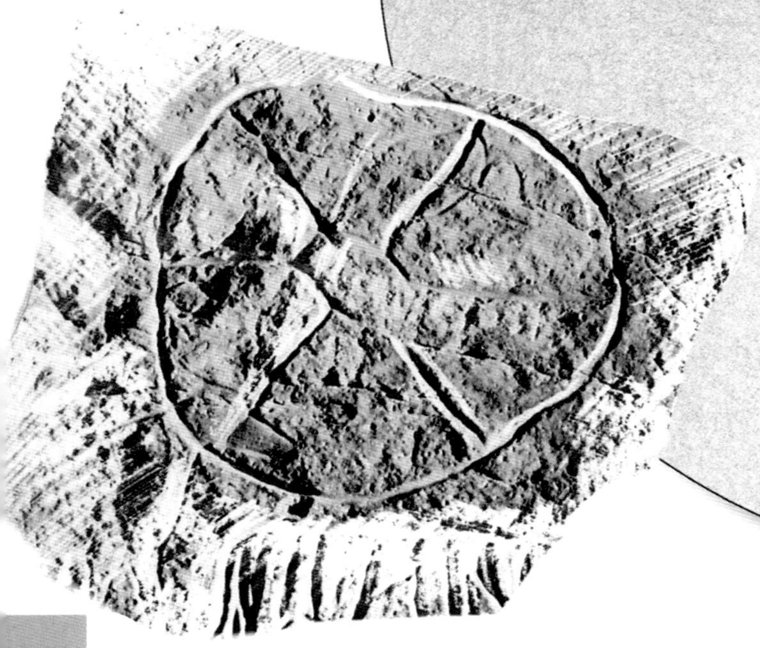

Homo erectus became a superpredator, taking over the role of the big cats. The technique of hunting in groups brought in large quantities of meat which, when combined with the products of gathering (wild tubers and fruit), provided the species with a considerable food surplus. Tranquil and well-fed, *Homo erectus* spent his free time engaged in the rather more pleasurable activity of reproduction. Over time the demographical increase generated an imbalance between the resident population and the available resources. The Rift Valley began to seem overcrowded, and at this point a new mechanism was set in motion. As happens with lions, the young males were gradually emarginated. Obliged to seek out new resources, they followed the migrations of the herbivores and ventured into unknown territory. They became nomads. The most innovative among them, those least tied to stereotypical patterns of behavior, preceded the other members of the group: these were the first explorers. The environmental conditions and the high scarp slopes of the Rift Valley obliged the hominids to proceed along the North-South axis. Generation after generation, the nomadic hunters moved along the valley until they reached the Red Sea in the Danakil. The desert failed to halt the migration of *Homo erectus*, and by following the coast, he eventually reached the Mediterranean. One million years ago the species could be found in North Africa and the Middle East. Three hundred thousand years later *Homo erectus* had reached Italy. Isernia La Pineta is in the Molise region. In 1979 an amateur naturalist was passing the construction site for the Napoli-Vasto motorway when his attention was caught by a strange object protruding from a wall of earth brought to light during the excavations. The object was a fossilized elephant tusk. Further research has revealed a paleosoil of extraordinary richness: thousands of bones and stone tools piled up in an area of over 24,000 square yards. This was no accidental deposit: the bones, belonging to bison, rhinoceroses, elephants, bears, and deer, appear to be have been selected according to their shape and arranged to form a kind of trellis. The evidence of human activity is incontrovertible, but what was it that persuaded *Homo erectus* to engage in such titanic labors? Unfortunately, so far we have only been able to formulate hypotheses: Isernia could be all that remains of a scheme to reclaim a swamp. Alternatively the abundance of skulls and long broken bones suggest that it might have been the site of a tannery (the Bushmen of the Kalahari still use raw brain and bone marrow, which contain tannin, in the preparation of their skins). Furthermore, traces of red ochre have been found on a rock. This substance was used by most primitive people in rituals. This suggests that besides killing pachiderms and breaking bones with rocks, *Homo erectus* was taking his first steps in the spiritual world as long as 700,000 years ago. The sites of Tautavel, in the eastern Pyrenees, and Torralba and Ambrona on the Spanish plateau, bear witness to the expansion of our ancestors into the temperate regions of the Mediterranean

Above: This stone arrowhead is prehistoric and was found at Al Fayyum, Egypt. The production of stone tools opened up new horizons for our ancestors, allowing them to butcher the carcasses of large animals (otherwise inaccessible without suitable claws and teeth), thus providing them with large quantities of meat and bone marrow. The flaked-stone technology survived until very recent times in various regions of the Earth.

Right: The prints at Laetoli, including the one in this picture, are between 7 and 10 inches long, which allows us to deduce that they were made by individuals not more than five feet tall. The photogrammetric survey also allows us to establish beyond all reasonable doubt that the Laetoli hominids had achieved a fully erect posture three and half million years ago.

basin around 400,000 years ago. Fossil finds in the Ambrona valley have provided evidence of epic elephant hunts in which the animals were forced into nearby swamps by fires lit by the hominids. *Homo erectus* had learned to use fire to his own advantage, and such dangerous hunting activities undoubtedly required a high degree of social organization. Even more has been found at Terra Amata on the Côte d'Azur near Nice: the excavations, begun in 1966, have brought to light traces of numerous huts, 35,000 common utensils, and the first domestic hearth. There are no hominid fossils at Terra Amata, but *Homo erectus* left a footprint in the sand. The shape of the foot is similar to that of the tracks left in the ashes of Laetoli. Physically the species had not altered very much, but the inhabitants of the prehistoric Nice of 380,000 years ago were the protagonists in a decisive change of course: *Homo erectus* was beginning to take on a social lifestyle and make his first artistic impressions. After having overcome deserts, prairies, and mountains, and while the

European hominids successfully settled in the Mediterranean area, another branch of the migratory stream was tackling the journey eastward, across the Asian flatlands. We do not know what route *Homo erectus* followed to reach the mountains of Yunnan and northern China, but we do have proof that the caves of Choukoutien near Beijing were inhabited as early as 500,000 years ago for a period that lasted over 250,000 years. The hominids took refuge from the severe winters in the Choukoutien caverns, taking fire with them. A layer of ash 6 meters deep testifies to the fact that *Homo erectus* was skilled in managing fire and knew the secrets of combustion, even though he might not have been able to light a new blaze. The tools found at Choukoutien demonstrate constant technological progress: the efficacy of the techniques used for sharpening stone is highlighted by the huge quantiy of fossils, almost all of them being the bones and horns of the giant deer, a large fast animal and by no means an easy prey. In China as in France, *Homo erectus* was now the master of

his terrain. The time was ripe for the appearance of a new player, one ready to make an early great leap forward into history: *Homo sapiens* our great-grandfather. As with all fables, the story had a happy ending, albeit one with an uncomfortable appendix. *Homo erectus* continued his march South from China, entering the jungle of Indonesia, as many fossil discoveries prove. Up until this point our story has progressed smoothly. It is a pity that the discovery of a skull attributed to *Homo erectus* close to the village of Modjokerto in Java, upset the proverbial applecart. These fossils have, in fact, been dated to 1,900,000 years ago, and are therefore much older than the remains coming from Africa. Even though no fossil remains of *Homo erectus'* ancestors have yet been found on Java, the African model no longer appears so watertight and we need to presume that there were at least two separate crucibles of hominization. While we await further developments, we will continue to regard *Homo erectus* as the first explorer of the Earth.

15

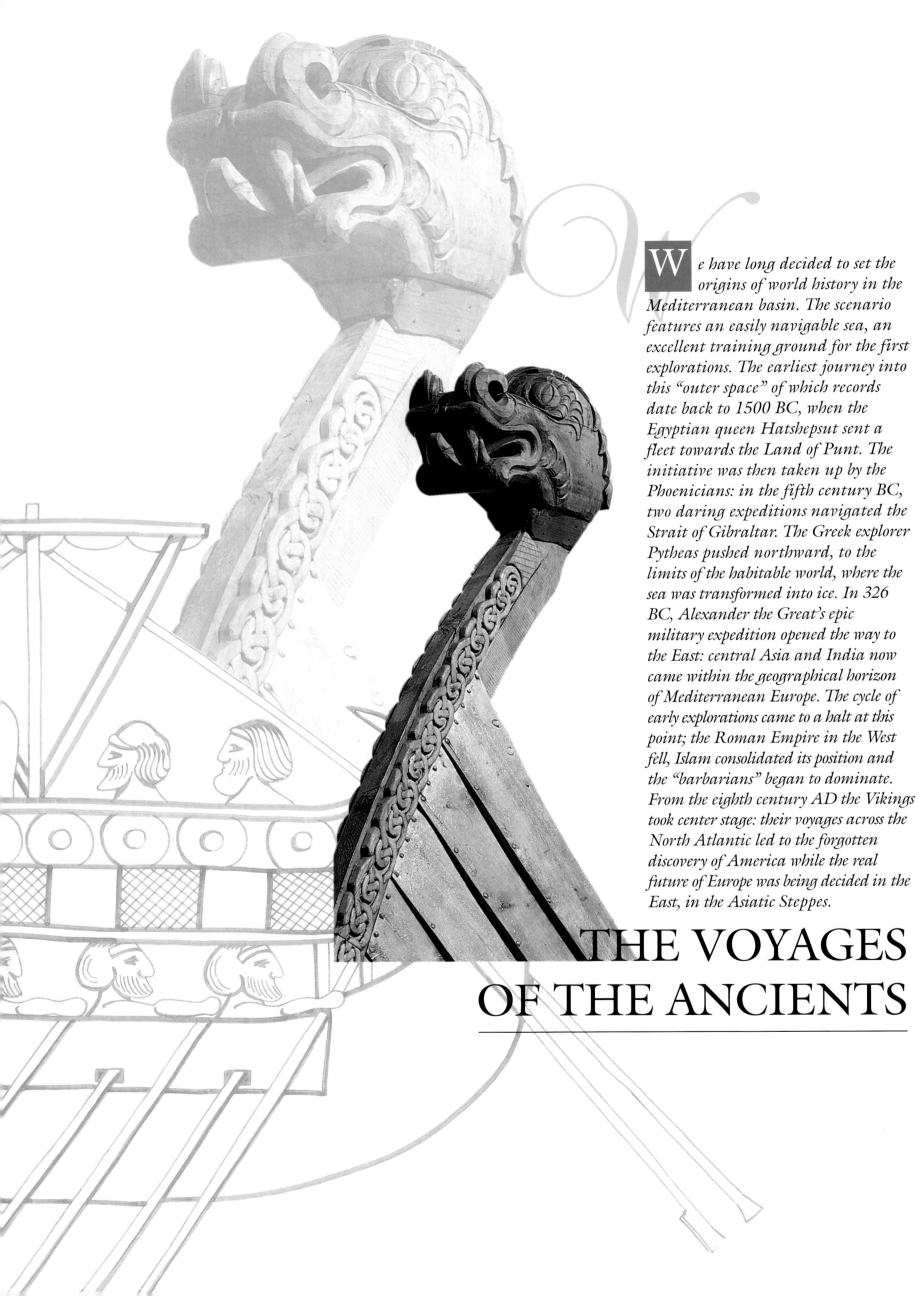

We have long decided to set the origins of world history in the Mediterranean basin. The scenario features an easily navigable sea, an excellent training ground for the first explorations. The earliest journey into this "outer space" of which records date back to 1500 BC, when the Egyptian queen Hatshepsut sent a fleet towards the Land of Punt. The initiative was then taken up by the Phoenicians: in the fifth century BC, two daring expeditions navigated the Strait of Gibraltar. The Greek explorer Pytheas pushed northward, to the limits of the habitable world, where the sea was transformed into ice. In 326 BC, Alexander the Great's epic military expedition opened the way to the East: central Asia and India now came within the geographical horizon of Mediterranean Europe. The cycle of early explorations came to a halt at this point; the Roman Empire in the West fell, Islam consolidated its position and the "barbarians" began to dominate. From the eighth century AD the Vikings took center stage: their voyages across the North Atlantic led to the forgotten discovery of America while the real future of Europe was being decided in the East, in the Asiatic Steppes.

THE VOYAGES OF THE ANCIENTS

THE EGYPTIANS

"Successful departure eastward. Successful arrival of the Soldiers of the Two Lands in the Land of Punt. According to the orders of the Lord of the Gods, Amun, to bring him precious goods… worthy of the magnificence of his love… Queen Makare has done this for her father Amun-King. Nothing similar has ever been accomplished by a sovereign of this country…
A vast portion of the Land of the Gods… Which the Egyptians only knew of through hearsay…"
The hieroglyphics at the Temple of Dayr al-Bahari, near the city of Thebes, relate the story of the celebrated journey ordered by Queen Hatshepsut, or Makare, to the Land of Punt around the year 1500 BC.
In reality Punt was not completely unknown to the Egyptians: as early as the year 2500 BC the pharaoh Sahure had sent an expedition to the Land of the Gods that had returned laden with precious goods: 80,000

Top: This bust of Queen Hatshepsut in painted plaster was found in the Temple of Dayr al-Bahari. The queen's name is synonymous with the great expedition to Punt organized on her orders, the story of which is recorded in the bas-reliefs decorating the Temple of Dayr al-Bahari.

Opposite: The prow of a drakkar, *the fast and agile Viking warship, decorated with a fearsome dragon's head as protection against the sea spirits. As well as the principal deities, Odin, Thor and Freyr, the Viking religion also included a huge cast of elves, demons, and evil and benign beings capable of influencing all aspects of daily life.*

Above: A detail of the reliefs at Dayr al-Bahari: an Egyptian ship is completing the loading of a cargo of precious goods from the Land of Punt. The hieroglyphics indicate the various types of goods: "Ebony, ivory, pure gold from Amu, scented wood, Kesit wood, incense from Ahem, sacred resin, dog-headed apes, long-tailed apes, dogs, leopard skins and natives of the country and their children."

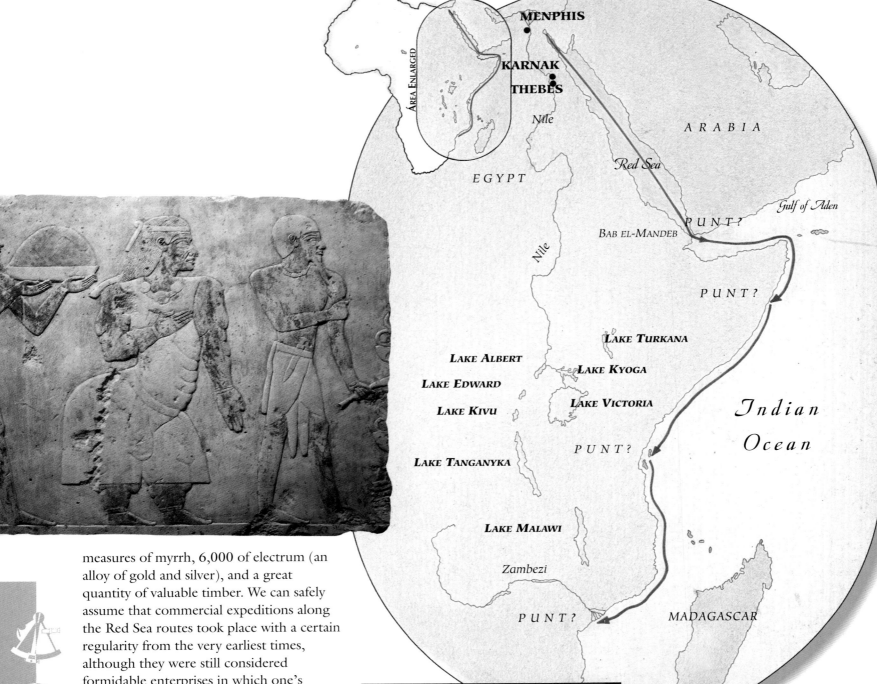

measures of myrrh, 6,000 of electrum (an alloy of gold and silver), and a great quantity of valuable timber. We can safely assume that commercial expeditions along the Red Sea routes took place with a certain regularity from the very earliest times, although they were still considered formidable enterprises in which one's descendants could glorify. Hatshepsut thus followed a route that was already known to her predecessors, albeit one that had become the stuff of legends. Her merit lies in having left a detailed description of the expedition's itinerary, establishing its place in history for the first time. Reaching the Punt, wherever it was, was no easy matter: from Thebes, an eight-day march through the desert separated the Nile Valley from the arid coastline of the Red Sea. The first great task was to transport all the timber and other materials required for the construction of a fleet to the coast. Furthermore, sailing in the Red Sea was by no means easy as insidious banks of coralline rock and capricious winds were constant threats and there were no opportunities for reprovisioning. The Land of Punt probably included the vast area extending to the southeast of Egypt, from the Strait of Bab el Mandeb to the

Top Left: In the reliefs at Dayr al-Bahari one can observe the king and queen of Punt, when they met the Egyptians. In the great obesity of the queen some observers have identified an example of steatopygia, a condition in which there is an accumulation of fat on the buttocks typical of the native peoples of southern Africa. More probably it was a case of pathological obesity.

Bottom: This capital, found in the temple of Dayr al-Bahari, depicts Queen Hatshepsut, "She whom the god Amun embraced, the first among nobles." Hatshepsut, who ascended to the throne after the death of her half-brother Thutmose II, governed Upper and Lower Egypt for around twenty years from 1501 to 1480 BC.

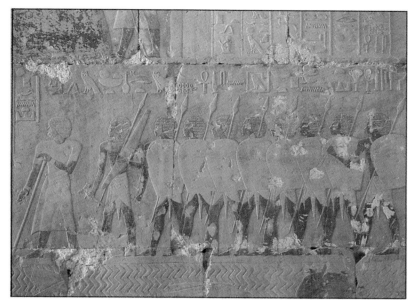

Somalian peninsula and even further down along the east coast of Africa. Those fabulous regions were the source of rare exotic products and aromatic essences. With the precision of a diary, the bas-reliefs and inscriptions at Dayr al-Bahari portray the day-to-day life of the royal expedition. Five ships reached the Land of Punt and were acclaimed with wonder by the inhabitants who asked themselves whether the Egyptians had really traveled by sea or had been carried "on the rays of the sun."
A king and his incredibly fat queen (in whom many have claimed to recognize Hottentot traits) received Hatshepsut's gifts of jewels and swords in a village of huts erected among the palms and myrrh trees. The Egyptian ships then took on board great quantities of "marvellous goods": apart from the carefully packed myrrh trees destined to be planted in the gardens of the temple of Amun, the tribute from the Land of Punt comprised incense, elephants' tusks, gold, ebony, baboons, and cheetahs trained to the lead. With all due respect to Hatshepsut, the maritime expeditions were not Egypt's only links with the distant southern countries: explorers and emissaries had earlier penetrated the interior of the continent. In the period between 2280 and 2240 BC, Hirkhouf, a noble citizen of Aswan, had brought back a "dancing dwarf" from his travels to the south, a flesh-and-blood Pygmy no less, from a remote "land of the inhabitants of the horizon." We have no precise information on Egypt's relationship with the rest of Africa, but the Nile Valley was certainly not so isolated from the "black" civilizations as was until recently believed. While we await the results of archaeological research, it would be better to be prudent. Were the contacts and influences between Egypt and Africa always one-way? There are far more doubts than certainties.

*Top to bottom: In the reliefs at Dayr al-Bahari can be seen palms, incense- (or myrrh-) producing trees, tropical fish and pointed huts.
The location of Punt remains a mystery. Many have claimed that it lay on the coast of Arabia or the Somalian peninsula (which would explain the presence of aromatic plants), although the shape of the huts,*

probably grain stores, suggest more southerly latitudes. Perhaps the name Punt simply identified the long stretch of African coastline from the Bab el-Mandeb strait to the mouth of the Zambezi.

THE PHOENICIANS

As from the last millennium before Christ, with the Mycenaean competition having relaxed its hold, the people known as the Phoenicians assumed the undisputed supremacy over the Mediterranean routes. The Phoenician ships, sailing out of the ports on the Lebanese coast, established flourishing colonies along the coast of North Africa, in Sicily and in Spain, pushing on beyond the Strait of Gibraltar, the so-called Melkart colonies. Phoenician navigational expertise was recognized throughout the Mediterranean basin and many countries made use of Phoenician ships and crews for their boldest commercial enterprises. The Bible contains the story of a mythical journey to Ofir, the mysterious land of gold, completed in the year 945 BC. by a fleet from Tyre in collaboration with the king of Israel, Solomon: the explorers returned with no less than 19 tons of the precious metal. Rivers of ink have been expended with regards to the position of Ofir: the source of the gold has been variously located in Japan and Zimbabwe, and we will probably never know for sure exactly where it was or even whether it actually existed. The story of a Phoenician expedition on behalf of the pharaoh Neco in the seventh century BC and narrated by Herodotus is even more extraordinary: the royal ships left the Red Sea and headed south until they rounded the Cape of Good Hope and, three years later, reappeared in the Mediterranean claiming that while "circumnavigating Libya they had had the sun to their right," that is to say to the north, as would be the case in the Southern Hemisphere. Herodotus doubted the claim, the only "proof" of the journey. In 660 BC, the fall of Tyre to the Assyrians, and the recommencement of the Greeks' maritime activities in the Aegean, shifted the epicenter of the Phoenician

Top: This bas-relief depicts a Phoenician ship from Lebanon and dates from the 2nd century BC. Little is known about the Phoenician trading ships. The material that is available, mostly of Egyptian and Greek origins, *lacks any technical detail that could help in reconstruction of a model. Although sturdy, the Phoenician vessels probably lacked keels and ribs as they were not fitted with the reinforcing cable that linked the prow and the stern posts.*

Bottom: These necklace ornaments were made with glass paste. The Phoenicians achieved a considerable degree of skill in the production of glass pendants and *beads. From 800 BC Carthage became the center for the production and distribution of precious goods exported throughout the Mediterranean region.*

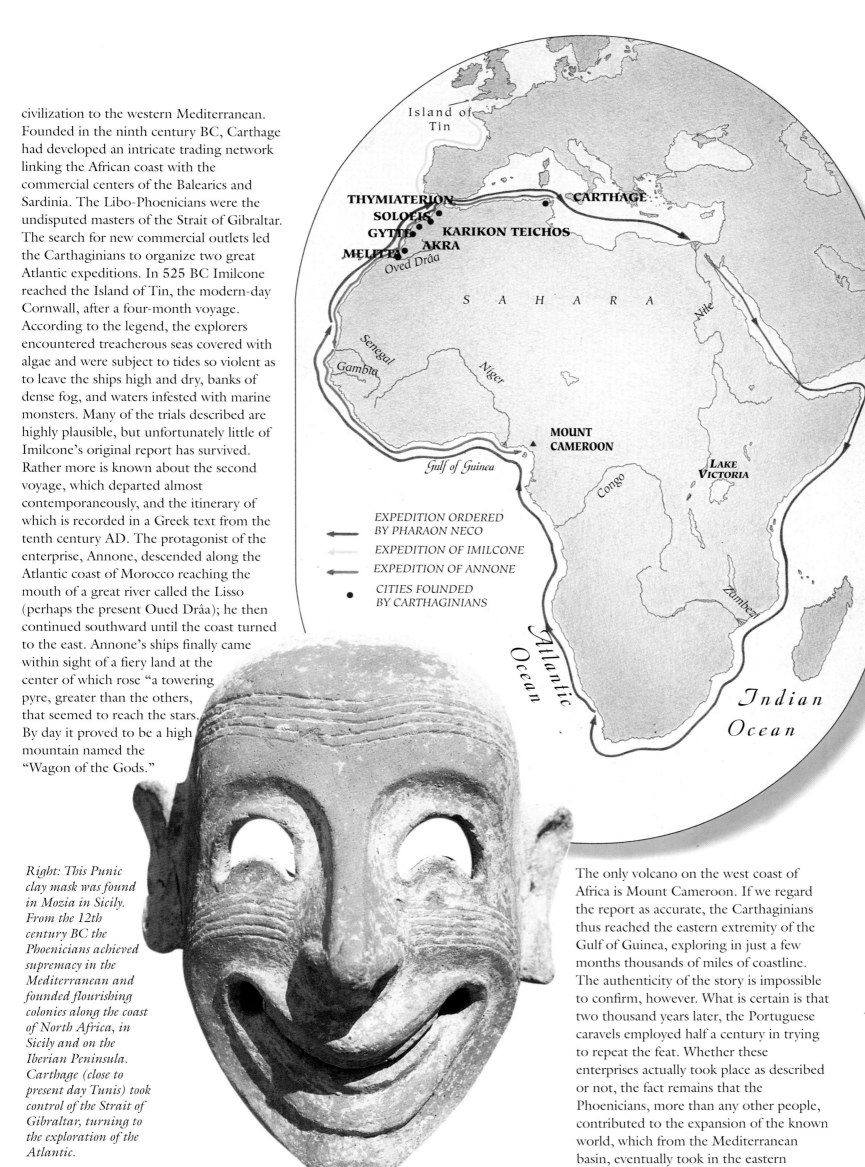

civilization to the western Mediterranean. Founded in the ninth century BC, Carthage had developed an intricate trading network linking the African coast with the commercial centers of the Balearics and Sardinia. The Libo-Phoenicians were the undisputed masters of the Strait of Gibraltar. The search for new commercial outlets led the Carthaginians to organize two great Atlantic expeditions. In 525 BC Imilcone reached the Island of Tin, the modern-day Cornwall, after a four-month voyage. According to the legend, the explorers encountered treacherous seas covered with algae and were subject to tides so violent as to leave the ships high and dry, banks of dense fog, and waters infested with marine monsters. Many of the trials described are highly plausible, but unfortunately little of Imilcone's original report has survived. Rather more is known about the second voyage, which departed almost contemporaneously, and the itinerary of which is recorded in a Greek text from the tenth century AD. The protagonist of the enterprise, Annone, descended along the Atlantic coast of Morocco reaching the mouth of a great river called the Lisso (perhaps the present Oued Drâa); he then continued southward until the coast turned to the east. Annone's ships finally came within sight of a fiery land at the center of which rose "a towering pyre, greater than the others, that seemed to reach the stars. By day it proved to be a high mountain named the "Wagon of the Gods."

Right: This Punic clay mask was found in Mozia in Sicily. From the 12th century BC the Phoenicians achieved supremacy in the Mediterranean and founded flourishing colonies along the coast of North Africa, in Sicily and on the Iberian Peninsula. Carthage (close to present day Tunis) took control of the Strait of Gibraltar, turning to the exploration of the Atlantic.

The only volcano on the west coast of Africa is Mount Cameroon. If we regard the report as accurate, the Carthaginians thus reached the eastern extremity of the Gulf of Guinea, exploring in just a few months thousands of miles of coastline. The authenticity of the story is impossible to confirm, however. What is certain is that two thousand years later, the Portuguese caravels employed half a century in trying to repeat the feat. Whether these enterprises actually took place as described or not, the fact remains that the Phoenicians, more than any other people, contributed to the expansion of the known world, which from the Mediterranean basin, eventually took in the eastern and Atlantic regions.

Right: This fresco of the 16th century BC found on the island of Santorini, depicts a ship about to enter port. The Greek migration from the Aegean to the western Mediterranean reached its peak in the period between the 8th and 6th centuries BC. The colony of Massilia, the present-day Marseille, from which Pytheas departed for his voyage toward the northern seas, was founded around 500 BC.

Opposite: This 15th century map, inspired by Ptolomeic theories, depicts the North Atlantic. Britain, Ireland (Ibernia Insula), and the European coast with the Danish peninsula and the Baltic Sea can be recognized. Between Greenland and a rather distorted Scandinavia lies the unknown and inaccessible Mare Congelatum *or Frozen Sea.*

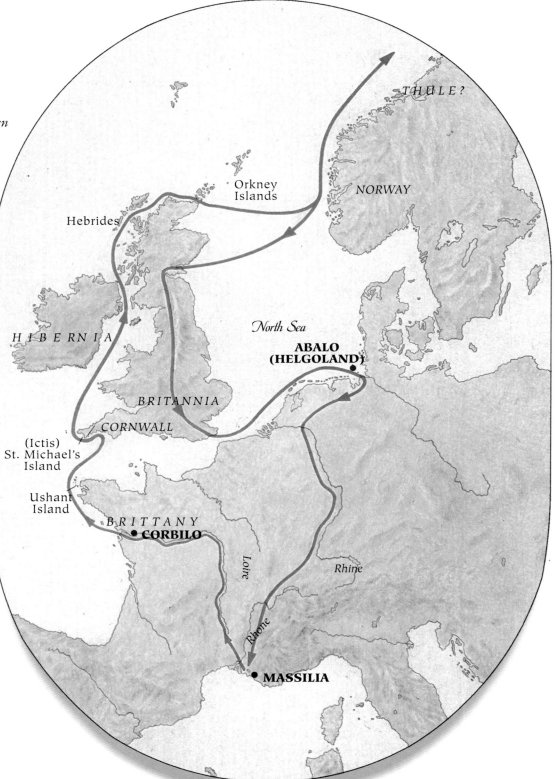

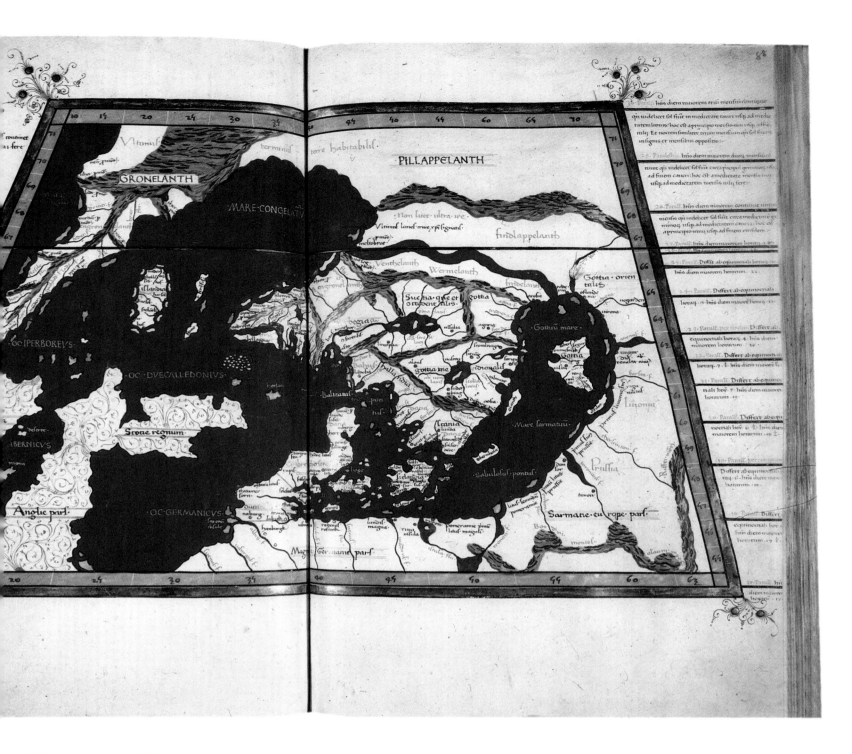

PYTHEA, THE GREEK

Pythea was born at Massilia, the present-day Marseille around the year 380 BC. The Greek colony, strategically situated at the mouth of the Rhone, was then a flourishing market for the products arriving from northern Europe; amber, precious metals, and especially tin. It was undoubtedly motives of commercial exploration which persuaded Pythea, a cultured and wealthy citizen, to undertake his voyage across the North Atlantic. The documentation relating to his enterprise is scarce, and what is available is of doubtful value for the very date of his departure is uncertain. The itinerary on which his wanderings took him is very controversial and based on mere hypotheses. Considering that the Strait of Gibraltar was then under the control of Carthage, the great rival to Massilia, Pythea perhaps preferred a land route along the trade ways which followed the course of the Rhone and the Loire and

eventually reached the Celtic port of Corbilo in Brittany. From Corbilo he set sail for Ouxisame (the island of Ouessant), crossed the English Channel, and reached the coast of Cornwall. There he observed how the inhabitants of Britain extracted and refined the tin. Cast in fist-sized ingots, the metal was transported, taking advantage of the low tide, to the island of St. Michael (Ictis), the obligatory landing place for the merchants, who were afraid of approaching the mainland due to the bellicose locals. Pythea continued along the stretch of sea separating Wales from Ireland, skirting the Scottish coast and visiting the Hebrides and the Orkney Islands. Then, according to the records, he sailed northward for a further six days until he came within sight of "the most distant of all the lands," the legendary Thule, perhaps Iceland, but more probably the coast of Norway. Beyond Thule, the sea was transformed into a

dense material "on which it was neither possible to walk nor to sail," and the sun never set. At this point Pythea turned southward: he sailed along the east coast of England, part of which he also explored on foot, and then headed into the North Sea, to the Amber Islands off the Danish coast. From Abalo (Helgoland) he returned to Massilia, perhaps following the Rhine and Rhone valleys. While his itinerary is a matter of conjecture, we can be sure that Pythea approached the Arctic Circle: his descriptions of the frozen sea and the interminable Arctic summer days are incontrovertibly precise, even though those very descriptions were ridiculed at the time. He undoubtedly circumnavigated Great Britain which he recognized as an island, complaining about its dreadful climate, but praising the quality of its beer. For centuries Thule remained the northern edge of the world.

23

ALEXANDER THE GREAT

In 336 BC Alexander, the son of Philip II, the king of Macedonia, ascended the throne. Just two years later, with the various Greek states unified under his authority, Alexander moved eastward at the head of a formidable army with the intent of defeating the Persian empire once and for all. At that time, Greek culture was at the height of its splendor: Alexander had been a disciple of the great Aristotle from whose teachings he had derived his taste for scientific and geographical investigations. On his orders a large group of scholars, historians, and astronomers followed in the footsteps of the fighting men. Thus the campaign of conquests also became an explorative expedition. Alexander rapidly conquered Phoenicia, Egypt, and Asia Minor, forcing the Persian king Darius beyond the Tigris. At that time little was known of the vast eastern regions of the Persian empire that extended as far as the

Above: Alexander the Great is often idealized as an exquisitely handsome youth with a pensive expression. Alexander was a disciple of Aristotle, the most famous Greek philosopher of the era, whose teachings inspired his enthusiasm for scientific and geographical investigation.

Right: This piece of a mosaic, which is conserved entirely in the National Museum of Naples, depicts the battle between Darius and Alexander at Issus and shows the pugnacious, aggressive character of the Greek adventurer.

borders of India. By way of the Iranian uplands, Alexander reached the shores of the Caspian Sea and, with the death of Darius, followed his successors through the Steppes of Battriana, the modern-day Afghanistan. From Nuristan he crossed the Hindukush range, descending into the valley of the Oxus (the Amudar'ja). His raids against the Scythians, nomadic herders of western Turkistan, led him beyond the Syrdar'ya River. Central Asia was by now at the feet of the Macedonian sovereign, and he turned his attentions southward. The conquerers crossed the Indus, then the Idaspe (the Jhelum) before eventually halting on the banks of the Ifasi, now the Beas River, a confluent of the Sutlej in the Punjab region. Beyond this point extended the endless plain of the Thar Desert, the gateway to the Ganges valley and the extreme frontier of the world where "the great Ocean River encircles all the Earth." There Alexander harangued his troops, inciting them to proceed eastward. However, his lesson in epic geography failed to convince soldiers weary of wandering the interminable footpaths of Asia. To avoid a mutiny, Alexander decided to turn back. He had a great fleet constructed and set sail, descending the Idaspe and then the Indus to its outflow into the Indian Ocean. The journey was difficult and tortuous:

Top: Having reached the Indus, Alexander had a fleet constructed and descended the river to its mouth. After his vessels had been repaired following a violent storm, he decided to reach Persia via land, ordering one of his generals, Nearco, to proceed with the exploration of the coast of the Indian Ocean as far as the mouth of the Euphrates. Nearco sailed for 130 days encountering schools of whales and people, who fed on fish alone, whom he named the Icthyophages.

Above: In this Limoges enamel 16th century Alexander the Great is depicted on the back of an elephant. Once past the Indus and having reached the course of the Idaspe (the Jhelum in the Punjab region), Alexander's army was confronted with the fierce resistance of the local ruler Poro. Poro's forces included 200 war elephants that ran the Macedonian cavalry ragged. Alexander eventually won the ferocious battle thanks to the efficiency of his archers.

25

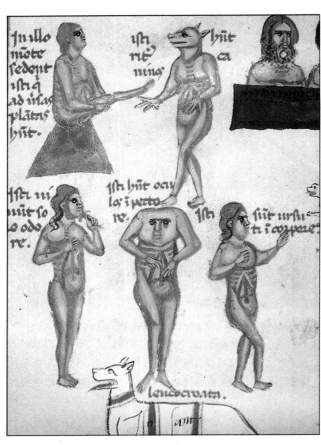

Top left: In this page of the Cosmografia by Julius Solinus, 16th century, Alexander is close to his favorite horse, Bucephalus. The legendary mount of the Macedonian conquerer was killed during the battle with the forces of King Poro on the Idaspe. In his honor Alexander founded the city of Alexandria Bucephalus on the site of the battle.

Top right:
The fabulous inhabitants of the remote lands of the East, from the Cosmografia by Julius Solinus: men without heads, Cyclops, cynocephalae and beings with one foot. The exotic monsters appear in all the poetic celebrations of the exploits of Alexander.

Above: The events in the life of Alexander the Great are surrounded by an aura of the supernatural. Having reached the farthest corners of the Earth, the Macedonian hero could hardly have avoided encountering monsters and fantastic beings. Here we see him tackling ranks of turtles.

the waters of the river, swollen by the spring rains, were flowing rapidly, constantly threatening to overturn the boats. Close to the river's mouth, a violent tidal current to which the Mediterranean sailors were not accustomed, swamped a number of vessels, throwing them onto the banks. It was clear that in spite of the crocodiles, the river had little in common with the Nile. Alexander nevertheless felt that the eastern sea into which it flowed must, in some way, be linked to the Red Sea and perhaps with the Caspian Sea. Gripped by the "violent desire" to discover a navigable route from India to Persia, he decided to divide his forces. Along with the major part of his

army Alexander himself was to follow the Gedrosia (Baluchistan) route until he reached the Persian Gulf, while one of his generals, Nearco, was given orders to proceed by sea as far as the mouths of the Euphrates. Nearco sailed through unknown waters for 130 days, encountering primitive peoples who lived on fish alone whom he named the Icthyophages, and schools of whales. Alexander's journey along the desolate coasts of Iran was much harder: thousands of soldiers died of hunger and thirst before reaching Babylon, the city that the king of Macedonia wanted to elect as the capital of the new empire. After 10 years of battles and exploration Alexander fell ill

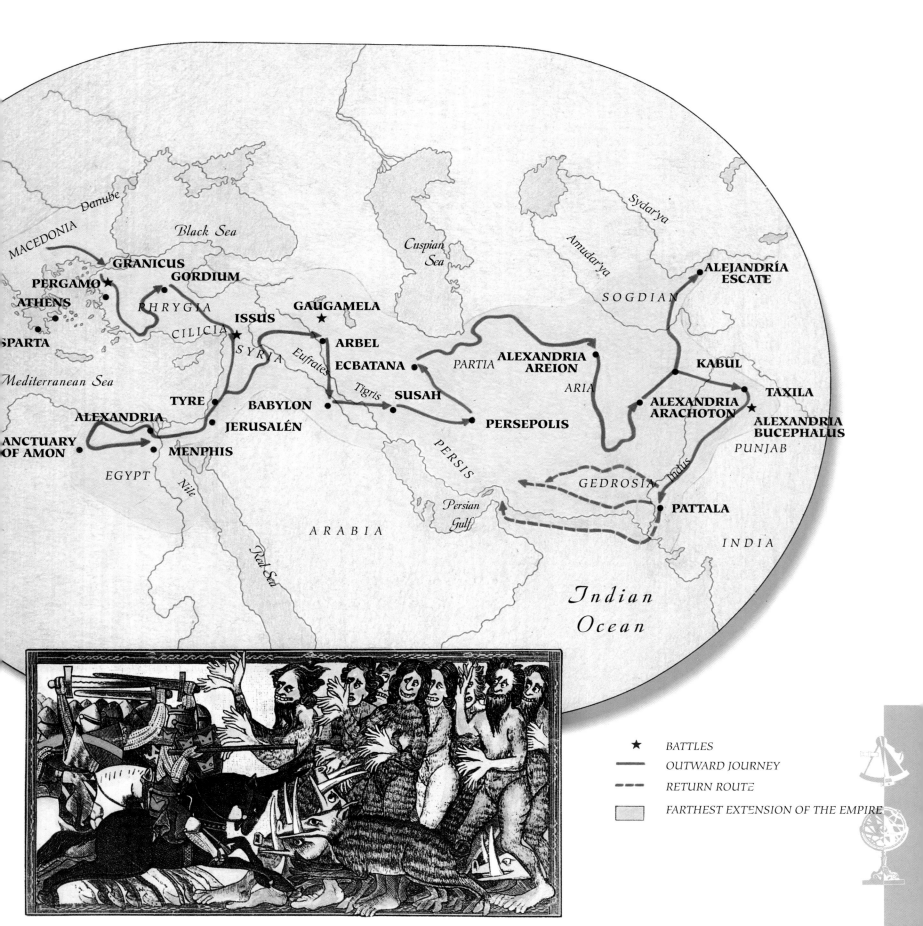

MACEDONIA
Danube
Black Sea
GRANICUS
PERGAMO ★
GORDIUM
ATHENS
PHRYGIA
SPARTA
CILICIA
ISSUS
GAUGAMELA ★
SYRIA
Eufrates
ARBEL
Mediterranean Sea
ECBATANA
Tigris
SUSAH
TYRE
BABYLON
ALEXANDRIA
JERUSALÉN
PERSEPOLIS
ANCTUARY OF AMON
MENPHIS
EGYPT
Nile
ARABIA
Red Sea
PERSIS
Persian Gulf

Cuspian Sea
Amudar'ya
Sydar'ya
SOGDIAN
ALEJANDRÍA ESCATE
PARTIA
ALEXANDRIA AREION
KABUL
ARIA
TAXILA ★
ALEXANDRIA ARACHOTON
ALEXANDRIA BUCEPHALUS
PUNJAB
GEDROSIA
Indus
PATTALA
INDIA

Indian Ocean

★ BATTLES
— OUTWARD JOURNEY
--- RETURN ROUTE
▭ FARTHEST EXTENSION OF THE EMPIRE

and died, perhaps drained by his exertions. This was in the year 323 BC. The long Asian campaign had brought the Greek armies to the borders of India and into the very heart of the continent, adding a vast portion of terrain to the known world.

Above: These two illustrations shows some of the adventurous enterprises that Alexander the Great had to face during his great expedition in Asia. In the above image the Macedonian leader fights men with six hands. In the bottom one he battles dangerous animal-headed beasts.

27

Top left: Alexander's army, with its 30,000 infantrymen and 5,000 mounted warriors, reached Mesopotamia after having conquered Asia Minor, Phoenicia, Syria, and Egypt. Having crossed the Tigris and the Euphrates, as the illustration taken from a manuscript of the 15th century shows, Alexander faced the Persian forces and defeated them at Guagamela. This victory opened the gateway to the East for the Macedonian sovereign.

Bottom left: This miniature in the Gothic style was produced by the Flemish artist Loyset Liedet for a French edition of the Alexander story by Quinto Curzio Rufo. It shows the Macedonian explorer camping at the Siwa Oasis. Alexander the Great was revered as the son of the god Ammone and was himself regarded as something of a god-king.

Opposite: Alexander's fleet, having reached the mouth of the Indus, was surprised by a violent tidal surge that swamped and destroyed many of the vessels. With invincible tenacity the men recovered the wrecks, repaired the major damage, and after a sumptuous sacrifice to the gods of the sea, the expedition could finally set sail on the unknown waters of the Indian Ocean.

Bottom left: Legend has it that Alexander the Great had himself lowered into the sea in a glass barrel, so as to explore the mysterious submarine world. Apart from being a military campaign, Alexander's expedition was a true journey of exploration. Not satisfied with having investigated what lay in the depths of the oceans and spurred by insatiable curiosity, the sovereign also attempted to ascend into the sky, tightly bound to the claws of two griffons.

Bottom right: Alexander's battle against the army of King Poro in the Punjab was perhaps the only military episode of note during the Macedonian sovereign's long advance toward the confines of the known world. He succeeded in getting the better of the terrible war elephants only thanks to the skill of his archers.

THE VIKINGS

At the end of the eighth century AD the Viking raiders from the inhospitable coasts of Scandinavia commenced their bloody advance through Europe. In AD 793 the monastery on Lindisfarne on the east coast of England suffered the first devastating attack by the "Men from the Sea." Over the following years the number of attacks grew rapidly. In their remarkably seaworthy ships, the *drakkars*, the Vikings reached Ireland and, sailing up the Seine, fell upon Paris, sacking the city in AD 855. Other groups headed south, devastating the Spanish and Portuguese Atlantic ports and penetrating the Mediterranean. To the east the Swedish Vikings, the so-called Rus, followed the Volga and after having conquered Novgorod and Kiev, eventually threatened Constantinople and the cities of Syria. There was more to their enterprises, related in the Scandinavian sagas, than acts of piracy and bloodthirsty warmongering. The Vikings were also the protagonists in authentic voyages of discovery. As early as AD 815, the Norwegians had settled in Iceland, establishing a permanent colony that in a little over a century numbered 60,000 inhabitants. Demographic pressure and the island's insufficient economic resources soon created a new class of exiles. The hunger for virgin lands and the desire to escape social constraints led to a systematic exploration of the North Atlantic. In AD 982 Eric the Red, found guilty of murder, was expelled from the Icelandic colony and left in search of a legendary western land of which earlier exiles had signalled the presence. After sailing 450 miles through the freezing Arctic seas, Eric came within sight of a desolate, ice-bound coast which he followed southward until, after having rounded Cape Farvel, he reached a protected haven. The environment there appeared to be less hostile: there were even pastures, albeit of poor quality, and the waters of the fjord were crammed with fish. Eric returned to Iceland full of stories of a fabulous "green land" — today's Greenland of course — and decided to return to found a colony. Hundreds of people agreed to follow him in the hope of a better future. The Viking settlements on the western coast of the great island had a hard life: there were

Opposite top:
The Oseberg longship, found in a funeral mound at Oseberg in Norway in 1903. Over 72 feet long and 16 feet wide, the ship is constructed in pine and oak and dates back to around the year AD 800. Her structure and notable dimensions suggest that she was designed as an ocean-going vessel.

Opposite center:
The Viking drakkars, here depicted under full sail, were exclusively used for war and raiding. For trading

expeditions and voyages of exploration the Vikings preferred the larger and more robust knorr, built in pine and oak and capable of carrying a crew of 30 men as well as the supplies necessary for a long ocean voyage. It was probably aboard a knorr that Leif Eriksson reached the coasts of Labrador and Newfoundland.

Opposite bottom:
This engraved stone dated form the 9th shows the dead Vikings undertaking their last journey beyond the tomb.

Right: This miniature from the 12th century presents a Viking ship affronting a gigantic sea monster. The perils of the North Atlantic routes followed by the Viking colonists to reach Iceland, Greenland, and finally the coast of Canada, were anything but imaginary. Fog, violent storms, and the constant threat of icebergs made navigation close to the Arctic Circle an enterprise fraught with dangers.

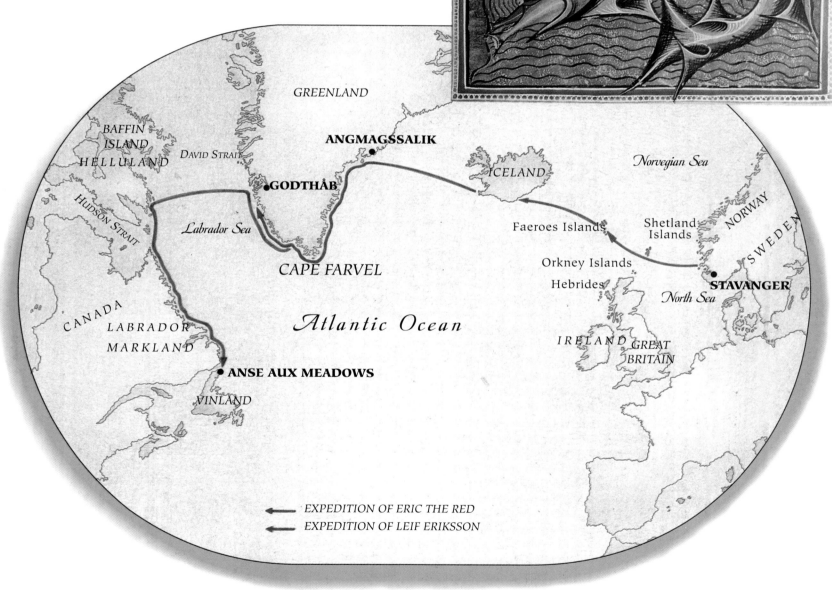

EXPEDITION OF ERIC THE RED
EXPEDITION OF LEIF ERIKSSON

no trees suitable for shipbuilding and the unbelievably harsh winters gave no quarter. Further explorations confirmed that the greater part of the island was uninhabitable. Were there other lands to the west? In AD 986, Bjorn Herjulfson, thrown off course by a storm, claimed to have sighted "a flat region" covered with forests. His affirmations were enough to persuade Leif Eriksson to undertake a new voyage of

exploration. Leif left Greenland in AD 992. Some time later the frozen rocks of Helluland (possibly Baffin Island) appeared on the horizon. Leif continued southward until he encountered the coasts of Labrador and Newfoundland. The abundance of shrubs, rich in wild berries, convinced the Vikings to name the island Vinland, the "land of wine." Leif and his companions spent the winter on the northern tip of

Newfoundland, at the present-day Anse aux Meadows, setting sail for Greenland as soon as the temperatures were a little milder. Without knowing it, the Vikings had discovered America, five centuries before Columbus. The subsequent attempts at colonization, obstructed by the hostile behavior of the native *screlingi* (literally "ugly people") were unsuccessful and the New World was rapidly forgotten.

In the mid-thirteenth century the Mongol hordes turned their attention to Europe, sowing terror in their wake. However, the horsemen from the Steppes were responsible for rather more than just blind destruction. For the first time the mysterious frontiers of Asia were opened to European travelers. The first to venture in the direction of the court of the Great Kahn were the missionaries. In the decade between 1246 and 1255 the Franciscans Giovanni da Pian del Carpine and William of Rubruk reached Karakorum, the capital of the Mongol empire. Their journeys paved the way for Marco Polo's epic adventure. Departing in 1271, the Venetian remained in Asia for no less than twenty-five years, in the service of the omnipotent Kublai Kahn, the dominator of a territory extending from Hungary to the Pacific. The memories of his travels, set down in The Travels of Marco Polo, *revealed a whole new world and a sophisticated and powerful civilization to skeptical Europe. Cathay and its incredible riches triggered one of the greatest explorations in recorded history.*

FAITH AND COMMERCE: ASIA REVEALED

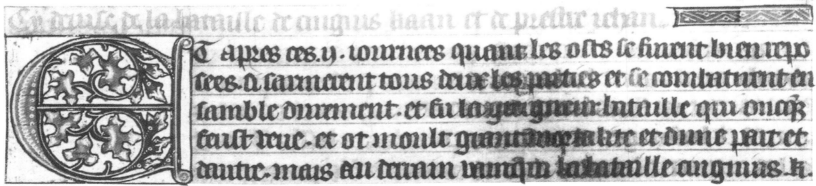

Missionaries Among The Mongols

The Mongol invasion fell upon Europe's eastern frontiers like a hurricane. After having suddenly appeared out of the endless Asian plains and having put Russia to the torch, the "sons of hell" rode roughshod over the resistance put up by Poland and Hungary, destroying everything that lay in their path. By 1241 their advance parties were threatening Vienna and the cities on the Dalmatian coast. It appeared that nothing could stop them. Then, inexplicably, the surge faded and the Mongol armies retreated eastward. The Great Kahn Ogodai had died, thereby saving Europe from destruction. But for how long? One of the aims of the Congress of Lyons, convened by Pope Innocent IV in 1245, was that of defending Europe against another invasion. At all costs

contacts had to be established with the Mongols, or Tartars as they were known in the west, so as to commence negotiations for peace and, if at all possible, convert them to Christianity. Suitably indoctrinated and set on the road to salvation, the nomadic pagans could have become welcome allies in the fight against Islam. It was thus that in the April of 1246, at the age of sixty-three, the Franciscan monk Giovanni da Pian del Carpine, left Lyons on his long and perilous journey into the east. The monk carried with him a letter from the Pope warning the Mongol kahn to cease his persecution of Christians and to appease "with suitable penitence, the divine fury." After a brief stay

in Prague, Giovanni and his companions headed towards Poland, and continued eastward across the desolate Russian Steppes as far as Kiev, a city which still bore the signs of its recent sacking. Early in February, 1247, the group encountered the first patrols of Mongol horsemen and were escorted to the banks of the Dnepr, and the encampment of Batu, the Governor of the Khanate of the Golden Horde. Batu welcomed them with benevolent condescension, inviting them to continue their march toward Karakorum, the capital of the empire. Weakened by their Lenten fast and tormented by the cold and the privations of the journey, the monks

Opposite: This world map is from a Book of Psalms from the 13th century. The image of the world comes from the blending of the geographical knowledge of the ancient Greeks and Romans with biblical elements: East is to the top, identified by the figure of Christ and the Garden of Eden, while to the Northeast the iron fence built by Alexander the Great keeps back the hordes of Gog and Magog, the forces of evil and the Anti-Christ, the ever-present threat to the Christian world.

Above and below: The legend of Prester John (top, with a number of his followers), the sovereign of a powerful Christian realm at the shoulder of Islam, was long-lived in Europe. Originating in the middle of the 12th century, it persisted for almost three hundred years, contributing to Portuguese fervor for the exploration of the African coasts. The realm of Prester John was from time to time localized in central Asia, in India, and in Ethiopia, and Marco Polo himself referred to the legend, telling the story of an epic battle between the Mongol troops and the Christian forces, illustrated below in an engraving taken from Livre des Le Merveilles.

GIOVANNI DA PIAN DEL CARPINE

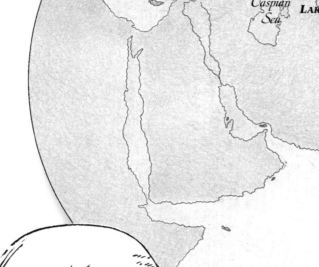

followed the trail used by the Mongol messengers. Changing their horses as many as seven times a day, they rapidly covered the monotonous plain that extended from the Volga to the Aral Sea. They left the Syr Darja heading eastward and, skirting the northern buttresses of the Tien Shan chain, penetrated the semidesert regions of Dzungaria. On the 22nd of June they reached the kahn's residence located not far from the modern city of Ulaabaatar in Mongolia. The assembly that was to ratify the nomination of Guyuk as the successor to Ogodai was in full swing, and Giovanni was allowed to participate in the complex ceremonies preceding the election of the Mongol emperor. Supplied with food and lodgings, he remained in that vast city of tents for four months before Guyuk deigned to receive him. The Franciscan obtained permission to depart on the 13th of

November. The Great Kahn's reply to the Pope's requests left no room for doubt: Guyuk declared himself to be invested with divine powers and ordered Innocent IV to recognize his authority. If not, ran the message, "we will consider you our enemies." In November, 1247, Giovanni was once again in Lyons. The diplomatic mission had failed, but his observations, collected in the *Historia Mongalorum*, revealed to the West for the first time the face of central Asia: apart from a few digressions into the fantastic, the data gathered by the monk was an inexhaustible mine of information on lands and people that was previously unknown. Giovanni described with spy-like precision the customs, social structure, shamanistic rituals, and military tactics of the Mongols. There was no hope of converting them into faithful servants of God he concluded

Above left: Giovanni da Pian del Carpine, portrayed here in an engraving taken from antique Chinese documents, was sixty-three years old when he began his journey into the Mongol territories. Born in Italy in 1182, in the Lake Trasimeno region, he already had considerable experience as a missionary. In the opinion of a contemporary, man of the faith, he was a "pleasant man, humorous, educated, very eloquent, and skilled in many things."

Above right: The men with dogs' heads, in an illustration from Livres des Le Merveilles, *and the crowds of legendary creatures that were thought to populate the extreme confines of the habitable world, rarely feature in the account by Giovanni da Pian del Carpine, whose descriptions were generally precise and remote from the contemporary taste for the fantastic.*

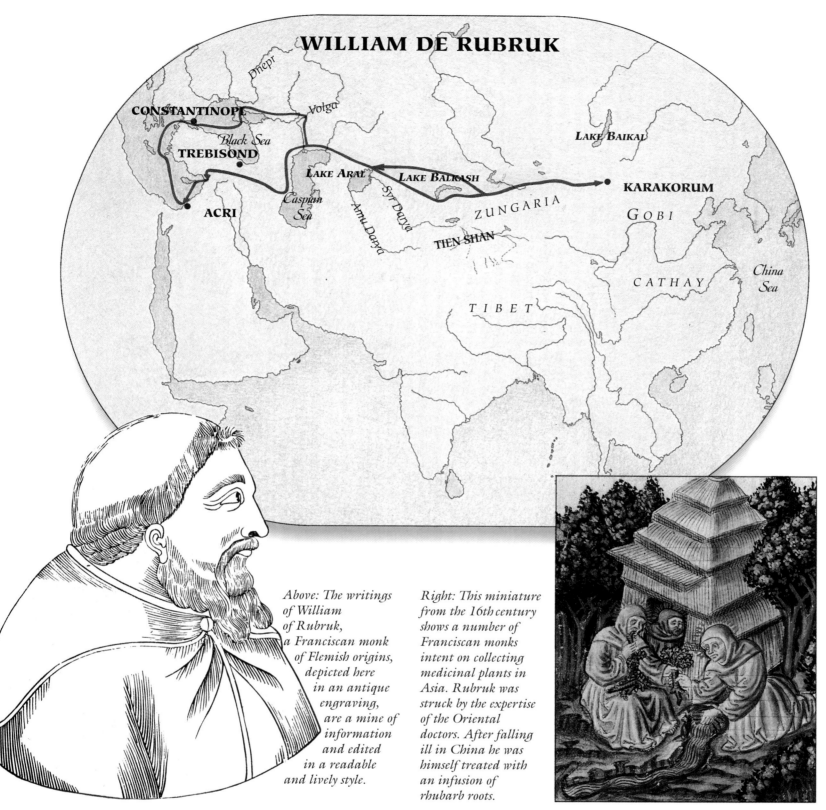

WILLIAM DE RUBRUK

Above: The writings of William of Rubruk, a Franciscan monk of Flemish origins, depicted here in an antique engraving, are a mine of information and edited in a readable and lively style.

Right: This miniature from the 16th century shows a number of Franciscan monks intent on collecting medicinal plants in Asia. Rubruk was struck by the expertise of the Oriental doctors. After falling ill in China he was himself treated with an infusion of rhubarb roots.

bitterly. They therefore had to be fought and in his report he suggested how. In spite of Giovanni's pessimism, Western Christianity refused to be discouraged. Other ambassadors, this time sent by the canonized French king Louis IX, departed for the East. Among the many rumors that filtered through to Europe, passing by word of mouth, was one claiming that Huyuk Kahn had been converted to Christianity. The rumor was of course unfounded, but was sufficient to convince the French king to send further emissaries to Karakorum. The mission of the Dominican monk André de Longjumeau was unsuccessful: Guyuk was dead and his widow claimed the right to demand weighty tributes in gold from all the kings and princes of Europe. Negotiations were going nowhere, but Louis IX was not yet ready to concede defeat. In 1252 he

commissioned a Franciscan monk, William of Rubruk, to undertake yet another journey to the land of the Mongols. William was to have acted as a missionary rather than an ambassador, thus protecting the king from further diplomatic embarrassment. The small party left Constantinople the following year. Their route was not significantly different to that followed by Giovanni da Pian del Carpine, but William of Rubruk was an acute observer and proved to have a taste for the new and the exotic. His *Journey through the Empire of the Mongols*, pervaded by a subtle vein of irony, is rightly considered a classic in the literature of travel. Blessed with a healthy dose of realism, William was the first to recognize that the Caspian Sea was landlocked and not a gulf in some ocean, thereby flying in the face of the geographical dogma of the times. The

capital of the Mongol empire failed to impress him: Karakorum, he wrote, "with the exception of the Kahn's palace could not match even the borough of Saint-Denis" (a Parisian quarter). A theological debate, organized by Mangu Kahn so as to compare the Christian faith with the other religions practised (and all tolerated) within his realm, was resolved without drama: "Everything having been concluded, the Nestorians and the Saracens sang out loud together and afterwards everybody drank copiously." William of Rubruk's mission marked the beginning of a period of peaceful relations between East and West. The physical and human geography of Asia began to be better known. The road had been opened up and was difficult but practicable. The time was ripe for the missionaries to make way for the merchants.

MARCO POLO

In 1269 brothers Niccolò and Maffeo Polo reentered Venice for the first time in almost fifteen years. They had just completed one of the most sensational trading expeditions in history. From Constantinople where they owned an emporium, they had traveled to Sarai on the Volga, the capital of the Golden Horde before heading on toward Bukara. Crossing the desert of Dzungaria, they eventually reached Cambaluc (Beijing). There they were sympathetically received at the court of Kublai Khan, the Mongol emperor. The Great Khan was eager to hear about the mysterious countries of the West from which his guests originated and wanted to be instructed in Christian doctrine. Before he allowed the Venetians to leave, he extracted a promise: Niccolò and Maffeo were to return to Cambaluc with a message from the Pope and above all in the company of "one hundred scholars learned in the seven arts," capable of illustrating the knowledge and faith of Europe for the benefit of the court. The Polo brothers were determined to honor the pledges they had made. They waited until the new Pope Gregory X had been elected before leaving for Asia once again in 1271. They were laden with gifts for the Great Kahn and in the company not of one hundred scholars, but of two monks, charged by the Pope with carrying the authority of the Roman Church to those remote regions. Niccolò decided that on this trip he should be accompanied by his seventeen-year-old son Marco. The three Venetians reached Laiazzo, a port in southeast Turkey (now Yumurtalik) and from there they proceeded in a caravan toward the Black Sea coast and Armenia. The monks, alarmed by the dangers of such a long journey, turned back shortly after the departure. The Polo family headed toward Hormuz, the famous spice port on the Persian Gulf, with the intention of setting sail for China. However, unknown motives persuaded them to follow an overland route through the turbulent regions of Khorasan. They passed through the ruins of the ancient city of Balkh, sacked half a century earlier by Genghis Kahn, before eventually reaching the Wakhan corridor in what is now

Above: In this 1857 engraving of a Venetian school painting, Marco Polo is a grown man.

Below: Piazza San Marco was the true political and economic heart of Venice. At the time of Marco Polo, Venice was not just a trading city, but a veritable republic of merchants in which economic and political power were intertwined. The government controlled the volume and alternation of traffic, oversaw and regulated the life of the commercial associations, and regulated the quality and quantity of goods imported and exported, thus creating perfect harmony between public and private interests.

Above: This miniature taken from the Roman d'Alexandre *depicts Marco Polo's departure from Venice.*

Bottom left: In the late Middles Ages the term spices was used to describe a vast assortment of substances used in cooking, as medicines, as perfumes, and as cosmetics. Sugar, in the form of loaves, as can be seen in this illustration, was also considered a spice. A trade manual of the 14th century recognizes no less than 11 different types.

Bottom right: This illustration depicts a priest with a thurible in his hand, buying incense. Incense came mainly from Arabia and the Somalian peninsula and was in demand in Europe not only for ritual purposes, but also for use as a medicine and an antiseptic. It had long been used to treat diseases of the respiratory system. Marco Polo described how the resinous product of trees similar to "small pines" dripped from cuts in their bark and then hardened.

Afghanistan, between the towering ranges of the Hindukush and the Pamir plateau, the source of "beautiful precious gems," rubies and lapis lazuli. The crossing of the Pamir required forty days of hard labor. The mountains, furrowed by deep valleys, were almost completely uninhabited, the realm of wolves and strange animals. Marco Polo noted and described the magnificent Pamir sheep *(Ovis poli)* weighing all of four-hundred pounds and whose spiralled horns could reach lengths of up to five feet. Descending from the plateau, the Venetians followed the caravan trails that led to Kashgar, one of the destinations of the Silk Road. In front of them extended the deserts of Takla Makan, apparently inhabited by

Above: In this detail from Charles V's Catalan Atlas compiled in 1375, one can see Marco Polo's caravan during his journey into the fabulous East.

invisible, malign spirits that confused the minds of travelers until they lost their 0bearings. However, it took more than a regiment of ghosts to stop a Venetian merchant, and the Polos crossed the Takla Makan without mishap and reached Kanchou, the westernmost city of China, where they waited for a year for orders from the Great Kahn. In the May of 1275, they finally encountered the emperor in his summer residence at Shang tu, around 38.180 miles north of Cambaluc. Kublai Khan received the Venetians warmly and was immediately impressed by the young Marco. For his part, Marco was struck by the magnificence of the court established within an immense park in which deer and other wild animals wandered freely. "The King of Kings," he related, "is of medium stature, neither tall nor short. He has well formed limbs and is well proportioned in all his

figure. His skin is light, occasionally flushed with red like the luminous tint of a rose, which adds much grace to his appearance. His eyes are black and attractive, his nose well shaped and prominent."

A kind of unspoken affinity was established between the two men, perhaps from that very first meeting. Kublai brought Marco into his entourage, choosing him as his confidant and trusted aide, having the Venetian accompany him on hunting trips and during ceremonial events. Marco was also entrusted with public commissions in the farthest-flung provinces of the empire. He gradually learned the Asian languages and the secrets of the state administration. The civilization facing him was not found wanting in a comparison with the sophistication of his native Venice. Via a network of messengers, the Great Kahn could send orders to the most remote

Center: Taking his leave of the Polo brothers, the Emperor of the Mongols presented them with a tablet of gold, a guarantee of safe-conduct and a symbol of his personal protection in a territory extending from the Pacific to the Danube. Kublai Kahn obtained from the Venetians a promise that they would return to his court at the head of a caravan of priests and scholars, expert in all the arts, who would reveal to the Mongol sovereign the mysteries of the Christian West.

Opposite: This portrait of Marco Polo in Tartaria is taken from The Clothes of the Venetians of Almost Every Ere, collected and painted in the 18th century, 1754. The legendary adventures of the Venetian traveler in Asia have stimulated the imaginations of artists and writers of all eras. In this illustration Marco Polo is depicted in Mongol costume, armed with bow and arrows and a sabre.

Bottom: This miniature shows the roads and canals of Chinsai, the Heavenly City. It so excited the imagination of Marco Polo that he claimed "the city of Quinsai has a circumference of 10 miles."

Opposite: A boat loaded with exotic goods from India and China approaching Hormuz, the famous spice port on the Persian Gulf. The Polos left Venice in 1271, and after having crossed Turkey and Armenia, headed for Hormuz, from where they were due to have embarked for China. For unknown motives they abandoned the idea of a sea passage, preferring an overland route along the trails of northern Persia.

outpost of his domain in a matter of days or weeks. Marco Polo saw paper money, the making of which seemed to him to be more a question of alchemy than an administrative necessity. In the imperial mint at Cambaluc, the Great Kahn accumulated vast quantities of mulberry bark, which once "soaked, is then ground in a mortar until it is reduced to a paste and then transformed into a paper similar to that produced from cotton, but completely black. When it is ready for use, he has it cut into pieces of money of different values, almost square, but slightly longer than they are wide." The banknotes, impressed with the royal seal, were then officially authenticated and falsification was "punished as a capital offence."

As an envoy of the emperor, Marco Polo traveled the length and breadth of China, reaching the Yun Nan and on beyond the confines of Burma.

For three years he performed ill-defined public duties at Chinsai (modern-day Hangzhou, not far from Shanghai), which he considered to be the most beautiful and richest city in the world. The wonders of Chinsai were not limited to the streets paved in stone or the squares and the canals crossed by an incredible number of bridges (no less than 12,000). Chinsai, according to Marco, was also a paradise of love, and those foreigners that were able, even just once, to frequent its courtesans, "skilled and perfect

in the art of flattering caresses," could never forget their appeal and, "intoxicated by sensual pleasure, on returning home they reported that they had been to Chinsai, the Heavenly City, and eagerly awaited the moment in which they could return to that paradise."

Nothing is known of how Niccolò and Maffeo Polo spent those long years in their gilded exile: both disappeared from the pages of *The Travels* immediately after their arrival at Cambaluc. The two merchants were perhaps keener than Marco to return to Venice. By now twenty years had passed since their second departure from Europe. Kublai Kahn was reluctant to let the Venetians go as they were by now considered an integral part of his entourage. The perfect opportunity finally arose: the Great Kahn entrusted them with the task of accompanying a delegation of ambassadors on their return journey toward distant Persia. Marco had recently returned from a mission to the seas of Indochina: his proven fidelity and knowledge of the difficult route dispelled the emperor's last doubts.

The Polos left the Chinese coast in 1292. The fleet of 14 large, ocean-going junks reached the strait separating the Malay Peninsula from the island of Sumatra and entered the Indian Ocean.

After having skirted Ceylon and southern

Opposite bottom left: Le Livres de Merveilles, *produced in Paris in 1375, contains precious miniatures illustrating the most significant episodes of Marco Polo's journeys. This particular miniature shows the men of the Great Kahn conquering the island of Cipangu, modern-day Japan.*

Opposite bottom right: An Eastern sovereign, probably the Great Kahn himself, witnessing a commercial transaction. The silver ingots are being exchanged for paper money. Marco Polo had the opportunity of seeing the production of paper money made out of mulberry bark. It seemed to him more an alchemical process than an administrative necessity.

con
el se
ho o
le qu
caro u
te brach
del suo reg
che regend
tri liuomi
numero d
uanti e da
tutti ipiace
ui del mo

Above: Marco Polo's enthusiastic interest in the diversity of the world makes Il Milione (or The Travels of Marco Polo) a true Book of Wonders as the title of one of the best known versions of the volume reads. Between the lines of the descriptions of epic battles, hunts, curiosities, customs, and ethnological annotations, legends and fantasy, can be seen the practical nature of the merchant, which confers an air of realism upon the account, differentiating it from the tastes of its day and making it an authentic piece of travel writing.

Center: This miniature taken from Livre des Le Merveilles *portrays the fabulous inhabitants of the remote lands of the East: men without heads, Cyclops, and beings with a single great foot, which they used as parasols to bring themselves a little relief from the summer heat. These monsters form part of the exotic Medieval tradition and, although absent from Marco Polo's narration, were illustrated in some of the many different editions of Il Milione.*

Bottom: Marco Polo stayed on the Malabar coast of southern India during his return voyage to Europe. This illustration shows a group of dark-skinned and bearded men harvesting pepper, which the Venetian described as "of a naturally serpentine form." Pepper (Piper nigrum), a native species of the region, was among the most sought-after and expensive spices in Europe.

India during their two-year voyage, the ships eventually tied up in the port of Hormuz. Niccolò, Marco, and Maffeo continued overland, through Persia and Armenia until they reached the shore of the Black Sea. In 1295 they finally came within sight of Venice. Three years later, a prisoner of the Genoese, Marco Polo embarked on a new adventure, this time of a literary nature. His extraordinary experiences, related in *The Travels of Marco Polo*, provided a portrait of the East for centuries.

The fabulous wealth of Cathay and Cipangu (Japan) were to be the lure for one of the most exciting phases of European exploration.

Below: Visiting the ever-crowded and cosmopolitan ports of China and the Indian Ocean, Marco Polo took careful note of the number of ships, the volume and quality of the goods traded and commercial practices. His estimates, influenced by sincere wonder, appeared exaggerated to his disbelieving fellow Venetians who gave him the nickname "Ser Milione."

Bottom: The Great Kahn, on the occasion of the Polos' departure, prepared a fleet of "fourteen ships, each of which had four masts, and many were propelled by twelve sails," crewed by a total of 600 men and stocked with provisions for two years. The Polos navigated the seas of the Indonesian archipelago, taking in Sumatra, Ceylon, and the Malabar coast of India before reaching Persia after a voyage lasting two years and three months.

THE TRAVELS OF MARCO POLO: A BEST-SELLER IN THE LITERATURE OF TRAVEL

In 1298 Marco Polo was captured by the Genoese during a naval battle off the island of Curzola on the Dalmation coast. Imprisoned, he shared his three-year incarceration with a certain Rustichello da Pisa, a writer of tales of knightly adventure. Perhaps as a way of passing the time, Marco began to recount the story of his travels in Asia, which the Pisan transcribed in a Franco-Italian language typical of a certain literary genre. Thus was born *The Travels of Marco Polo, or The Description of the World* as the original title ran. The book was immediately successful and the number of manuscript versions of the work, more or less faithful to the original text, soon increased to 143. Considering the extremely high cost of production, the diffusion of *The Travels* was remarkable and can be compared with a modern best-seller printed in hundreds of thousands of copies and translated into the principal European languages. *The Travels* spoke to a varied audience: it appealed not only to that group of knights, ladies, and aristocrats who were avid consumers of spicy, imaginative tales, but also the wealthy bourgeoisie and men of the church. The structure of the work is original and differs in form and content with respects to the literary norm of the era. *The Travels* is in equal measure

a story, a guide for traders and a historical and ethnographical treatise, with the necessary concessions to traditional exoticism.

The 234 chapters are arranged according to a discontinuous narrative structure which does not take into account the itinerary followed by the traveler who, with no forewarning, frequently describes places of which he has only heard others speak. Even though *The Travels* never deals directly with commerce, Marco Polo was apparently obsessed by quantification: numbers are more important than any other form of observation; how many bridges or squares there were in a city; the distances between various places; the quantities of goods bought or sold. The numbers are always extreme, which led to the coining of the nickname Ser Milione for Marco Polo, which was later applied to the book as well. The fabulous riches of Cathay,

Bottom: Marco Polo is depicted in this frontispiece from Il Milione *published in 1477.*

Eofm
breue
ctona
ð ɑɒ

painstakingly enumerated, inflamed the dreams of a Europe torn by struggles between relatively insignificant and poverty stricken states. *The Travels* offered an idealized image of a centralized, strong, and well organized power, reviving the ancient ideal of a universal empire.

The curtain of mystery concealing the East was raised for the first time. Asia was no longer an unknown land populated by monsters and diabolic hordes. *The Travels* revealed the presence of another civilization that was perhaps even superior to that of Europe. The geographical horizons suddenly exploded and the influence of *The Travels* far outstripped its author's intentions.

The geography of Marco Polo appeared on maps for centuries, inspiring generations of cosmographs and explorers who, searching for Cathay and the Spice Islands, circumnavigated Africa and discovered a new continent, America.

Opposite and above: "... All of you who wish to know the variety of the human races, and the variety of the realism, provinces and regions of all parts of the East, read this book and you will find the great and astounding characteristics of the peoples above all of Armenia, Persia, India and Tartaria, who are distinctly referred to in this work by Marco Polo, wise and cultured citizen of Venice." These are words that open Il Milione, one of the most famous books of all times. Its diffusion was in relative terms as rapid and wide- spread as a modern best-seller. In a brief space of time, 143 editions were published in various languages and all more or less faithful to the original text.

Top left: In this miniature of the 15th century taken from one of the innumerable editions of Il Milione, Marco Polo is portrayed on horseback while receiving a precious gift.

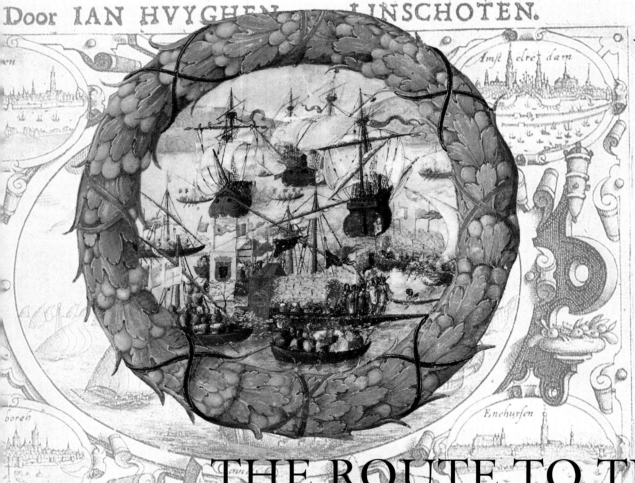

*I*n search of gold and the mythical Christian Kingdom of Prester John, Portugal sent explorers into the uncharted Atlantic Ocean. Descending along the seemingly endless coast of West Africa, swarms of fragile caravels rounded Cape Bojador and reached the Gulf of Guinea and the mouth of the Congo. Diogo Cão pressed on as far as the deserted coasts of southern Africa, preparing the way for the final assault by Bartolomeu Dias. In 1488 the Portuguese ships rounded the Cape of Good Hope for the first time and entered the waters of the Indian Ocean. The route to the East and the spice markets was now open. Ten years later Vasco da Gama's fleet reached the port of Calicut in southern India. A new era commenced following his expedition. From the early sixteenth century, a long-lived Portuguese trading empire was established in the East.

THE ROUTE TO THE INDIES: THE PORTUGUESE NAVIGATORS

The stretch of coast between Lagos and Cabo de São Vicente is one of the most suggestive in the whole of the Algarve, the southernmost region of Portugal. That desolate promontory pointing finger-like southwestward really can look like the very end of the world. The Atlantic waves beat incessantly against the rocks and the nudity of the barren, wind-blown land heightens the loneliness of the place. It was there that Prince Henry the Navigator was perhaps stimulated and encouraged to hunt for the "hidden things," the mysteries concealed beyond the gray horizon of the sea. Much further south, on the west coast of Africa, another cape, no more than a long tongue

of sand, marked the boundary of the human universe. South of Cape Bojador, the ocean was considered to be unnavigable: from that point began the horrors of the equatorial zone. Ships that dared to enter that Sea of Shadows would have been remorselessly sucked into soupy waters inhabited by monsters. The sun was so hot that the sea boiled and, legend had it, white men were turned into blacks. We do not know exactly what it was that prompted the young prince to dedicate his entire wealth and all his life to an exploration of the African coast. There was undoubtedly the lure of riches, but not solely. Henry cultivated medieval ideals and was a knight

rather than a merchant. His primary objective was the propagation of the faith. No business man would have risked energy and capital in an enterprise with such poor prospects. The real motivation behind the exploration was a crusading spirit: the same spirit that in 1415 had carried the prince to the walls of Ceuta, a Muslim stronghold on the Mediterranean coast of Morocco. The conquest of Ceuta marked the beginning of the African dream that, for almost a century, was to absorb much of the human and economic resources of Portugal. Although Henry is famous as "The Navigator," he never actually participated in the Atlantic expeditions in person, nor can it be said

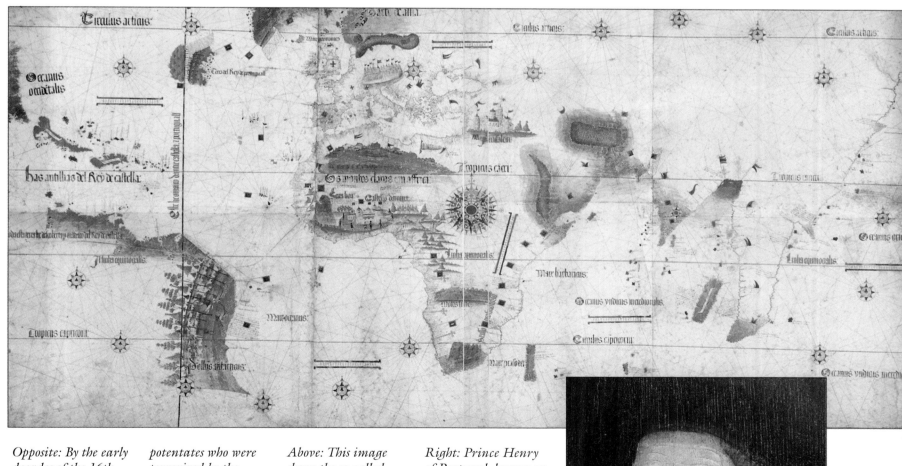

Opposite: By the early decades of the 16th century, the Portuguese fleet, here portrayed in a miniature from 1513, enjoyed almost total control over the Indian Ocean routes. The area was conquered with brutal rapidity, crushing the resistance of the local

potentates who were terrorized by the unrestrained audacity of the Portuguese adventurers on whose arrival "all the ships fired and even the birds stopped flying" as Alfonso de Albuquerque wrote on the occasion of the attack on Aden.

Above: This image shows the so-called Cantino Map from the name of the man who fled from Portugal to deliver it to the Duke of Ferrara in 1502. The map reproduces the globe as it was represented at the time: it is evident in many cases the profile of the coast is missing.

Right: Prince Henry of Portugal, known as "The Navigator," here in a 15th century portrait by Nuno Goncalves, throughout his life was the supporter of the expeditions along the African coast. He died in 1460, leaving his successors with the task of completing his ambitious explorations.

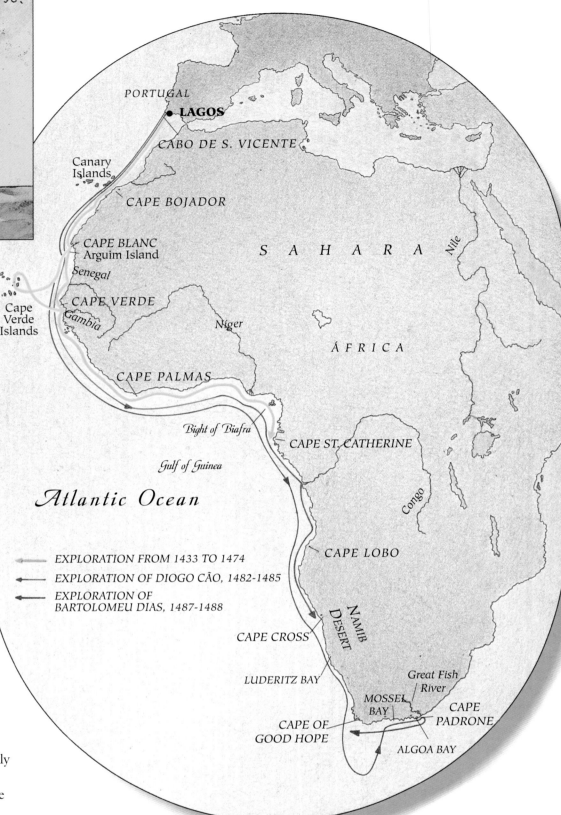

Nau redonda - 1498.

PORTUGAL
● LAGOS
CABO DE S. VICENTE
Canary
Islands
CAPE BOJADOR
SAHARA
Nile
CAPE BLANC
Arguim Island
Senegal
CAPE VERDE
Cape
Verde
Islands
Gambia
Niger
ÁFRICA
CAPE PALMAS
Bight of Biafra
CAPE ST. CATHERINE
Gulf of Guinea
Congo
Atlantic Ocean
CAPE LOBO
⟵ EXPLORATION FROM 1433 TO 1474
⟵ EXPLORATION OF DIOGO CÃO, 1482-1485
⟵ EXPLORATION OF
BARTOLOMEU DIAS, 1487-1488
NAMIB
DESERT
CAPE CROSS
LUDERITZ BAY
Great Fish
River
MOSSEL
BAY
CAPE
PADRONE
CAPE OF
GOOD HOPE
ALGOA BAY

that from the beginning he conceived of a route to the Indies, which at the time vaguely meant all the lands to the east of the Muslim empire. Perhaps, like his successors, he really did believe in the existence of a powerful Christian kingdom, that of the legendary Prester John, which the cartography of the times placed deep in the African interior. Whatever it was, mystical obsession or lucid calculation, the prince's exploration fever never waned. In 1419 he was named the regent of the Algarve and assumed the direction of the Order of Christ (the heir to the Templar traditions), whose wealth enabled him to finance the first expeditions. From then on Henry commissioned ships and crews to round Cape Bojador almost every year. Nevertheless, for almost a decade, none of the them were successful nor did they seriously attempt to break down the barrier of superstition that protected the region. With his debts mounting, the prince decided to make his authority felt and ordered his squire, Gil Eannes to venture beyond the fatal promontory without further ado. Evidently Eannes was more concerned about his sovereign's reactions than the threat of the boiling seas as he duly rounded the cape without encountering any great difficulties. He landed on the desert coast without encountering any form of life other than the odd shrub which he collected and brought back with him as tangible proof of his enterprise. That was it: no signs of men and none of monsters. The way was now open. The following year Alfonso Baldaya pushed on a few hundred kilometers further south, heaving to in a bay foaming with fish and seals. He mistook the inlet for the mouth of a river which he baptised the Rio de Ouro, the River of Gold. He returned to Portugal

48

Top left: Pottery of the Sagres school depicting a Portuguese nauredonda *of the late 15th century: as you can clearly see the traditional lateen rig of the caravel has been modified with the addition of square sails that were more efficient on long ocean voyages. The* nauredonda *also had larger holds than the caravel and was more suitable for commercial voyages.*

with a cargo of seal skins and a remarkable piece of news: on the sand he had seen traces of man and other tracks which may have been made by camels or horses. Above all, it had been discovered that navigating in the Atlantic was much easier that had been thought. Officers and men soon began to understand the rhythms of the winds and currents, while the rudimentary open fishing boats were replaced by a new type of ship with a more versatile rig and a greater loading capacity, the caravel. From 1437 Prince Henry was embroiled in internal problems, and for five long years no ships cast off from the port of Lagos. The new King Pedro's ascension to the throne gave new life to the exploration: in 1441, Nuno Tristão and Antão Gonçalves left once again for the River of Gold. This time they met the natives, probably nomadic Berbers, and succeeded in capturing a small group of them. One ship set sail for Portugal with the prisoners, while Tristão headed south until he reached Cape Blanc and the island of Arguin close to what is now called Greyhound Bay in Mauritania. The African coast was arid and inhospitable, but the expeditions began to bear their first fruit. Salt, furs, exotic curiosities, and above all men. Once converted to the true faith and brought back to their homelands, they in turn would become the ambassadors of the Good Book, the first Christians in the land of Islam. Other ships set sail for Arguin, and the races of the interior were the source of increasing numbers of slaves. In 1444, five caravels returned to Lagos with 165 prisoners whose sale partially covered the expedition expenses. Missionary zeal was thus flanked by the profit motive. The following year was marked by the discovery of the mouth of the Senegal River. The desert gave way to tropical Africa and the Portuguese were faced by a completely different landscape. The vegetation was florid and the banks of the river were lined by palms and tall trees. There were numerous birds and some of them, such as the swallows, were identical to "those that migrate from Portugal."

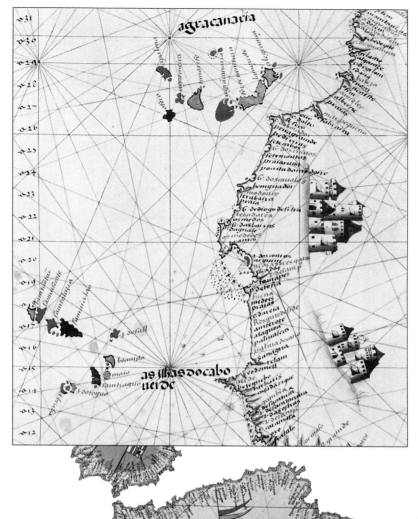

Opposite: The Portuguese explorers' first contacts with the kingdom of Congo, then one of the most advanced civilizations on the African continent, were based on reciprocal friendship and respect. The "greatly powerful and excellent King of the Congo" (as the Portuguese sovereign addressed his African colleague), shown here conceding a hearing to the European envoys, agreed to convert to the Christian faith and sent ambassadors to Lisbon.

Top: This map from 1514 shows the Atlantic coast of West Africa, the theater of the early Portuguese explorations. The navigators who ventured beyond Cape Bojador in Morocco had to cope with serious technical and psychological problems. There began the Dark Sea, where according to the medieval geographers, fantastic creatures were waiting to devour seamen and where the sun was so hot that the waters boiled. It was said that all the white men who passed that point would instantly be transformed into blacks.

Above: This detail from the Cantino Map depicts the interior of West Africa, then completely unknown, and is rich in imaginary features (apart from the very real Portuguese outpost of La Mina on the Gulf of Guinea), but the coastlines are crammed with names and navigational notes, testimony to the regularity of the Portuguese expeditions to the area in the late 15th century.*

Top: The Portuguese were not always forced to take control of the Indian ports. Frequently their envoys were warmly welcomed by the local leaders, who were competing among themselves, and eager to be free of the control of the Islamic traders.

Bottom: The port of Lisbon in the 16th century; color engraving by Theodore de Bry. Lisbon, on the Tagus estuary, was the point of departure for all the great Portuguese expeditions to the African coast, the Cape of Good Hope and, finally, the Indies. Until the late 16th century, Portugal enjoyed a virtual monopoly of the Indian Ocean routes and the lucrative spice trade.

The inhabitants of this region were also different: the color of their skin was much darker than that of the men from the north and they appeared to be less docile. The crews that tried to capture them were met by a shower of poisoned arrows. Tristão himself was fatally wounded as he sailed up the Gambia River he had discovered in 1446. In less than 15 years since Gil Eannes had rounded Cape Bojador for the first time, dozens of caravels had followed in his wake. Twelve hundred miles of unknown coastline had been explored. A success from a geographical point of view, but an economic disaster. Slaves and salt were not enough to clear the debts racked up by the prince. None of the explorers had yet found either gold or spices, and Henry was facing ruin. The latest war with Castile put an end to all thoughts of exploration for a period of ten years. The first official expedition to return to the West African coast was entrusted to two Italian merchants, Aloisio Cadamosto, a Venetian, and Antonieotto Usodimare, a Genoese fleeing from his creditors. Between 1456 and 1458 Cadamosto and Usodimare discovered the Cape Verde Islands and navigated the Gambia River. Their trading with the natives was perhaps not as profitable as they had hoped, but Cadamosto, an acute observer, brought back startling news. He had seen enormous trees (baobabs) "whose circumference at ground level measured seventeen ells," elephants and a hippopotamus, "which the natives call the water-horse: it is over ten feet long and has very short legs and cloven hooves. On its horse-like head it has, like the wild boar, two tusks each almost as long as a forearm." Henry the Navigator did not live to see the latest progress: he died in 1460. The following year Pedro da Sintra navigated as far as Sierra Leone, opening the way to the Gulf of Guinea. The coast gradually curved away to the east, suggesting the idea of an easy circumnavigation of the continent, in accordance with the maps of the era. The exploration was entrusted to private monopoly in exchange for a share in the profits and a commitment to the continued exploration of the coastline. By the end of 1475, year by year, the Portuguese had explored the entire coast between Libya and Cameroon, identifying the various sections according to the goods they produced: the Pepper, Ivory, and Slave Coasts, and finally the Gold Coast located in modern day Ghana. This discovery led to the construction of a stone fortress called Elmina, the mine. In reality, by far the most profitable trade remained slaves. In any case, the coast of the Gulf of Guinea became one of the principal sources of wealth for Portugal. When it was discovered that beyond the Niger delta the African coast continued southward, precluding the hoped-for direct route to the Indies, the Portuguese monarchy concentrated on safeguarding its trading rights. A new war with Castile definitively established Portuguese supremacy on the African

coast. King John II, who ascended to the throne in 1481, now had the means and political stability to reactivate Henry the Navigator's exploration project begun 60 years earlier. The first expedition left the Tagus estuary in 1482 under the command of Diogo Cão, a Captain with considerable experience of navigating in the tropical seas. According to the king's instructions, Cão was to head as far south as possible until he found a passage to the east, and to erect *padrões*, stone pillars engraved with the arms of Portugal, on the most significant points of the coast. Following a stay at Elmina, the caravels proceeded toward the Bight of Biafra and the waters of Cameroon and Gabon. Cão was now sailing in unknown waters beyond the line of the equator. At a certain point he noted that the sea had changed color and a strong, murky current was forcing the ships away from the shore: he had discovered the estuary of the Congo. He sent ashore a party of men with orders to explore the area and proceeded as far as the site of the modern city of Benguela in Angola. Cão then inexplicably turned back. Perhaps he believed himself close to the extreme tip of Africa and was anxious to present his discoveries to John II. Portugal afforded him a hero's welcome and, in 1485, just a year after his return he was sent to sea once again. During this second expedition he reached the desolate coasts of the Namib Desert: he left a *padrão* at the Cape Cross and once more headed back northward. Cão was never to reach his homeland again, but his men brought discouraging news to the king: the African coast was apparently endless. Some time earlier John II had rejected the project of a Genoese captain, a certain Christopher Columbus, who held that it was possible to reach the Indies by sailing westward across the Atlantic. The king's advisors had excluded any such possibility and stubbornly insisted that the route to the Indies lay to the east. In 1487, a small fleet of caravels under the command of Bartolomeu Dias set out from Lisbon with high hopes and a more flexible strategy. Cão's expeditions

had demonstrated that the southern coast of Africa lacked resources and was virtually uninhabited. One of the new expedition's three ships was dedicated to the transport of provisions, and once its stores had been exhausted, it could be abandoned and destroyed. At the same time the king dispatched an overland mission with orders to find Prester John and eventually reach

India. The chosen men, Pedro da Covilhão and Alfonso di Paiva, spoke fluent Arabic and, disguised as merchants, would with a little good fortune have been able to cross the vast Muslim territories safely and to return with precious information. While Covilhão was landing in Egypt, Dias's ships were crossing the Atlantic on a new route avoiding the doldrums of the Gulf of

Below: A sea serpent engraving from 1558: one of the monsters thought to infest the waters of the Atlantic. The real dangers to be faced by ships sailing along the African coast were in fact far worse: offshore currents, sudden and violent storms, and the impossibility of procuring regular supplies.

Guinea and heading directly for the mouth of the Congo. From that point on Dias faithfully followed the route pioneered by Diogo Cão: with the support ship left anchored in a sheltered bay in southern Angola, he headed on toward the Cape Cross, where Cão had erected his last marker. The voyage along the coast was arduous due to adverse winds and the Benguela current, which at those latitudes passes very close to the coast. After a final pause in Lüderitz Bay, Dias decided to head out into the open sea, plotting a broad curving route that would quickly take him southward. Exploiting the westerly winds which blow constantly at around the 40th parallel, he could now head easily toward the African coast. The caravels sailed swiftly eastward before the wind, but no land appeared on the horizon. Dias maintained his route for a number of days, but there was still no sighting. What was happening? According to his calculations the coast should have been sighted some time ago. He decided to head northward again, and in early February, 1488, the lookout sighted land. Dias had gone beyond the tip of the continent without realizing it. He dropped anchor in what is now known as Mossel Bay (248 miles east of the Cape), where he was able to reprovision with fresh water and

meat. The natives, he noted, were negros *de cabello revolto* (curly-haired) like those of Guinea, but less welcoming. Their manifest hostility persuaded the captain to leave the bay. The coast extended east to west, but beyond Algoa Bay (the site of the present day Port Elizabeth) it curved northward. Dias was sure that he was sailing in the waters of the Indian Ocean. India, the dream of many generations of explorers, was within reach, and yet he had to resign himself to turning back. The crew was exhausted and supplies were running critically low. The return voyage was long and gruelling. The captain followed the coast until he reached the magnificent buttresses of the Cape of Good Hope and headed to the north, finally reaching his support ship. Just three surviving sailors were there to greet him. The rest had all died of scurvy. After having transferred the supplies, Dias torched the unseaworthy ship and set sail directly for Portugal. His enterprise had resolved a fundamental question in the exploration of the seas: the Atlantic and Indian Oceans were connected and beyond the Cape of Good Hope extended a new world. The reports sent back by Covilhão were very detailed: far from being empty, the Indian Ocean was criss-crossed by a

CAP·DE·BONNE-ESPERANCE.

Above: Dias reached the extreme tip of Africa, depicted here in a Dutch engraving from the 17th century, in the spring of 1488. Caught unawares by a storm, he baptized it Cabo Tormentoso or Cape of Storms. This name was later changed by King John II to the rather more optimistic Cape of Good Hope.

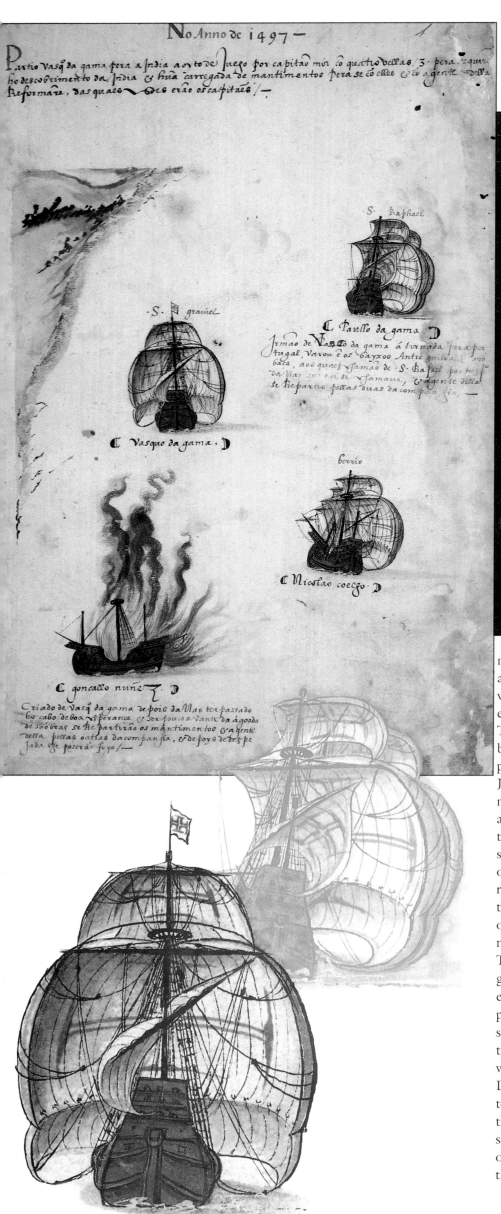

S. Raphael

C. Pavllo da gama D

S. Graviel

C. Vasquo da gama D

borrio

C. Nicolao coello D

C. goncallo nunes D

network of traffic linking important cities and ports. After such great efforts Portugal was unwilling to let the rewards of years of expense and labor slip from its grasp.

The rich spice markets were highly prized by the Spanish who, it appeared, were also preparing important oceanic enterprises. John II requested and obtained papal mediation and in June, 1494, he came to an agreement with the king of Castile whereby they would divide the Atlantic into separate spheres of influence. According to the Treaty of Tordesillas, the Lusitanian monarchy retained all the geographical discoveries to the east of an imaginary line cutting the ocean vertically at a distance of over 248 miles from the Cape Verde Islands.

The time was now ripe for Vasco da Gama's great expedition. The expedition's purely explorative motives were overlapped by new political and commercial demands. The selection of the commander himself revealed the conviction that in the Indies a diplomat would be more useful than a good sailor. Da Gama was of noble origins and had the temperament necessary for the complex task that he had been given. The fleet that set sail from Lisbon in July, 1497 was composed of four ships with specially modified rigging: the lateen (triangular) sails were replaced or

Left: Da Gama's fleet reproduced in a catalog of Portuguese ships from the 16th century. Notice that the traditional lateen rig was modified to accommodate the square-sail system that was more efficient on long ocean voyages with constant winds. In contrast with Dias, da Gama did not hug the interminable African coastline, but from the Cape Verde Islands, he headed south almost as far as the latitude of the Cape of Good Hope before turning due east.

Right: In this portrait, painted shortly before his death, Vasco da Gama appears calm and benevolent, a rather different figure to the cruel man described in contemporary reports.

integrated with a system of square sails
better suited to sailing on the high seas.
Dias's experience had in fact suggested that
the best routes lay out to sea rather than
along the coast. Da Gama left the Cape
Verde Islands in early August, heading due
South; then, in the region of the Tropic of
Capricorn, he turned east, sailing until he
came within sight of land. Three months
later his fleet dropped anchor in St. Helena
Bay, around 124 miles north of the Cape
of Good Hope: da Gama had completed
the longest ocean crossing ever attempted
by a European navigator (at least a third
longer than Columbus's voyage), and
established a new route to the Indian
Ocean. Africa, until that moment the
focus of the explorer's attention, now
became an obstacle to be overcome on
the way to India. Having rounded the
cape, the Portuguese hugged the coast
of South Africa, following the route
established by Dias as far as the Great
Fish River. On the 25th of December, in
uncharted waters, they found themselves
faced by the cliffs of Pondoland, which
they called *Terra do Natal*, a name which

55

*Above: This
engraving from 1800
shows one of the ships
that accompanied
Vasco da Gama
during his voyage
towards the Indies.
In spite of the great
expense of the
expedition, both in
human and
monetary terms, the
handful of gold and*

*spices that reached
Portugal with da
Gama's vessels
aroused the
enthusiasm of the
sovereign Manuel I:
the wealth of the East
appeared to be
guaranteed and the
discoverer of the
Route to the Indies
was acclaimed as a
national hero.*

*Right: This portrait
of Vasco da Gama
comes from an old
Portuguese
manuscript conserved
in the National
Library, Paris.
Hard-headed and
determined in
character, da Gama
led the first Portuguese*

*expedition to reach
the coast of India in
1498. Subsequently
he commanded two
further campaigns
of conquest as an
admiral in the Far
East. He died at
Cochin on the
Malabar Coast
in 1524.*

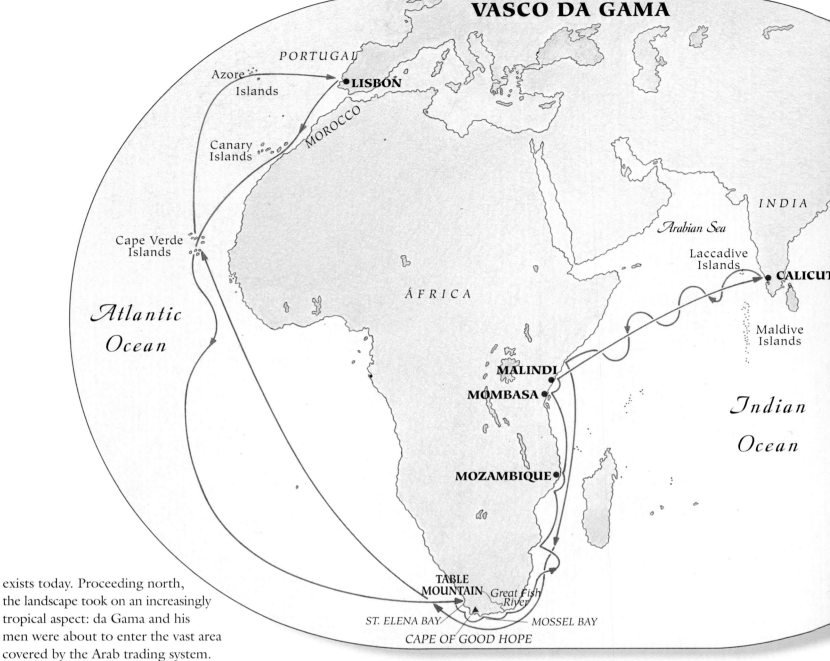

exists today. Proceeding north, the landscape took on an increasingly tropical aspect: da Gama and his men were about to enter the vast area covered by the Arab trading system. Mud hut villages were replaced by stone-built towns the ports of which were crowded with vessels from the farthest reaches of the Indian Ocean. The Sultanates of the East African coast enjoyed considerable prosperity and were constantly at war amongst themselves. The Portuguese first stopped in Mozambique and then Mombasa, where they encountered a hostile reception. Nearby Malindi, in contrast, offered help and hospitality.

The local Sultan procured food and water for da Gama and, most importantly, a pilot with knowledge of the rhythms of the dominant winds. Taking advantage of the spring monsoon, the small fleet reached the Malabar coast in the south of India in just 27 days: this was in late May, 1498. The Portuguese ships dropped anchor off the city of Calicut (now Koshikode), and some days later da Gama was invited to present himself to Zamorin, the local lord. Initially, relations were friendly, even though the Portuguese gifts were considered to be little more than baubles. Soon however, pressure applied by Muslim merchants, who considered the foreigners to be a threat to their trading monopoly forced Zamorin to

Left: Vasco da Gama paying homage to the ruler of Calicut, then an important commercial port on the Malabar coast of southern India. The tributes presented by the Portuguese, glass beads, feathered hats, and other similar items, were not appreciated by the king and his retinue, who, according to a contemporary report, "laughed at the sight of the gifts."

Opposite: This Flemish tapestry woven around 1525, celebrates the arrival of Vasco da Gama's expedition in the port of Calicut (now Kozhikode on the Malabar coast) in 1498. The Portuguese, greeted by a composed and sumptuously dressed crowd, are loading their ships with exotic animals from the furthest corners of the Earth: ostriches, camels, and even a unicorn. The buildings of Calicut have been transformed in accordance with the European style of architecture and the whole scene is dominated by an imaginary exoticism.

Top: A view of Goa on the west coast of India, conquered in 1510 by Alfonso de Albuquerque, one of the principal artificers of the Portuguese empire in the East. In just a few years Goa was transformed from a simple trading port into a flourishing colony and a stronghold controlling the most important Indian Ocean routes.

modify his attitude. The Calicut market was rich in spices and other goods precious in Europe, but the Portuguese were unable to barter successfully, partly due to their lack of suitable goods of exchange and partly due to the hostility surrounding them. After three months of vain attempts, da Gama decided to leave Calicut and set sail for Portugal. The return voyage, sailing into the teeth of the monsoon, was completed with great difficulty: it took no less than three months to reach the coast of Africa. The men were exhausted and dying, one by one, of scurvy. When da Gama finally reached Portugal in the summer of 1499, he had lost two ships and half of his men. From a commercial point of view the expedition had been a failure: no gold and no spices, apart from a handful of peppercorns and cloves. But they had finally reached India, and the feat was acclaimed as a triumph. Da Gama's accounts revealed that there was no Christian kingdom in the East and that the Muslim dominion extended from the coast of Africa to the Far East. If Portugal wanted spices she was going to have to acquire them by force. Vasco da Gama's three-year journey, with its three hundred days of straight sailing on the open sea, had unwound a slender thread that, from the gray solitude of the Atlantic, rounded the southernmost tip of Africa and led to a new, equally vast and mysterious

Top left: In 1557, the Chinese authorities granted the Portuguese merchants of Malacca permission to establish a permanent base at Macao, on the estuary of the River of Pearls, shown here in an engraving by Theodore de Bry from 1598. The city of Macao was for three centuries the fulcrum of European trade with Far East Asia and Japan. The last outpost of the Portuguese empire in the East, Macao will return to China in 1999.

Top right: In just a few decades a series of audacious coups gave the Portuguese control over all the strategic strongholds of the Indian Ocean, from Malacca to Hormuz, together with the principal commercial routes between the West and the East. Their Islamic rivals were crushed in the process. The illustration shows the port of Aden at the entrance to the Red Sea.

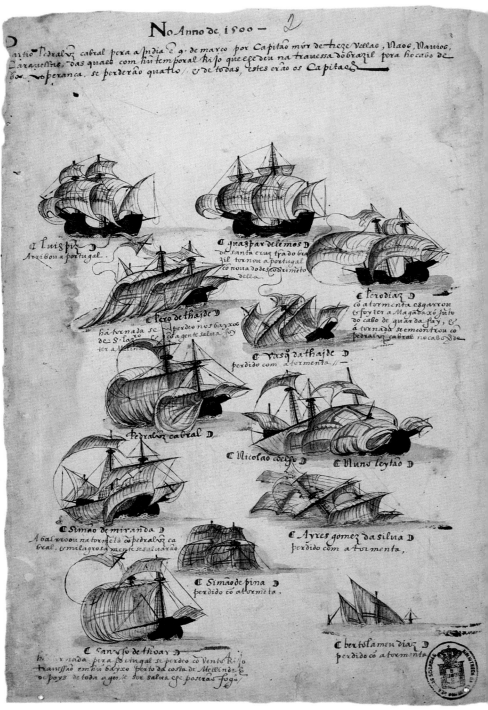

ocean. The Carreira da India, the route to the Indies, was a long and anything but easy voyage: Lisbon was 9,920 miles from the Malabar coast, six months sailing in either direction with all the inherent risks that were entailed. What the undertaking of such a trip really meant, leaving aside the minor inconveniences of illness, mutiny, and the privations of shipboard life, can be seen from the estimates relating to shipwrecks, with a vessel being lost every 80 miles. However, enthusiasm was rampant in Portugal: with the help of God, and after untold sacrifices, the doors to the Orient had finally been opened, and King Manuel I was determined to pursue the seafaring destiny of the nation come what may. Not six months had passed since the return of da Gama before a new expedition heading for Calicut was ready to leave the Tagus estuary: it was commanded by a nobleman of little more than thirty years of age, Pedro Alvares Cabral. Cabral actually had little experience of long ocean voyages, but was assisted by Bartolomeu Diaz, a veteran of the explorations of the African coast and the discoverer of the passage to the south of the Cape of Good Hope. Cabral was at the head of a 13-strong fleet and 1,200 men, many of whom were professional soldiers. Exploiting the pattern of Atlantic winds known to Diaz and proven by da Gama, Cabral unhesitatingly headed south to the Cape Verde Islands, and then veered westward. He actually sailed too far on his westerly course, and six weeks after the fleet had left Lisbon, an imposing unknown coastline appeared on the horizon. Cabral had discovered Brazil, landing about 124 miles south of present-day Bahia. According to the treaty of Tordesillas, the new land was located, as it happened, within the Portuguese sphere of influence. We do not know whether Cabral had been supplied with secret information, or whether the discovery was in fact made by pure chance and the unbridled force of the trade winds blowing across the South Atlantic. The fact remains that as far as was possible, he scrupulously, dedicated himself

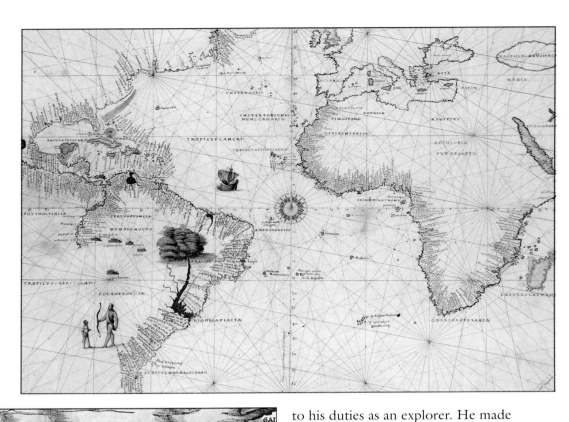

Top: The portolan of Battista Agnese, 1553 (chart VI, South America). The east coast of the continent was by now well charted, even though the lands to the south of the Strait of Magellan are shown with prudently indefinite outlines. Central America appears, from east to west, marked with a continuous coastline: it had now been confirmed that there was no strait linking the Atlantic and the Pacific. South America is inhabited by the legendary giants.

Center: This copy of the Tabula Terra Novae from the 16th century shows a still very uncertain outline of the coat of the northern Brazil. The inner continent is still completely unknown, and it is inhabited by ferocius beasts and people: among the many fantasious notes on the map, one inscription reads "antropophagi hic sunt."

to his duties as an explorer. He made a brief survey of the coastline and took possession of the land in the name of Portugal, noting in his log that the country was inhabited by naked savages decorated with colored feathers, the first description in history of the Tupinamba natives. After a few days stop, the fleet set sail once again for India where the rather more prosaic duties of the professional soldier awaited Cabral. Using diplomacy or cannons as the situation demanded, he obliged the principalities of the Malabar coast, firstly Calicut and then Cochin, to sign a series of agreements that gave the Portuguese crown the right to trade freely and to establish permanent bases. Cabral returned to Lisbon in the summer of 1501 with only half of his original fleet of ships and with his crews decimated. He did however bring with him an enormous cargo of precious spices, the first tangible evidence of the wealth of the Orient, and

Bottom:
The penetration of the Brazilian interior by the Portuguese began over a century after Cabral's accidental discovery. In 1637, Captain Pedro Teixeira left Belém close to the mouth of the Amazon with a fleet of 47 boats, 70 soldiers, and a thousand faithful natives. In contrast to the impression

given by the illustration, the resistance put up by the Amazon tribes was weak and sporadic: in eight months' travel Teixeira reached the Spanish settlement of Quito, and around thirty years later the Portuguese built a fort at Barra on the Amazon, where the future city of Manaus was to rise.

above all the certainty of having established a bridgehead in the distant Indies. The foundation stones of an empire had been laid: Cabral's successors, Francisco de Almeida and Alfonso de Albuquerque were to follow in his footsteps with remarkable efficiency. In less than twenty years, the Portuguese fleets controlled all the key ports of the Indian Ocean from Mombasa to Malacca, from Hormuz to Goa. Malacca, conquered in 1511, became the base for further expansion toward the Moluccas, China and Japan. In 1557, the merchants of Malacca, who had for some time been involved in profitable smuggling, succeeded in persuading the Chinese government to allow them to establish a presence in Macao. Trade with Japan was formalized shortly afterwards: in 1571 the Portuguese set up a base at Nagasaki where they were to remain for the next seventy years. Goa became the capital of an immense trading empire based on the control of the ports and the key routes: an ambitious monopoly that was, however, destined to collapse as new and more aggressive pretenders made their appearances. Under the combined weight of attacks from the Dutch and the British, the Portuguese were gradually forced to retreat, losing the mainstays of their empire one by one. By 1666, all that remained of the Portuguese empire of the Indies were Goa and Macao. However, a new era of European domination in Asia was to emerge out of the ruins of a Lusitanian dream that originated among the bleak rocks of the Algarve.

Top: This illustration taken from a Dutch edition of The Journey of Fernão Andrade in China, *by Joao de Barros, shows the first landing on Chinese soil that took place in 1517. Note the Portuguese captain offering gifts to a group of Mandarins.*

Bottom: This illustration shows the flourishing port of Banten in Java, a vital staging post on the trading route to China and a center for the collection and distribution of spices from the archipelagos of the Far East. In 1603 the English captain, James Lancaster succeeded in concluding a commercial treaty with the ruler of Banten, laying the foundations for the future British expansion in Asia.

61

Left: This Japanese screen from the 16th century is decorated with a number of scenes depicting the arrival of a Portuguese ship and the unloading of goods. In 1570 the Portuguese founded Nagasaki, the first European settlement in Japan, and the terminus of the trading route that, from Goa by way of Macao, extended into the Far East.

SPICES

In the late Middle Ages the term spices was used to indicate a whole range of natural substances used as condiments, medicines, deodorants, and preservatives. Some of them, like saffron, had also been cultivated for some time in Mediterranean Europe, but most, the most precious and sought-after products, were only to be found in the tropical regions where conditions were hot and wet enough for them to thrive. Cloves, the dried flower buds of *Eugenia caryophyllata*, a tree similar to the myrtle, was only found on certain islands of the Molucca archipelago. They had been prized for centuries in China and India thanks to their thaumaturgical properties in the treatment of caries and stomach upsets. In Europe they were used to preserve meat, and, suitably packed in a gold shell, they were thought to be efficient talismans against infection with the plague. Pepper, *Piper nigrum*, originated in southern India and Malaysia and was itself considered to be "a good antidote to poisons," and widely used as a condiment. It was hugely expensive and the expression "peppercorn rent" was coined to describe particularly high rents. Equally precious were nutmeg, *Myristica fragrans*, and cinnamon from Ceylon, the bark of the *Cinnamomum zeylanicum*. Up until the mid-fourteenth century, spices were regularly brought to Europe by the caravans that crossed the Asian continent. With the fall of the Mongol empire and the explosion of the Great Plague, the traditional supply channels suddenly dried up. The Arab and Persian merchants monopolized the Eastern trade and prices shot through the roof. The precious goods from the Far East arrived at the market at Alexandria, where the Venetians had managed to retain a commercial foothold via the ports of the Persian Gulf and the Red Sea. A very restricted quantity of pepper and other spices thus continued to reach Europe, but prices were prohibitive and profits vast. Goods bought in India at reasonable prices could be resold in Europe for up to eighty times their original value, with payments being made in silver or gold. Given this situation, spices were one of the pressing motives that persuaded the Spanish and Portuguese navigators from Vasco da

Left: The most sought-after and valuable spices were all to be found in the tropical regions of eastern Asia: pepper, cinnamon, nutmeg, and cloves (considered to be excellent protection against infection with bubonic plague) were all treasured for their medicinal properties and sold at remarkably high prices in European pharmacies.

Gama to Columbus and Magellan, to risk voyages through unknown oceans. When, in 1501, Cabral's fleet reached the Indian ports visited by da Gama, its intentions were clear. Cabral returned home with a cargo of 150 tons of spices: he had forced Islam's commercial blockade and laid the basis for the Portuguese domination in Southeast Asia that was to last for centuries.

Center: The seed of Myristica fragrans, known as nutmeg (enlarged in this illustration), was one of the most sought-after and expensive spices in Europe. Nutmeg and its derivative mace (the outer covering of the seed) was almost exclusively found in the Banda Islands and, as well as being used as condiments, were employed as medicines: among other things they were said to be useful for eliminating freckles.

Bottom: A spice trader from Tractatus de herbis, late 15th century, Estense Library, Modena. Spices, rare and very valuable goods in Europe, almost exclusively came from India and the Far East. Profits from the trade were astronomical: goods bought cheaply on local markets would be sold at up to eighty times their cost price on the European markets.

Overleaf: An imaginatively portrayed hail of flying fish surrounds a vessel heading for the Americas in an engraving by Theodore de Bry from the late 16th century. Even though the voyages of Columbus and the conquistadores had swept away the fears of marine monsters, an Atlantic crossing was still a major test for the European navigators.

63

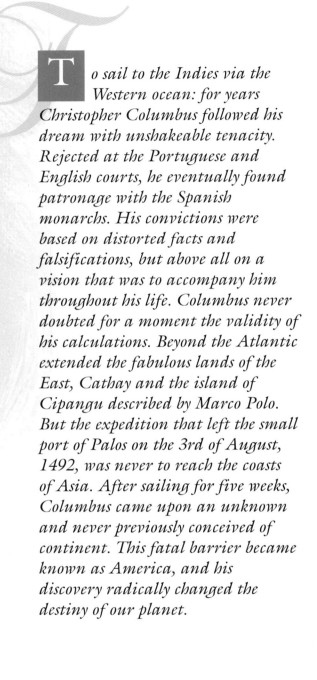

T o sail to the Indies via the Western ocean: for years Christopher Columbus followed his dream with unshakeable tenacity. Rejected at the Portuguese and English courts, he eventually found patronage with the Spanish monarchs. His convictions were based on distorted facts and falsifications, but above all on a vision that was to accompany him throughout his life. Columbus never doubted for a moment the validity of his calculations. Beyond the Atlantic extended the fabulous lands of the East, Cathay and the island of Cipangu described by Marco Polo. But the expedition that left the small port of Palos on the 3rd of August, 1492, was never to reach the coasts of Asia. After sailing for five weeks, Columbus came upon an unknown and never previously conceived of continent. This fatal barrier became known as America, and his discovery radically changed the destiny of our planet.

THE FATAL ERROR: COLUMBUS DISCOVERS AMERICA

In December, 1488, Bartolomeu Dias's caravels slowly sailed up the Tagus towards Lisbon. Among the crowds of onlookers lining the banks of the river a mysterious, middle-aged figure watched the proceedings. After years of stubborn attempts, the Portuguese had finally opened the gates to the East and as far as he was concerned Dias's success wiped out his last remaining hopes. Nobody was likely to take him seriously anymore and his proposal for a western route to the Indies would once more fall on deaf ears. Not even England, before whose monarch he had explained his project, appeared to be interested. Christopher Columbus, born at Genoa in 1451 and boasting a solid seafaring experience, had spent the last few years of his life migrating from one court to the next, searching for approval and support for his ideas.

By now he was resigned to his fate, all that remained was to wait for the response of the king of Castile. No less than 12 years had passed since he had been shipwrecked on board a pirate ship off Cabo de Sao Vicente and had managed to swim to shore. Since then he had made his home in Portugal.
The colony of Genoese merchants at Lisbon had welcomed him with open arms. Naturally he had had to keep quiet about the fact that his ship had been sunk during a skirmish with the Genoese fleet. Subsequently he was to invent a less embarrassing past and an illustrious genealogy. In Portugal he learned to read and write and picked up the local languages, Castilian and Latin. He became

Center: This request of 100 gold castellanos signed by Columbus himself, was addressed to the Granata Treasurer Alonso de Morales.

67

a good cartographer and married a local girl of noble origins. His trips to Madera, the seas of the north, and to Guinea made him an expert in the ocean winds and currents, and it was in those years that he became convinced that the lands of the East, the Indies, and the Cathay of Marco Polo, could easily be reached by sailing westward across the Atlantic. His convictions were based on theoretical data deriving from studies of the most authoritative cosmographical texts of the era. In order to demonstrate his hypothesis of a "narrow" Atlantic, Columbus selected those facts that corroborated it and combined them so as to obtain the result he desired. According to Ptolemy, dry land accounted for half the Earth's surface with the rest being covered by the oceans. However, in his treatise the Imago Mundi, Cardinal Pierre d'Ailly claimed that Ptolemy was mistaken and, making reference to other classic authors, he increased the extension of the continents by over a tenth. According to this procedure, Asia was seen to be larger than

previously believed. But not large enough for Columbus, who added another 60 degrees of longitude by considering the immense island of Cipangu (Japan) described by Marco Polo. In this way the distance between the coasts of Portugal and Asia appeared to be 77° : by departing from the Canaries and rounding up the figure, the distance could be reduced to 60°. But the Atlantic was still too vast. Columbus therefore had to discover the lowest linear measurement per degree of longitude and chose that of the Arab geographer Al Farghani (a little over 56 nautical miles), and arbitrarily adopted the length of the Italian mile (4,884 feet). In this way a degree of longitude at the equator measured just 51,5 miles. On the route plotted by Columbus this value was further reduced, and the distance between Asia and Europe could therefore be calculated at around 2,728 miles (just a quarter of the actual distance). It was a long, possibly arduous voyage, but one that was undoubtedly feasible. Columbus had expounded his theories to

Above: Columbus's caravels are painted on this ceramic by Zuloaga. None of the vessels had a dead-weight greater than 80 tons. The Niña, *the* Pinta, *and the* Santa Maria *were rigged with square sails that were better suited to the winds of the mid-Atlantic and carried crews of around 90 men. The* Niña, *a robust oak-built ship, was 30 feet long with a beam of 70 feet.*

Right: This wall painting by Bejarano, Palos, La Rabida monastery, shows Christopher Columbus in conversation with the physicist Garcia Hernandez at the La Rabida monastery. The first known globe was constructed by Martin Behaim in 1492, the year Columbus departed for America. It is therefore highly improbable that Columbus had ever seen one, despite the evidence of this painting.

John II of Portugal, but the commission of scholars charged with examining the proposal judged it to be impractical.

In 1485, the Genoese moved to Castile. There he had to start from scratch: he was once again a foreigner to be wary of. With remarkable tenacity and ability Columbus succeeded in taking on a new identity and striking up important new friendships in just a few months. After little more than a year he was introduced to the court and obtained his first audience with the king and queen of Spain. Isabella immediately took him under her wing, but in those years the Spanish monarchy was involved in the conquest of Granada, and Columbus's requests were turned over to the examination of a commission of experts. There followed five interminable years of academic disputes during which time a response failed to arrive. During that period even Columbus's determination wavered at times. In 1492, with the Arabs finally driven from the Iberian Peninsula, it appeared that things may have finally taken a turn for the better, and Columbus once again began to hope for a favorable response. In the meantime, he had never stopped pleading his cause with a number of influential figures close to the court including the Duke of Medinaceli and Luìs Santàngel, the patron of the Santa Hermanadad, a powerful political-military confraternity. Columbus was finally convocated for the court's final verdict: a unanimous no, accompanied by disturbing accusations of heresy.

The threat of the inquisition hung over Columbus at this point.

While the Genoese was taking into consideration the possibility of yet another exile in France, Santàngel decided to help him: ably circumventing the problem of financing,

Above: Columbus, in this anonymous painting from Palos, La Rabida monastery, explains his plans to the Franciscan monks of Granada. Having arrived in Spain in 1485, for many years Columbus searched in vain for somebody who believed in his ideas. Only thanks to the friendship and support of the Andalusian clergy did the Genoan finally succeed in attracting the attention of the Spanish court.

Bottom left: This gold coin bears an effigy of Ferdinand II of Aragon and Isabella of Castile. The marriage between the two sovereigns united the most powerful realms of the Iberian Peninsula, marking the birth of the Spanish nation.

Bottom right: This hourglass dates from the 15th century. Fragile and imprecise, in that era the hourglass was the only instrument for measuring time available to navigators.

69

which implied direct collaboration on the part of the crown, he reformulated the question in a new light. The involvement of the king and queen would be restricted to the supply of the ships and the payment of the crews, while the Santa Hermanadad would provide Columbus with his fee of 250,000 *maravedis*. The total figure of around two million *maravedis* can hardly have seemed much to Santàngel. It was more or less equal to the monthly income of a Castilian nobleman. Columbus was unwilling to modify any of his rather extravagant requests. He insisted on the title of Viceroy of all the lands discovered for him and his descendants, a tenth of the wealth and an eighth of the commercial proceeds deriving from the expedition as well as a number of other rewards. Nevertheless, as he was careful to point out, his true objective was not the conquest of fame and riches but rather the propagation of the Christian faith. After some hesitation, the queen gave her consent to the project. The city of Palos was obliged by royal decree to supply two ships, the third was to be hired from a local owner. Palos was a lively commercial port, although much less important than nearby Cadiz, and was perfectly suited to a low-key departure. When all was said and done Columbus's enterprise was not an official expedition and should it have proved to be a failure, the crown would have avoided compromising its reputation. The small fleet, two caravels and a square-sailed nao, left the Spanish coast on the 3rd of August, 1492. The captains of the 80-ton vessels were chosen from among the leading families of Palos: Martin Alonso Pinzon commanded the *Pinta* and his brother, Vicente Yanez Pinzon, the *Niña*. Columbus sailed on the *Santa Maria*. The crews numbered ninety men, including a converted Jew who spoke Arabic. It was thought that his skills as an interpreter would have been useful in the realm of the Great Kahn to whom Columbus was carrying a letter bearing the seal of the King of Spain. Ten days later the fleet came within sight of the Canary Islands. During the fleet's stay in the port of Gomera, modifications were made to the *Niña's* sails, unsuited to ocean crossings. With the last preparations having been made and the ships fully provisioned, Columbus gave the order to weigh anchor: according to his calculations a straight route due west should within a few weeks have brought them to Antilla, one of the imaginary islands filling the

gaps in his maps of the Atlantic. Beyond Antilla, and lying on the same latitude there had to be Cipangu. Columbus always displayed absolute faith in his calculations, but he must have known, at least in part, that he was heading into the unknown. The only concrete fact was the constant presence of a northeasterly trade wind that, at least initially, would have rapidly pushed the ships out to sea. Too rapidly as it happened. Foreseeing problems with the crew, the expedition leader decided from the outset to falsify the ship's log, reducing (as was his wont) the number of miles covered each day. If Asia proved to be further away than expected, in this way the sailors would never have known and, Columbus concluded, nobody "would have been frightened." The crew and the officers were in fact Spanish, and Columbus was a foreigner. How long would he have been able to maintain his authority? Everything depended on the duration of the voyage. The ships sailed on through the blue vastness of the Atlantic, the lookouts ever alert for signs of land on the horizon. On the 16th of September, the sea suddenly changed in appearance, and all around there were "numerous tufts of bright green grass that seemed to have been recently torn from the ground and led the entire expedition to believe that

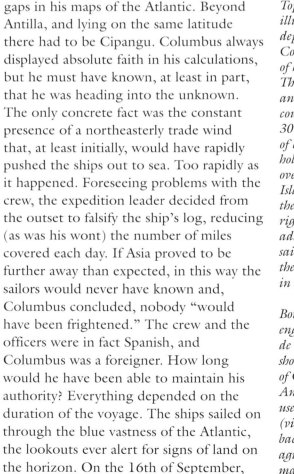

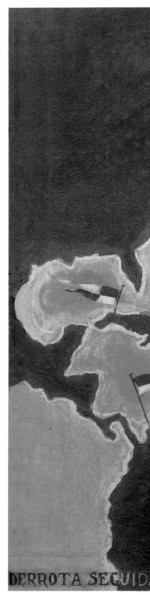

DERROTA SEGUIDA

Top: This painting illustrates the departure of Columbus and two of his caravels. The Niña, *70 feet long and 30 feet broad, could carry a crew of 30 men and 51 tons of cargo stowed in her hold. During the stop-over at the Canary Islands, Columbus had the traditional lanteen rig modified with the addition of square sails better suited to the dominant winds in mid-ocean.*

Bottom: This engraving by Theodore de Bry from 1594, shows the departure of Columbus for America. The caravels used by Columbus (visible in the background) were agile, fast, and highly manoeuvrable vessels derived from those traditionally used for fishing and coastal trading.

70

TOBAL COLON EN SU PRIMER VIAJE

Top center:
The outward and return route of Columbus's first voyage (Palos, La Rabida monastery). In spite of the limitations of the technology available to him and his lack of knowledge of the Atlantic winds, the route followed by Columbus, whether deliberately or not, still today appears to be one of the best possible.

Bottom:
The departure of the three caravels from the port of Palos on the 3rd August, 1492 is depicted on this wall painting by Bejarano, La Rabida monastery, Palos. The Franciscan monks of the La Rabida monastery were from the very beginning among the most enthusiastic supporters of Columbus's plans and introduced to important figures in the Castilian nobility.

Above: On the 10th of October, 1492, after over a month's sailing on the open sea, Columbus was faced with an attempted mutiny aboard the Santa Maria, *as can be seen in this colored engraving by Amati, 1890. His own self-belief helped him to defuse the situation: the Indies, he claimed, were now within reach and all they had to do was to "keep to their route until, with the help of God, they had reached them." He was lucky: just three days later the lookout on the* Pinta *sighted the first American headland.*

71

they were close to an island." They had in fact reached the Sargasso Sea. The men could believe what they liked, but Columbus's predictions did not foresee land so soon: they were only halfway to Cipangu. The algae, dense as it was, did not impede the fleet's progress, and the ship's maintained their westerly heading. On the 25th of September a lookout on the *Pinta* thought that he had spotted land. "It was nothing but sky," noted Columbus, while discontent began to spread through a crew tired of sailing through this emptiness. On the 7th of October great flocks of birds were spotted high in the sky heading toward the southwest. Columbus gave order to follow them and this proved to be a fortunate decision. Had he kept to his planned route the fleet would sooner or later have encountered the Gulf Stream, which would have dragged them to the

north and eventually taken them out to sea again. Instead, just five days later, the lookout reported a sighting of land. The Indies! It was only a small island (Watling Island, now known as San Salvador Island in the Bahamas), but to Columbus it was just the first of the many islands, over 7,000 of them, of which Marco Polo wrote in *The Travels*. Beyond that great archipelago lay the continent. Cipangu and Cathay could not be far. By pure chance Columbus had stumbled across land exactly where he had expected to find it: the sum of his errors led to a remarkable discovery. After 36 days at sea, the navigator landed and, falling to his knees on the beach, named the island San Salvador, taking possession of it in the name of Spain and "in honor of God who guided us and saved us from many perils." The Taïnos natives (part of the Arawak group) gave the

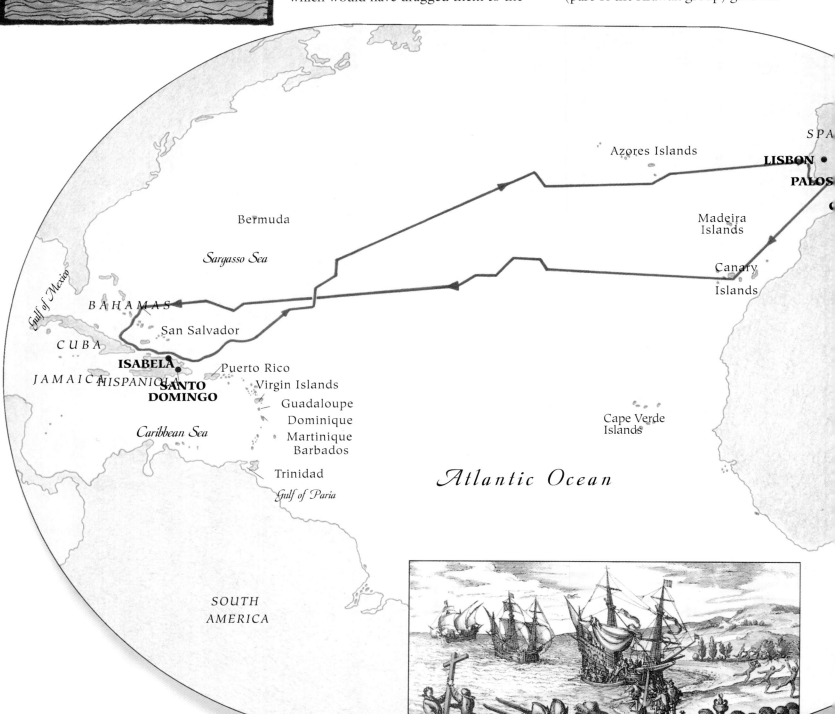

foreigners a friendly welcome: they were all naked and appeared to conduct a simple life. There were no signs of walled cities or golden temples, but the landscape was lush and attractive. Columbus was moved to contemplate that scenic paradise: towering trees, brilliantly colored birds and flowers. But where was Cipangu? The interpreter spoke to the Indians in Arabic but gained no reply. None of them had ever heard of the Great Kahn and his realm, but some wore small gold coins as jewellery. Where did that gold come from? Undoubtedly to the south, as only in the warmer southern countries, it was then believed, could the precious metal be found. To the south, he believed to understand, lay a great island. After having cruised through the Bahamas archipelago for a couple of weeks, Columbus reached the northern coast of Cuba which he followed for some days

ÁFRICA

Opposite: In this illustration from Columbus's letter De Insulis Indie Inventis, *1493, Columbus lands on the coast of the Insula Hyspana, or Hispaniola, welcomed by a group of naked girls. The nudity of the natives, women included, surprised but did not scandalize the Spaniards. For Columbus it simply represented the proof of their innocence and was due to the natural state in which they lived while awaiting elevation to a higher level of humanity through faith.*

Opposite: This tinted engraving by Théodore de Bry, 1596 depicts Columbus while landing in the Bahamas, on the island he named San Salvador. Columbus immediately took possession of the island in the name of the king and queen of Spain and had a cross raised on the beach. The Tainos natives proved to be friendly, but they had only food and water to offer their rapacious guests rather than (in contrast to what is shown in the illustration) the mythical gold of Cathay.

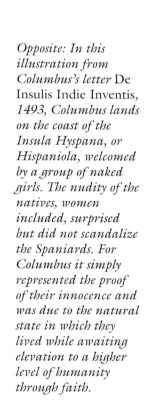

Top: On the 12th of October, 1492, after 36 day's sailing, Columbus set foot in the New World for the first time.
The Spaniards were captivated by the extraordinary beauty of the Bahamas archipelago, and

Columbus declared that he had never seen anything more beautiful: "Everything is green and the vegetation is like that in Andalusia in April. The singing of the birds is so sweet that truly one would never leave this place."

Above: The first mass celebrated in the Americas, in the Bahamas archipelago, painted by Pharamond Blanchard in the 19th century. There were no clergymen aboard Columbus's ships during his first voyage. The problem of the

mass conversion of the "pagans" of America was postponed until the second expedition of 1493: Columbus set out with a fleet of 17 ships and 1,200 men, with the explicit task of converting the peoples of the New World.

Top: This profile
of the coast of
Hispaniola was
drawn by Columbus
himself. Columbus
reached the island
from Cuba early
in December 1492.
Giving way to his own
desires, he initially
mistook it for Marco
Polo's Cipangu, the
legendary land of
gold. Hispaniola
hosted the first
European Colony
in the New World,
Navidad (marked
on the map), though
the settlement was
tragically short-lived.

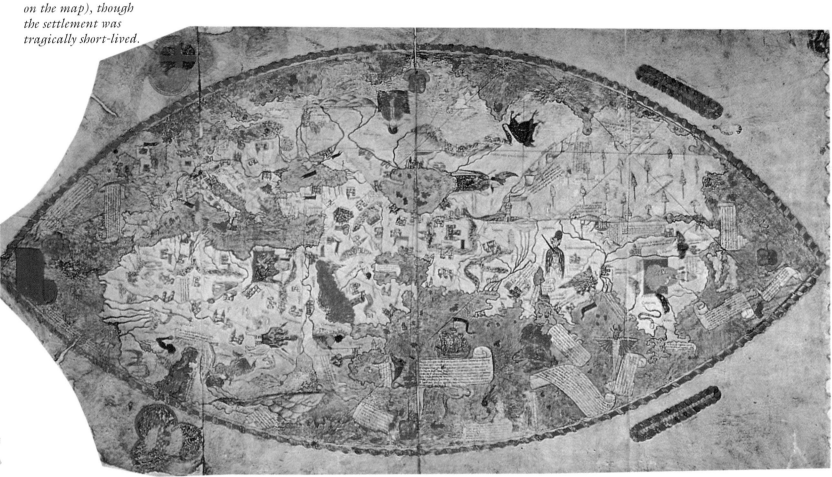

74

Center: The so-called
Toscanelli Planisphere
(circa 1457) is
attributed to the
Florentine physician
and geographer Paolo
del Pozzo Toscanelli.
Africa had yet to be
circumnavigated,
and the American
continent had not
even been dreamt of.
The work of
Toscanelli, who
championed the cause
of the westward route
to the Indies, had
considerable
influence on
Columbus's schemes.

Left: The colony of
Navidad, on the
north coast of
Hispaniola, is here
represented in an
edition of Columbus's
letter to Santangel of
1493. Navidad,
founded after the
sinking of the Santa
Maria, was in reality
a rough fort, built
from the wreckage of
the lost ship. On his
return during the
second expedition
Columbus found
nothing but ruins.

before dropping anchor in a sheltered bay.
An expedition on foot into the interior
failed to produce the hoped for results:
neither gold nor spices, just a few villages
of huts. The fleet continued eastward, and
early in December reached the coast of
Hispaniola: the inhabitants, noted
Columbus, were more diffident but also
richer. Their gold coins were larger and
more sophisticated. The gold, they told
him, came from Cibao in the East. Lost in
his personal vision, for Columbus, Cibao
was transformed into Cipangu. The Indian
leaders on Hispaniola warned the Spaniards
about the *caniba*, ferocious cannibal
warriors who terrorized the island. It was
only natural that Columbus should mistake,
through one of his habitual phonetic
interpretations, the caniba for the subjects
of the Kahn. In his mind all the pieces of
the great mosaic were falling perfectly into
place: Cathay was to hand and sooner or

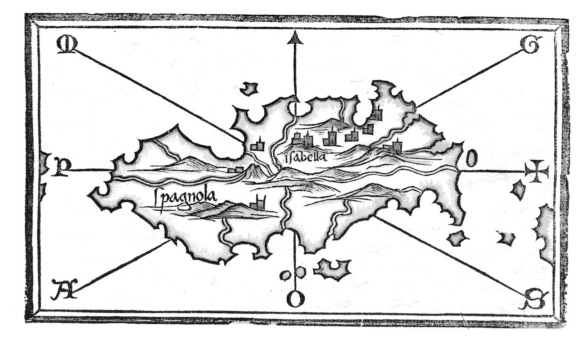

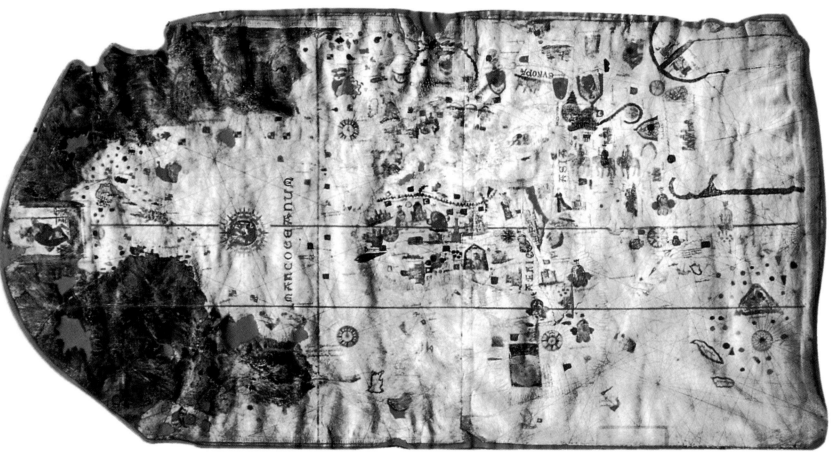

later they would have reached it. It was just a question of time. In the meanwhile, he tried to obtain as much gold as possible, exchanging it for the goods he had brought from Spain. During Christmas night a serious incident brought Columbus back down to Earth: the *Santa Maria*, left unmanned, ran aground on the coralline rocks close in to the coast. The great navigator realised that the ship was irreparably damaged and with the help of the natives he unloaded supplies and equipment before deciding to destroy the hulk. There was no room for the crew of forty men on the *Niña* or the *Pinta* and so the timber salvaged from the wreck was used to construct a shelter. This was the origin of Navidad, the first European colony in the Americas. Columbus assured the men that he would return the following year and exhorted them to make use of the intervening months by searching for gold.

On the 4th of January, 1493 the surviving caravels set sail for Spain. Once again Columbus hit on the correct route, instinctively heading northward until he found favorable winds for the return crossing. A storm when the ships were close to the Azores threatened to swamp the vessels and ruin the expedition just as it entered its final stages. In that moment of danger Columbus wrote a brief report of his voyage, enclosed it in a sealed barrel and consigned it to the waves. Perhaps one day some one would have found it and his discovery would not have been made in vain. At last, on the 18th of February, the *Niña* succeeded in gaining the refuge of a port in the Azores. There was no trace of the *Pinta* with whom all contact had been lost some time previously. Fate appeared to be turning against the great navigator: off the coast of the Iberian Peninsula another storm once again forced the *Niña* off course, and

Top: This map of Hispaniola from the Isolario of Benedetto Bordone, dates 1528. Compared with the sketch of the northeast coast of the island executed by Columbus at the time of the discovery but found and published relatively recently, the outline of Hispaniola is far from accurate.

Above: The first map depicting the recently discovered New World drawn on a sheepskin by Juan de la Cosa, Columbus's guide, in around 1500. West is to the top. The Caribbean islands can clearly be seen, while the coasts of North and South America are drawn with no thought as to accuracy. The well known shape of Africa is in the center. At the bottom the Indian peninsula is barely hinted at.

He wanted an overseas empire and the promised gold. However, there was no gold on Hispaniola, or very little, and the Navidad colony had been massacred by the Indians. Columbus headed to Cuba, exploring the southern coast. He never admitted that it was an island and obliged his men to sign a declaration confirming his folly: Cuba was a peninsula of the continent, a province of the vast empire of

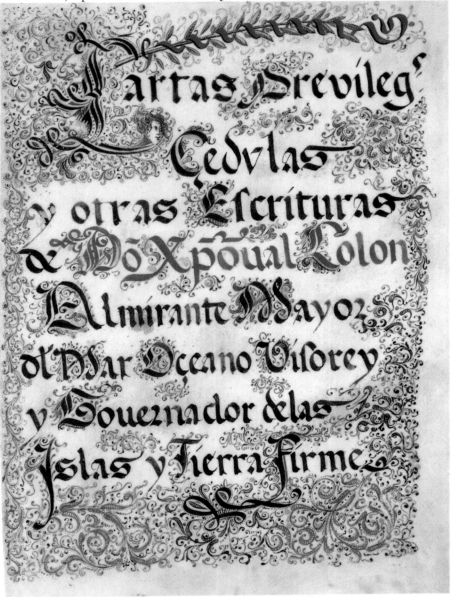

Columbus was forced to make repairs in the port of Lisbon. The situation was rather delicate: relations between Portugal and Castile were problematic and Columbus realized that he risked being arrested.
He was taken to John II and presenting himself as an admiral of Castile, succeeded in coming away unscathed.
The king of Portugal did not demonstrate any great interest in his discoveries and preferred not to run the risk of a diplomatic incident. In the meantime the *Pinta*, which had been forced on the coast of Galizia by the fury of the seas, was heading for Palos. The two ships entered the port on the same day, the 15th of March, 1493.
Columbus immediately sent news of his great discovery to the court at Barcelona. Ferdinand and Isabella's reply could hardly have been more explicit: it was addressed to "our Admiral of the Ocean" and urged a meeting as soon as possible.
Columbus was acclaimed in triumph.
He presented himself to the king at the head of a magnificent parade, surrounded by the Taïnos Indians and bearing exotic gifts. The gold that he carried, he said, could give but a poor idea of "the wealth of those lands."
"The skeptics will say I exaggerate regarding the quantities of gold and spices to be found over there but, in all truth, we have seen but a hundredth part of the splendours of those realms... I know that we will find enormous gold mines if only His Highness would permit me to return";
Six months later Columbus departed once more at the head of a fleet of 17 ships and a host of colonists: the king of Spain had taken his words as gospel.

Cathay. Whoever dared claim otherwise would be punished with a fine and have his tongue cut out. Columbus was to depart for the Americas on two further expeditions.
He was to fall into disgrace only to rise again. He was to discover other islands and eventually the continent, close to the Orinoco delta. In 1502 he reached the coast of Honduras. He was never to find gold and, for better or for worse, he remained true to his convictions.
Columbus died on the 19th of May 1506, still believing that he had discovered Asia.
Seven years later Balboa was to cross the forests of Panama and discover the southern sea, the immense Pacific Ocean. The Indies drew farther away from the Spanish horizon and a New World appeared on the maps.

Top left: The coat of arms assigned to Columbus, "Admiral of the Ocean Sea" by the king of Spain. The two figures at the top, the castle and the lion, represent the realms of Castille and Léon. At the bottom left appear a group of islands and the coastline of a hypothetical continent; they are the newly discovered lands. The gilded anchors on a blue ground refer to the rank of Admiral, conferred upon Columbus in 1493.

Opposite center: The frontispiece to The Code of Privileges, *which was conceded by the Spanish monarchs to Columbus, decorated with the titles of "Admiral of the Ocean Sea, viceroy and governor of the islands and the* continent" discovered by him. Dazzling the court with the wonders of the New World and promising gold and riches, Columbus succeeded in obtaining all the rewards that had been agreed upon prior to his departure.

Below: In this painting Columbus presents the treasures of the New World to the Spanish monarchs. Received in triumph, Columbus immediately headed for Barcelona to meet Ferdinand and Isabella.

He presented himself at court at the head of a sumptuous parade, bringing with him a group of Caribbean natives, parrots, exotic objects and, above all, promises of the future discovery of "enormous gold mines."

Bottom left: This colored engraving taken from Columbus's letter De Insulis Indie Inventis *shows the flagship that accompanied the Italian navigator on his successful voyage in search of the mythical lands of Cathay.*

Bottom right: This engraving of Columbus's letter to Santangel of 1493 shows a caravel sailing in an absolutely imaginary scene, off the islands discovered by Columbus during his first voyage, Fernandina, Isabella, Hispaniola, Concepcion and San Salvador.

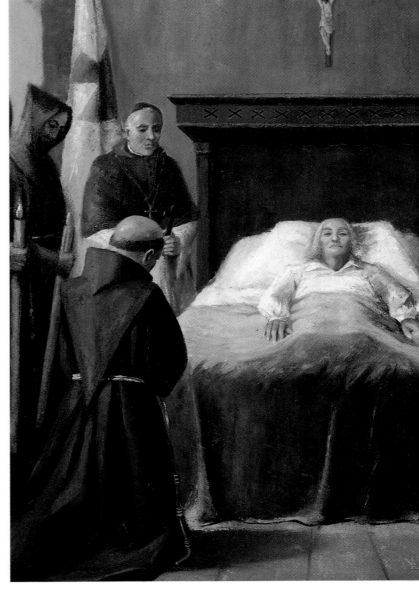

Above: This colored engraving shows Columbus being taken back to Spain in chains. After having violently quelled a rebellion by Spanish colonists on the island of Hispaniola, Columbus was arrested by the new governor sent to investigate the affair. Only in 1502 was the Genoan able to obtain partial rehabilitation within the Spanish court and set out on his fourth and final voyage.

Right and opposite: This map was drawn in 1505 by the brother of Christopher Columbus, Bartholomew, who took part in the navigator's fourth and last voyage in 1502. Testimony to the confusion that reigned among the cartographers of the early 16th century, South America (the Mondo Novo) is separate from the islands of "Jamaicha, Guadelupa, Spagnola, and Dominica, but still solidly attached to Asia, or rather the "Serica Provincia" or China. Many decades were to pass before America was recognized as an independent continent.

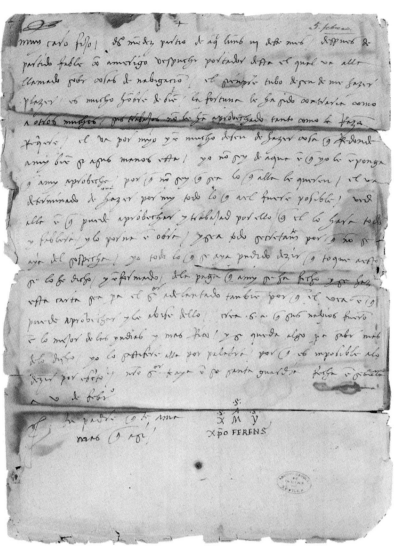

THE DISCOVERY OF THE "OTHERS"

Left: This acquatint by D. K. Bonatti (1792) is one of the many portrayals of Columbus's first meeting with the natives. The exchange of gifts with the natives did not bear the desired fruit: only on Hispaniola did Columbus manage to obtain even modest quantities of gold, but this only fuelled his conviction that he was close to the wealthy lands of Cathay described by Marco Polo.

Many of the lands discovered by the European navigators at the turn of the fifteenth century were already inhabited. The maps of Asia and Africa depicted legendary creatures: men with tails, Cyclops and cynocephalae. Marco Polo described distant populations and strange customs. Something was already known of the African continent: its inhabitants were perhaps considered to savages but not lacking a historical and social dimension. The discovery of America was an unexpected event. Nobody had ever hypothesized the existence of a continent on the other side of the Atlantic. Just as European culture was unprepared for the New World, it could hardly have imagined its inhabitants. Columbus's encounter with the Americans was different, for example, to that of the Portuguese with the Africans or the Asian Indians. It was a relationship based on absolute otherness. Columbus thought he was in Asia, not far from the legendary realms of Cipangu and Cathay, the sites of a civilization which in some ways could be compared with that of Spain. He moved in an uncertain world, created by his own desires. His overwhelming sensation was one of wonder. Columbus came from a multiracial society. He was accustomed to foreigners, whether they were Moors of Jews: they may have been infidels but they were still men. The native of the Caribbean apparently had no faith. To what extent were they human? Columbus was unable to decide. In his eyes the islanders from the Bahamas and Hispaniola appeared as "wonders," just as did trees, birds, flowers, and other natural phenomena. He failed, or refused, to recognize the signs of humanity in a society so different to his own. He noted the beauty and nudity which he immediately associated with the idea of an Earthly paradise. Even though he was unable to understand a word of their language, he claimed that the Indians were timid creatures and free of malice, raw material to be humanized through conversion to the Christian faith. Their good nature would lead them to obedience: once saved from the spiritual limbo in which they lived they would make excellent servants. Compared with the Spaniards they were inferior by definition: Columbus's ethnocentrism was absolute, at least initially, and free of economic or cultural motivations. In the act of discovery there were no practical reasons to support or justify this claim inferiority. But, as soon as the Indians tried to oppose the invasion, the scheme was suddenly upset: inferiority naturally gave the invaders the right to conquest. Ethnocide commenced after that first voyage of discovery by Columbus: a few decades later just a tenth of the native American population remained.

Center: This illustration of Caribbean warriors comes from Columbus's letter "De Insulis Indie Inventis" of 1493. The initial contacts with the people of the New World were peaceful. Columbus considered them to be innocent creatures to be humanized through the faith and treated them with condescension. However, as soon as the Indians rebelled against the forced labor and the pillaging of their goods, they became ferocious, cannibalistic savages to be fought an conquered. Thus began the ethnocide.

Right: This scene of cannibalism shows the Tupinamba of Brazil. The Spaniards were in no doubt about the fact that the Caribbean people, the Caniba from which the term cannibal derives, fed on human flesh. As Doctor Chanc, the physician with Columbus's second expedition narrates, "They say that human flesh is so good that there is nothing better in the world."

Bottom left: In this engraving by Theodore de Bry from 1692 can be seen an Indian ceremony of the Tupinamba people of Brazil. The custom of body painting and tattooing, common to many native American peoples, had a particular impact on the Spaniards. The description that follows is taken from Stories of the Life and Events of Christopher Columbus *written by his son Fernando on his return from the fourth and final expedition, and refers to the inhabitants of Nicaragua: "They have their arms and bodies decorated with Moorish designs made with fire that make them appear strange; others have painted lions, others deer, others fortified castles... still others blacken their eyes. Thus they adorn themselves to appear beautiful, and yet they look like devils."*

Opposite: This wall painting by Cesare Dell'Acqua (19th century) depicts Columbus and the discovery of America. The map in the background shows the dominions of Charles V (1500-1558) in the Americas.

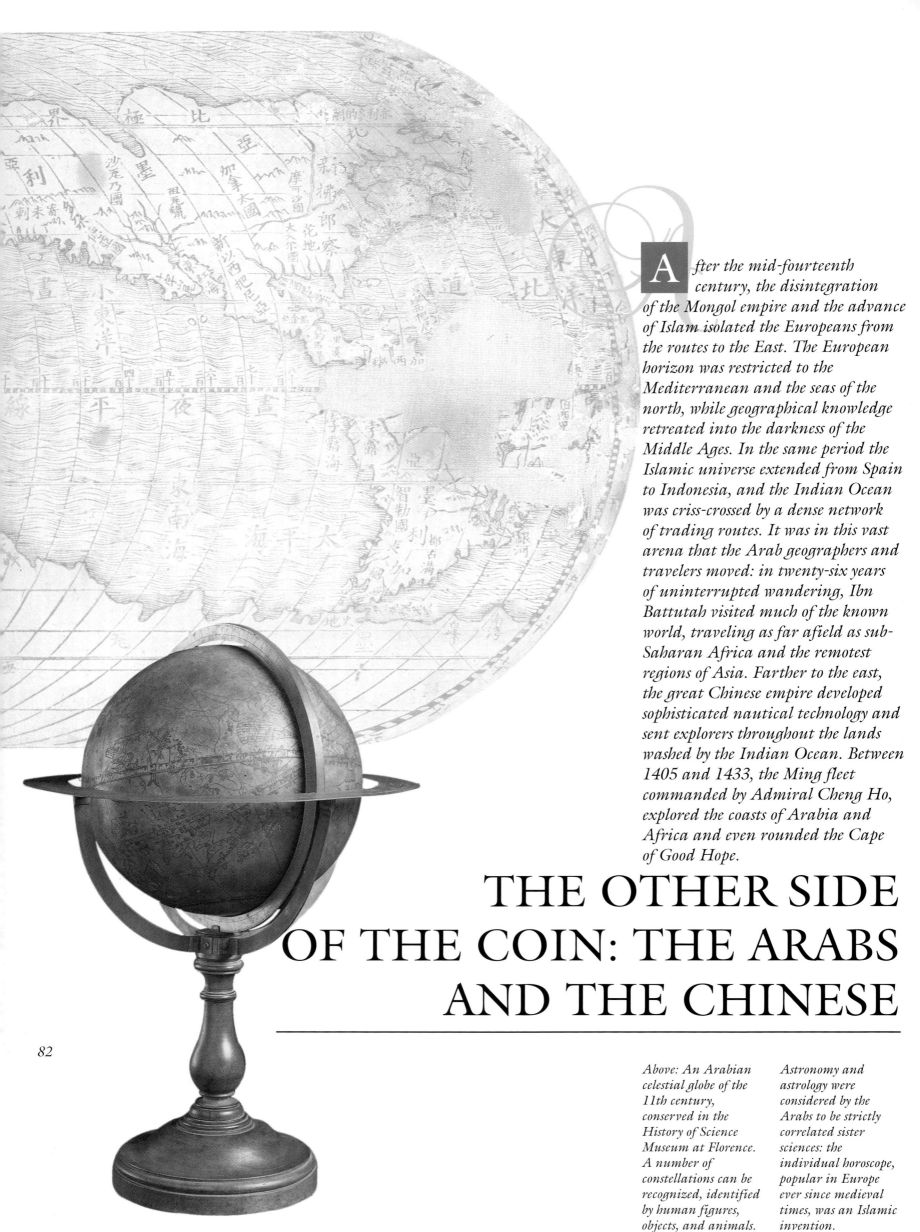

After the mid-fourteenth century, the disintegration of the Mongol empire and the advance of Islam isolated the Europeans from the routes to the East. The European horizon was restricted to the Mediterranean and the seas of the north, while geographical knowledge retreated into the darkness of the Middle Ages. In the same period the Islamic universe extended from Spain to Indonesia, and the Indian Ocean was criss-crossed by a dense network of trading routes. It was in this vast arena that the Arab geographers and travelers moved: in twenty-six years of uninterrupted wandering, Ibn Battutah visited much of the known world, traveling as far afield as sub-Saharan Africa and the remotest regions of Asia. Farther to the east, the great Chinese empire developed sophisticated nautical technology and sent explorers throughout the lands washed by the Indian Ocean. Between 1405 and 1433, the Ming fleet commanded by Admiral Cheng Ho, explored the coasts of Arabia and Africa and even rounded the Cape of Good Hope.

THE OTHER SIDE OF THE COIN: THE ARABS AND THE CHINESE

Above: An Arabian celestial globe of the 11th century, conserved in the History of Science Museum at Florence. A number of constellations can be recognized, identified by human figures, objects, and animals.

Astronomy and astrology were considered by the Arabs to be strictly correlated sister sciences: the individual horoscope, popular in Europe ever since medieval times, was an Islamic invention.

IBN BATTUTAH

Below: There are no contemporary portraits of Ibn Battutah: this water-color, executed in recent times, portrays him with a beard and regular features. In the course of over 25 years' traveling, the famous "traveler of Islam," visited 45 different countries, reaching as far as the frozen steppes of Siberia.

"I have just arrived from Almeira in Spain. Your Moroccan colleague Fès has sent me a gold ingot, undoubtedly coming from the Sudan, in order to buy Spanish silk for you. However, I do not believe this to be a good idea and I am sending you the gold instead. At the same time, a friend of your colleague sent me a certain quantity of gray amber which I am sending to you by the same means. He wants you to send him five flasks of musk of the same value."

Thus wrote, circa the year 1100, an Egyptian merchant to his partner in Cairo regarding a routine business transaction in goods coming from the Far East, from Europe and from Africa. The vast Islamic trading system of the time extended from Spain to Indonesia, linking unbelievably distant lands in an intricate network. It was within the ambit of this commercial network that, over 200 years later, Ibn Battutah, the world's greatest traveler, commenced his wanderings.

His journeys lasted 26 years, and were they to be superimposed onto a modern map, they would stretch for at least 74,400 miles and cross the borders of 45 nations. Ibn Battutah traveled through almost all the Islamic lands, as well as making a number of incursions into the countries inhabited by the Christian and Buddhist infidels (Constantinople, Sardinia and China). He wrote a detailed report of what he saw, thanks to which we can follow his itineraries. In June, 1325, at the age of 22, he left Tangiers on a pilgrimage to Mecca. Reaching Cairo he headed toward the Nile Valley and the Red Sea looking for a ship that would carry him to Jiddah. However, communications with Arabia had been interrupted by a war and Ibn Battutah, "spurred by an irrepressible and long-nurtured desire," decided to reach the holy city by land. He therefore returned to Cairo and, crossing Syria, descended the Red Sea coast to Mecca. Then, in the company of a caravan of merchants, he headed towards the Euphrates. He visited Bassora, Shiraz,

Left: An Arab map of the Mediterranean Sea, taken from the Book of Countries compiled in the 10th century by the geographer al-Istakhri. Knowledge of the Mediterranean, here depicted in extremely stylized form, was essential to the political and cultural expansion of Islam. North is to the right. To the left is the coast of North Africa and Lebanon, interrupted by the Nile Delta. The three circles at the center of the map represent, from the top, Sicily, Crete, and Cyprus.

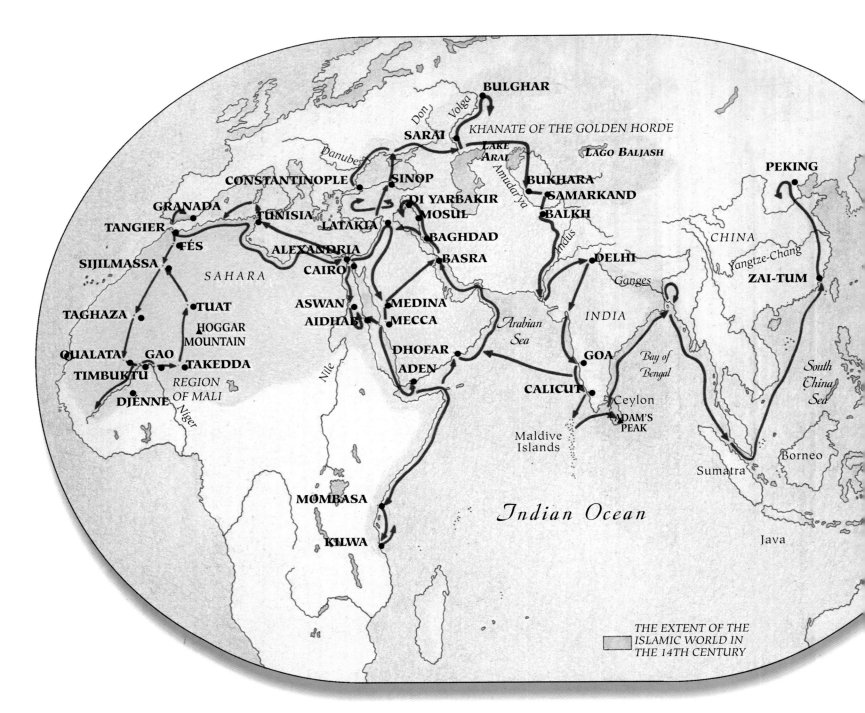

THE EXTENT OF THE
ISLAMIC WORLD IN
THE 14TH CENTURY

Baghdad and the fortified city of Diyarbakir on the banks of the Tigris. Returning to Mecca, he stayed for two years studying law the profession which was to permit him to earn a living during his future travels. In 1330 he set sail with a large retinue of servants and concubines and headed toward Aden, the famous trading port at the entrance to the Red Sea. There he saw the great tanks for the collection of rainwater which still exist today, and he marveled at the crowds of merchants filling the city. Aided by the favorable monsoon winds, he left Aden for the East Africa coast, reaching Mombasa and Kilwa, where he admired the architecture and beautiful wooden houses. After a third pilgrimage to Mecca, Ibn Battutah decided to leave for India. Long sea voyages did not appeal to him and once again he plotted an overland route which was to lead him through Syria, the "Land of the Turks" and southern Russia as far as the Volga. From Sarai, the capital of the Mongol Khanate of the Golden Horde, he traveled upstream as far as Bulghar at a latitude of 54° north. He would have liked

to have proceeded further, but the bitter cold and lack of food persuaded him to turn back. Ibn Battutah continued his march towards the East, skirting the northern shore of the Aral Sea and visiting Samarcanda and Bukhara. At Kunduz in the mountains of Afghanistan, he camped for forty days while waiting for the snow to melt on the high passes of the Hindukush. During the trip, his caravan was attacked on more than one occasion by bandits but, "by the grace of God," and with a little good fortune, he came through without a scratch. At last, having crossed the Indus, he arrived at Delhi, the principal Muslim city of the East, whose omnipotent Sultan was famous for the generosity and cruelty which he dispensed in equal measure. Ibn Battutah was received benevolently and was even assigned a post as a judge. The wonders of Delhi left him awe-struck: the Sultan was preceded by a court of "two hundred soldiers dressed in armor, sixty sumptuously saddled horses and fifty elephants adorned with silk and gold." He saw the magical arts of the fakirs, men capable of surviving

buried below ground and of levitating at will: the spectacle shook him to the point that he actually fainted twice and his servants had to use powerful drugs to bring him round. Suddenly one day the Sultan suspected him of instigating a conspiracy and had him arrested. Ibn Battutah was well aware of his master's bloody habits. The least he could hope for would be to be torn apart by elephants specially trained for the task. Thus for five days he fasted and read the Koran from start to finish. It is said that this act of extreme faith saved his life and earned him the favor of the court once again. The now benevolent Sultan sent him to China at the head of a delegation comprising hundreds of servants, singers, dancer, and precious gifts for the Chinese emperor. A few miles out of Delhi the caravan was ambushed by infidel rebels (in this case Hindus) and Ibn Battutah returned to the Sultan cap in hand. A second expedition, this time by sea, was destroyed by a tempest in front of the port of Calicut. Ibn Battutah was the only survivor and this time he decided that it would not be wise to return to Delhi and instead made his own

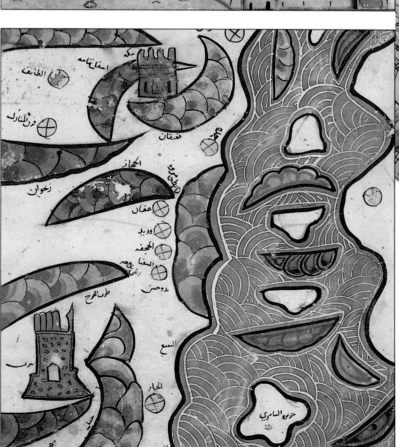

Top: Muslim pilgrims traveling to Mecca (Istanbul, Topkapì Palace Library). Within the great al-Haram mosque, stands the black stone of the Kaaba, which according to the Islamic creed was handed to Abraham by the Archangel Gabriel. Pilgrimage to the holy shrines, obligatory for all good Muslims, marked the beginning of Ibn Battutah's wanderings.

Bottom: This map of the Red Sea and the holy cities was drawn in the 12th century by the Arab geographer and traveler al-Idrisi for King Roger II of Sicily. It was part of a treatise that supplied maps and information on around 70 previously unknown areas of the world. Al-Idrisi, born at Ceuta in 1100, also produced a planisphere engraved on a sheet of silver.

Above: This Arabian astrolabe of the 10th century, can be found at the History of Science Museum, Florence.

The astrolabe, or something similar was already in use in classical times (the Arab term asturlab derives from the Greek astrolàbos).

85

way to the Maldives. While in the islands, he noted that thanks to a diet based on "honey, coconut milk, and fish, the natives have a notable and unmatched sexual vigour." Battutah himself had six wives whom he zealously satisfied each night, establishing a strict rota. After a year of this cure, he left for Ceylon which he explored inch by inch, climbing the Peak of Adam on the summit of which was an enormous footprint said to have been made by the father of humanity. He sailed along the coast, visiting Malaysia, Java, and Sumatra before finally reaching China. He stayed in Beijing, admiring the wealth of the city, but China did not agree with him: the local cuisine made him shudder and the people worshiped stone idols. In 1349, at the age of 45, he returned to his homeland, but his thirst for knowledge had yet to be quenched. The following year, on the orders of the Sultan of Fès, he left to explore the legendary lands of gold beyond the Sahara Desert, the fabulous kingdom of Mali. When Ibn Battutah reached Timbuktu,

the city was at the height of its splendor: the country was wealthy and well governed, and the roads were safe. But, as Battutah observed critically, such wealth was not translated into similar munificence. He was presented with neither gold not silk but, "Would you believe it! There were three buns, a piece of beef fried in oil, and a marrow in sour milk." On more than one occasion Ibn Battutah was to regret ever having left home, even though he stayed in the city on the banks of the Niger for seven months. At Gao he joined a caravan directed towards Ahaggar in the middle of the Sahara: there he saw the mysterious veiled men, the Tuaregs, whom he described as a group of incompetents and time wasters. In December, 1354, he returned to Sijilmassa in southern Morocco in the middle of a violent snowstorm. His career as a traveler was over. A sedentary old age awaited him in his native Morocco, "the most beautiful of all countries, where one can always find an abundance of fruit, spring water, and nutritious food."

Above: A Muslim traveler in his tent. Within Islamic society, journeys undertaken for faith, curiosity or trade was the norm rather than an exception. Travel writing became a separate literary genre with an enjoyable blend of reality and fantasy, from which it is still possible to draw precious historical, geographical and ethnographic information.

Top left: Islamic astronomers and geographers working in the observatory constructed at Istanbul in the 16th century by the Sultan Murad III (contemporary miniature). Arab astronomical knowledge, which was very advanced for the time, filtered through to Europe via Sicily and Spain.

Bottom left: This astrolabe dates back to the 13th century. The Muslims undoubtedly perfected the astrolabe, transforming it into a versatile and useful instrument for calculating the positions of the various celestial bodies, without the need for complex operations.

Bottom right: A caravan in a miniature by al-Wasiti, Baghdad, 1237. A dense network of well-worn caravan trails punctuated by refreshment points and caravanserai stretched throughout the Islamic lands from the Sahara to Central Asia. Ibn Battutah, who did not like long sea voyages, frequently joined the trading caravans, following tried and trusted routes.

THE CHINESE

Ten Lung, the Lantern, sparkled in the southern sky. Like an outstretched arm, that wild promontory indicated the south to the junks, the direction symbolic of fortune and power. Beyond that nameless cape the coastline turned brusquely northward, lapped by a new sea. The Chinese navigators turned for home so as to return to their emperor and report the position of the new borders of the known world. While in Europe tales abounded of boiling oceans and sea monsters, the Chinese were inventing the compass and developing quite remarkable marine technology. The court cartographers had been aware for some time of the position of the Southern Cross (the shape of which does actually resemble a lantern) and the southern coast of Africa which appears on splendid maps painted as early as 1320. It is very probable that the Chinese navigators had already rounded the Cape of Good Hope, beating the Portuguese by over a century. The Chinese explorative fervor was never motivated by expansionist objectives and experienced its most fertile period in the first decades of the fifteenth century. Apart from the official motivations such as the search for political and commercial alliances, the Chinese maritime explorations were undertaken as a means of exporting Chinese prestige to distant lands and of demonstrating the empire's wealth and splendor to the outside world. In the years between 1405 and 1433 at least seven important expeditions set out from Chinese ports led by the famous navigator Cheng Ho, known as the Eunuch of the Three Jewels. In that period the Ming dynasty assembled one of the greatest fleets in history: sixty large ocean-going junks carrying 27,000 men. As well as the crews, the vessels housed ranks of civil, and military administrators, scientists, doctors, and interpreters capable of speaking all the known tongues of the ports of the Indian Ocean, from Arabic to Vietnamese. The records of the explorations, known as "The Triumphant Vision of the Boundless Ocean," contain detailed descriptions of the itinerary followed. During the first three expeditions Cheng Ho sailed along the coasts of Indochina and Malaysia,

Below: Chinese cartography has distant origins: the first geographical atlas was compiled as early as AD 267, and contained 18 different maps of the regions of China. With the advent of the Mongol dynasties, while European science was stagnating during the Middle Ages, the Chinese developed a sophisticated cartographic system based on a rectangular grid, which allowed the correct representation of distances between various points on the map and their position with respects to each other.

Bottom: An ancient Chinese nautical compass. The phenomenon of magnetic polarity was known in China ever since the 8th century, and rudimentary compasses were used in geomancy, the art of aligning buildings, beds, and tombs in correspondence with the energy lines that surround the Earth. Subsequently, around the year 1000, the compass was adapted to the needs of navigators. It only entered general use in Europe in further developed form three centuries later.

Opposite: This engraving shows a Chinese river and a number of junks being prepared for voyages to the most distant ports of the Far East. Under the Ming dynasty, and especially during the first decades of the 15th century, China experienced an intense commercial and explorative expansion. The Chinese fleets reached India, the Red Sea, and the African East coast as far as the Cape of Good Hope.

Atlantic Ocean

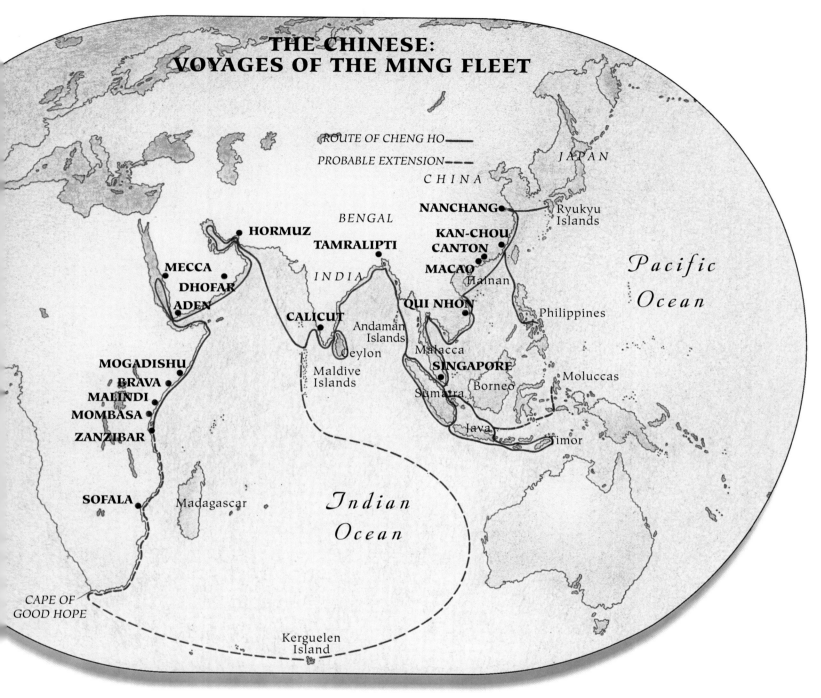

THE CHINESE:
VOYAGES OF THE MING FLEET

ROUTE OF CHENG HO ———
PROBABLE EXTENSION - - -

JAPAN

CHINA

NANCHANG • • Ryukyu
Islands

BENGAL KAN-CHOU
HORMUZ • CANTON •
TAMRALIPTI MACAO •
MECCA • Hainan
DHOFAR • QUI NHON
ADEN • *INDIA*
CALICUT • Andaman *Pacific*
Islands *Ocean*
Ceylon Malacca
MOGADISHU • Maldive SINGAPORE •
BRAVA • Islands Borneo Moluccas
MALINDI • Sumatra
MOMBASA • Java
ZANZIBAR • Timor
Philippines

SOFALA • Madagascar *Indian*
Ocean

CAPE OF
GOOD HOPE
Kerguelen
Island

exploring the Indonesian archipelago and
the Nicobar Islands. Part of the fleet
reached southern India and Ceylon, while
a number of junks were sent ahead toward
the distant ports of the Arabian Peninsula.
During the fourth voyage between 1416
and 1419, the Chinese vessels sailed as far
as the Persian Gulf and Aden. From that
point it could not have been difficult for
Cheng Ho to descend along the East
African coast and, hugging the shore and
visiting the cities of Mu-ku-tu-shu and Pu-
la-wa, modern day Mogadishu and Brava,
in Somalia. To the Chinese, Africa did not
represent that fabulous land populated by
fantastical creatures that was such a part of
the European tradition. Mogadishu was
described with a notable sense of reality
and a degree of disappointment: "If one
looks around, outside the city, where there
are brick-built houses four or five floors
high, inhabited by argumentative people,

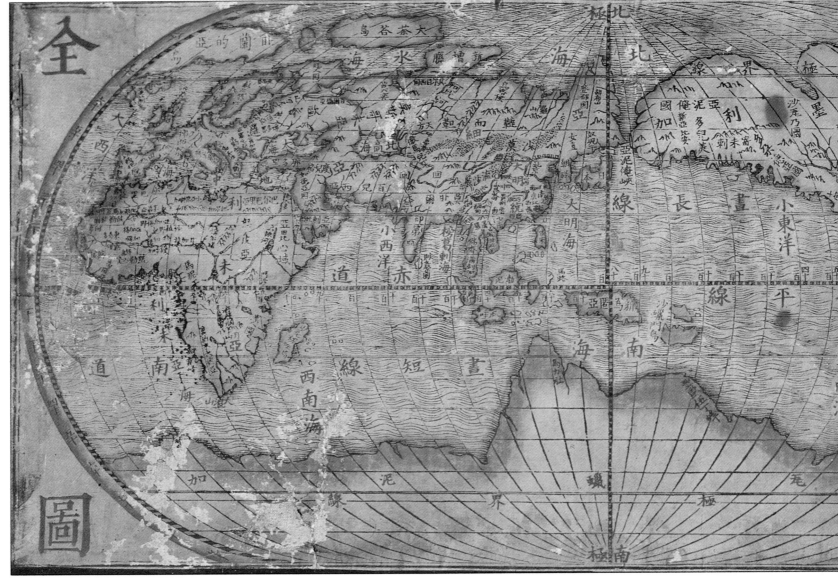

ones gaze is drawn to the horizon, there is nothing to be seen but sand." Cheng Ho continued southward as far as Ma-lin (Malindi) whose sultan, a few years earlier, had sent a live giraffe as a gift to the emperor. The documentation of the Eunuch of the Three Jewels' African adventures ends with the coast of Kenya, but it is reasonable to presume that the Chinese continued their exploration and reached the farthest tip of the continent. Other fleets were in the meantime heading into the Pacific toward the Philippines, the Moluccas and the Ryukyu Islands southwest of Japan. The last expedition sailed out of the port of Nanjing in 1431: Cheng Ho's junks entered the Red Sea, reaching Jiddah and Mecca. The admiral and many of the fleet's commanders were Muslims and visited the holy sites. They entered the great mosque in which is conserved "a black stone which is said to have come from heaven." Cheng Ho died during he return trip. From that moment China closed in on itself, leaving the leadership in marine exploration to the Christian West.

Top: In this planisphere compiled by Giulio Aleni, a pupil of the Jesuit Matteo Ricci, with Chinese characters, China appears as the center of the world. The Jesuits, present in Asia since the second half of the 16th century, borrowed heavily from Chinese cartography which under the Mongol dynasties reached extraordinary technical and figurative levels.

Above: The port of Canton in southern China was for centuries the favored terminus of the route that, crossing the Indian Ocean, linked the Persian Gulf with the South China Sea. Following Cheng Ho's last great expedition, the Ming emperors prohibited commercial voyages toward the west, leaving the initiative to the European traders.

THE CHINESE OCEAN-GOING JUNK

Those European travelers of the Middle Ages who had the opportunity of visiting China, spoke in wonder of the sophisticated marine technology behind the construction of the ocean-going junks. During his stay in the ports of the Fukien region, Marco Polo was amazed by the sight of huge ships with covered decks and sumptuously furnished cabins, capable of carrying up to three hundred men and great quantities of goods. Furthermore, with the expert eye of the Venetian sailor, he noticed that the junks had "up to thirteen bulkheads or divisions in the holds formed from interlocking boards. Their role is that of protecting the vessel in the case of an accident such as striking a rock or being struck by a whale in which she takes on water." The Chinese had used this system of watertight compartments since the year 1200. This feature, which drastically reduced the risk of sinking, was only adopted by European shipbuilding yards six hundred years later. The ocean-going junks used by Cheng Ho were probably around a 330 feet long and 132 wide (the contemporary Iberian caravels measured around 66 feet) and could be fitted with up to nine masts rigged with large rush-matting or canvas sails, strengthened with bamboo cross pieces. The vessels were flat-bottomed and reinforced by a longitudinal beam known as "the dragon's backbone." A large central rudder was fixed to the stern which ensured that the junks were manoeuvrable. As well as the watertight bulkheads, the junks had a system of floodable compartments, which could be deliberately filled with water to ballast the vessel and increase its stability in rough seas. Chinese nautical treatises illustrate, alongside the ocean-going junks, a series of different model adapted to the most diverse uses: from the 990 feet long warships covered with metal plates (the "turtle-ships") to those fitted out as bordellos (the so-called "flower-ships"). Other vessels were equipped with mobile masts and rigging so that they could invert direction rapidly and sail stern- as well as prow-first. Compared with the Arab and European vessels of the time, the junks were far more efficient and much safer. They were equally at home on the open seas as they were navigating coastal waters. The Chinese sailors were skilled in the use of the compass at sea as early as the eleventh century and could rely on accurate charts. It is clear that the sudden abandonment of oceanic exploration was not due to a lack of ability or suitable ships, but rather the result of a precise political policy. In 1848 a Chinese junk left the port of Shanghai for London. In spite of the difficult sea conditions, the long voyage was completed without mishap: the vessel was navigated according to modern criteria, but the techniques of its construction were not dissimilar to those used for the ships of Cheng Ho, four hundred years earlier.

Above: The ships used by Admiral Cheng Ho for his voyages of exploration, were considerably more impressive than the junks depicted in these illustrations, models from a much later period. Probably over 330 feet long, the ocean-going junks of Fukien could be equipped with up to nine masts and featured a central rudder and a system of water-tight compartments, which drastically reduced the dangers of sinking. The contemporary Portuguese caravel, little more than 66 feet long, was a veritable nutshell in comparison.

On the 20th of September, 1519, five ships left the port of Seville for an unknown destination. The commander of the fleet, a Portuguese exile named Ferdinand Magellan, was perhaps the only member of the expedition to have a clear idea of the enterprise that they were about to undertake. His plan, honed during years of assiduous study and based on the collection of confidential information, involved reaching the so-called Spice Islands through a hypothetical sea passage to the south of the American continent. Mutinies, shipwrecks, and all kinds of complication failed to erode his determination: Magellan discovered the strait that still bears his name, heading into the immensity of the Pacific Ocean and reaching the eastern borders of Asia. He was to die in the Philippines during a battle with the natives. Only one ship with eighteen men aboard made it home to Spain three years later. This was the first vessel to complete a circumnavigation of the globe.

MAGELLAN AND THE FIRST CIRCUMNAVIGATION OF THE GLOBE

Above: The Victoria *was the only vessel of the five that were part of Magellan's fleet, to return to Spain in May 1522. Of the 250 crew members of the fleet only 18 survived the difficulties of the long voyage.*

Below: Stubborn, courageous and desperate for glory, Magellan was born in Portugal circa 1480. He fought bravely in the East and Morocco, but subsequently emigrated to Spain after differences with the Portuguese crown, and there succeeded in finding support for his explorations.

Bottom: A portrait of Charles I (the future Emperor Charles V) at the age of 16. In spite of his youth, the Spanish king recognized the potential of Magellan's enterprise and support his projects from the outset, committing himself to supplying 5 ships and underwriting the expenses of the expedition. Magellan also obtained the rank of captain ceneral and a fifth of any profits deriving from the future discoveries.

In the years following Vasco da Gama's expedition, the Portuguese consolidated their supremacy in the Indian Ocean. Hormuz and Goa were easily conquered and in 1511 a powerful fleet, commanded by Alfonso de Albuquerque, attacked Malacca. The city fell after a long siege, opening up new horizons for the Portuguese. Apart from being an important trading center, Malacca was an ideal base for the exploration of the vast, unknown spice-producing archipelagos. In that same year Antonio de Abreu and Francisco Serrão departed on a reconnaissance trip toward the eastern seas. Close to the Banda Islands one of the ships sank during a storm and Serrão was fortunate to survive, reaching Ternate on an improvised raft. He was the first European to land in the Moluccas, the legendary Spice Islands. Serrão was

afforded a warm welcome by the local sovereign and decided to remain on the island as his advisor, foregoing all opportunities to return to his homeland. His only contacts with Portugal were through the correspondence he exchanged with his old friend Ferdinand Magellan, the man who had saved his life during the battle of Malacca. Born into a noble family of Porto around 1480, Magellan had personally taken part in all the decisive battles for the control of the Indian Ocean. Having returned to Portugal, in 1513 he took part in the assault on the Moorish fortress of Azamor in Morocco. The wounds he received made him lame for the rest of his life. He had faithfully served his country for many long years and now awaited suitable recompense. However, the king of Portugal rejected all his requests. He refused Magellan an increased pension and refused to listen to his projects. Magellan's theory was not very different to that of the Genoese Christopher Columbus who, over twenty years earlier, had attempted to reach the Indies via a western route. The voyages of Cabot and Vespucci had demonstrated that there was an enormous continent between Europe and the lands of the East, although it was not yet clear whether the New World was actually a vast appendix to Asia. Balboa had certainly seen another ocean with his own eyes in 1513, but no one was yet aware of its true extension. Magellan believed in the existence of a southern passage linking the Atlantic with the South Sea, as the Pacific was then known. However, this strait as yet only existed in Magellan's imagination and in any case the Portuguese sovereign had no wish to risk ships and capital on an enterprise that even if successful could only have led to problems for Portugal in its eastern stronghold. Once again the king's response was no: the route to the Indies was via the Cape of Good Hope, and the Portuguese were unwilling to give up their monopoly. Magellan was not the type of man to accept rejection easily: he

93

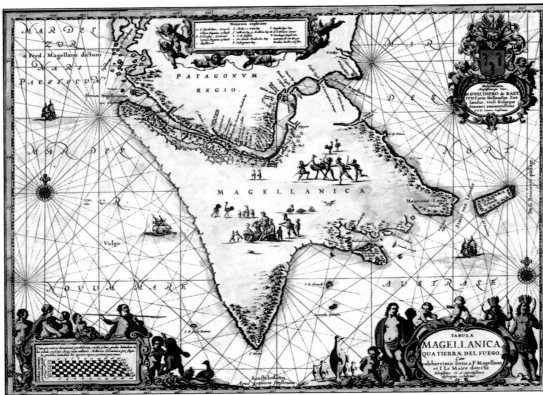

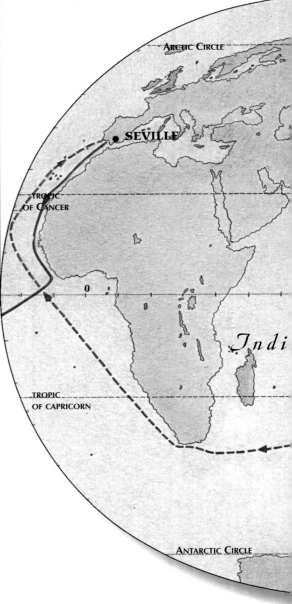

Below: left: A map from the 17th century published after the epic journey of Schouten and Le Maire. In 1616 the Dutchmen, having passed through the Magellan Strait, continued southward until they doubled a promontory "entirely composed of high snow-covered mountains" that they named Cape Horn. Beyond Tierra del Fuego, whose insular nature was proven, extended open water: a new, more practical route to the Pacific.

considered his bonds of loyalty to the Portuguese crown to have been absolved and, like Columbus, decided to transfer his allegiance to Spain. There his arguments carried considerable weight. The information sent to him by Serrão suggested that the Spice Islands were situated much farther to the east than was actually the case. Extending the dividing line established by the Treaty of Tordesillas into the upper hemisphere, the Moluccas would have inevitably fallen within the Spanish sphere of influence. Magellan's project aroused immediate interest in Seville: a number of important political figures and businessmen were excited by the idea of a possible southern passage and the commercial advantages it implied. Through the support of Juan de Fonseca, the omnipotent bishop of Burgos, Magellan succeeded in obtaining a hearing at the court of the young King Carlos I (the future Carlos IV), who enthusiastically welcomed the exile's project. It was established that the crown would be responsible for the fitting out of the ships, while the German Fugger bank would provide the commercial financing for the expedition. The cargo carried by the fleet on the outward trip would not have been restricted to the usual baubles to be exchanged with the native savages, but would have comprised goods of value destined for the sophisticated kingdoms of the East. As a security measure a Spanish commander, Juan de Cartagena, was to accompany Magellan so as to supervise the operation. The expedition's mandate imposed by the Spanish government expressly forbade the ships to invade the Portuguese sphere of influence. The fleet was composed of five ships, the *San Antonio*, the *Trinidad*, the *Concepción*, the *Victoria* and the *Santiago*, all small vessels in rather poor condition. The crews numbered around 250 men of diverse nationalities, including an Englishman and a couple of Malays. An Italian nobleman, Antonio Pigafetta from Vicenza, was taken on unpaid. If, as many suspected, he was a Venetian spy, he never revealed the truth: in any case his presence was a stroke of fortune for the historians of the future as he left a diary rich in observations and notes that is an indispensable aid to reconstructing the story of the voyage. Magellan left the port of Seville on the 20th of September, 1519. He followed the African coast for a long stretch, coming dangerously close to the waters of the Portuguese-held Gulf of Guinea, before turning his prow westward. On the

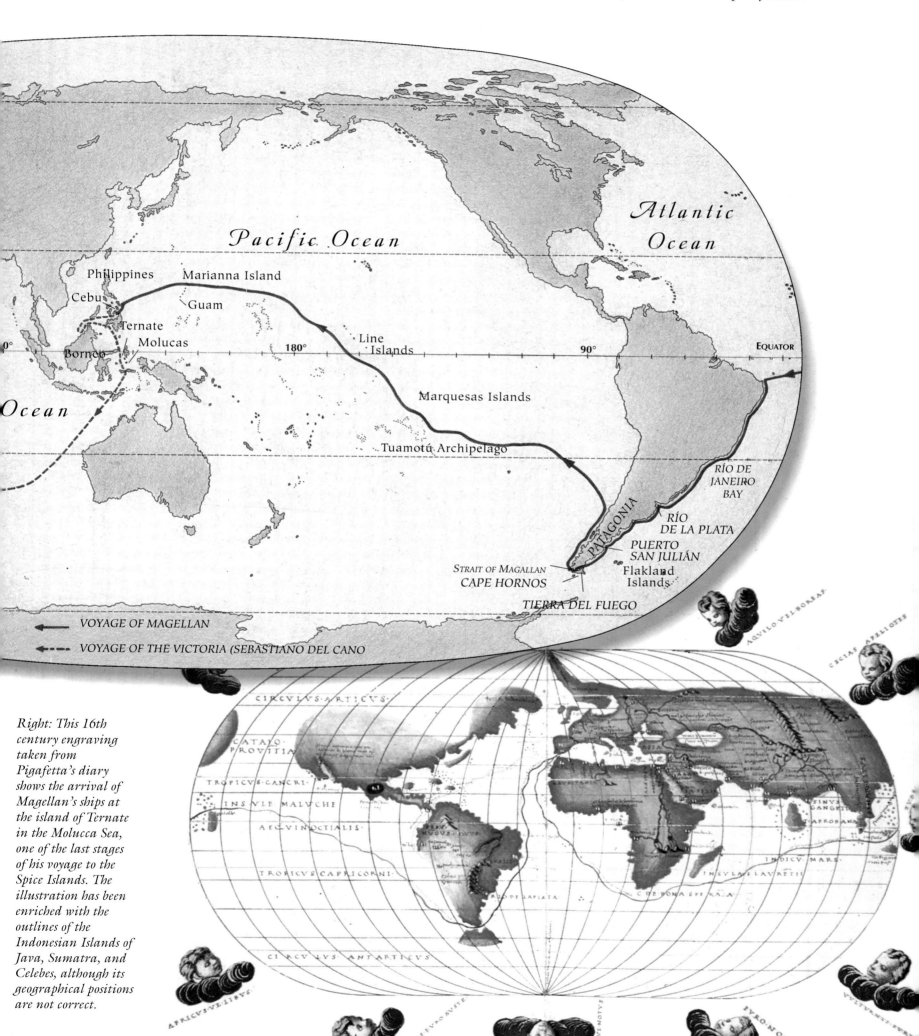

Below: A map from
1536 drawn by
Battista Agnese.
The explorations of
Dias, Columbus, da
Gama, Vespucci, and
Magellan (whose route
is marked on the map)
revealed the true
vastness of the world,

although the Pacific
was still a mystery,
and the extension of
the continents only
approximated.
The outline of North
America was
uncertain and
Australia was
completely absent.

Atlantic Ocean

Pacific Ocean

Philippines
Cebus
Marianna Island
Guam
Ternate
Molucas
Borneo
0°
180°
Line Islands
90°
EQUATOR
Ocean

Marquesas Islands

Tuamotú Archipelago

RÍO DE
JANEIRO
BAY

RÍO
DE LA PLATA

PUERTO
SAN JULIÁN

PATAGONIA

Flakland
Islands

Strait of Magallan
CAPE HORNOS

TIERRA DEL FUEGO

⟵ VOYAGE OF MAGELLAN

⟵--- VOYAGE OF THE VICTORIA (SEBASTIANO DEL CANO)

Right: This 16th
century engraving
taken from
Pigafetta's diary
shows the arrival of
Magellan's ships at
the island of Ternate
in the Molucca Sea,
one of the last stages
of his voyage to the
Spice Islands. The
illustration has been
enriched with the
outlines of the
Indonesian Islands of
Java, Sumatra, and
Celebes, although its
geographical positions
are not correct.

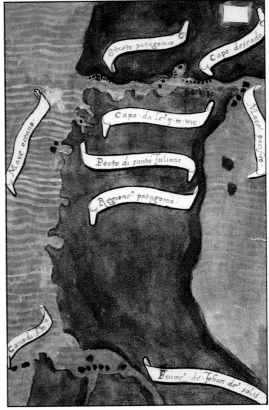

Top left: The
Magellan Strait from
the Pigafetta codex.
The Italian, Antonio
Pigafetta took part in
Magellan's expedition,
keeping a detailed
record of the events
rich in precious data
on the islands and

inhabitants of the
Pacific. Pigafetta and
his role remain rather
mysterious, and some
writers have suggested
that he was acting on
behalf of the Venetians,
who were obviously
extremely interested
in the spice trade.

Top right: A map
showing the extreme
tip of the American
continent and the
Strait of Magellan.
The map was drawn
up following
Magellan's voyage
and prior to Drake's
circumnavigation.

It hypothesized open sea
to the south of Tierra
del Fuego. Drake was
dragged off course by
a tempest and
presumed that Tierra
del Fuego was not part
of the mythical
southern continent,
but rather an island.

Above:
This engraving on
wood from 1880
depicts the passage
of Magellan's ships
through the strait
that bears his name.

Below: Magellan exiting the strait that bears his name between Patagonia (right) and Tierra del Fuego in an engraving by de Bry, late 16th century. The allegorical image shows the navigator calculating his position, aided by a balanced Apollo and the God of the Winds. A Patagonian "giant" is, for some obscure reason, portrayed in the act of swallowing an arrow; the monstrous fish, mermaids, and an enormous bird of prey holding an elephant in its talons symbolize the dangers of the uncharted ocean.

29th of November, the fleet dropped anchor off the coast of Brazil close to the modern-day bay of Rio de Janeiro. The Guaranì Indians proved to be friendly and the ships were able to restock with wood and fresh food, while Pigafetta recorded the natives' strange customs in his diary. Magellan proceeded south, along the interminable Atlantic coast of South America. The vast estuary of the Rio de la Plata momentarily deceived the crews into thinking that they had finally reached the fatal strait. By the end of March, the freezing cold of the southern winter began to be unbearable and the discontent of the men and some of the officers grew rapidly. Magellan thus decided to wait out the winter in a sheltered bay, which he called Puerto San Julian. The mutiny exploded without warning: the homogeneity of the crew and the ambiguity of the double command had created problems from the very outset of the voyage and now

threatened the entire enterprise. On the 1st of April, Juan de Cartagena and a group of rebel officers took three of the ships by force inviting Magellan to concede defeat. The expedition leader acted quickly and astutely: he set up negotiations to gain time and then, following a precisely worked out strategy, he seized the *Victoria*, killing her master in cold blood. He then blocked the entrance to the bay with his ships. After a feeble attempt at resistance, and dispirited by Magellan's brutal reaction, the mutineers surrendered. The leaders of the rebellion were executed and their mutilated bodies were displayed as a deterrent. Juan de Cartagena, the instigator of the plot, was abandoned on a deserted stretch of the coast. Pigafetta's records deal sketchily with the episode, preferring to go into great detail about the native Patagones (the "Big Feet"). The Italian's imagination was captured by the great stature of these men giving rise to the enduring legend of the Patagonian giants. During a reconnaissance trip along the coast, the *Santiago* was swept against the rocks by heavy seas and sank. The survivors managed to return to base by land and on the 18th of October, Magellan left Puerto San Julian. A few days later the monotony of the unchanging coastline appeared to have been interrupted: in front of the ships there opened a deep inlet, a funnel of shattered rocks that penetrated snow-covered mountains. Navigation through those gray, stormy waters appeared impossible. Was it a strait leading to open sea or just a dead end? The channel might have transformed into an inescapable trap, but Magellan decided to accept the risk of an exploration. The *Trinidad* and the *Victoria* headed into the inlet while the rest of the fleet awaited their return

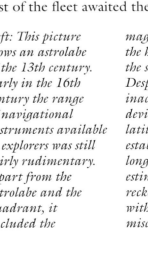

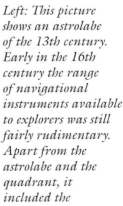

Left: This picture shows an astrolabe of the 13th century. Early in the 16th century the range of navigational instruments available to explorers was still fairly rudimentary. Apart from the astrolabe and the quadrant, it included the magnetic compass, the hour-glass, and the sounding line. Despite their inaccuracy these devices allowed latitude to be established, but not longitude, which was estimated by dead reckoning, frequently with serious miscalculations.

anchored off the rocky shore. After what seemed to be an interminable period, the two ships returned to base with good news: at the end of the bay there opened another passage and then another bay... Magellan gave orders to proceed. The mountains appeared to open up miraculously before his very eyes. Some days later the channel divided once again into two branches. Magellan headed southwest, sending the *San Antonio* and the *Concepcìon* to explore the southeast branch. Only one ship returned to report the negative findings of the exploration: the *San Antonio* had taken advantage of the situation to flee. Magellan proceeded along the strait with his three remaining ships and finally, on the 28th of November, 1520, the fleet found its way out of the labyrinth and into the open sea. After 38 days sailing, the Spanish had entered the legendary South Sea. The point at the end of the strait was named Cabo Deseado, Cape Desired. Magellan followed the coast of Chile northward until the 30th parallel and then headed northwest. The fact that no storms impeded the fleet's progress across the new ocean led to it being named as the Pacific, but as the days and week passed not a single island appeared on the horizon. Magellan could have had no idea of immensity of the Pacific, the area of which is equal to that of all the dry land put together, and he was unable or unwilling to stock up on water and food before attempting the crossing. In three months and twenty days the fleet encountered nothing more than

Top and center: Long, primitive-looking rafts made of closely tied rushes were the vessels used by the inhabitants of islands of the South Sea that the explorers met during their voyages and that they described with the precision of entomologists.

98

uninhabited rocks, in spite of passing close to the major Polynesian archipelagos, not far from the island paradises of Tahiti and Tuamotu. The living conditions on board the ships, recorded Pigafetta were frightening: they ate all the biscuits they had, and when they were finished they ate the vermin-infested crumbs, which smelled strongly of urine, and drank yellowish water that had turned bad many days previously. They even ate a number of hides in which some of the ship's great ropes were wrapped." Many of the men fell ill with scurvy and were barely able to stand. When, on the 6th of March, 1521, they came within sight of the island of Guam in the Marianas, they were so exhausted that they were even unable to react to the invasion of the natives who clambered the length and breadth of the ships, stealing whatever they could make off with. The islanders' kleptomania took Magellan by surprise, and he named the Marianas the Islands of Thieves. The disappearance of a whaler infuriated the expedition leader who ordered an immediate reprisal: a large group of armed men landed and sacked the nearest village without pity.

The rations they pillaged, sweet potatoes, coconuts, and fresh vegetables allowed the crews to regain their strength. The *Victoria*, the *Trinidad* and the *Concepcion* proceeded on their westerly course until, a week later, they came across the island of Samar in the Philippines. The first contact with the natives was friendly. This encouraged Magellan to enter the archipelago and at the end of March,

Opposite bottom: A pair of penguins, from the Report on the Journey *by Beauchesne, late 17th century. Keeping to his course along the coast of South America, in February of 1520, Magellan reached a bay populated by*
strange birds, incapable of flight and equipped with a long bill similar to that of crows. Penguins were an easy prey for the hungry crews. Half a century later Drake observed that their flesh was excellent, "similar to that of a fat goose."

Below: Patagonian natives in a water-color from the Beauchesne report, late 17th century. Pigafetta described the Patagonians as being so tall "that we only reached their waist" and capable of eating a basket of biscuits in the blink of an eye and
drinking half a bucket of water in a single swallow. "They even ate rats," he observed, "without skinning them." Drake was later to put these claims into perspective, but the fame of the Patagonian giants survived in Europe for a couple of centuries.

Left: An encounter with a sea lion, from the Beauchesne report, late 17th century. Even though Magellan had personally ensured that sufficient supplies for a long voyage were loaded, the provisions soon began to run short, obliging the crews to take advantage of whatever resources presented themselves. During the interminable crossing of the Pacific, hunger and scurvy decimated the men, seriously threatening the success of the enterprise.

99

escorted by the native canoes, the ships approached the large island of Cebu. One of the Malayans in the crew was able to understand the local language, definitive proof that they really had reached Asia. The Moluccas could not be far. And nor could the Portuguese warships. At all costs the fleet had to avoid being intercepted and captured. Magellan realized that if they were unable to stop and reprovision their ships, the return voyage toward Europe would have been long and difficult. He decided to prolong the fleet's stay in the Philippines until the men had recovered sufficiently to be able to tackle a long ocean crossing. In the meantime he established friendly relations with the local sovereign, putting himself forward as the "protector" of the island in the name of Spain. A display of cannons and armor impressed the rajah of Cebu who readily accepted the protection offered by his powerful new foreign ally. It was thus that Magellan found himself involved in the struggle between Cebu and Mactan, a neighboring island whose chief refused to submit to the authority of the rajah of Cebu. On the 27th of April, sixty Spaniards, followed by a few hundred local warriors landed on Mactan. The shallow waters of the bay deprived Magellan of his artillery support. The king of Mactan, Lapulapu, was determined to repel the invaders and with the strength of numbers in his favor, he attacked suddenly. Finding themselves showered with rocks and spears, the Spaniards retreated in disorder leaving their leader isolated with a handful of men: "seeing this his enemies turned against him, and one of them with a great sword similar to a large scimitar, struck the Captain a great blow on the leg which felled him." Magellan was massacred by the Indians. The tragedy left the Spaniards confused and unable to react. A few days later the rajah of Cebu enticed 27 men onto dry land and slaughtered them. Over the following months the survivors wandered aimlessly from one island to the next: there were insufficient men to sail all three ships and it was decided to sacrifice the *Concepcion*. The vessel was set on fire off the island of Bohol. The remaining two ships reached the Moluccas on the 8th of November, 1521. Having loaded the

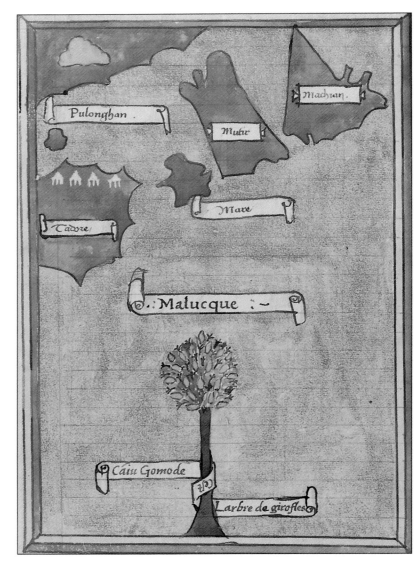

Top: A map of the Moluccas drawn up according to Pigafetta's indications. Only two of the five ships that left Seville reached the celebrated Spice Islands in November, 1521, and only one managed to return to Spain with its precious cargo. At the bottom is a rather stylized illustration of the plant that produces cloves (Eugenia caryphillata).

Bottom: An antique version of Pigafetta's account in French, rich in superb illustrations. Alongside the text is portrayed a map of the Mariana Islands in the Pacific, then known as the Ladrone Islands. The versatility and sea-worthiness of the outrigger canoes used by natives impressed the Spaniards. The Marianas were the first islands encountered by Magellan after three months' uninterrupted navigation.

Opposite: Magellan's adventure in the Philippines. The print depicts the moment in which he planted a cross on Cebu — the last time he was to do so. He was killed by the subjects of Lapulapu, the sovereign of Mactan whom the conquistador had challenged in defence of the rajah of Cebu.

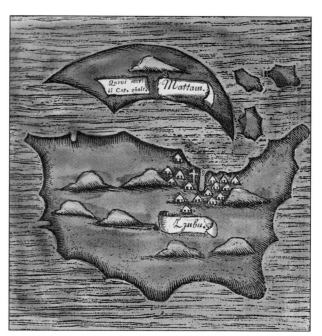

Top right: This illustration taken from the diaries of Pigafetta, shows the islands of Cebu and Mactan in the Philippines where Magellan was killed. Lapulapu, the ruler of Cebu, rejected Magellan's ultimatum to surrender and courageously stood up to the invaders armed with muskets and cannon. Today, considered the first Filipino to have successfully countered the European invasion, he is celebrated as a national hero.

Below: The death of Magellan. Caught up in the struggle between the rulers of the islands of Cebu and Mactan, the Spaniards fought under unfavorable conditions and were massacred while trying to retreat to their ships. According to Pigafetta's account, Magellan fell fighting, surrounded by a group of adversaries.

largest possible cargo of cloves, they decided to leave for Europe in mid-December. The *Trinidad* was in terrible shape; it appeared clear that she would never be able to tackle the crossing of the Indian Ocean and the storms of the Cape of Good Hope. The crew's only hope was to reach Panama. The *Victoria*, commanded by Sebastiano del Cano was to continue westward, following a southern route as far away as possible from the Portuguese controlled waters. The return voyage was a nightmare: del Cano refused to stop over at Mozambique, fearing arrest, and pushed on toward the Cape which he rounded on in May, 1552. The *Victoria* returned to Seville early in September. Of the 250 men who set out, only 18 returned home alive. In the meantime, the *Trinidad*, repelled by a storm, was forced to return to the Moluccas where she was captured by the Portuguese and destroyed. The first circumnavigation of the globe had been completed, albeit at a phenomenally high price. Virtually an entire fleet had been lost and its commander killed during the voyage. The western route to the Indies was too long to be economically advantageous. Five years later Spain officially renounced all claims to the Moluccas in favor of Portugal in return for a cash indemnity. The Portuguese remained the undisputed masters of the East, while the Spanish crown turned its rapacious attentions toward the riches of America.

In the course of just half a century, following the death of Columbus, the Spaniards explored and conquered vast areas of the New World; their dominion extending from Colorado to Chile. Conquest is a rapid, brutal process, shrouded by a veil of lucid folly. Mercenaries or minor landowners, noblemen or illiterates, the Conquistadors were driven by an implacable desire for wealth and a missionary zeal. In 1513 Balboa crossed the forests of Panama to reach the Pacific, founding the first European colony on the American mainland. A few years later Cortés and Pizarro, leading an army of a few hundred men, sacked the Inca and Aztec capitals. Others such as Coronado marched to the north in search of the fabulous Seven Cities of Cibola. When, in 1545, the mines of Potosí were discovered, all that remained of the great Amerindian civilizations were ruins. Vast quantities of American silver then began to flow into Europe, destabilizing the world economy and heralding a new historical era.

ADVENTURERS IN THE AMERICAS

VASCO NUÑES DE BALBOA

In 1510 a ship commanded by Fernando de Enciso left Hispaniola for the Gulf of Uraba in modern-day Colombia. Enciso's task was to go to the aid of the survivors of an expedition that attempted to establish a base for the colonization of the continent. There was a stowaway on board, legend has it that he hid in a barrel with his dog. His name was Vasco Nuñes de Balboa, a pig breeder hounded by his creditors and determined to seek his fortune in unexplored lands. Enciso

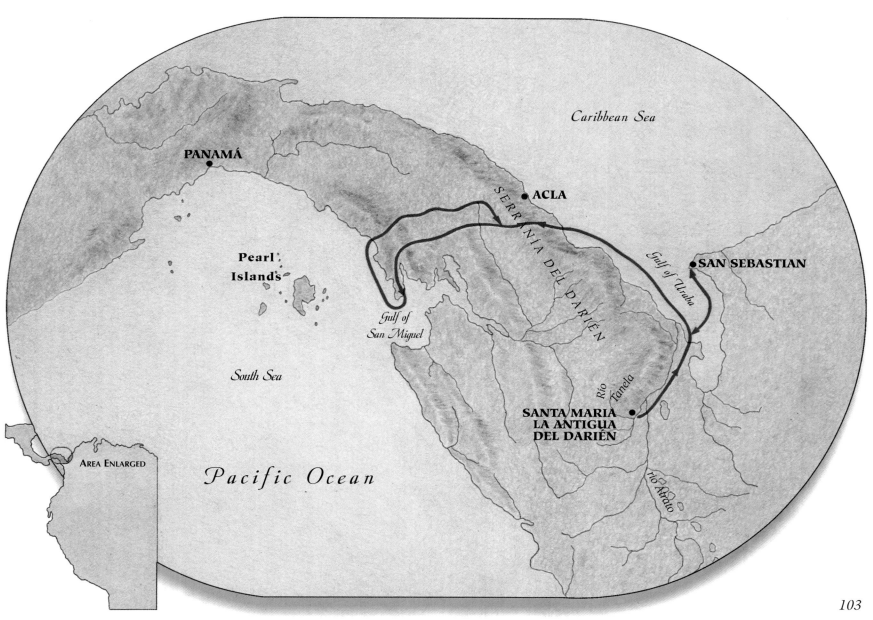

Caribbean Sea

PANAMÁ

ACLA

SERRANÍA DEL DARIÉN

Pearl Islands

Gulf of Uraba

SAN SEBASTIAN

Gulf of San Miguel

South Sea

Río Tanela

SANTA MARIA LA ANTIGUA DEL DARIÉN

AREA ENLARGED

Pacific Ocean

Río Atrato

103

Opposite: This boat conserved at the Bogota Museum of Gold symbolizes the legend of Eldorado. It is an artifact of the Muisca civilization, an Amerindian people belonging to the Chibcha group.

Top: In this 16th century engraving, Vasco Nuñez de Balboa can be seen while taking possession of the South Sea. Balboa, of humble origins, reached America traveling as

a stowaway. In 1510 he left the island of Hispaniola, hounded by his creditors, to seek his fortune on the mainland. Three years later he led an expedition through the impenetrable

forests of the Panamanian isthmus and came within sight of the Pacific Ocean, which he named the South Sea. Having fallen from grace he was executed at Acla in 1519.

decided to spare his life: Balboa knew that coast and his experience was deemed to be useful. It was probably on Balboa's advice that the survivors of the Uraba disaster were transferred to the Darién region where the natives were less aggressive. This led to the foundation of Santa Maria la Antigua, the first Spanish colony in America. The strength of Balboa's personality soon came to the fore and Enciso was sent back to Hispaniola. Once he returned to Spain, Enciso devoted his energies to blackening the name of Balboa. Anyway, Balboa was titled governor of Darién. It was clear that there was only one way of keeping the post: by finding the gold that the royal treasury so needed. Balboa had not been standing idle in the meantime and the Santa Maria colonists recognized his qualities as a wise leader and relations with the natives were peaceful. During a reconnaissance trip into the interior, Balboa had come across an Indian village hidden in the forest. The village chief had shown him many gold ornaments. According to the chief, the metal came from the rivers flowing into a sea just the other side of the mountains. On the 1st of September, 1513, Balboa left with 190 men, hundreds of porters and a pack of war-dogs determined to reach the new ocean. The rainy season had just begun, but Balboa had no time to lose: he had received news that the king would soon be sending an emissary to inspect his achievements. The gold had to be found before his arrival. The expedition landed at Acla, about 50 miles north of Santa Maria and headed into the forest covering the Serrania de Darién mountains. Impeded by their heavy armor and tormented by insects, the Spaniards cut their way through the impenetrable undergrowth for miles. The marshes and swampy rivers

104

that flooded the valleys obliged them to wade "stripped naked, though the water for one, two, or even three leagues with their clothes carried above their heads on their shields." Following a final battle with the Indians, Balboa came within sight of a clearing and "preceeding his men, he climbed a bare hill and from the summit sighted the South Sea." The Spaniards fell to their knees around a cross erected for the occasion and sang the *Te Deum*. Three days later, on the 29th of September, 1513, the expedition reached the Pacific. Balboa named it the South Sea because in that area of the coast (the Gulf of San Miguel) it extended southward. Balboa waited for high tide, entered the water with his sword drawn and formally took possession of the ocean and all the lands washed by its

Top left: This gold breastplate was also made by the Calima master goldsmiths: the abundance of elaborate detail demonstrates the excellence of their metal working skills.

Top right: This delicate gold breastplate, featuring an animal relief in the center, was made by Central American people of the Tierradentro civilization.

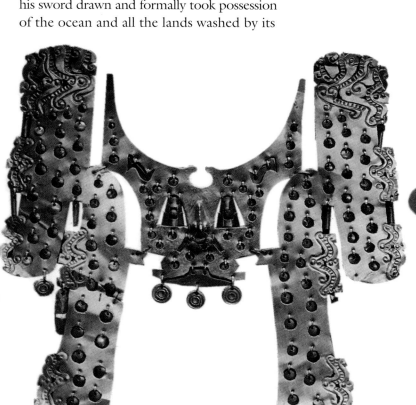

waters. In mid-January 1514, the party re-emerged from the jungle at the point from which it had departed and returned to Santa Maria. In June the new governor, Pedrarias, reached the coast of Darién. Relations between the two conquistadores were strained from the outset. It was only after he had overcome considerable difficulties that Balboa was able to return to the shores of the South Sea, navigating as far as the Pearl Islands. His journeys had demonstrated the existence of another ocean, and had rekindled the hopes of a sea passage leading to the Indies. However, the expedition had not brought wealth, and Balboa was unable to regain the favor of the Spanish court. Eventually Pedrarias found a pretext on which to arrest him and he was executed in the square at Acla. The man who captured him performed his duty with unwavering decision: his name was Francisco Pizarro.

Right: The Dominican monk Bartolomé de Las Casas reached America in 1502, and was the leading figure in the ecclesiastical opposition to colonial oppression. In his will he wrote "I believe that due to these godless, evil, and ignoble acts perpetrated in such an unjust, barbarous, and tyrannical manner, God will direct his ire and fury upon all Spain, as all Spain has taken its part, large or small, of the bloody wealth usurped at the price of much ruin and many massacres."

Right: This portrait of Herman Cortés was painted after his death. Born in 1485 at Medellin in Estremadura, Cortés was 34 years old when he began his extraordinary Mexican adventure. Following the conquest of the Aztec empire he became the governor of the colony of New Spain, the hub of Spanish power in Central America. In 1540, having fallen out of favor with the court, he returned to Spain where he died a few years later.

"When we saw many towns and villages constructed on the water and other towns on the dry land and that great road on the embankment that led to Mexico, so straight and flat, we were astounded as they were like the enchantments we read about in the legend of Amadigi, with their the great towers and temples and buildings rising from the water, all built of stone. And our soldiers asked themselves if all those things they saw were just a dream." This was how, in the words of Bernal Diaz, Hernan Cortés's Spanish forces saw Tenochtitlan, the fabulous capital of Aztec Mexico, one of the largest cities in the world at that time. This was on the 8th of November, 1519: from that day onward the wonder of discovery was replaced by

106

Bottom: The Oaxaca valley in southern Mexico was an important hub of autochthon civilizations. On Mount Alban, the capital, rose a necropolis with frescoes and funerary urns. This large gold breast-plate depicting a figure with a feathered head-dress and a number of mysterious symbols came from this site.

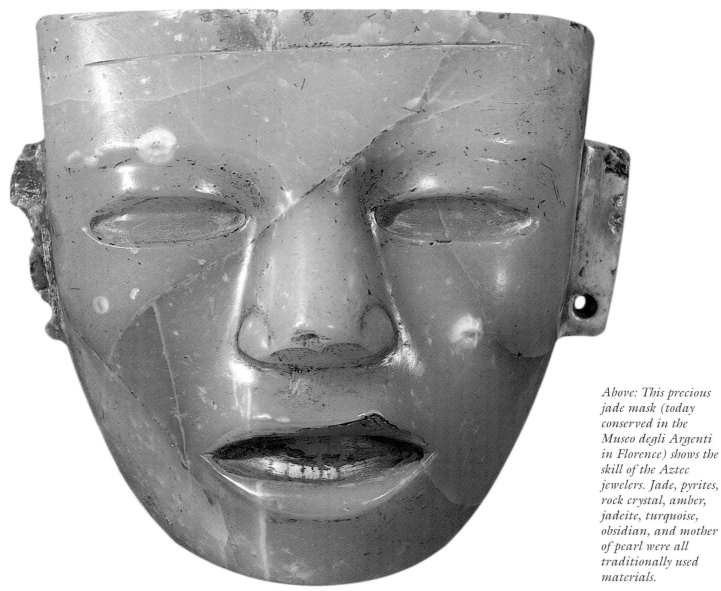

Above: This precious jade mask (today conserved in the Museo degli Argenti in Florence) shows the skill of the Aztec jewelers. Jade, pyrites, rock crystal, amber, jadeite, turquoise, obsidian, and mother of pearl were all traditionally used materials.

the brutality of conquest. Tenochtitlan fell nine months later after a bitter struggle. Cortés, a failed law student lacking military experience, had left Cuba at the end of 1518. He commanded a fleet of eleven ships sent by Velasquez, the governor of the island, to explore the coasts of the Yucatan Peninsula. While he was searching the region for gold and riches, Cortés had heard talk of a great empire whose dominions extended into the interior to the west. A chance meeting with a fellow countryman, shipwrecked on that coast some years earlier, and with a slave who had been presented to him by the Indians of Tabasco but who was originally from Mexico, confirmed the rumours. Aguilar and the girl, known as Doña Marina, became his guides and interpreters and helped him to understand the complex political situation in Mesoamerica. Having landed on the Mexican coast close to the present-day Veracruz, Cortés's first act was to free himself of his ties to Velasquez: he sank his ships and claimed his future discoveries in the name of the king of Spain. He would brook no intermediaries between himself and glory. On the 16th of August, he commenced his march inland. His column of 15 horsemen, 400 soldiers

Right: Montezuma, the Aztec emperor, bears the symbols of his rank. According to the account of Bernal Diaz, an eye-witness to the conquest, "The great Montezuma was about forty years old, he was well built and proportioned, with slim legs... His hair was not long, only just covering his ears: his sparse beard was well shaped and thin. He had a rather long face, but with a spirited expression and benevolent eyes and his appearance and manners revealed both tenderness and, when necessary, gravity."

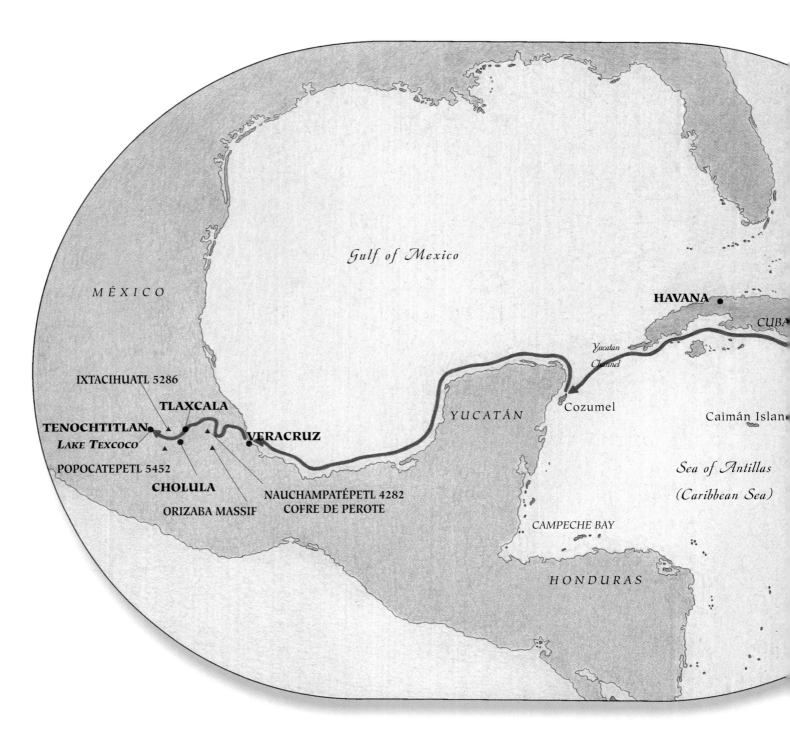

MÉXICO

IXTACIHUATL 5286

TLAXCALA

TENOCHTITLAN
Lake Texcoco

POPOCATEPETL 5452

CHOLULA

ORIZABA MASSIF

VERACRUZ

NAUCHAMPATÉPETL 4282
COFRE DE PEROTE

Gulf of Mexico

HAVANA

CUBA

Yucatan
Channel

Cozumel

YUCATÁN

Caimán Island

Sea of Antillas

(Caribbean Sea)

CAMPECHE BAY

HONDURAS

Above: An Aztec look-out witnesses the arrival of Cortés's ships on the Mexican coast (from the Historia de las Indias *by Diego Duran, 1579). Montezuma's spies described the Spanish as demi-gods covered with iron, with long beards, and frightening weapons capable of spitting fire and filling the air with a pestilential smell "like that of putrid slime."*

IAMAS

ANTIAGO DE CUBA

AMAICA

Left: This painting, on copper, of the late 18th century depicts the first meeting between Cortés and the envoys of Montezuma at Veracruz. The Aztec emperor, tormented by dark premonitions, tried all he knew to halt the advance of the mysterious strangers that had arrived from the sea, sending ambassadorial tributes. However, the sumptuous gifts, discs of worked gold, and fabrics and masks set with turquoise, only served to arouse the avidity of Cortés.

Right: Diego Velazquez, the governor of Cuba, entrusted Cortés with the command of a fleet departing for Mexico. The expedition, the largest that had ever left the island, had the official objective of exploring the Yucatan. However, having landed on the Mexican coast, Cortés immediately freed himself of Velazquez's tutelage and sank his ships, obliging his men to follow him on his march toward the heart of the Aztec empire.

and a few hundred porters tackled the steep scarp slope leading from the coast to the upland regions. The route had been chosen so as to avoid encounters with the Aztec militia but was extremely arduous. The mountainous region between Cofre de Perote and Oriziba was inaccessible and uninhabited. The slopes covered with volcano detritus made walking difficult for the men and horses, and the deserted valleys were swept by freezing winds and hail storms. The Spaniards eventually came within sight of Tlaxcala, the only city independent of the authority of Montezuma, the Aztec emperor. After a bloody opening skirmish, Cortés succeeded in exploiting the rivalry between Tlaxcala and Tenochtitlan, sealing a pact with the leaders of the former. He now had a real army and was in a position to march towards the heart of the Aztec empire. However, he first launched an attack on the city of Cholula, mercilessly massacring its inhabitants whose loyalty he doubted. To the west of Cholula rose the snow-covered

109

peak of Popocatépetl. At that time the over 16,500-foot-high volcano was still active and the plume of smoke that rose from the summit made it sacred and fearful in the eyes of the Indians. Cortés decided to send a group of men to explore the mountain. The ascent of Popocatépetl was not particularly difficult from a technical point of view, but given the unsuitable equipment and clothing of the day it was still quite a feat. The Spaniards were forced to halt a few dozen yards from the rim of the crater: the Earth trembled beneath their feet and as they headed back they were showered with ashes. From the summit of the mountain the explorers had spotted another, less frequented route that descended into the Mexican valley. In spite of Cortés's precautions, the Aztec had beens monitoring his movements from the outset via their efficient spy system, and yet they failed to counter the foreigners' advance.

Montezuma may not have mistaken the Europeans for supernatural beings, but he certainly feared them and was tormented by obscure premonitions. Until that moment, he had attempted to sway them with gifts and diplomacy but, faced with the determination of Cortés, he had to resign himself to accepting the Spaniards' arrival in the capital. The story of the destruction of the Aztec empire is well known and amply described. What happened after the first few days of November, 1519, no longer had anything to do with exploration. Cortés first tried to convince Montezuma to declare his submission to the Spanish crown, but then, fearing the worst, he took the emperor hostage, demanding a ransom in gold from his subjects. When he was informed that the governor of Cuba had sent an armed expedition to arrest him, Cortés left his lieutenant Alvarado at

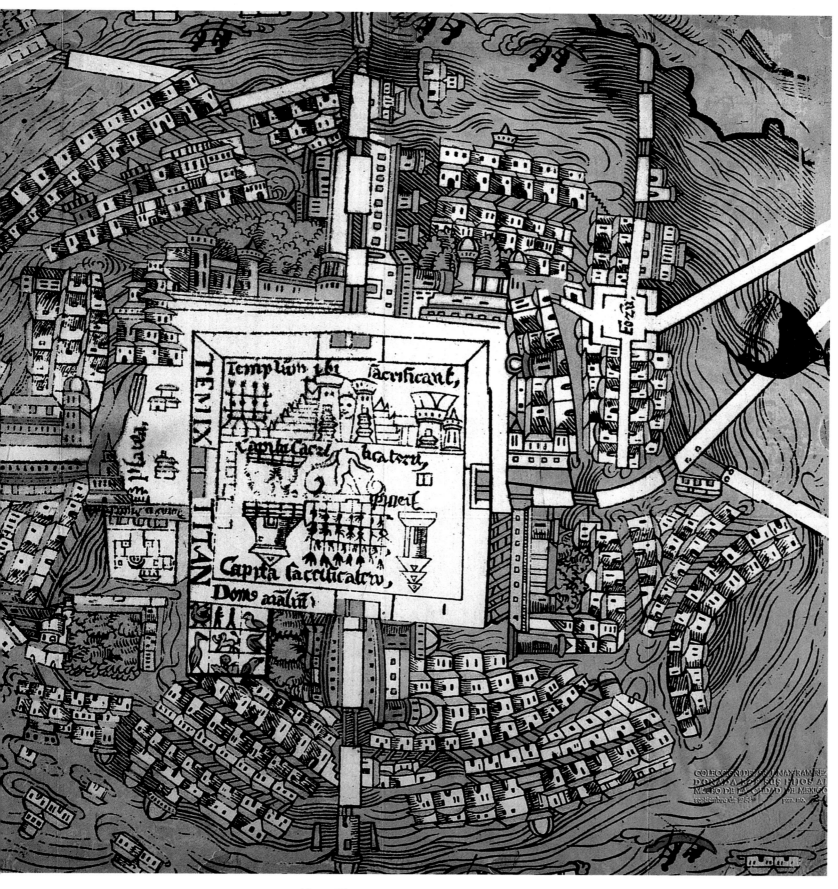

Above: These illustrations of Tenochtitlan and Lake Texcoco are attributed to Cortés himself. The Spanish conquistador and his men were greatly impressed by the size of the lake city, linked to dry land by a system of elevated roads.

Right: This illustration of Tenochtitlan appeared in a German publication of 1594. In 1519 the capital of the Aztec empire housed 200,000 persons and was probably larger than any Spanish city of the period.

111

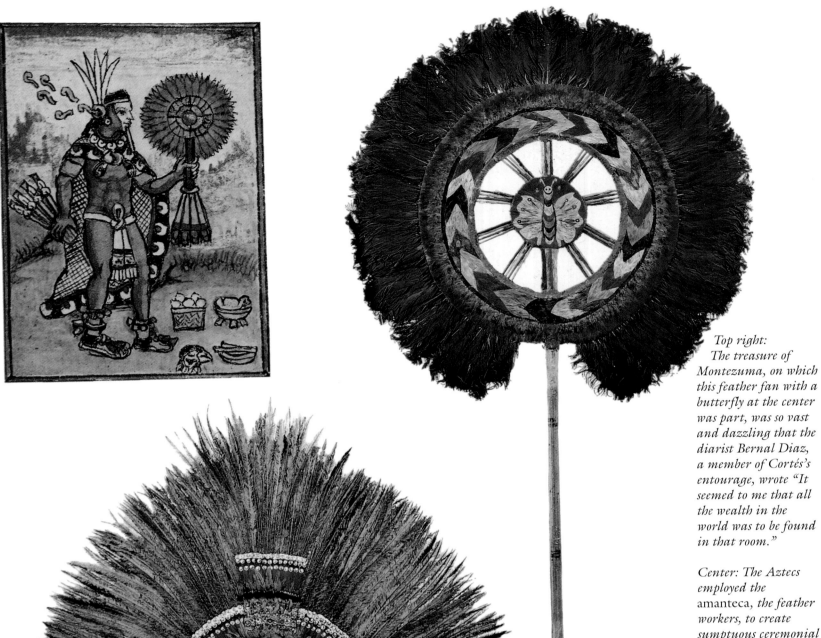

Top right:
The treasure of
Montezuma, on which
this feather fan with a
butterfly at the center
was part, was so vast
and dazzling that the
diarist Bernal Diaz,
a member of Cortés's
entourage, wrote "It
seemed to me that all
the wealth in the
world was to be found
in that room."

Center: The Aztecs
employed the
amanteca, *the feather*
workers, to create
sumptuous ceremonial
decorations for the
high ranking
dignitaries and
military chiefs. It is
thought that this
headgear once
belonged to
Montezuma.

Top left: In the
Historia de las Indias
by Diego Duran can
be seen this Aztec
prince in ceremonial
dress with a large
feather fan in his
hand. The splendor of
the Aztec civilization
stupefied even Cortés,
a man not easily
impressed: "... these
people live almost like
the people of Spain,
in equal harmony
and order, and
considering that they
are barbarians and
so far removed from
a knowledge of God
and lacking in all
contact with civilized
nations, it is truly
surprising to see what
they have achieved in
all manner of things."

Left: On the 8th of
November, 1519, the
Spanish troops came
within sight of
Tenochtitlan and
were received by the
emperor in person,
followed by a court
of 200 dignitaries.
Cortés presented
Montezuma with a
collar of pearls and
"glass diamonds,"
receiving in return
two necklaces from
which hung "eight
gold prawns executed
with great perfection
and a span in
length."

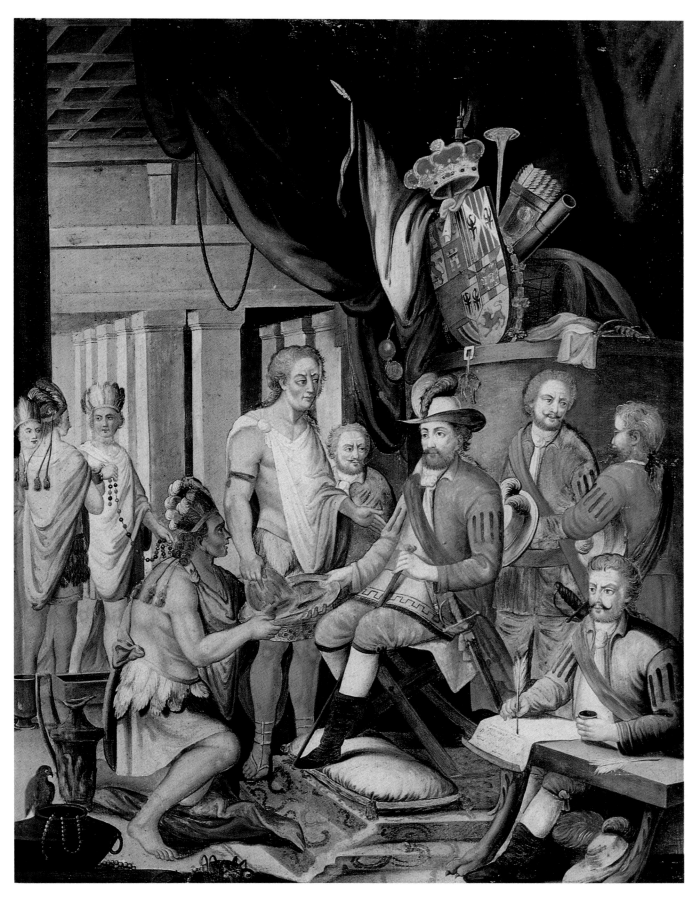

Above: In this painting on copper dated late 18th century, Cortés receives from Montezuma the tributes demanded in the name of the king of Spain. Montezuma's treasure of leggings, shields, bracelets, and heavy necklaces in solid gold of incalculable value were piled up in the central square at Tenochtitlan and melted down into ingots. Cortés, after having set aside the portion due to the Spanish crown, divided the rest of the booty among his men.

Tenochtitlan and dashed to the coast where he succeeded in persuading many of the soldiers to desert and throw in their lot with his forces. When he returned to Tenochtitlan, he was faced with a desperate situation: Alvarado had given orders for the senseless massacre of hundreds of Indians gathered for a religious ceremony.

The massacre had led to an insurrection. The Aztec emperor Montezuma was unable to calm matters and was killed while trying to restore order. Cortés was thrown out of the city and during the disastrous retreat, recorded in history as the "Night of Sorrows," half of the Spaniards lost their lives along with thousands of Indians. The conquistador did not allow the tragedy to interfere with his plans. Back in Tlaxcala he reorganized his army and laid siege to Tenochtitlan. The city eventually fell after a period of desperate resistance. Mexico was now at Cortés's feet and he was appointed as governor of the vast territory. Renamed as New Spain, over the following years the former Aztec empire became the base for successive explorations toward Honduras, Guatemala, and the Pacific Coast. Cortés himself participated in an expedition that reached the Gulf of California. Then, in 1540, Cortés fell out of favor with the Spanish court and returned to Spain where he died seven years later.

The history of the conquest of Mexico has been reconstructed on the basis of contemporary accounts by eye-witnesses and others, and the letters sent by Cortés himself. While such sources may be reliable, they are by no means objective, influenced as they are by personal interest and a celebratory tone. The testimony of the Aztec authors, even though it was collected and transcribed by the Spanish missionaries in the years following the conquest, offers a different perspective, one colored by the resignation and bitterness aroused by defeat. The landing of the Spaniards on the Mexican coast had not worried Montezuma.

Top left: Coalticua, "she who is dressed with serpents," was the goddess of the Earth, the mother of Coyolxauqui, goddess of the moon, and the incarnation of darkness and the constellations, and above all of Huitzilopochtli, the sun god, the triumphant, also and the symbol of Aztec domination over other people — until the arrival of the Spanish conquistadors.

Top right: The legendary Tula from where the stone statue of the warrior came from, was the capital of the Toltecs, a Mexican people from the central plateau. Toltec art was permeated by a bellicose spirit which was also reflected in the bloody religion practised by the followers of the ferocious Quetzalcoatl, the "Serpent of Clouds."

Bottom: This mask, frightening in its simplicity, is composed of a human skull and a sacrificial flint knife driven in place of the nose.

115

Above: Bernadino de Sahagan, a missionary in Mexico from 1529, was the author of various works in Spanish and Nahuatl, the local language. The best known of these is Historia de las cosas de Nueva Espana, *the rich iconographical* apparatus of which illustrates numerous scenes of Aztec life. In this work the existence of the native people appears to be profoundly conditioned by their obsession with their gods, war, and continual sacrifices to the sun god, of whom the Aztecs considered themselves to be the offspring. The sacrifices were necessary as the deity guaranteed the survival of the world each day, fighting against the night; his efforts were repaid with human blood.

116

Above: The pages of the work by Bernadino de Sahagun also contain a meticulous review of the complex Aztec pantheon. Among the numerous deities reproduced was the mysterious figure of Quetzalcoatl, the Feathered Serpent.

As was the case with the sun, many other gods were thirsty for human blood, the precious fluid.
In order to obtain victims, the Aztecs organized special military expeditions in which their soldiers participated with no fear of death as falling in combat would have guaranteed their immediate ascension to the heaven of the heroes. This accounts for the unending sequence of wars and massacres that characterise Aztec history.

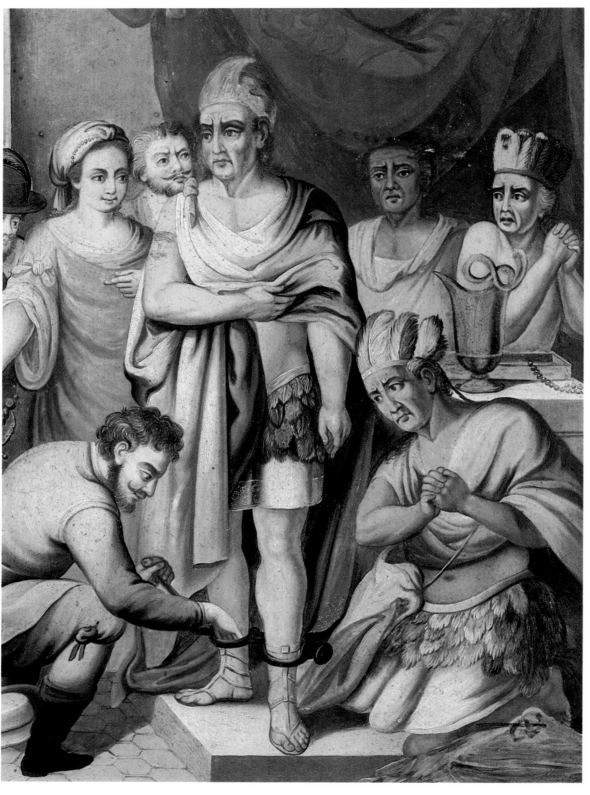

Above: This painting on copper of the late 18th century shows Montezuma taken prisoner and shackled. The murky details of the conquest were narrated in the Historia general de las cosas de la Nueva Espanã *by the Franciscan missionary Bernadino de Sahagún, who reached Mexico eight years after the fall of Tenochtitlan. His work, the fruit of long and patient investigations, drew on Indian sources and put forward a very different reading of the events than the official historiography of the time: it shows the point of view of those conquered, the other side of the coin.*

The spies he sent to keep watch on the foreigners described their appearance for the emperor: "they dress in metal; they cover their heads with metal, the swords are metal, their bows are metal, their shields are metal, the lances are metal. And those that carry them on their backs, the deer, seem as high as the terraces of houses. They cover their bodies on all sides, leaving only their dead white faces exposed, they have faces as white as chalk. They have yellow hair. Some, however, have black hair; their beards are long and yellow." The description was precise and realistic and, in spite of Montezuma's obsession, it is improbable that the Aztecs considered the Spaniards to be divine beings. Locked into a cyclical conception of time in which events were destined to repeat themselves, they would have failed to recognize the uniqueness of the situation. The white foreigners may well have been formidable adversaries, but as the events of Tlaxcala proved they could be challenged and defeated. Not even Cortés's entrance into Tenochtitlan was seen as the advance of a legendary hero (as it is depicted in many European paintings) but rather as a timid incursion. The Spaniards, impressed by the magnificence of the capital and the power of the Aztecs, realized that they were running serious risks and proceeded cautiously, looking to the left and right in fear of an ambush. Cortés wisely kept to the rear. As far as the Aztecs were concerned, the violence of the Spaniards, divorced from any form of ritual, was incomprehensible and gratuitous. Welcomed as guests, the bearded foreigners had no hesitation in killing Montezuma (the Spaniards blamed their adversaries) and at that point the Indians rebelled. The retreat of Cortés during the Night of Sorrows, was seen

as a victory by the Aztecs. In their disorderly haste to escape, the Spaniards trampled underfoot their casualties whose bodies filled the streets of Tenochtitlan, and they were relentlessly assaulted by the Aztec soldiers. The white men then returned and the empire crumbled in a sequence of tragic events: the horrors of a smallpox epidemic, the siege and tenacious resistance street by street, the retreat and the massacres. The Aztec accounts became the sad elegy of an irreversible defeat: "Where are we going? Oh friends/ we are abandoning the City of Mexico:/ the smoke is rising; the fog is spreading.../ Weep, friends,/ and know that with these events/ we have lost the Mexican nation."

Top left: Francisco Pizarro was born in Estremadura, like Cortés and Balboa, around 1475. An experienced, but poor and illiterate adventurer, he was 50 years old when he began his exploration of the Pacific Coast of America. The discovery of the Incan empire that he conquered with brutal rapidity brought him sought-after fame and wealth. He was assassinated at Lima in 1541.

While Cortés was organizing the administration of the new province, other adventurers were exploring the Pacific Coast to the south in search of fortune. Were there other Teochtitláns in the New World? The mirage of the legendary kingdom of Birù had aroused Spanish enthusiasm for years. In 1522, Pascual de Andagoya had followed the coast of Panama beyond the borders of modern-day Colombia: Andagoya failed to find gold, but his reports confirmed the existence of a rich and powerful country in the far south. However, Peru was not easily accessible, isolated by the formidable barrier of the Andes and the immense Amazonian forest, it was practically impossible to reach from the east. Navigation along the Pacific Coast was made difficult by adverse currents and the coastal regions were inhospitable and unhealthy. The exploration of the area nevertheless proceeded, albeit slowly. In 1526, thirteen exhausted and starving men awaited reinforcements on the desolate

Gorgona Island off the Colombian coast. Their commander, Francisco Pizarro was determined to advance at all costs. Pizarro was born into an extremely poor family in Estremadura. He was around fifty years old, illiterate but an expert soldier and courageous to the point of insanity. He knew that this was his last chance for fame and fortune: his first attempt at exploration had failed miserably and should he fail again his sponsors would have refused to provide fresh funds. His companion in arms, Diego de Almagro, as avid and courageous as Pizarro, had nothing to lose: Pizarro knew that he would return. Almagro arrived seven months later, with fresh supplies and a handful of men. Together they continued southward. They crossed the broad Gulf of Guayaquil and dropped anchor close to Tumbes, an outpost of the Inca empire, a well built town with paved streets and irrigation canals. The Spaniards were well received: such a small company could hardly have

Top right:
The working of metal reached extremely advanced levels in the Chimú civilization. Jewelery, religious artifacts, and funerary masks were produced using an unusual alloy of gold and copper called tumbaga. *Precious stones were also often used as in this ritual knife in gold and emeralds.*

Left: The famous "pact" for the discovery of Peru, sealed on the 10th of March, 1526 at Panama between Pizarro, Almagro and the priest Hernando de Luque, the venture's financier, is depicted in this engraving by Theodore de Bry, 1596. In the course of that year, Pizarro and Almagro explored the Pacific coast of Peru, reaching the Incan city of Tumbes: the modest quantity of gold and silver they brought back to Panama was sufficient to attract the attention of the Spanish court and the consequent authorization for the conquest.

Top: This gold funerary mask belonged to the Chimù culture and shows a number of polychromatic traces, while small emeralds are applied as eyes.

Right: The emperor Atahualpa is going to meet the Spaniards sitting on a sedan chair. A writer of the era described him as "around 30 years old, attractive, robust, with a pleasant face, and an imposing and proud expression."

When Pizarro reached Cajamarca in the November of 1532, Atuhualpa's authority was being challenged by his brother Huascar, and the Incan empire was lacerated by a bloody civil war between the opposing factions.

Caribbean Sea

PANAMA
PANAMA

VENEZUELA

Orinoco

Pacific Ocean

COLOMBIA

MOUNTAINS

ECUADOR

Putumayo

Gulf of Guayaquil

Napo

Amazon River

TUMBES

Maraño

Ucayali

BRASIL

CAJAMARCA

HUASCARÁN 6768

LIMA

ANDES

CUZCO

AREA ENLARGED

LAKE TITICACA

122

Left: Atahualpa is taken prisoner by Pizarro in this engraving by de Bry, 1596. The Incan king tried to buy his liberty by offering a fabulous ransom: 9,900 lbs of gold and 19,360 of silver.

Opposite: Pizarro gives the signal to attack Atahualpa in the central square at Cajamarca. The ambush was prepared with icy determination and had success.

Opposite bottom left: In 1535 Almagro, in search of wealth, left Cuzco with 500 men and 1,000 porters, eventually reaching Chile. The crossing of the Andes proved to be very arduous: many Spaniards, weighed down by their armor and lacking clothing suited to the altitudes, died. Beyond the mountains there was no new Eldorado, and Almagro returned to Peru the following year.

Opposite bottom right: Atahualpa was accused of idolatry, wastage of public funds, adultery, and rebellion. Even though accusations were groundless, he was found guilty and condemned to be burnt. Padre Valverde convinced the emperor to embrace the Christian faith: he would be strangled rather than burnt. He accepted this and was executed on the 29th of August, 1533.

Above: The Amerindian Mochica people lived in an area that is, today, situated between Ecuador and Peru. The arts of gold and silver smithery were, together with agriculture and war, their principal activities. The earring in this illustration is of gold with a turquoise mosaic and represents a threatening warrior.

Right: This female statue in pure gold was produced by the Tolita civilization. The extensive use of precious metal has permitted a number of pre-Columbian funerary artifacts to survive up to the present day, despite the pillaging of the conquistadors who violated innumerable tombs to collect gold objects for melting down.

aroused the Indians' suspicions. Pizarro exchanged his goods for cloth, ceramics, and gold and silver jewels. What he had was sufficient for the moment: the inhabitants of Tumbes belonged to an advanced, wealthy society. He returned to Panama and from there set sail for Spain. The Spanish court, gathered at Toledo, was still dazzled by the riches that Cortés had brought from Mexico, and it was not difficult for Pizarro to obtain a mandate for a new expedition. He was given explicit permission for conquest and the title of Governor of the future Peru. He left Panama late, in 1530, in command of three ships and 180 men. A couple of weeks later he landed on the coast of northern Ecuador: the exploration of the swampy, disease-ridden coastal area required two months of unmitigated suffering. Having reached the Gulf of Guayaquil, the overland column met up with the fleet and moved on to Tumbes. The Spaniards found the city in ruins, devastated by the civil war being fought by Atahualpa and his brother Huascar. The country appeared deserted, but Pizarro learned that Atahualpa's army was not far away. The emperor was at Cajamarca, on the other side of the mountains. Crossing the Andes was a severe test for the Spaniards with their heavy armour and lack of suitable clothing for the bitter cold at high altitudes. However, early in November, having tackled the last mountain pass, Pizarro came within sight of the city situated in a grandiose natural amphitheatre and surrounded by fields of

Above: A portrait-vase in gold from the Chimù civilization. The immense mineral wealth of Peru encouraged the Spanish conquistadors to carry out audacious and bloody expeditions culminating in the massacre of the Incan aristocracy by Pizzarro in 1531.

Right: This finely worked gold crown is also a product of the Chimù civilization. It was the abundance of gold that gave rise to the legend of the fabulous city of Eldorado.

maize and tobacco. Cajamarca also appeared deserted, with no sounds enlivening the stone buildings and the silent squares swept by freezing winds from the uplands. Atahualpa, with his army of 30,000 men had camped well away from the city itself. The following day the emperor agreed to come into the city to meet Pizarro. The events that followed echoed those that occurred in Mexico. Atahualpa was captured and kept as a hostage until he was of use. Once he had obtained the fabulous ransom demanded for Atahualpa's release, Pizarro had him killed. The conquest of the Inca empire, deprived of its leader and lacerated by profound internal conflict, proceeded rapidly. A year later, a few hundred Spaniards led by Almagro and Pizarro launched an attack on Cuzco: the political and religious capital of the Incas fell after a brief siege and the empire's efficient road network aided the occupation of the vast and otherwise inaccessible Andean territories. In 1535 the Spaniards founded Lima, the administrative center of the new colony. Almagro, dissatisfied with the rewards he had obtained, headed to Chile, and three years later challenged Pizarro's authority and attacked him below the walls of Cuzco. His defeat was to cost him his life. Pizarro himself was assassinated by Almagro's followers at Lima in 1541. A few years later, the Spanish colonists began to exploit the Potosì silver mines, and immense wealth flowed into Spain, triggering a process of inflation that was to shake the economy of the whole of Europe and give rise to a new historical era.

Above: In this engraving by Theodore de Bry, 1596, can be seen the conquest of Cuzco. In reality, except for sporadic episodes, the resistance offered by the Incan armies never seriously troubled the Spaniards.

In contrast with de Bry's illustration, on the 15th of November, 1533, Pizarro's troops entered Cuzco without bloodshed. The city was sacked and the booty divided among the soldiers in the best traditions of conquest.

Center: This gold cat is yet another Chimù masterpiece: even the ruthless conquistadors were astounded by these extraordinary examples of the goldsmiths' art, but few were allowed to escape the plundering.

Opposite: The noble city of Cuzco in an engraving by Theodore de Bry from 1592. This imaginary view is based on the inaccurate information that had reached Europe. In reality Cuzco, although divided into quarters, was not surrounded by a wall and was of a more irregular plan. The Incan capital, constructed on the outskirts of the empire, was served by an extensive network of paved roads thousands of miles long.

Overleaf: A Chimù funeral mask in gold with polychromatic traces, now kept in the Lima Museum of Gold. The Chimù were organized in a powerful theocratic state and the quality of the manufactures that have survived bears testimony to the heights their civilization achieved.

CVSCO, REGNI PERV
IN NOVO ORBE CAPVT.

FRANCISCO VASQUEZ DE CORONADO

Above: Francisco Vasquez de Coronado demonstrated all the typical traits of the minor Spanish land-owning nobility: fearlessness, individualism, and boundless faith in his own abilities. In 1540, dissatisfied with his career in the colonial administration, Coronado left Mexico in search of the wealth of Cibola, a fabulous realm that was said to be found in the unexplored regions of the north. He never found the gold but was the first European to penetrate the Southwest of the present-day United States of America, reaching the Colorado River and the prairies of Kansas.

Center: This painting by Jan Mostaert, a Dutch painter of the 16th century, shows the Spaniards attacking a pueblo of the Zuñi Indians. The artist has represented the Indian village with a certain degree of realism but used his imagination for the rest. The Zuñi are portrayed completely naked and some of them are bearded, while the trees and animals are those of the European countryside.

Francisco Vasquez de Coronado, the Governor of the northern provinces of New Spain, arrived in Mexico in 1535. He had enjoyed a brilliant career, as befitted a Castilian nobleman, but this was not enough. Coronado wanted gold and glory, just like Cortés and Pizarro, the conquistadores of the fabulous Peru. The riches of the New World appeared to be inexhaustible. Increasingly insistent rumors had been circulating for some time about another fabulously wealthy kingdom north of the Mexican frontier, beyond the desert: the legendary Seven Cities of Cibola. In 1539 the viceroy of Mexico, Mendoza, had sent a Franciscan monk, Marco of Nice, to verify how much truth there was to the legend. He failed to reach Cibola but returned with exciting news: his report spoke of cities larger and more sumptuous even than Tenochtitlán, stone buildings ten floors high, and temples with turquoise-covered facades. And, of course, gold, in quantities to put the treasures of Atahualpa well and truly in the shade. The monk's report coincided perfectly with what Mendoza wanted to hear and he immediately set about organizing a full-blown expedition. Leadership of the party was entrusted to Coronado. In February, 1540, everything was ready and the party of 250 horsemen, seventy foot soldiers, and a thousand Indians, followed by a huge herd of pack and meat animals, set off toward Cibola. Marco of Nice, with his cross in his fist, led the procession. Should Coronado have gotten into difficulties he could have turned toward the Gulf of California where a support fleet would be waiting: the hypothetical meeting place was at the mouth of the Colorado River the approximate position of which was known to the Spaniards. The expedition made slow progress and it took forty days to

reach Cualicán, the northernmost outpost of the Spanish territories. The landscape became more and more desolate as each day passed: the men and animals suffered from thirst and the march became a nightmare. The Indians they met along the trail were friendly but had no food to offer the armored foreigners, and they had heard of neither towering cities nor gold. Beyond the valley of the Sonora River, Marco of Nice had promised a land "rich in greenery" and irrigated fields. In reality the expedition was about to enter the inhospitable desert of what is now Arizona. The men were exasperated, and it was only Coronado's authority that saved the monk from being lynched. On the 8th of July, the column finally reached the area inhabited by the Zuñi Indians, but the people of Hawikuh with their terraced houses accessed via long rope ladders were very different to what the Spaniards had been expecting. There was no legendary city of gold before their disenchanted eyes, just a miserable mud-hut village. Where were the celebrated riches of Cibola, for which they had suffered three months' worth of fatigue and privation? As if this was not enough, the Indians were hostile and attacked the expedition "like men possessed." Following a brief but bloody battle, "Cibola" was conquered and Coronado, wounded in the foot by an arrow, entered the city. It was clear that Marco of Nice had lied: "the realms of which he had spoken had not been found, nor had the teeming cities, the gold or the precious stones." In recompense the Spaniards could at least placate their pangs of hunger, pillaging the stores of food accumulated in the pueblo. The men were exhausted and Coronado decided to stop in the village for a couple of months. In the meantime he sent his lieutenants to explore the vast and unknown surrounding areas. Diaz pressed on as far as the mouth of the Colorado only to discover that after a prolonged wait the support fleet had returned to Mexico. Lopez de Cárdenas, marching westward had discovered the Grand Canyon. A great river, the omnipresent Colorado, flowed through the gorge, one of the deepest in the world. A number of men attempted to descend along the walls of the great chasm, but without success. Alvarado, on the other hand, returned from his reconnaissance trip with more interesting news: he had followed

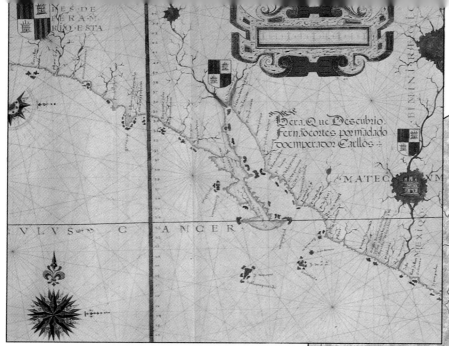

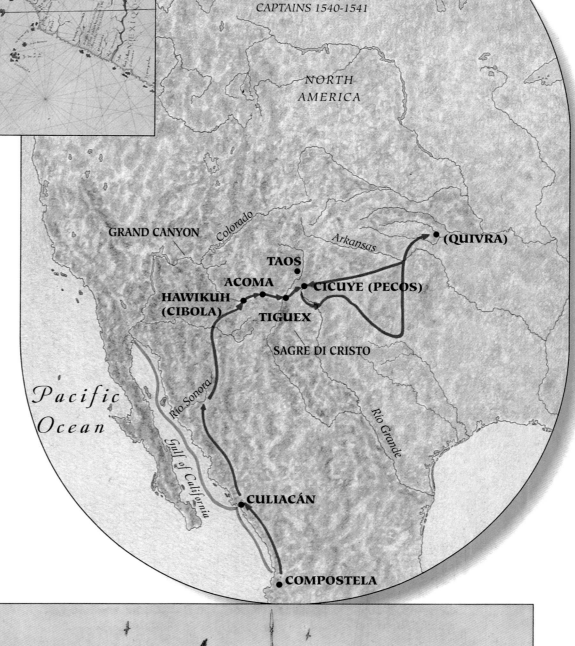

SUPPORT FLEET 1540
CORONADO AND HIS CAPTAINS 1540-1541

NORTH AMERICA

GRAND CANYON

(QUIVRA)

TAOS

ACOMA

HAWIKUH (CIBOLA)

CICUYE (PECOS)

TIGUEX

SAGRE DI CRISTO

Pacific Ocean

Colorado

Arkansas

Río Sonora

Gulf of California

Río Grande

CULIACÁN

COMPOSTELA

the valley of the Rio Grande, discovering other villages and penetrating as far as the "regions of the cattle" (the buffalo) in the great plains of the American Midwest. He was accompanied by new guides who assured him that in the distant west there was a realm called Quivira: there the Spaniards would have found the gold they so ardently desired. Coronado decided to spend the winter on the banks of the Rio Grande close to the pueblos of Tigeux, where food was more abundant. In April, 1541, the expedition departed in search of Quivira: the guides led the Spaniards beyond the Sangre de Cristo Mountains and the valley of the Pecos River until they reached the vast plains of Kansas. The plains Indians were very different to those the Spaniards had so far encountered. They led nomadic lives in tents and hunted the buffalo that roamed the region in their millions. Coronado continued his advance as far as the territory occupied by the Wichita Indians. Quivira did not exist, and the expedition had once again proved to be a failure. All that remained for the Spaniards to do was turn for home. Following another winter on the Rio Grande, the expedition returned to Mexico. There was no El Dorado in the north but Coronado had at least established the basis for the future colonization of the American Southwest region which was to be dominated by the Spaniards over the following two centuries.

Top: This map, taken from the Hydrographical Atlas by Fernand Vaz Dourado, published in 1571, shows the coasts of Southern California and Mexico washed by the Pacific Ocean as Magellan had named the expanse of water in spite of the storms that had made the crossing of the strait that bears his name so difficult.

Right: This drawing by Charles M. Russell shows Francisco Vasquez de Coronado advancing with his armed men on the legendary city of Cibola, in reality a pueblo in the American Southwest.

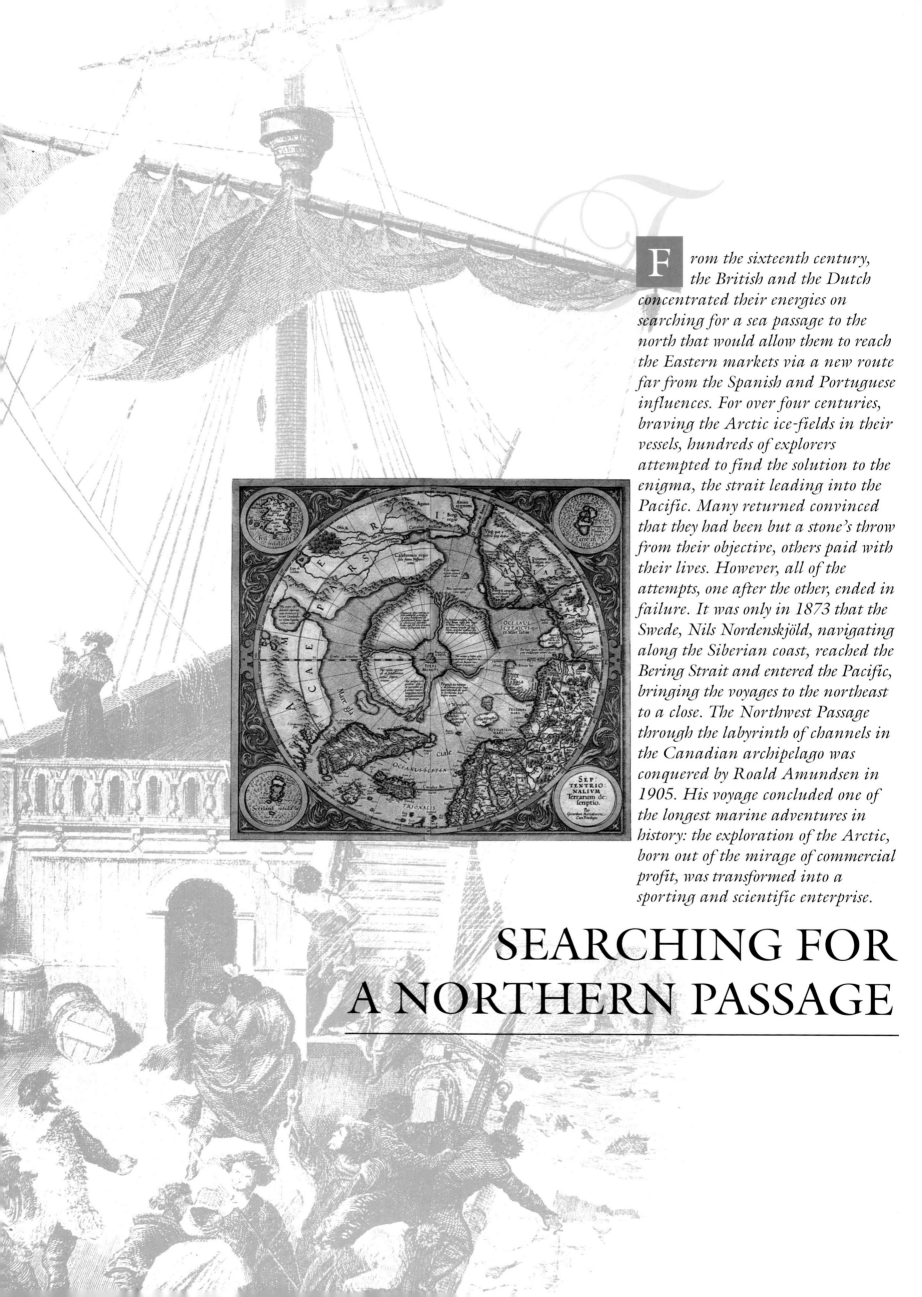

From the sixteenth century, the British and the Dutch concentrated their energies on searching for a sea passage to the north that would allow them to reach the Eastern markets via a new route far from the Spanish and Portuguese influences. For over four centuries, braving the Arctic ice-fields in their vessels, hundreds of explorers attempted to find the solution to the enigma, the strait leading into the Pacific. Many returned convinced that they had been but a stone's throw from their objective, others paid with their lives. However, all of the attempts, one after the other, ended in failure. It was only in 1873 that the Swede, Nils Nordenskjöld, navigating along the Siberian coast, reached the Bering Strait and entered the Pacific, bringing the voyages to the northeast to a close. The Northwest Passage through the labyrinth of channels in the Canadian archipelago was conquered by Roald Amundsen in 1905. His voyage concluded one of the longest marine adventures in history: the exploration of the Arctic, born out of the mirage of commercial profit, was transformed into a sporting and scientific enterprise.

SEARCHING FOR A NORTHERN PASSAGE

THE NORTHWEST PASSAGE

In 1495, Henry VII of England received a visitor from Italy, a Venetian citizen originally from Genoa. The Italian's proposal once again concerned the search for a western route to the Indies. Some years earlier Henry VII had rejected the requests of another Genoese, Christopher Columbus, a rejection which subsequently he bitterly regretted. He was determined not to let this second opportunity slip through his fingers. It was thus that Giovanni Caboto set out from Bristol in May, 1497, heading for Cathay. After sailing for about a month, Caboto reached the Canadian coast, which he mistook for Japan. Convinced that he had reached the eastern confines of Asia, he set out again the following year. However, the results of his second voyage were disappointing: quite by chance, he had discovered the world's richest fishing grounds off the coast of Newfoundland, but there were no traces

Below: Giovanni Caboto, a Venetian citizen in the service of the English crown, was perhaps the first European to reach the coast of North America. In spite of being well organized and generously financed, his second expedition of 1498 failed tragically and Caboto himself disappeared with his ship in the Atlantic Ocean.

of the fabulous wealth of Cathay.
In 1508, Sebastiano Caboto followed in his father's footsteps: sailing northward he encountered "great mountains of ice floating on the sea and almost constant daylight." How far did the new northern lands extend? Was there perhaps a strait farther to the north? It was no more than a hypothesis, and initially nobody paid any attention to his stories, but Caboto's voyages had opened a breach and triggered one of the longest and wildest adventures in the history of exploration: the search for a Northwest Passage to Asia. While the Iberian powers were concentrating their attention on the Southern Hemisphere, France and Britain gradually turned their attention to the North. In 1524, Giovanni da Verrazzano explored a vast stretch of the American coast on behalf of the French crown, dropping anchor in the bay that today houses New York. Ten years later, Jacques Cartier sailed up the estuary of the St. Lawrence, hoping to find route through to the new ocean discovered by

Lef: Sebastiano Caboto, who left England in 1508 for the mythical Cathay of Marco Polo, found himself sailing in seas infested with mountains of floating ice, and where the light of day never faded. It is not known at what point the Italian came upon the coast of North America (perhaps the Hudson Strait), but his voyage marked the beginning of the interminable search for a Northwest Passage to Asia.

133

Right: Jacques Cartier, born at Saint Malò in 1491, was the first European to ascend the St. Lawrence River. His three trips, while important from the point of view of exploration, did not lead to the sought-after passage to Cathay nor to the wealth of the legendary realm of Saguenay. Following the failure of his last expedition, Cartier fell out of favor with the court and died forgotten in his hometown in 1557.

Magellan. Then, after a few decades of stagnancy, the torch was taken up by the British explorers. The wealthy London merchants had been pleading for a search for a sea passage to the north of the American continent for some time. Their arguments, bound in a weighty tome entitled *Discussion on the Discovery of a New Passage to Cathay*, highlighted the extraordinary advantages that such a discovery would present to the British economy. Such fervor could hardly be ignored by the court, and Queen Elizabeth eventually assented to a new program of exploration. The man chosen to conduct the enterprise to a fruitful conclusion was Martin Frobisher, virtually illiterate and with a reputation as a pirate, he was nevertheless a respected navigator. Frobisher left England in June, 1576: a month and a half later, having rounded the southern tip of Greenland, he came within sight of an unknown land (Baffin Island) whose coast opened in "a great inlet, a bay or a passage, separating two large

Center: In September of 1535 Cartier attempted to ascend the St. Lawrence, thinking that the great river was the key to the Northwest Passage to the Pacific. With the help of Indian guides, Cartier penetrated far upstream until he reached the site of present-day Montreal. He was then obliged to turn back due to the presence of insuperable rapids.

Below: This map of New France, drawn with the South to the top, shows Jacques Cartier at the head of a group of colonists about to take possession of Canada. In reality, the attempts to found a colony in the new lands failed miserably.

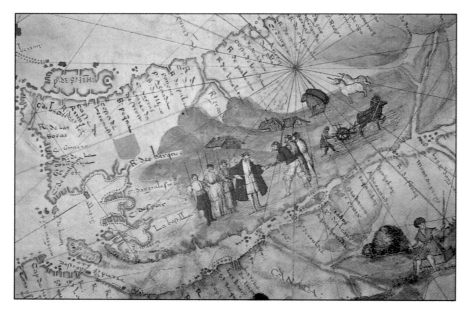

territories, not to say continents." It was in fact no more than an inlet, but Frobisher did not investigate his discovery further, being distracted by the Eskimos whose Mongol traits convinced him that he had landed in some remote province of Asia. Then something rather more significant caught his attention: the island or continent was full of sparkling stones. Gold: everywhere and in unheard of abundance! Frobisher rushed back to England with his extraordinary news. He set sail again the following year with orders to fill his holds with the precious metal. When he reached England with two hundred tons of what he believed was gold-bearing rock he was acclaimed in triumph. Questions of exploration faded into the background, and in 1578 Frobisher was sent with a fleet of 15 ships to the Meta Incognita as Baffin Island was mysteriously called. This time he penetrated the true strait leading to the Hudson Bay, but the discontent of his crews and adverse weather conditions soon helped to concentrate his attention on the mission's primary objective. Loaded with mineral ore, the ships set sail for Britain. In the meantime, however, the bitter truth had been revealed: the ore contained not gold but common pyrites or Fool's Gold

good for paving streets at best. Frobisher disappeared from circulation but his failure had not dampened enthusiasm for exploration as the discovery of the Northwest Passage appeared imminent. The search continued. When the voyages were obstructed by ice, it was thought sufficient to attempt more northern routes: it was believed that in the higher latitudes, where the days never ended, the seas were free of pack-ice. The heat of the sun prevented the formation of ice, or at least that was what the geographers of the day claimed. The following voyages confirmed this theory: in 1587 John Davis followed the western coast of Greenland, finding open sea at 73° latitude North. Davis returned to England convinced that he was on the right track: "The passage is almost certain, the sailing easy" he claimed without hesitation. Had Henry Hudson survived he might have had something to say about such claims. Hudson had considerable experience of sailing in the Arctic seas and in 1610 he was commissioned to continue the exploration from where Frobisher had left off. The stretch of sea separating Baffin Island from the Labrador coast appeared to be a promising route. In the June of that year Hudson entered the strait, but strong

Above: Martin Frobisher, an adventurer and pirate in the service of the British crown, was the protagonist in a series of voyages across the North Atlantic that, from 1576 to 1578, took him as far as the Hudson Strait and Baffin Island. Frobisher returned to England with a 200-ton load of of iron pyrites, believing that he had found gold ore.

Right: Relations with the Eskimos (here fancifully depicted) were initially good but were inevitably soured when Frobisher tried to capture a number of them to take back with him as trophies. The appearance of the natives, he observed, was similar to that of the Tartars, "with their long black hair, round face and flattened nose." This reinforced the Briton's conviction that they had finally landed on the coast of Asia.

135

Top left: The Englishman Henry Hudson is portrayed here on the deck of his ship the Half Moon, the tragic scene of the mutiny that cost the explorer his life. He departed in search of the Northwest Passage in 1607, completing the exploration of the Svalbard archipelago previously visited by Barents and reached the waters off Novaja Zemlja. He died in Hudson Bay in 1610.

currents obliged him to seek refuge in Ungava Bay. The passage was obstructed by great sheets of floating ice, a mortal danger for his fragile sailing ship. In spite of the heated protests of his crew, Hudson decided to try his luck. A month later he entered the vast bay, which today carries his name. No land appeared on the horizon and Hudson, believing that he had finally reached the Pacific, followed the coast to the south. Seven hundred miles later he found himself bottled up in James Bay, a dead end. Rather than turn back or continue with his reconnaissance, he wandered for months around that desolate inlet until the precocious polar winter trapped his ship in an icy grip. There was nothing to be done but to ration the food supplies and wait for spring. During those seven months of enforced immobility Hudson's relations with his crew deteriorated beyond repair. Hunger and scurvy decimated the men and the captain's mental stability was severely shaken. Early in the summer, during preparations for their departure, a mutiny broke out: Hudson, a number of faithful seamen, and his sixteen-year-old son were

THE NORTHWEST PASSAGE

Artic Ocean

FROBISHER 1578
HUDSON 1610-1611
BAFFIN 1616

Ellesmere Island

GREENLAND

Devon Island

BAHÍA DE BAFFIN

LANCASTER SOUND

Bylot Island

DAVIS STRAIT

Baffin Island

BAY OF FROBISHER

Labrador Sea

NORTHWEST TERRITORY

HUDSON STRAIT

Atlantic Sea

LABRADOR

UNGAVA BAY

AREA ENLARGED

HUDSON BAY

ST. JAMES BAY

Left: The expression of sufferance on Henry Hudson's face expresses his resignation to the sad fate that awaited him: on the 23rd of June, 1611, his crew mutinied, abandoning their captain, with his sixteen-year-old son and eight faithful men, on a drifting boat. Nothing further was ever heard of them. An inquiry was opened into the episode, but the guilt of the mutineers was never fully proven. The mysterious disappearance of Hudson left unanswered the question as to whether the Northwest Passage had been found.

Top left: John Ross
was the leader of two
important Arctic
expeditions: in 1818
he meticulously
explored the western
coast of Greenland
and the coast of
Baffin Island,
penetrating deep
into the labyrinth
of the Canadian
archipelagos.
From 1829 to 1833
his ship was locked
into the ice for no
less than four
consecutive winters.

Top right: An Eskimo
from the Boothia
Peninsula to the West
of Baffin Island. The
drawings and notes
in Ross's log carefully
document all aspects
of the daily life of the
Eskimos. Their
hunting skills and
their ability to
survive in such a
hostile environment
aroused the
admiration of the
British seamen;
"None of us,"
observed Ross,
"would be capable
of harpooning a
seal through a hole
in the ice."

set drifting in a small boat and nothing more was ever heard of them. When the survivors returned to England they were put on trial but eventually absolved due to lack of evidence against them. There remained one doubt: had Hudson discovered the Northwest Passage? Over the following years a number of other expeditions followed in his wake until it became clear that the bay was completely landlocked. Subsequent voyages to Baffin Island revealed that neither the strait navigated by Hudson, nor the great bay that opened West of Greenland led to the open ocean. Exploration fever gave way to the commercial exploitation of the lands that had been discovered: the Hudson Bay Company was formed in 1670 and concentrated on hunting and trapping the fur animals that thrived in the boundless territories of the Great Canadian North. However, in 1725 news from the Pacific revived interest in the search for a Northern Passage. Vitus Bering, a Dane in the service of the Czar, had been exploring the coast of Siberia and had discovered the strait separating America and Asia. Then, in 1768, James Cook had navigated the strait sailing eastward to Cape Icy on the northeast coast of Alaska. Cook's reports confirmed the existence of a viable route from the Pacific to the Arctic seas, but put a definitive end to the tales of the melting of the ice by the sun. The ice was there, and in great quantities, and it was the principal obstacle that had to be overcome. In the meantime, overland exploration continued: in 1769 Samuel Hearne left the Hudson Bay and eventually followed the Coppermine River to its outlet on the Arctic coast of Canada. Around twenty years later MacKenzie reached the Beaufort Sea. By the end of the century much of the Canadian coastline had been explored and the time was ripe for Arctic exploration to be revived in grand style. With the Napoleonic Wars having ended, the question of the Northwest Passage was tackled with renewed enthusiasm. In 1818 John Ross completed a painstaking survey of Baffin Bay. He came across the Lancaster Sound (the true key to the passage) but, deceived by dense fog, judged it to be a dead end. A year later William Parry was more fortunate: he

Center:
The relationships of Ross's crew with the inhabitants of the Arctic were from the outset, based on reciprocal trust. In order to seal their friendship, the English team offered the Eskimos of Baffin Island, who had never before seen a European, knives, mirrors, and other items. The mirrors proved to be a very welcome gift: stunned by the sight of their own reflected faces, wrote Ross, "the Eskimos loosed a sudden cry and then exploded in gales of laughter, a sign of joy rather than surprise."

Above: This drawing by John Ross shows a rather unusual phenomenon that captured the imagination of the British explorer: the roseate coloring of the Arctic ice. During his 1818 expedition Ross actually sent a number of sailors ashore to investigate the causes of this coloration, but was unable to solve the mystery. Only later was it discovered that the pinkish tint was caused by a unicellular plant Chlamydomonas nivalis that only flowers in cold damp climates.

entered the sound and, with no great problems, reached Melville Island located at a longitude of 112° on the threshold of the open sea. In front of the ship's prow stretched an endless barrier of ice and Parry, trapped by the perpetual polar night, prepared to sit out the winter in a sheltered bay. Under a large tent pitched on the deck of the ship, the men waited for the summer. By mid-August the ice had not yet melted and it appeared as though the pack would be insuperable. Subsequently Ross and Parry were to search unsuccessfully for a passage further to the south. The Arctic archipelago appeared to be a labyrinth with no way out. Nevertheless, the pieces of the mosaic were gradually falling into place: the continental

Left: Casting doubt on the claims of Ross, Parry held that Baffin Bay was a dead end. He penetrated Lancaster Sound and sailed west for 600 miles until he reached the coast of Banks Island, going beyond the 110° longitude threshold. Success now appeared at hand, but in the August of 1820, the expedition's advance was finally thwarted on the threshold of the perennially frozen Beaufort Sea. Parry's second voyage was in search of a passage to the north of Hudson Bay, but also ended in failure.

Center left: Among the ethnographic finds and curiosities brought back to Europe by the Arctic explorers were these rudimentary but efficient Eskimo "sunglasses" made of suitably shaped soft wood incised with a narrow fissure. In the absence of colored lenses, they served to protect the eyes from the reflection of the sun on the snow.

coastline had by now been almost completely charted and other explorers demonstrated that it was navigable, albeit with some difficulty. The problem was how to link the northern routes with the more practicable routes following the Canadian coast. In 1844, the Royal Navy decided to examine a problem which had now become a question of national pride: a meticulously organized new expedition was launched and it was hoped that it would provide a definitive solution. The expedition was commanded by Captain John Franklin, a veteran of audacious explorations along the coast west of the Coppermine and MacKenzie Rivers. Franklin departed in May, 1845: he entered Lancaster Sound, determined to proceed westward at all costs. However,

138

Center right: Vitus Bering, an expert Danish navigator in the service of the Russian navy, was the first man to verify the existence of a passage between Asia and America (the Bering Strait). During a subsequent expedition he reached the coast of Alaska and Aleutian Islands; exhausted and suffering from scurvy he died on an island off Kamchatka.

Bottom: Sir John Franklin also searched for the legendary Northwest Passage in the 19th century, and he too, like Hudson, came to a tragic end. Setting out in 1845 with two vessels for Baffin Island, nothing more was heard of him after he had reached Lancaster Sound. His remains were not found until fifteen years later.

Top: The committee
formed by the
admiralty to
organize the rescue
mission for the
Franklin expedition,
comprized the most
famous British Arctic
explorers, including
William Parry and

George Back,
recognizable for
his heavy sideburns
(left, consulting a
map), James Clark
Ross, the nephew of
John Ross, standing
below a portrait of
Franklin himself
(left).

having ventured into Barrow Strait he was
obstructed by ice. He then searched for a
route to the north, which would allow him
to skirt round Melville Island, but once
again encountered impenetrable pack-ice.
Franklin now had no alternative but to
head south: he finally reached open water
and if he could have found a way past
King William Island he would have
reached previously charted routes. Success
appeared to be beckoning, but once again
the pack implacably closed ranks in front of
the ship and Franklin resigned himself to
sitting out his third polar winter. The
anticipated thaw never arrived and the
members of the expedition died one by
one. Almost a year passed before news of
the latest tragic failure filtered through to
Britain. The first rescuers did not leave
until 1848. In the decade following the
disappearance of Franklin at least forty
expeditions combed the desolate Arctic

*Center left:
The tragedy of the
Franklin expedition
in a painting by W.
Thomas Smith from
1895. The
disappearance of John
Franklin had a great
impact on public
opinion and
officialdom: the
British government
offered a reward of
20,000 pounds to
whomever brought
news of the explorer.
From 1848 onward,
over 40 expeditions
combed the Canadian
Arctic, but the destiny
of Franklin was only
resolved 10 years later.
Jules Verne's* The
Englishmen at the
North Pole *was
inspired by the episode.*

*Center right:
The MacClintock
expedition found a tin
cylinder containing a
double message:
alongside a normal
report from 1847 can
be read a number of
phrases from 1848 that
reveal the terrible
conditions of
Franklin's expedition.*

*Bottom: In 1859
the MacClintock
expedition dedicated
to the search for John
Franklin came across
a mound of stones on
the west coast of King
William Island.
The members of*

*Franklin's
expedition, now on
their last legs, had
left all their
superfluous
equipment here in
the hope of moving
southward more
quickly.*

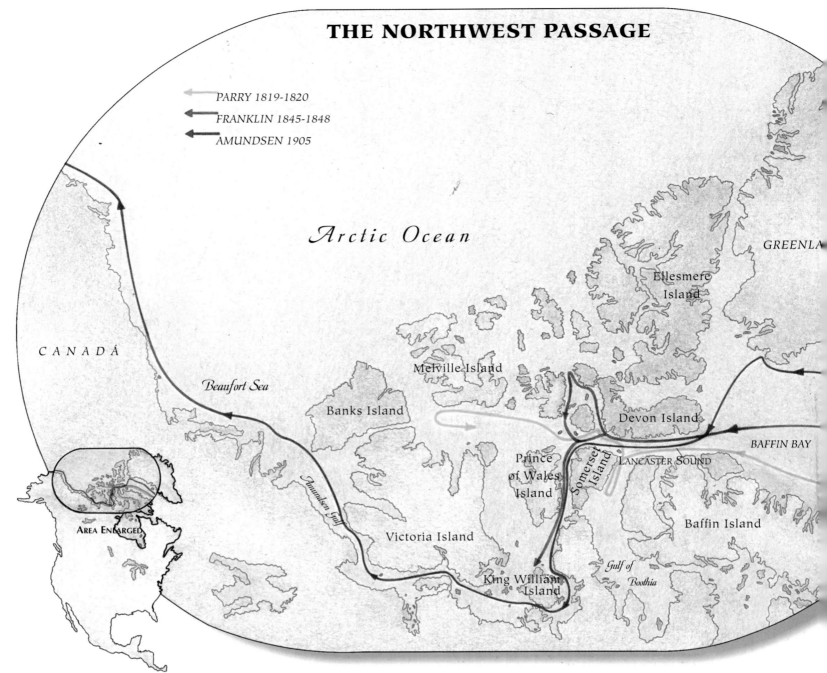

THE NORTHWEST PASSAGE

PARRY 1819-1820

FRANKLIN 1845-1848

AMUNDSEN 1905

Arctic Ocean

GREENLA

Ellesmere
Island

CANADÁ

Beaufort Sea

Melville Island

Banks Island

Devon Island

AREA ENLARGED

Amundsen Gulf

Prince
of Wales
Island

Somerset
Island

LANCASTER SOUND

BAFFIN BAY

Victoria Island

Baffin Island

King William
Island

*Gulf of
Boothia*

Left: The expedition that went to John Franklin's rescue had faced grave danger and big difficulties. Some of the would-be rescuers soon had to be rescued themselves: among these, the Irishman McLure aboard his ship the Investigator *was imprisoned in the ice for three consecutive winters.*

Opposite top left: Captain Robert McClure, seen here wearing typical Arctic clothing, was responsible for the search for Franklin. However, hoping to find traces of the legendary Northwest Passage, he disobeyed his orders and sailed solo for 1,000 miles from the Bering Strait eastward. Due to this reckless decision he was locked into the ice for three winters off Banks Island.

Top right: Attracted more by the glory deriving from the sporting enterprise than the seduction of scientific investigation, the Norwegian Roald Amundsen can nevertheless rightly be considered one of the greatest polar explorers.

Center: The conquest of the Northwest Passage after centuries of incessant attempts brought Amundsen (the first on the left in this photo taken on his arrival in Alaska) into the public eye. He ably exploited the fame achieved thanks to the Gjöa enterprise to find financial backing for his polar exploration projects.

wilderness searching for him. In 1852, the Irishman McClure, trapped for a third successive winter on the northern coast of Banks Island, was rescued by another expedition arriving from the west. McClure and his men walked over the ice to the rescuing ship, thus becoming the first men to cross the Arctic from East to West. However, in spite of the systematic exploration of the region, which was by now accurately charted, no ship had yet managed to complete the entire crossing. It was not until 1905 that Roald Amundsen succeeded in forcing the defenses of the Northwest Passage, concluding centuries of fruitless attempts. The discovery had no practical consequences: Amundsen's route was not commercially viable. His success was nothing more than a sporting record. During the long months he spent in the Arctic, Amundsen had carefully studied the customs of the Eskimos, their clothing, and their use of sled dogs.

This information was to be of great value to him in the future. Amundsen was already cultivating other projects.

Right: The Gjöa arriving in Alaska in August, 1906. After almost four centuries of attempts and sacrifices, it was left to Roald Amundsen, the future explorer of the Antarctic, to navigate the Northwest Passage for the first time. The Gjöa, a suitably modified fishing vessel, was not so very different to the ships used for earlier Arctic expeditions: nearly 70 feet long, she carried a crew of 6 and enormous quantities of provisions.

THE NORTHEAST PASSAGE

Left: The Swede, Nils Nordenskjold was the first to reach the Bering Strait from Europe, tracing the route of the Northeast Passage to the Pacific. Despite the fact that the ship he chose, the Vega, was equipped and fitted with a 60-horsepower steam engine, Nordenskjold found himself imprisoned by the ice and had to pass the winter on the Siberian coast.

"By eleven in the morning we were in the strait linking the Arctic Ocean with the Pacific Ocean, and we saluted the Old and New Worlds from the *Vega* by raising the Swedish flag and singing the national anthem. We had finally reached the objective longed for by many nations ever since Sir Hugh Willoughby, amidst artillery salvoes and the hurrahs of his smartly dressed men, and in the presence of a celebrating crowd, inaugurated in 1553, certain of his triumph, the long series of Northeast voyages." These words described the scene on the 19th of July, 1879, when the ship of Baron Nils Nordenskjöld sailed into the waters of the Bering Strait, a year and a half after setting sail from Sweden. The search for a Northeast Passage to the Pacific had begun three centuries earlier, guided by the same motives that inspired the first explorers of the Canadian Arctic: finding a passage giving access to the riches of the East that was far from the areas controlled by the Spanish and Portuguese. The route to the East appeared more promising that the one to the West: the waters of the Siberian seas were less subject to ice than the narrow channels separating the myriad islands of the Canadian archipelagos. However, when Willoughby left the coast of England in 1553, the ocean beyond the North Cape was completely unknown. Nevertheless, the faith of his financiers was such that his ships were dressed with sheets of lead as protection against the shipworms that were known to infest the waters of the Indies. A very different destiny awaited Willoughby however: his fleet was scattered by a storm off the northern coast of Norway and only one ship succeeded in entering the White Sea and landing on the coast of Russia. The Englishmen were well received and their commander, Chancellor,

Opposite bottom: The crew of the Vega, *here photographed on their arrival in the port of Naples on the 14th of February, 1880, was composed of 20 people: besides Nordenskjold and the other officers and seamen there was a group of scientists, whose research and observations provided for the first time an exhaustive picture of the Arctic environment. The exploration of the polar regions, until then regarded as a struggle against the unknown, entered into a new and fascinating phase.*

Center: On the 19th of August, 1878, the Vega *and the* Lena *reached the Tajmyr peninsula, the northernmost tip of the Asian continent, a low tongue of land besieged by the ice. In the words of Nordenskjold it was nothing more than the "most uniform and most deserted land that I have ever seen in the Polar regions." The ships celebrated the event by raising their flags and firing salvoes of cannon shot. From that moment the expedition split up and the* Vega *headed alone toward the Bering Strait.*

traveled overland to Moscow. His gifts, intended to establish a solid trading link between the two countries, were accepted by the Czar, Ivan the Terrible. In the meantime, Willoughby had been forced to winter on the uninhabited coast of the Kola Peninsula where he died with all his crew. The expedition's only achievement was the founding of the Moscow Company: the fur trade with Russia was undoubtedly more profitable than exploration. The few expeditions that were to follow failed to progress beyond the western coast of Novaja Zemlja, and a few years later Britain abandoned the project. At this point the initiative was taken up by

Bottom left: The Christmas party aboard the Vega *imprisoned in the pack-ice. Apart from particular anniversaries such as Christmas, the winter passed slowly.*

Bottom right: In the well heated and illuminated assembly room aboard the Vega, *the crew occupied their free time reading, playing games, or sorting the data gathered during the day.*

*Right: The brief
survey of the bird-life
on Novaja Zemlja
provided the zoologists
of the* Vega *with a
number of pleasant
surprises: this image
shows three different
razor-bills.*

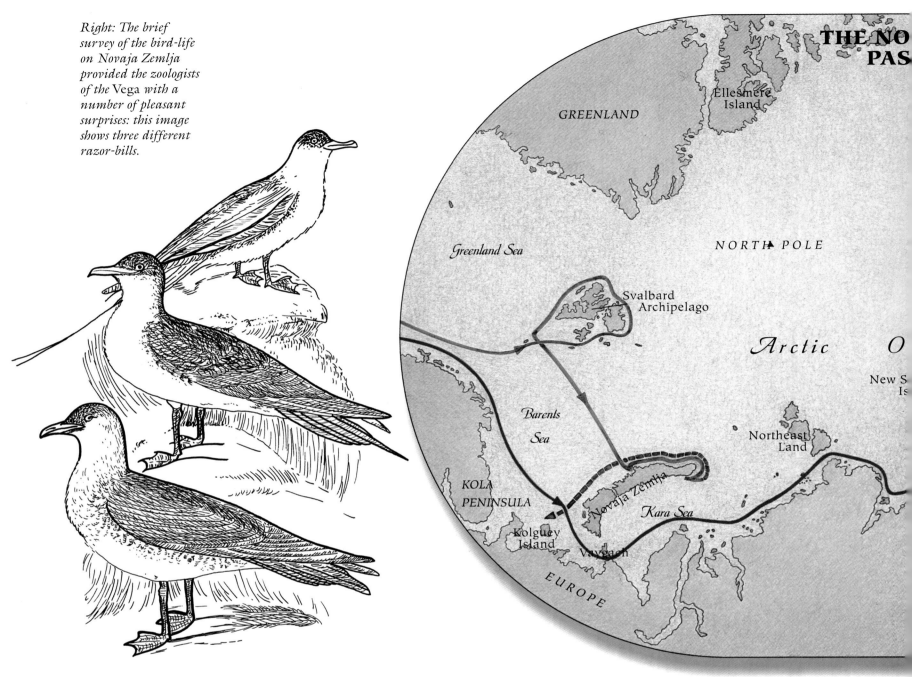

GREENLAND

Ellesmere
Island

Greenland Sea

NORTH POLE

Svalbard
Archipelago

Arctic O

New S
Is

Barents
Sea

Northeast
Land

KOLA
PENINSULA

Novaja Zemlja

Kara Sea

Kolguey
Island

Vaygach

EUROPE

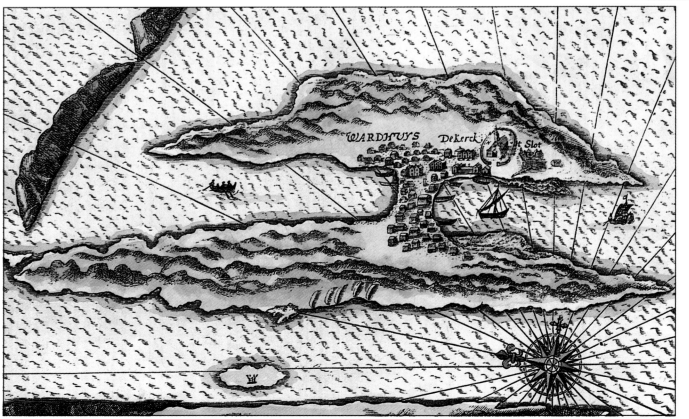

WARDHUYS   DeKerck   t Slot

*Left: The winter of
1878 saw the* Vega *on
the threshold of the
Bering Strait, with
success close at hand.
The ship was trapped
in the ice and risked
being crushed.
Fearing disaster,
Nordenskjold had
much of the supplies
of food and
equipment
transferred onto the
pack-ice so that if the
ship sank, the crew
would not be left
without resources.
Fortunately the* Vega
*came through her
trial undamaged,
and in July, 1879
recommenced her
voyage towards the
Pacific.*

ALASKA

BERING STRAIT

Bering Sea

KAMCHATKA

ASIA

BARENTS 1596-1597 →
YAGE OF SUPERSTITI 1597 ⇢
JORDENSKJÖLD 1878-1879 →

Top right: The Swede Nils Nordenskjöld, portrayed here, passed the Bering Strait on 19th of July, 1879, and reached Yokohama in Japan only on the 2nd of September, 1879, a year and a month after his departure from Stockholm.

145

Bottom right: The clothing of the crew of the Vega was specially designed to cope with the severe Arctic temperatures that frequently dipped below -40° C. Apart from the traditional Lapp clothes, the expedition members had a set of heavy woollen underwear, a jacket of windproof canvas, large canvas boots (that were filled with dry grass), a felt cap and seal- and deer-skin gloves. They were also all issued indispensable sunglasses.

Above: Nordenskjold carefully studied the history of the voyages in search of the Northeast Passage, compiling a detailed summary in his diary. He located close to Wardoe (shown here on a Dutch map of 1594) in the White Sea not far from the mouth of the Dvina, the anchorage where the Englishman Willoughby and his crew died in the winter of 1553.

Top left: In addition to the flocks of swans, geese, ducks, auks, petrels, and razor-bills, five species of gulls were observed, two of which, the Larus rossii *and the* Larus sabinii, *were extremely rare and barely known to science.*

Center: When Nordenskjold undertook his voyage along the Siberian coast, the great herds of walruses, the object of ruthless hunting for almost half a century, had practically disappeared from the coasts of Novaja Zemlja and were found in declining numbers in all the eastern Arctic regions. On Bear Island, where a few decades earlier a single hunter could kill a thousand animals in a week, the explorer saw "not so much as a shadow."

Bottom right: Examples of these crabs (Chionoecetus opilio) were collected by the scientists aboard the Vega *in the waters north of the Bering Strait. On the 8th of July, towards the end of the winter, a fishing trip* was organized in a coastal lagoon that was "still a block of ice, neither melted nor broken, on which there was a layer of water one or two meters deep": to the amazement of Nordenskjold who could not understand how they could survive the winter, those waters teemed with fish of a previously unknown species. Part of the catch was preserved in alcohol in favor of science, the rest was, more prosaically, cooked and eaten.

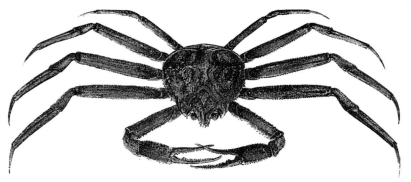

Opposite top and top right: Nordenskjold photographed the Ciukci of the Siberian coast with the intention of establishing the "standard type" of the race (for what such a term is worth today). In his words they were of: "Medium height, with coarse, strong black hair, a sloping forehead, a slim nose, often squashed, horizontal and not small eyes... Beard frequently very sparse." The young women, he added, "make a good impression, supposing that one can overcome the natural repugnance aroused by the dirt."

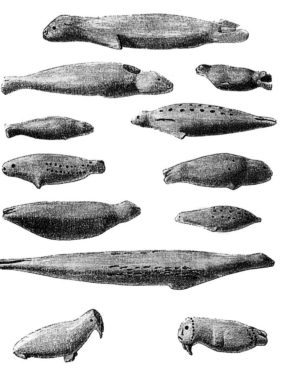

Above: Ciukci natives fishing. Among the native Siberian tribes, the Ciukci (literally the "rich in reindeer") were those who resisted the Russian expansion to the east the longest. Similar to the Eskimos, they were pastoral nomads and occupied the inhospitable territories between the Anadyr and Kolyma Rivers. Nordenskjold devoted particular attention to the Ciukci, studying their habits and customs and compiling a concise dictionary of their language.

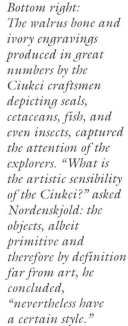

147

Bottom right: The walrus bone and ivory engravings produced in great numbers by the Ciukci craftsmen depicting seals, cetaceans, fish, and even insects, captured the attention of the explorers. "What is the artistic sensibility of the Ciukci?" asked Nordenskjold: the objects, albeit primitive and therefore by definition far from art, he concluded, "nevertheless have a certain style."

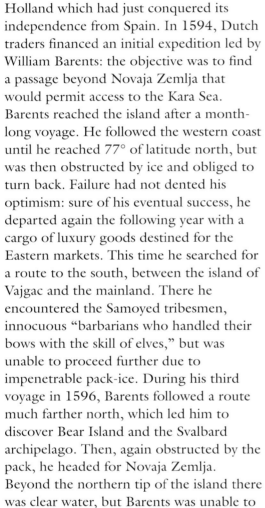

Left: Barents's ships were taken by surprise by the early onset of winter and vainly tried to open a way through the ice and reach the open water visible to the east of Novaja Zemlja. The pack-ice, then locked in tight around the hulls, and the men were obliged to spend the long Arctic night ashore. The solar rings depicted in this illustration are due to a refraction of the light, frequent in high latitudes.

Holland which had just conquered its independence from Spain. In 1594, Dutch traders financed an initial expedition led by William Barents: the objective was to find a passage beyond Novaja Zemlja that would permit access to the Kara Sea. Barents reached the island after a month-long voyage. He followed the western coast until he reached 77° of latitude north, but was then obstructed by ice and obliged to turn back. Failure had not dented his optimism: sure of his eventual success, he departed again the following year with a cargo of luxury goods destined for the Eastern markets. This time he searched for a route to the south, between the island of Vajgac and the mainland. There he encountered the Samoyed tribesmen, innocuous "barbarians who handled their bows with the skill of elves," but was unable to proceed further due to impenetrable pack-ice. During his third voyage in 1596, Barents followed a route much farther north, which led him to discover Bear Island and the Svalbard archipelago. Then, again obstructed by the pack, he headed for Novaja Zemlja. Beyond the northern tip of the island there was clear water, but Barents was unable to gain the open sea. The ice locked in around him, pushing the ship toward the shore. Nobody had ever faced the prospect of a polar winter at such latitudes: Barents died of starvation on the 20th of June, 1597, just as the ice began to melt. The survivors managed to reach the coast of Siberia aboard two small boats and were rescued by the Russian fishermen, who in that era, habitually fished the waters between Archangel on the White Sea and the Kara Sea and the mouth of Yenisey River. Their boats, known as *kochi*, were smaller and more manageable than the European ships, and when necessary they could be hauled over the ice. The exploration of Siberia occupied the Russians for almost a century. In 1648 the Cossacks reached the Kolyma River and Semyon Dezhnev had ventured beyond

the Bering Strait. Following the death of Barents, the Dutch abandoned their search for a Northeast Passage to the Pacific as they lacked the resources to challenge Portugal for control of the East. The Arctic seas became the domain of fishermen and the hunters of whales and walruses whose ships traveled increasing distances in their search for virgin waters. The Russians and Scandinavians sailed from the Svalbards to the Kara Sea and by the time Nordenskjöld departed, the northern ocean was well known. Nevertheless, the *Vega* was caught in pack-ice just short of her objective and Nordenskjöld was obliged to spend the winter on board, waiting for the spring thaw. His well equipped and carefully prepared expedition inaugurated a new method of Arctic exploration. For the first time scientists, cartographers, and naturalists brought back reliable images of a difficult yet fascinating world.

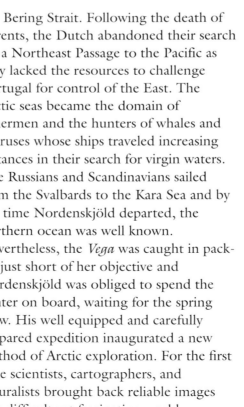

Left: The death of a polar bear, engraving by Gerrit de Veer, 1609. Early in June, 1596, Barents came within sight of an unknown island to the north of Norway that he named Bear Island. According to the Dutchman, the strength and ferocity of the polar bears greatly exceeded "all that has been heard about lions and other beasts."

Bottom: A map of the Arctic region compiled by Willem Barents in 1588. The Dutch voyages to the Northeast, undertaken in the attempt to find a route to the Indies that was far from the Spanish and Portuguese spheres of influence, did not provide the hoped-for results. Barents died in 1597, trapped in the pack-ice off the coast of Novaja Zemlja after having discovered and circumnavigated the Spitsbergen archipelago.

Opposite center: A portrait of Willem Barents. A skilled cartographer and a good observer, Barents was one of the most audacious navigators of his times. In the course of three voyages between 1594 and 1597 he explored the Spitsbergen archipelago and the north coasts of Novaja Zemlja and the island of Vajgac. The routes he traced opened the way for the Dutch and British fishermen and whalers who exploited the immense resources of the Arctic seas for over a century and a half.

Opposite bottom: Barents's ship imprisoned in the ice. Taken unawares by the early winter, the Dutchmen vainly attempted to cut their way through the ice to reach the open water visible to the east of Novaja Zemlja. The pack then locked in around the hull, breaking the ship's rudder and the men had to resign themselves to spending the long Arctic night ashore.

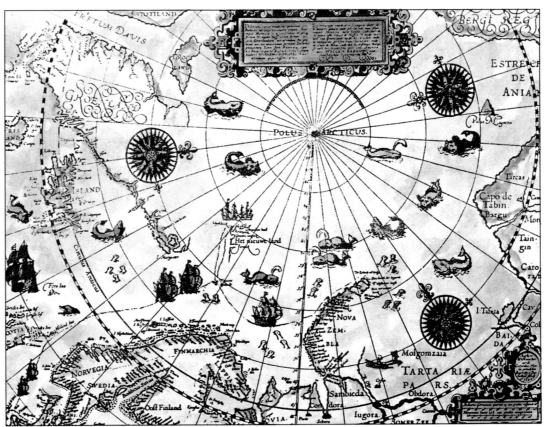

149

Right: This engraving shows a number of Barents's crew carrying the timber needed to build the hut that would house them for the winter.

Below: The refuge constructed by Barents on the north coast of Novaja Zemlja measured 33 feet by 20 and housed around 20 persons during the long winter of 1596. The bath was made out of a barrel (right), and the chimney could act as an emergency exit should the snow have buried the hut. The hunting of the fortunately numerous polar bears provided the Dutchmen with furs with which to make suitable clothing for the climate and provided fat for their lamps.

Top: This engraving shows another episode in the daily life of the Dutch crew. A number of men are skinning a polar bear that supplied no less than 99 lbs of fat for the lamps and a warm pelt. In the background a man is preparing a trap for foxes.

Center: When the Arctic ice began to melt at the end of May, 1597, Barents's men made ready to set sail southward. The preparations for their departure were interrupted by the passage of a large number of polar bears who, wrote de Veer, "appeared to have scented that we were about to depart and wanted to taste a little bit of one of us."

Bottom: In this illustration, Barents's men are searching for a route through the ice so as to transport goods and ships towards the open sea.

151

Navigating in Arctic Waters

The British and Dutch navigators who first ventured into the Arctic seas had about as much knowledge of what they were about to encounter as the Iberian explorers during their ocean voyages. The charts of the North Atlantic were based on mere conjecture: Zeno's chart, drawn up in Venice in the mid-sixteenth century was dotted with imaginary islands, while Greenland appeared as a peninsula of Europe. Successful navigation in unknown waters was determined more by the skill and experience of the navigator than on astronomical calculations. The latitude was established by measuring the height of stars over the horizon with more or less accurate astrolabes and quadrants. The resulting figures, given the roll of the ship, were extremely

Left: The clothing of the first polar explorers was often inadequate protection against the severity of the climate: subsequently, following the example set by Nansen, in place of woollen clothes, the explorers adopted the dress of the Eskimos with clothing made from bear, fox, and reindeer skins capable of efficiently trapping body heat while allowing transpiration without freezing.

Center: A team of sailors attempt to haul a cutter over the ice-cap covering Ellesmere Island in the Canadian archipelago. Worn out after waiting for aid that never came, short of provisions, and exposed to the freezing polar climate, the crews of the ships locked into the pack-ice tried everything at their disposal to reach open water or the nearest inhabited area: desperate attempts that frequently ended in tragedy.

Bottom: The brief Arctic summer conceded some hope — that was not always fulfilled — to the crews of ships trapped in the pack-ice. Armed with saws and crowbars, the seamen attempted to cut an artificial channel through the pack, attempting to drag their ship towards open water where they could set sail once more.

imprecise. It was not until the end of the sixteenth century that John Davis, one of the Northwest Passage pioneers, developed a reflecting quadrant that was easier to handle and more reliable. Davis's quadrant remained in use in its various versions until the advent of sextants and octants around two hundred years later. Time was measured with fragile hourglasses that were completely useless for calculating longitude, a complex problem that was not solved until late in the eighteenth century with Harrison's invention of the marine chronometer. Apart from the difficulties of orientation, exasperated by the anomalous behavior of compasses close to the magnetic pole, Arctic explorers also had to cope with extreme environmental conditions. The lands of the far North were, and still are, also completely uninhabited and sterile: the chances of reprovisioning, with the exception of fish and the often inedible meat of bears, seals and seabirds, were practically non-existent. The pack-ice could lock expeditions indefinitely in regions lacking any resources whatsoever and the ships, all of very small tonnages, were obliged to take on board huge quantities of foodstuffs (Franklin set sail with supplies for a five-year voyage). The principal problem was, however, the ice, especially on the Northwest route. In the labyrinth of islands extending beyond Baffin Bay, the explorers risked being imprisoned for years in extremely arduous environmental and psychological conditions. As winter approached, the waters began to freeze, subjecting the hulls of the ships to unheard of pressure. In order to prevent them being crushed, the hulls had to be protected against the impact of the great icebergs by cutting a gap in the pack. When the ice began to melt, it was imperative that the ship be freed as soon as possible, cutting artificial canals to gain access to the open sea. Every single day was crucial and delayed departure could easily result in the failure of the mission. The whole crew was involved in these tasks, which were all executed by manpower alone, with the aid of the chisels, levers, hooks, and long saws that were indispensable tools for all polar explorers. The seamen were only too happy to comply with the orders to cut the ship free — the very idea of departure after months of enforced immobility was sufficient to galvanize their spirits.

Top: Being trapped in the ice could mean the end for the polar explorers: the ice floes that pressed around the flanks of the ship subjected the hull to unheard of pressures and could easily crush it. Shackleton's Endurance *(shown here), imprisoned in the frozen Weddell Sea during the winter of 1915, suffered this fate and had to be abandoned by her crew.*

Bottom: This photograph shows Ernest Shackleton and Frank Hurley in front of their tent, near a rudimentary stove burning seal fat. In 1915 Shackleton and his men spent six months stranded on an ice floe drifting in the Weddell Sea off the coast of Antarctica. With most of the crew left on desolate Elephant Island, Shackleton and five companions succeeded in reaching the whaling stations of South Georgia, 800 nautical miles away, and organized a rescue mission. Only after repeated attempts did the explorer manage to force a way through the ice fields and save all his men.

153

W hen Cook undertook his first voyage into the Pacific, much of the great ocean was still unexplored over two hundred years after Magellan. The discoveries made by the Spaniards and the Dutch were restricted to a few isolated islands and barely surveyed coastlines. The map of the South Sea was full of question marks. With the explorations of Cook and La Pèrouse the Pacific emerged from legend and took its place in the worlds of geography and science. Their voyages concluded the first great phase of maritime exploration. With the collapse of the illusion of a Terra Australis, the abandonment of the search for a northern passage and fading of the myth of the "noble savage," the Pacific became the arena for the colonial struggles of the great European powers. The first Protestant missionaries arrived, and profit, both religious and commercial, replaced the desire for knowledge which had characterized the Age of Enlightenment.

THE PACIFIC: A SCIENTIFIC PARADISE

ABEL TASMAN

Opposite top: This wooden octant was made in England circa 1750. The octant, like the quadrant but much more reliable, served to measure the height of the sun above the horizon and thus determine latitude.

Opposite bottom: This map from 1622 shows a fleet of Dutch ships riding the waves of a still empty Pacific. The Spanish and Dutch voyages had revealed the existence of new lands, but most of the great ocean was still unexplored.

Below: Abel Tasman, born in Holland in 1603, arrived in the East at the age of 30, in the employ of the Dutch East India Company. A skilled sailor and a prudent man, after having participated in a mission in the North Pacific, he was dispatched on a search for the legendary Southern Continent. His voyages, which led to the discovery of Tasmania and New Zealand, were judged unproductive and Tasman was subsequently relegated to routine duties. He died in Batavia in 1659.

From Magellan's enterprise onward and throughout the sixteenth century, the exploration of the Pacific was almost exclusively monopolized by the Spanish. This situation was, however, overturned early in the seventeenth century, and the journey undertaken by Quiros and Torres, which led to the discovery of the strait separating Australia from New Guinea, marked the end of the Iberian explorations and the rise of a new European power in the Southern Ocean, Holland. The Dutch navigators, organized by the powerful Dutch East India Company (founded in 1602), inaugurated a new concept of exploration. Indifferent to the missionary zeal of the Iberians, and only marginally interested in pure geographical investigation, they had but one aim: commercial expansion. As early as 1605, Willem Janzoon had left the port of Batavia (today Jakarta) on a reconnaissance trip along the southern coast

Above: The inhabitants of Tonga warmly welcomed Tasman's fleet: the Heemskerk *and the* Zeehaen *were immediately surrounded by a swarm of boats of all types, each loaded with gifts for the unexpected guests.*

These gifts included "pigs, chickens, coconuts and bananas wrapped in sheets of white cloth." The Dutchmen stayed in Tonga for a couple of weeks, delighted by the extraordinary beauty of the archipelago and the hospitality of its inhabitants.

of New Guinea and had been the first European to see the Australian coastline in the area of the Gulf of Carpentaria. A decade later, thanks to a navigational error, another Dutchman, Dirk Hartog, sailing from the Cape of Good Hope toward the Indonesian archipelago again stumbled across an unknown land. Was this perhaps the mythical Southern Continent, the dream of the greatest geographers of the era? To judge from the reports reaching Batavia, those inhospitable coasts held little promise of easy wealth, and the accidental discovery left the powers that be at the Company

rather unimpressed. Not even Le Maire's feat in tracing a new route to the south of the American continent and across the Pacific (Cape Horn takes its name from one of his ships) attracted the attention it deserved. With an eye to profit, the Company was searching for new markets and not fantastical lands that, in the short term, were not worth a bean. However, Australia was simply too large to be ignored for long. During the following decades the discoveries multiplied and early in 1640, in spite of the unpromising initial reports, the Dutch decided to investigate further. They therefore developed an exploration project that was both pragmatic and heroic: they proposed no less than to "find whatever still remains unknown on the terrestrial globe," keeping their eyes open, naturally, for any potential source of wealth. The instructions given to the expedition leader suggested an ethical code of behavior towards the natives, albeit one that allowed a certain leeway in terms of trader's cunning. In other words, if the natives possessed silver or gold, the explorers were expected to curb their greed and feign indifference to the precious metal, "as if they had no idea what to do with it, indicating copper, zinc or lead, as if those minerals were of greater value to us." This was not all: it would have been extremely useful to verify the existence of a direct route through the South Pacific to Chile that would have allowed the Dutch ships to surprise the Spanish colonies on the American continent and "snatch rich pickings from the Castilians who could hardly have dreamt of such an event." The man chosen to guide the ambitious expedition was of course a faithful servant of the Company, of manifest experience and seafaring skill. His name was Abel Tasman. He was provided with two ships, the *Heemskerk* and the *Zeehaen*, and a total of 110 men. As all the recent discoveries regarding the Southern Continent had been made during navigation from West to East, along the vague route linking the Cape of Good Hope with the Indonesian ports, Tasman left Batavia on the 14th of August, heading for the island of Mauritius, then a Dutch possession. He stopped there for over a month for repairs to his rather dilapidated ships before setting sail southward. The Dutchmen sailed beyond the 49° South latitude without ever sighting land: they found masses of seaweed and drifting logs, probably coming from the island of Kerguelen, but the cold and the fog of the Antarctic waters soon convinced Tasman to change course. After around three weeks of difficult sailing on an easterly heading along the 40th parallel, battered by constant storms and exhausted by the conditions on board, the explorers finally

came within sight of an unknown island on the 24th of November. Having found a sheltered bay in which to drop anchor, Tasman decided to despatch a patrol to make a brief survey. The rugged mountains of Tasmania, covered with dense forests, could not have been a welcome sight for the Dutchmen and they remained on the coast without venturing inland. Nevertheless, they noted that many trees had "notches cut into their trunks, five feet from one another." All around there were piles of empty shells, undoubtedly the remains of primitive banquets. The inhabitants of that land must have belonged to a mysterious race of giants. Then suddenly, "out of the forest came a chorus of strident voices, hearing which we returned nervously aboard and saw smoke rising from the tops of the trees." Tasman felt that it was not worth risking another landing: worried by the worsening sea conditions and who knows what else, he finally decided to entrust the ship's carpenter with the unenviable task of swimming to the shore and erecting a marker with the arms of the House of Orange. This formal act of possession concluded the episode of the exploration of Tasmania, named Van Diemen's Land in honor of the governor of the Company.

Below: The map of the western Pacific reproduced here clearly shows the extent of European knowledge following the voyages of Tasman and Dampier.

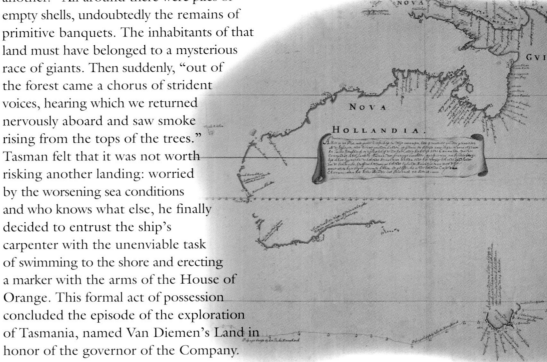

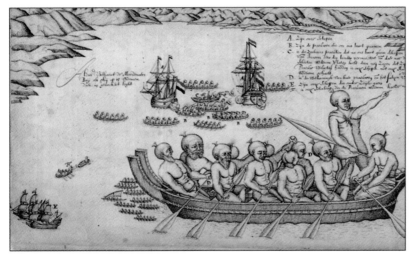

Above left: The first encounter between Europeans and the Maoris of New Zealand had a tragic conclusion: on the 18th of December, 1642, the natives ambushed a whaler from the Heemskerk, *killing four Dutch seamen. This image, taken from Tasman's diary, is a diagram of the dramatic events of Cape Farewell; in the foreground appears a pirogue carrying a group of Maori warriors.*

Above right: While his men took on water from a spring close to the beach, Tasman received a delegation of Tongan notables including a number of women: "Among them were two giantesses, one of whom had a moustache," he wrote, "They fell in love at first sight with our surgeon, throwing their arms around his neck, yearning for carnal love."

The Dutch expedition's indecision was a stroke of luck for the native Tasmanian Aborigines whose extinction, unbeknown to them, was postponed by a couple of centuries. The *Heemskerk* and the *Zeehaen* maintained their Easterly heading and, around a week later, reached the coast of New Zealand. Tasman was enthralled by the majesty of New Zealand's Southern Alps towering on the horizon and capped by clouds: perhaps, he thought, that "vast elevated land" was truly the edge of the fabled continent. He followed the coast northward as far as Cap Farewell, the extreme northern tip of South Island off which on the 17th of December he dropped anchor. However, that promising land was to provide the expedition leader with an

unwelcome surprise. The Maori natives immediately demonstrated their hostility to the intruders, and the following day, after a night charged with tension, a fleet of canoes loaded with warriors suddenly attacked a boat from the Heemskerk with seven men aboard. Four of the Dutch sailors were beaten to death before the rest of the explorers aboard the two ships could come to their aid. Tasman abstained from any form of retribution and decided immediately to leave the unhappily baptised Assassin's Bay. On the 4th of January, 1643, the explorers reached the extreme northern tip of North Island, which still today carries the name Cape Maria van Diemen. The search for a passage between the two islands, conducted in a hurried and superficial

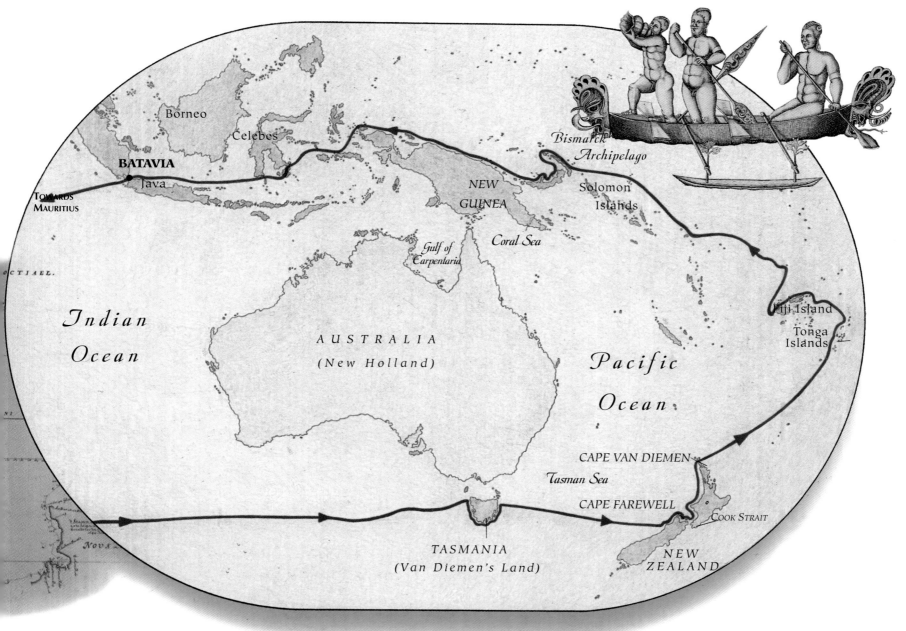

manner bore no fruits and the Cook Strait was mistaken for an inlet. Tasman now seemed eager to leave those seas and failed even to ascertain whether open water extended to the east of Cape Van Diemen, satisfying himself with mere supposition. The coast of New Zealand disappeared beyond the horizon without the Dutchmen ever having set foot on either of the islands. Two weeks later, land "similar to two woman's breasts" was sighted in the distance: this was Atu, the southernmost island in the Tongan archipelago. The natives welcomed the strangers with great celebrations, and Tasman could finally reprovision his ships with fresh food and water. The Tongans not only offered food and hospitality, but under the scandalized gaze of the Dutchmen, the native women demonstrated not the slightest hesitation in removing all their clothing. The most audacious, according to the account of the expedition's surgeon (himself the object of particular attention) "immodestly touched the sailors, indicating the front of their trousers, inviting them to make love to them, while the men encouraged the crew to perform such transgressions." The Puritanical Tasman was severely shaken: "They are good people," he wrote, "but excessively lascivious and unrestrained." The explorers left Tonga early in February heading west into the Fijian archipelago,

Right: In the 17th Batavia, thus named in memory of the "Holland of ancient times," became the headquarters of the Dutch East India Company and a flourishing center of the spice trade. This illustration depicts the town's port that was always crowded with ships.

which had until then been unknown to the Europeans. Tasman soon found himself caught up in a labyrinth of shallows and coral reefs and only his considerable skill as a sailor allowed the expedition to avoid disaster and regain the open sea. From Fiji the Dutchmen headed to the north of the Solomon Islands, toward the Bismark Sea and the already charted coast of New Guinea. Batavia was reached on the 15th of May, 1643, exactly nine months after the expedition had set out. In spite of the indisputable success of the difficult mission, the Dutch East India Company was not satisfied with the results obtained: Tasman had not revealed anything decisive with regards to the supposed existence of the Southern Continent, nor had he discovered a safe route to Chile. Above all, his reports

lacked commercial information. Van Diemen's disapproval was explicit: "He who is to investigate what the lands have to offer," he wrote, "must go to every place," while Tasman, perhaps due to excessive caution or a simple lack of exploration fever, had more or less restricted himself to observing the new lands from the sea. As the governor of the Company continued, "Consequently nothing profitable has been found if not some stunted tendrils with neither rice nor fruit of any worth, poor and in some places, wicked people." This was the severe epitaph to Tasman's career. After a final reconnaissance trip along the northern coast of Australia, the discoverer of Tasmania and New Zealand remained in active service with the Company until his death at Batavia in 1659.

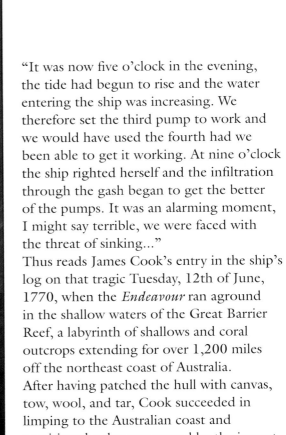

"It was now five o'clock in the evening, the tide had begun to rise and the water entering the ship was increasing. We therefore set the third pump to work and we would have used the fourth had we been able to get it working. At nine o'clock the ship righted herself and the infiltration through the gash began to get the better of the pumps. It was an alarming moment, I might say terrible, we were faced with the threat of sinking..."

Thus reads James Cook's entry in the ship's log on that tragic Tuesday, 12th of June, 1770, when the *Endeavour* ran aground in the shallow waters of the Great Barrier Reef, a labyrinth of shallows and coral outcrops extending for over 1,200 miles off the northeast coast of Australia. After having patched the hull with canvas, tow, wool, and tar, Cook succeeded in limping to the Australian coast and repairing the damage caused by the impact against the sharp spikes of coral. After being laid up for seven weeks, the *Endeavour* once again headed out into those treacherous waters which even today are treated with great respect by even the most experienced sailors. On the 20th of August he rounded Cape York and entered

Above: Captain James Cook at the age of 47 in a portrait by Nathaniel Dance three years before the death of the explorer. Capable, determined, and methodical, during his three long voyages Cook drew up charts of the entire Pacific Ocean, from the Antarctic coasts to the Bering Strait, definitively discrediting what he called the armchair geographers and their centuries of conjecture and fantastication.

Right: In spite of an elevated sense of duty that obliged him to take formal possession of all the new lands he discovered in the name of Great Britain, Cook always showed the greatest respect to the peoples of the Pacific for whom he reluctantly predicted an inevitable integration with the Western way of life. (Painting by Philip Fox).

Top left: This map of the "New discoveries made between 1765-67 and 79 in the South Sea," is taken from the Zatta atlas, printed in Venice in 1776. Cook was responsible for the greatest contribution to geographical and scientific knowledge of the Pacific: during his first voyage (1768-1771), he circumnavigated New Zealand and drew up accurate charts of the east coast of Australia.

Top right: Harrison's chronometer used by Cook determined longitude, by simply calculating the difference between the time indicated at a given point and the time at the meridian used as a point of reference.

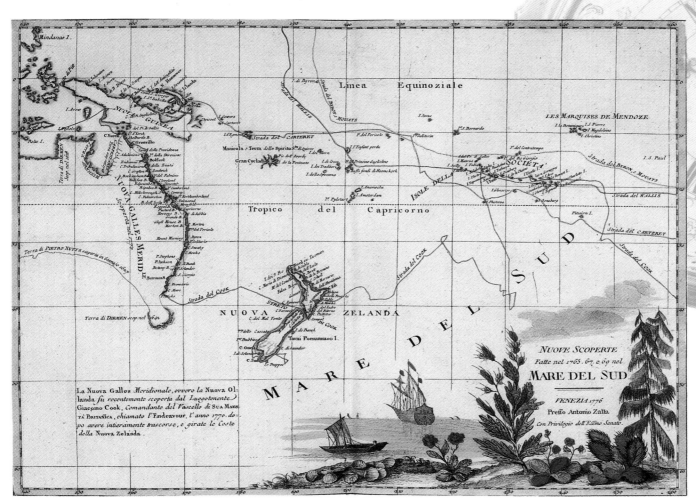

the Torres Strait, the stretch of sea separating New Guinea from Australia. His voyage home was now plain sailing: the course he would set for the Dutch East Indies and, crossing the Indian Ocean, the Cape of Good Hope and Europe, was by now a familiar communications and commercial route. His mission could be said to have been accomplished and James Cook, at a little over forty years of age, had embarked on one of the most glorious seafaring careers of all time. Fortune and ability had come together to mark his destiny. Had the *Endeavour* sunk on the Great Barrier Reef, Cook's life would have followed a different path. A shipwreck was undoubtedly the very worst thing that could happen to a sailor, the profession's ultimate tragedy. And yet Cook described those moments calmly, almost dispassionately, and we search his notes in vain for a hint of desperation or panic. Cook is always true to himself, rhetoric simply had no place in his character. It is difficult to identify in him any defects or to suggest better courses of action: Captain James

Bottom: As well as the octant, the azimuthal compass and a series of new precision instruments, on his second and third voyages Cook benefited from Harrison's famous No. 4 chronograph. A prototype is pictured here. This instrument, invented in 1759, was capable of keeping exact time without being affected by the rolling of the ship and the atmospheric conditions. It was indispensable for calculating longitude. This illustration shows the first instrument invented by Harrison in 1735: bulky and awkward, it weighed over 70 pounds.

159

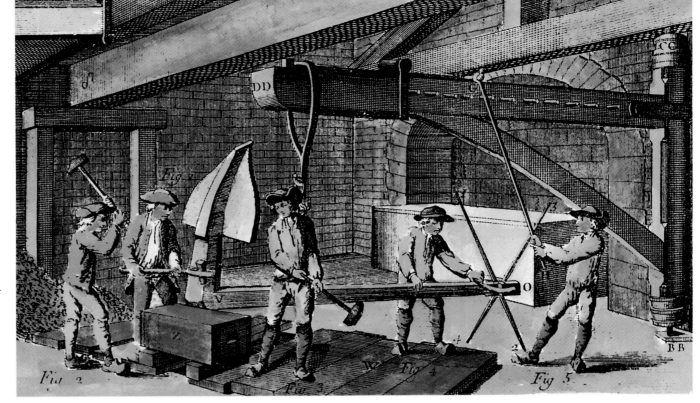

Top: This illustration, taken from the Encyclopedie, shows the making of an anchor. All the ships used by Cook during his voyages of exploration were built in the shipyards at Whitby in Yorkshire, then a lively commercial port on the North Sea: the Endeavour, the Resolution and the Adventure were all flat-bottomed colliers known as Whitby cats. Cook had sailed on these robust and easily maneuverable vessels for many years and had great faith in their capabilities.

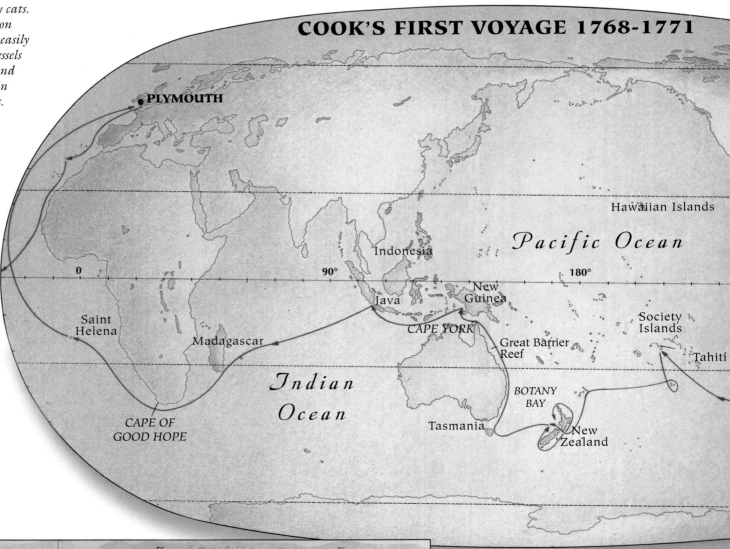

COOK'S FIRST VOYAGE 1768-1771

PLYMOUTH

Hawaiian Islands

Indonesia

Pacific Ocean

Saint Helena

Java

New Guinea

Society Islands

Madagascar

CAPE YORK

Great Barrier Reef

Tahiti

Indian Ocean

BOTANY BAY

CAPE OF GOOD HOPE

Tasmania

New Zealand

0   90°   180°

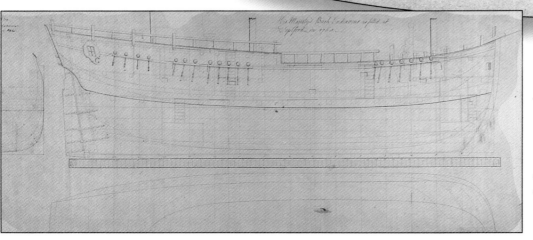

Left: The construction drawings for the Endeavour, the ship used by Cook on his first voyage. Originally a cargo ship, it was refitted under the supervision of the captain and equipped for long voyages. 105 feet in length with a breadth of a little over 26 feet, she could house around 100 men and carry enormous quantities of provisions. Below the water line the hull was dressed with a layer of pine carefully filled with broad-headed nails. This "armor" was intended to protect the planking against the ship-worms that infest tropical waters.

Cook was perfect in every situation. The accounts of historians and contemporaries concord in their universal praise: Cook is considered the greatest explorer of all time. His three Pacific voyages were responsible for distinguishing once and for all fact from geographical fantasy. Hundreds of new islands appeared on his charts, all plotted in their precise geographical positions, while the imaginary lands of the "armchair geographers," a species profoundly (but politely) despized by the rationally-minded Cook, were eliminated. It was not only the geographical profile of the Pacific that was brought into focus by Cook's voyages. The immense South Sea finally revealed its true face to Europe as an image of a world populated by exotic plants and animals took form, a lost paradise inhabited by contented people leading simple lives in direct contact with nature. People that Cook respected and whose demise he bitterly predicted as they came into increasing contact with Europe. Cook's

ships brought back to England not only thousands of botanical and zoological specimens, but also mountains of sketches and drawings precisely executed by the artist-naturalists that were fundamental elements in each crew. Cook's voyages inaugurated the practices of taking along on each expedition those "experimental-gentlemen," who in time were to become known as scientists. Darwin was to be the most representative example of these hunters of knowledge: his voyage aboard the *Beagle* concluded an era and altered our vision of the world.

The story of Cook's life is a parable: it is the edifying story of a self-made man who achieved fame without losing his innate modesty and who set himself precise goals. It would be an injustice to recount the story in any other way.

James Cook was born in a small Yorkshire village in 1728. His father managed a small farm belonging to a local landowner, but Cook was evidently not cut out for the

Walker brothers, took him on as a ship's boy, and Cook embarked on one of the heavy colliers sailing between Newcastle and London. It was a difficult and dangerous route, but an excellent maritime training ground. Aboard his ship (called *Freelove*, every sailor's dream) Cook gained invaluable experience, learning all the vices and virtues of the Whitby cats, robust working vessels designed to navigate shallow, stormy waters. Voyage by voyage, Cook's career blossomed. The Walkers promoted him to the rank of captain and his experience was such that he could have set up on his own. However, commerce was obviously not to his liking, as in 1749 he made the unusual decision to enroll in the Royal Navy. This inevitably meant low pay, a brutal environment, and no chance of a decent career for a twenty-seven year old man lacking the necessary family contacts. There was only one event that could have upset the rigid structure of the Royal Navy and opened the door to the

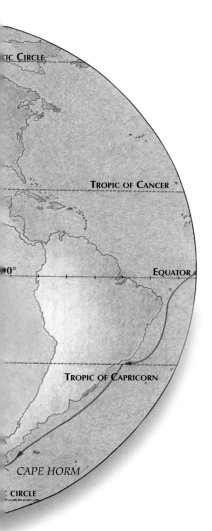

agricultural life: at the age of sixteen, equipped with a rudimentary education and a notably independent spirit, he moved to Staithes, a fishing village on the foggy North Sea coast. There he found work in a grocery and stayed for a year and a half. It is not difficult to imagine his life: apart from beer drinking, the most exciting pastime at Staithes must have been watching the great gray waves of the sea ceaselessly pounding the shore. Perhaps it was on one of those damp evenings when the fog settles thickly and the sea seems to be the only living thing for miles, that the young Cook was gripped by a desire to escape or, better yet, embrace the sea. He quit his job and moved to Whitby, then a lively commercial port and the home of a number of shipping companies. One of these, run by the

meretricious as well as the titled. That event came about, and it was perhaps the first world war in history: in 1756 the political wrangling between Britain and France exploded into the Seven Years War. Cook was sent to Canada, took part in the battles on the St Lawrence River and earned a reputation as a cartographer. His maps charted over 1,800 miles of the coast of Newfoundland and were masterpieces of accuracy. The powers that be at the admiralty began to take note of the skills demonstrated by the young seaman (who in the meantime had been promoted to the rank of Boatswain). The charts were published and became the indispensable instrument for coastal navigation in the region for over a century. Cook had by now become an expert in mathematical and astronomical calculations and was

161

Above: This painting depicts the Endeavour *entering Table Bay. Having doubled the Cape of Good Hope in the March of 1771, Cook stopped at Cape Town to take on fresh water and food. During his stay in the town, then a Dutch possession, he noted that the inhabitants were "generally well educated and very courteous to all strangers... this is in their interest as the whole town can be considered as a single great hotel equipped to welcome all those who come and go."*

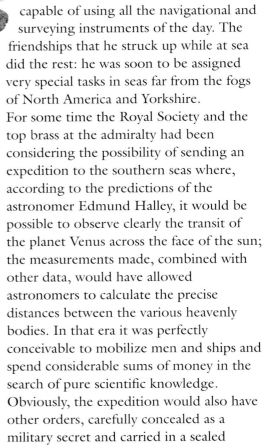

Top left: Sidney Parkinson embarked on the Endeavour *as a botanical illustrator at the age of 23. An acute and meticulous observer, he locked himself into the captain's cabin each day to reproduce with great precision the examples of new plants and the colorful animals discovered during the voyage. Unfortunately the young Parkinson died during the return voyage.*

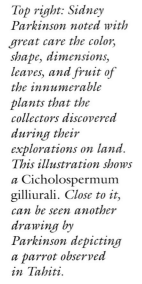

Top right: Sidney Parkinson noted with great care the color, shape, dimensions, leaves, and fruit of the innumerable plants that the collectors discovered during their explorations on land. This illustration shows a Cicholospermum gilliurali. *Close to it, can be seen another drawing by Parkinson depicting a parrot observed in Tahiti.*

Right: This watercolor by T. Gosse from 1770 shows the camp set up by Cook's scientists at Port Jackson, Botany Bay. The scholars on the first expedition succeeded, in spite of the continual hostility of the natives, in collecting a large number of new plants.

capable of using all the navigational and surveying instruments of the day. The friendships that he struck up while at sea did the rest: he was soon to be assigned very special tasks in seas far from the fogs of North America and Yorkshire.

For some time the Royal Society and the top brass at the admiralty had been considering the possibility of sending an expedition to the southern seas where, according to the predictions of the astronomer Edmund Halley, it would be possible to observe clearly the transit of the planet Venus across the face of the sun; the measurements made, combined with other data, would have allowed astronomers to calculate the precise distances between the various heavenly bodies. In that era it was perfectly conceivable to mobilize men and ships and spend considerable sums of money in the search of pure scientific knowledge. Obviously, the expedition would also have other orders, carefully concealed as a military secret and carried in a sealed

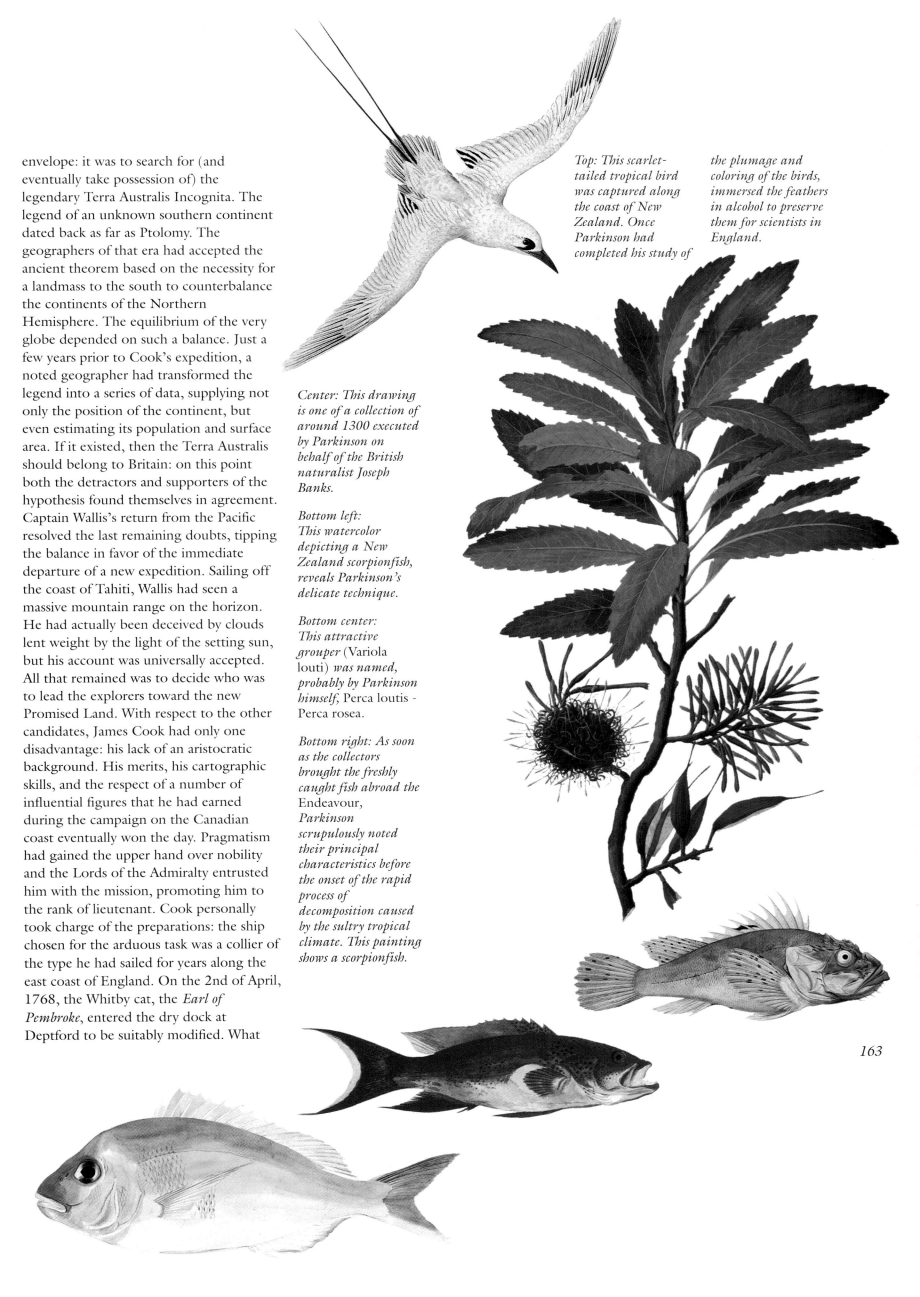

envelope: it was to search for (and eventually take possession of) the legendary Terra Australis Incognita. The legend of an unknown southern continent dated back as far as Ptolomy. The geographers of that era had accepted the ancient theorem based on the necessity for a landmass to the south to counterbalance the continents of the Northern Hemisphere. The equilibrium of the very globe depended on such a balance. Just a few years prior to Cook's expedition, a noted geographer had transformed the legend into a series of data, supplying not only the position of the continent, but even estimating its population and surface area. If it existed, then the Terra Australis should belong to Britain: on this point both the detractors and supporters of the hypothesis found themselves in agreement. Captain Wallis's return from the Pacific resolved the last remaining doubts, tipping the balance in favor of the immediate departure of a new expedition. Sailing off the coast of Tahiti, Wallis had seen a massive mountain range on the horizon. He had actually been deceived by clouds lent weight by the light of the setting sun, but his account was universally accepted. All that remained was to decide who was to lead the explorers toward the new Promised Land. With respect to the other candidates, James Cook had only one disadvantage: his lack of an aristocratic background. His merits, his cartographic skills, and the respect of a number of influential figures that he had earned during the campaign on the Canadian coast eventually won the day. Pragmatism had gained the upper hand over nobility and the Lords of the Admiralty entrusted him with the mission, promoting him to the rank of lieutenant. Cook personally took charge of the preparations: the ship chosen for the arduous task was a collier of the type he had sailed for years along the east coast of England. On the 2nd of April, 1768, the Whitby cat, the *Earl of Pembroke*, entered the dry dock at Deptford to be suitably modified. What

Top: This scarlet-tailed tropical bird was captured along the coast of New Zealand. Once Parkinson had completed his study of the plumage and coloring of the birds, immersed the feathers in alcohol to preserve them for scientists in England.

Center: This drawing is one of a collection of around 1300 executed by Parkinson on behalf of the British naturalist Joseph Banks.

Bottom left: This watercolor depicting a New Zealand scorpionfish, reveals Parkinson's delicate technique.

Bottom center: This attractive grouper (Variola louti) *was named, probably by Parkinson himself, Perca loutis - Perca rosea.*

Bottom right: As soon as the collectors brought the freshly caught fish abroad the Endeavour, *Parkinson scrupulously noted their principal characteristics before the onset of the rapid process of decomposition caused by the sultry tropical climate. This painting shows a scorpionfish.*

eventually emerged from the dock a few months later was a perfect vessel for exploration, rebaptised with the rather appropriate name *Endeavour*. Apart from the crew (almost all young men less than thirty years of age) the *Endeavour's* cabins accommodated the astronomer Charles Green, two draughtsmen (Sidney Parkinson and Alexander Buchan), Joseph Banks and Daniel Carl Solander. Banks was a young naturalist whose fabulous annual income (£6,000 when the entire *Endeavour* had been purchased for £2,800) allowed him to indulge his enthusiasm for science, in particular botany. Banks participated in the expedition in his capacity as a member of the Royal Society, of which he was later to become president. Solander, of Swedish origins, had studied under the great Linnaeus: from a scientific point of view he became the group's principal point of reference even though the nominal supervisor was Banks. Cook took particular care with regards to the quality of the ship's food supplies. It was not simply a question of loading sufficient provisions to feed a hundred men for two years, but also of providing a healthy, varied diet that would protect the men from scurvy, the bane of long sea voyages. Among the mountains of foodstuffs loaded onto the *Endeavour*, there were great quantities of pickled cabbage and vegetables, rich in vitamin C: Cook was obsessed with on-board hygiene and correct diet. Thanks to the cabbage, constant reprovisioning with fresh vegetables, and the ubiquitous "scurvy grass" (*Lepidium oleracum*) none of his men contracted scurvy. Cook had not discovered anything new: he had simply taken note of the problem and resolved it with the means and knowledge at his disposal. On the afternoon of the 2nd of August, 1768, the stubby profile of the *Endeavour* drew away from the quayside at Plymouth heading for the island of Madeira and the solitude of the Atlantic. Following a problematic stopover at Rio de Janeiro, where the arrival of a British ship could hardly fail to arouse the suspicions of the Portuguese authorities, the *Endeavour* headed without further delay to the Pacific. The true voyage of exploration had begun. Cook landed on the coast of Tierra del Fuego in order to take on fresh water and firewood. Banks insisted on landing "at all costs" and set off hunting for plants with Solander. The party was surprised by a snow storm and Banks's two black servants, probably after drinking, slept in the open and died of exposure during the night.

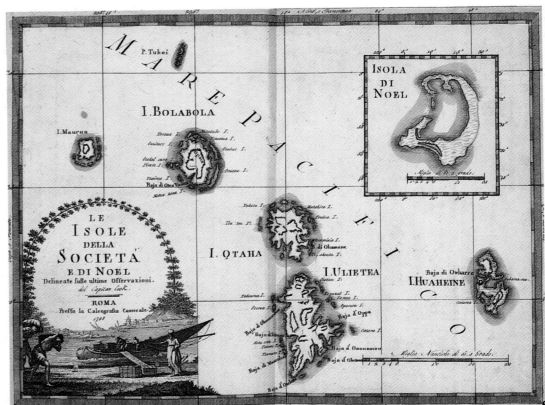

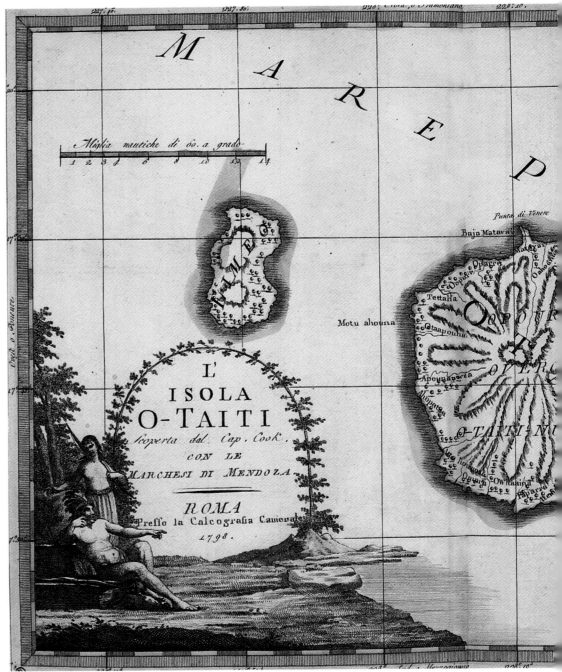

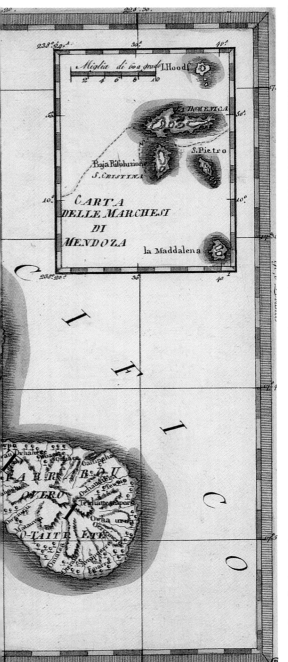

Opposite top: This map of the Society Islands, is taken from the Universal Atlas published in Rome in 1798. With his competent guide Tupaia, a native leader, Cook left Tahiti heading west, entering an unknown archipelago which he baptized the Society Islands as they were "situated close to one another within a chain of coral reefs."

Center: "The island of O-Taiti discovered by Captain Cook." In reality the first European to reach Tahiti was the Englishman Samuel Wallis in 1767. Cook landed on the island a couple of years later with the intention of observing one of the rare passages of Venus across the face of the sun.

The *Endeavour*, assisted by favorable winds, safely rounded the infamous Cape Horn and sailed to the northwest. Cook maintained this heading so as to able to verify the existence of the southern continent, which according to the maps should be found virtually beneath the ship's keel. The length of the waves and the lack of currents led Cook to deduce that there could be no land within a reasonable distance and he therefore set course for Tahiti. The island's unmistakable mountains appeared on the horizon on the 11th of April. Two days later the *Endeavour* dropped anchor in the splendid Matavai Bay. The Tahitians welcomed the visitors and brought goods and food to trade: the only problem was their irrepressible fascination with metal objects for which they would do anything. Cook immediately established a set of rules to limit the systematic thieving and the denuding of the ship. The women of Tahiti

Top: In this drawing by Sidney Parkinson can be seen a breadfruit tree from Tahiti. The breadfruit (Artocarpus altilis), a native species of India and Oceania, produces fruits that may weigh as much as 26 pounds from which an edible flour can be extracted.

Above: The inhabitants of Tahiti proved to be extremely hospitable, showering their guests with gifts and attention. Unfortunately, on more than one occasion, their irrepressible propensity for theft risked precipitating the situation and Cook's patience was severely tried.

were very well disposed toward the visitors, and an iron nail was sufficient to guarantee a night of pleasure. Wallis had seen his ship dismantled little by little, to the point where he risked not being able to depart. The South Sea paradise was capable of intoxicating the best of men, but not James Cook: between one theft and another he gave orders for the construction of a fort and the preparation of a portable observatory. Thus, he wrote in his diary, they could be "perfectly safe from anything

165

these people may attempt." His precautions were in vain however, cannons and palisades were of no use against the thieves: the stolen pistols and an embroidered waistcoat from Banks, Solander's binoculars, the ship's doctor's tobacco pouch, and even Cook's stockings. Finally one evening the expedition's precious quadrant, indispensable for the observation of Venus, also disappeared: this was the last straw, and Cook decided to sequester one of the island's leaders until the vital instrument had been returned. The situation was on the point of deteriorating into open hostility before Banks found the quadrant and the episode was concluded happily. In fact, the illustrious prisoner, convinced that he had escaped death by a miracle, wanted at all costs to present the captain with two pigs. The episode left Cook perplexed as to the mysteries of Tahitian customs.

On the 3rd of June everything was ready for the long-awaited passage of Venus: in spite of the torrid heat and the presence of a halo around the planet, the measurements were successfully completed. The system of calculation subsequently proved to be inaccurate, but as far as Cook was concerned the first part of his mission had been accomplished. During the laborious repairs that had to be made to the ship, Cook mapped the island while the draughtsmen and the naturalists (Buchan had died a few days after the expedition's arrival at Tahiti) continued with their work: Parkinson, probably the first European to be tattooed (the word derives from the local expression tattow), produced beautiful watercolors of the island's flora and fauna. The explorers were surprised to discover enormous dressed stone constructions, the marae, used for religious ceremonies: one of them measured 264 feet in length by 69 feet in width. Cook recorded in his diary every aspect of the life and social organization of the Tahitians, expressing his admiration for their large, ocean-going outrigger canoes and the quality of their cloth woven from vegetable fibers. The local food was excellent, and Cook discovered that the meat of dogs, when suitably prepared, was "almost as good as English lamb." What with the parties and banquets, life on Tahiti passed very pleasantly, and the crew were not all happy to depart. Cook was obliged to search for two sailors who had fled into the interior in an attempt to remain on the island with their lovers. Such sexual passion worried Cook who was concerned about

Left: This Tahitian dancer has been portrayed in heavily idealized form. The island of Tahiti became the standard image of heaven on Earth for all the Pacific navigators: a paradise immediately betrayed to Cook's great disappointment as he became a powerless witness to the rapid spread of venereal diseases carried by the European sailors.

Opposite top: This sketch by John Weber, the artist aboard the Resolution shows the preparations for a human sacrifice at Tahiti. Cook had the opportunity to witness such ceremonies during his third stay on the island, counting 49 skulls arranged on the stone plinth within the enclosure, but the significance of the rite remained incomprehensible, "given that the mysteries of almost all the religions are very obscure and not easily understandable, not even for those who practice them."

the transmission of venereal disease between the crew and the natives. Perhaps the cause of the infection was not directly linked to the arrival of his ship but, as he noted bitterly, "this is poor satisfaction for the many that must suffer due to the disease, and in time the infection could spread throughout the South Sea Islands, to the eternal shame of those that brought it with them."

On the 13th July 1769 the *Endeavour* left Matavai Bay with an extra passenger: Tupia (or Tupaia) was one of the island elders, and his detailed knowledge of the ocean would be of great help to the expedition leader. Tupia guided the *Endeavour* toward islands that were still unknown to the Europeans, from Bora Bora to Rurutu in the Austral Island archipelago. Cook headed ever further southward until he reached the 40th parallel: there was no trace of the southern continent. Not even an island interrupted the endless blue of the ocean. The *Endeavour* then turned her prow to the west. In 1643, the Dutchman Abel Tasman had discovered a new land, a large island of which he had surveyed the west coast:

New Zealand appeared on the charts of the Pacific as an abstract profile, a line without thickness that began and ended in empty space. Cook spent six months painstakingly exploring the irregular coastline that stretched for almost 2,500 miles.

New Zealand is James Cook's masterpiece: despite the considerable logistical difficulties, he circumnavigated the northern island, penetrating the strait which still carries his name, and headed south, rounding the southern cape and following the coast round to the Tasman

Center left: Ataongo, Otaga for Cook, was a Topngatapu notable. Cook was enamoured of the vegetation of the Tongas and admired the inhabitants: "It seemed to me like being on one of the most fertile plains of Europe," he wrote, "Not a square inch of land was left untilled, each fence occupied no more than 4 inches of land and even those 4 inches were not wasted as in many of the fences, fruit trees, and cotton plants were intertwined."

Center right: Otoo, an important Tahitian leader, is here portrayed by William Hodges. Cook returned to Tahiti during his second voyage (1772-75) and on that occasion he struck up a friendship with Otoo, whom he considered to be "a worthy man": in order to return the islanders' hospitality, Cook organized an evening fireworks display that provided Otoo with "great satisfaction."

Below: From Cook's diary, Thursday, 26 May, 1774 (Tahiti): "... Mr. F., during one of his botanical expeditions, has seen a place where dogs are buried that the natives call marai no te ore; *but I do not consider this to be a true custom as few dogs die of natural causes, generally being killed and eaten: nevertheless I do not see why a lady's favourite dog should not have a decent burial as in England."*

Sea. Describing an almost perfect figure of eight, the *Endeavour* sailed right round New Zealand, demonstrating that there were two islands rather than one and that the country was by no means a continent. The native Maoris had very different characters to the peaceful Tahitians, and Cook's encounters with them were never tranquil. As soon as the *Endeavour* approached the coast, she was immediately surrounded by a fleet of pirogues that could accommodate up to 100 warriors and whose prows were decorated with "a strange figure of a man with a frightening face, with a huge tongue hanging out of the mouth and enormous white eyes made of seashells." The Maori warriors' dance, a pantomime of lateral jumps, grimaces, and threatening songs (more or less identical to that performed by the All Blacks rugby team before each match) and the exhibition of arms and tattoos were unequivocal signs of their hostility to the strangers. On more than one occasion Cook was obliged to use force and a number of natives lost their lives. Nevertheless, there are no traces of acrimony in the ship's log. As far as the implaccable Cook was concerned the

167

Left: A map of New
Zealand from the
Universal Atlas,
Rome, 1798. The
surveying of the
tortuous coastline of
New Zealand
represented six months'
hard work for Cook. It
can safely be said that
New Zealand was

Cook's masterpiece: he
took the Endeavour
on an almost perfect
figure-eight course
around the islands
and established
beyond all doubt that
the supposed Southern
Continent was
nothing but a "castle
in the air."

Top and right:
Inhabitants of New
Zealand in a series
of contemporary
portraits. In spite of
the Maoris's hostility
to the Endeavour's
crew, Cook did not
consider it to be idle
wickedness, but rather
the reaction of a proud

race. He carefully
observed their habits
and customs, paying
particular attention
to the art of tattooing,
which was executed
with such skill that "if
they tattoo the whole
face one cannot see any
difference between one
side and the other."

Top: This Maori
fortress can be found
on the coast of New
Zealand. Cook
admired the efficient
defences of the native
villages constructed on
high spurs of rock sheer
to the sea and
surrounded on the
land side by trenches
and palisades.
"What nature has
left undone," he
wrote, "man has
completed."

natives were a proud race incapable of
betrayal, albeit unfortunately cannibalistic
in their habits. New Zealand was a land of
extraordinary beauty, and Cook had to
reign in the naturalistic ardor of Banks,
who was eager to explore the interior: the
expedition leader had other ideas and his
sense of duty led him to the west in the
direction of the unknown east coast of
Australia. By the end of March, 1770, the
Endeavour had left behind the profile of
New Zealand's mysterious Southern Alps,
crossed the Tasman Sea, and reached the
Australian coast. Banks must have still had
the lush green forests of New Zealand on
his mind as his first impressions of the new
land were hardly favorable: "this region
reminds me of the back of a scrawny cow...
in which the thin bones of the flanks
protrude more than they should." A few
days later the *Endeavour* dropped anchor in
the inlet which today houses the suburbs of
Sydney. Banks could finally satisfy his
scientific curiosity, collecting and pressing
examples of the extremely varied
indigenous flora. This abundant plant life
led to the inlet being named Botany Bay.
Here Cook met for the first time the
Aborigines whom he judged to be "timid,
inoffensive people." The voyage along the
coast proceeded without incident as far as
Cape Capricorn, where the shallows of the
Great Barrier Reef began. The *Endeavour*
risked sinking in the shallows to the north
of the promontory, which Cook called
Cape Tribulation, but this was the only
nautical accident in the whole of the three-
year voyage. During the long lay-up
necessary for the repair of the ship, the
explorers continued with their work. They
collected thousands of scientific samples
and 1,300 of these were previously unknown
species. The *Endeavour* reached Batavia
(today Djakarta) with its precious cargo
early in October. At this point the ship was
barely able to stay afloat and the crew had
reached the end of its tether. Cook was
forced to linger at Batavia for two months:
the unhealthy climate of the island, malaria,
and dysentery struck the crew down. During
the time spent there six crew members
died, and others were to die while crossing
the Atlantic. Finally, on the 10th of July,
1770, the lookout sighted the coast of
England. Before retiring into well deserved

Above: Cook always
tried to avoid conflict
with the natives of the
Pacific Islands,
conscious of trespassing
on the rights of others.
Given the age in
which he lived, it was
with great insight that
he wrote "We enter
their ports and try to
land peacefully. If this
is possible then
everything goes well,
otherwise we land
anyway secure in the
superiority of our
arms. How can these
people see us as
anything other than
invaders of their
territory?"

Below: A map of New
Holland and New
Guinea from the
Universal Atlas,
Rome, 1798. While
sailing along the east
coast of Australia,
the Endeavour ran
aground in the

labyrinth of channels
and coral of the Great
Barrier Reef (marked
on the map as "il
Labirinto"). Only
Cook's skill and
presence of mind
prevented the loss
of the ship.

Opposite top: This
image shows some
animals of New
Holland . The first
kangaroo (Macropus
canguru) was captured
by the naturalists
from the Endeavour
on the east coast of
Australia in July,
1770. Cook described

the animal, concluding
that, "with the
exception of the head
and the ears, similar to
those of a hare, it has no
similarities with other
European animals I
have seen." From a
gastronomic point of
view the kangaroo was
simply "excellent."

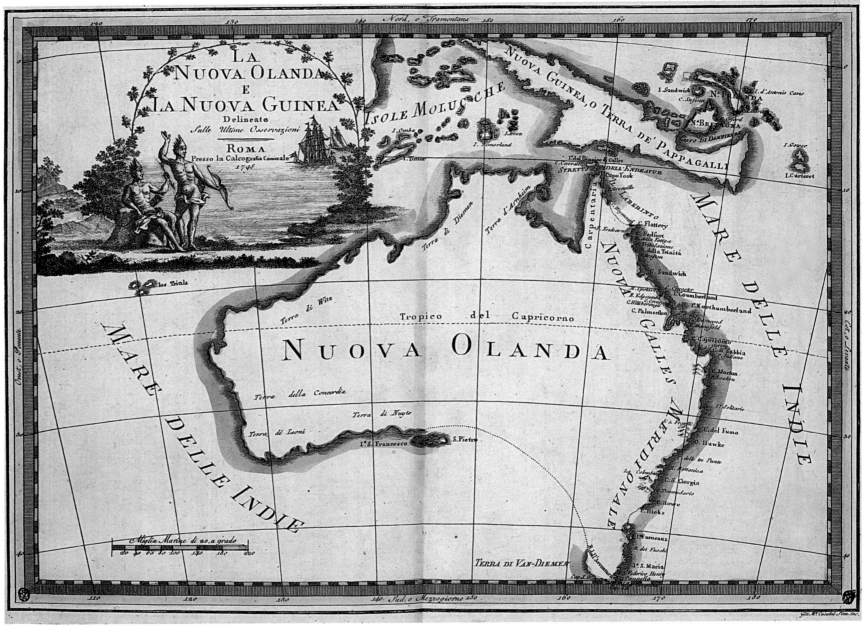

Right: Cook's first
meeting with the
inhabitants of
Australia took place in
April, 1770, at Botany
Bay, thus named for
the incredible variety
of plant species, close to
the present-day city of
Sydney. The Aborigines
threw a couple of
spears at the intruders
and then withdrew
into the bush. There
was no repeat of the
episode: the
Australians were not
hostile concluded the
captain, but were
simply jealous of their
privacy.

privacy, Cook consigned the ship's log and
his charts to the Lords of the Admiralty:
a footnote suggested how knowledge of
the Pacific could be amplified in the future:
"Thus the discoveries in the South Seas will
be completed." London's high society
received the explorers as heroes. Banks
grasped the opportunity for worldly glory:
in between receptions and conferences he
dropped his fiancée so as to launch himself
into the role of the great explorer. Fame
had gone to his head. Cook was promoted
to the rank of captain and was received at
court: the admiralty were keen to let him
know, in the restrained style of the Royal
Navy, that he could not have done better
and that his suggestions regarding possible
new discoveries in the Pacific were being
taken into consideration. A few months

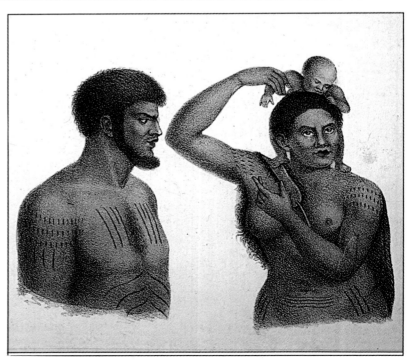

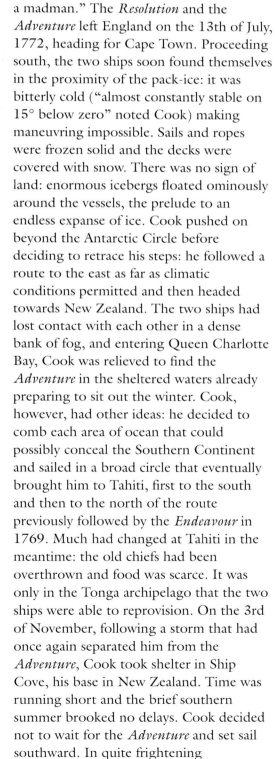

Center: These weapons of war and hunting belong to the Australian Aborigines. In his diary Cook described various types of spears and lances, equipped with points of wood, thorns and sharks' teeth, also remarking on the use of a propellant: when used with skill the "launching stick" allowed the spear to be thrown with greater force and "to hit a target at a distance of 40 or 50 yards almost as accurately as we do with a musket."

later he was despatched to take command of a new expedition on which this time he would have carte blanche. The usual sealed packet of secret orders again referred to the phantasmal Southern Continent. Cook was asked to establish its existence once and for all by sailing to the highest latitudes of the Southern Hemisphere. In short, he was to demolish the theory of the Terra Australis by circumnavigating the Antarctic. For this enterprise Cook was to be provided with two ships, both of them, like the *Endeavour*, built in the Whitby yards. No expense was spared in fitting out the *Adventure* and the *Resolution*: among the scientific equipment carried by the expedition was an extremely important innovation, an example of Harrison's famous No. 4 chronometer which had finally emerged from the bureaucratic jungle that had kept it idle for over twenty years. With Harrison's chronometer the problem of calculating longitude could finally be considered resolved. The sophisticated movement allowed time to be precisely measured in spite of variations in temperature and the rolling of the ship. All that was required to calculate longitude was to compare the local time with that of Greenwich. Cook was joined on this voyage by the painter William Hodges and two German-born naturalists, Rheinhold and Georg Forster. Banks, whose demands were incompatible with the organizational structure demanded by Cook, remained in

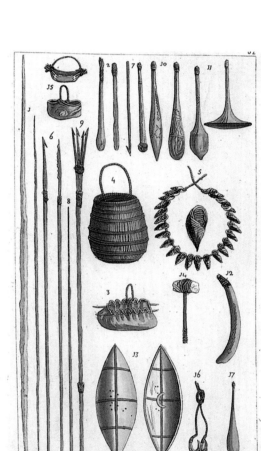
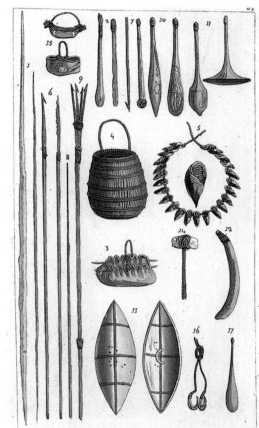

Left: "The natives of New Holland may appear to be the most unfortunate people on earth; in reality they are much more content than we Europeans. Wholly ignorant of the superfluous... it seemed as though all that we gave them was worthless and they were unwilling to let go any of their things in exchange for any object that we could offer."

England "to curse and stamp his foot like a madman." The *Resolution* and the *Adventure* left England on the 13th of July, 1772, heading for Cape Town. Proceeding south, the two ships soon found themselves in the proximity of the pack-ice: it was bitterly cold ("almost constantly stable on 15° below zero" noted Cook) making maneuvring impossible. Sails and ropes were frozen solid and the decks were covered with snow. There was no sign of land: enormous icebergs floated ominously around the vessels, the prelude to an endless expanse of ice. Cook pushed on beyond the Antarctic Circle before deciding to retrace his steps: he followed a route to the east as far as climatic conditions permitted and then headed towards New Zealand. The two ships had lost contact with each other in a dense bank of fog, and entering Queen Charlotte Bay, Cook was relieved to find the *Adventure* in the sheltered waters already preparing to sit out the winter. Cook, however, had other ideas: he decided to comb each area of ocean that could possibly conceal the Southern Continent and sailed in a broad circle that eventually brought him to Tahiti, first to the south and then to the north of the route previously followed by the *Endeavour* in 1769. Much had changed at Tahiti in the meantime: the old chiefs had been overthrown and food was scarce. It was only in the Tonga archipelago that the two ships were able to reprovision. On the 3rd of November, following a storm that had once again separated him from the *Adventure*, Cook took shelter in Ship Cove, his base in New Zealand. Time was running short and the brief southern summer brooked no delays. Cook decided not to wait for the *Adventure* and set sail southward. In quite frightening

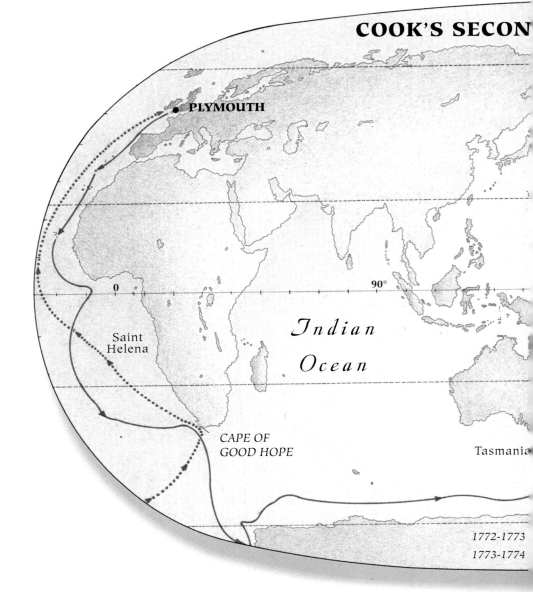

environmental conditions (especially given the clothing and equipment of the day) he headed resolutely beyond the Antarctic Circle, reaching 71° 10' South latitude. Nobody had ever before penetrated the barrier of ice surrounding Antarctica, and no one else would dare for the next fifty years. In front of the prow of the *Resolution* extended mountains of ice marching to the horizon, and the dazzling whiteness reflected onto the clouds gave the impression that the pack extended unbroken as far as the South Pole. "I do not say that it is impossible to proceed farther South at some point, but attempting to do so would be a dangerous and foolhardy enterprise... I, who have the ambition to arrive not only farther than any other before me, but as far as I think it is possible for man to arrive, was not sorry to have encountered this obstacle, that to a certain degree dispensed us from having to continue." In the months that followed Cook visited dozens of islands, plotting their exact positions on his charts. From Easter Island he once again sailed to Tahiti and the Tonga archipelago, which he named as the Friendly Islands. In July, 1774, the lookouts sighted the New Hebrides, an archipelago of volcanic origins that was already known but virtually unexplored: the inhabitants of the islands gave the British expedition a hostile welcome. Cook and his men were mistaken for supernatural beings, white spirits of the islanders' ancestors, who were to be avoided and repelled at all costs. In order to escape the attack, Cook was forced to use firearms and four natives were killed. This was Cook's first encounter with myth; the second in the Hawaiian Islands, was to be fatal. On the 19th of October the *Resolution* reached the haven of Ship Cove. Just five weeks after setting sail from New Zealand, the *Resolution* came within sight of Cape Horn: following a last, fruitless search, Captain Cook was able to draw up his conclusions. If it did indeed exist, the Terra Australis was uninhabitable and, as far as he was concerned,

172

Opposite top: January 1773: Cook's ships, by now close to Antarctica, reprovisioning with ice, a precious source of fresh water. Breaking the ice with axes so as to transport it more easily, in just a few hours a total of 24 tons was loaded. "The melting of the ice is a little tedious and requires some time," observed Cook, "otherwise it would be the quickest method of taking on water that I have come across."

Opposite bottom: The Adventure and the Resolution in this painting by William Hodges are at anchor in Matavai Bay, Tahiti. The bay had been named Port Royal by Wallis, the discoverer of Tahiti. Cook, who adopted it as his anchorage of choice, preferred the local name which is still used today.

ARTIC CIRCULO

TROPIC OF CANCER

Pacific Ocean

180° 90° EQUATOR

Society Islands

Tahiti

Tonga Archipelago Tuamotu Easter Island TROPIC OF CAPRICORN

Queen Charlotte Bay

CAPE HORN

ANTARTIC CIRTCLE

1774-1775

Bottom: A fleet of war canoes off Tahiti can be seen in this painting by William Hodges. When he landed at Tahiti in April, 1774, Cook was surprised to find himself greeted by an enormous fleet of canoes departing on a mission of war. The over 300 canoes "were decorated with flying flags and banners" and some of them were as long as the Endeavour. Cook judged that aboard the canoes there must have been no less than 7,700 men armed with spears and clubs and dressed in all their finery.

inaccessible. Shortly before he reached Cape Town, Cook learned from crew of a Dutch ship that the *Adventure* had returned home a year earlier, its crew decimated by the Maoris. On the 30th of July, 1775, after an absence of over three years, the *Resolution* reached the coast of Britain. Back in England Cook became a celebrity: he was a welcome guest at court, provided with an ample pension, and invested with a number of honorary titles. He was forty-seven years old, and thirty of those years had been lived to the full at sea. His remarkable career up to that point should have satisfied him. Instead he got bored and complained of the far too restrictive confines of English society. When he was called upon to give his opinion on a new expedition, it did not take him long to decide to depart. This time the objective concerned the famous Northwest Passage that would establish a new route between the Pacific and the Atlantic, that is to say a direct route to the commercial treasures of the East. Where many had tried and failed, Cook might well have succeeded. Attempting the impossible was his business. Following tried and trusted routes, Cook guided his ships (the redoubtable *Resolution* and the *Discovery*) toward New Zealand, Tonga, and lastly Tahiti. For the first time in his life Cook was running behind schedule: when he realized that there was not enough time to avoid the polar winter, he decided instead to rest in the favorable climate of the Tropics. Laziness had, for the first time, entered the vocabulary of the good Captain Cook, and he was not the man he once was. His health was impaired, he was no longer young, and he was possibly suffering from an undiagnosed disease (apparently an intestinal parasite) that affected his lucidity. Whatever the true state of affairs, it was not until early in December, 1777 (almost a year and a half after leaving Plymouth), that the expedition left the Society Islands. For the first time Cook crossed the equator in the Pacific and entered unknown waters.

173

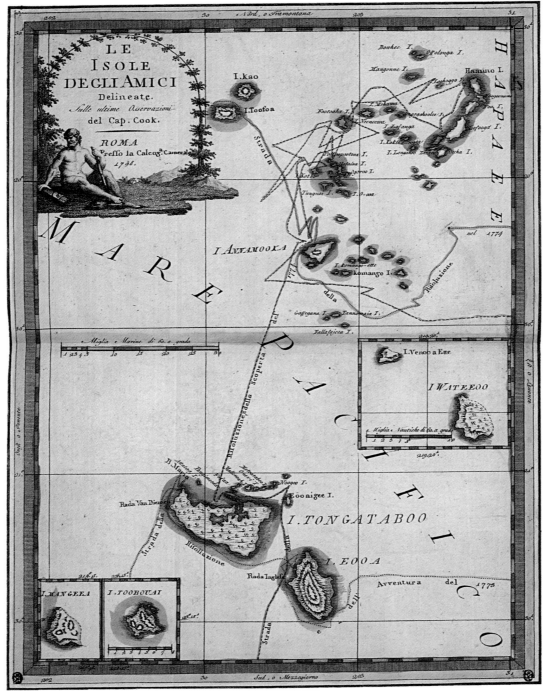

Heading for the coast of North America, he was surprised to encounter an unknown group of islands: he had discovered the Hawaiian archipelago which he named the Sandwich Islands. The welcome he received from the natives was friendly in the extreme: "they all fell prostrate and remained in that humble position until I gave them a sign to rise." Sailing from Hawaii, the *Resolution* and the *Discovery* reached the coast of the present-day state of Oregon, which they followed northward to Alaska and the Bering Strait. At a latitude of 70° North, the ships were obstructed by the ice and after a fruitless exploration of a fjord, Cook decided to return to Hawaii to pass the winter. On the morning of the 26th of November, 1778, the mountains of the island of Maui appeared on the horizon. Cook, however, for unknown motives, did not want to land and cruised around the islands for two months. By this time the men were exasperated, and Cook's stubbornness almost provoked a mutiny. Finally, in a state of considerable disrepair and escorted by hundreds of canoes, the ships dropped anchor in Kelakekua Bay. Cook was in a foul mood. The Hawaiians, however, treated their guest like a god: Cook passively submitted to the complicated rituals in which he was the protagonist, distributing a few baubles and receiving generous gifts. Too many gifts: realizing

Above: The Friendly Islands, taken from the Universal Atlas, Rome, 1798. During his third voyage Cook explored at length the seas around Tonga, before departing for the northern Pacific in search of the Northwest Passage. Many have attempted to identify that apparently pointless interlude as an early symptom of the failing physical and mental strength of the explorer, exhausted by trials of his brilliant career.

Right: Cook lands on the island of Middleburg Eua, Tonga, previously visited by Tasman in 1643. Cook was so struck by the gentleness of the Tongans that he wanted to baptise the archipelago the Friendly Islands. He wrote in his diary on the 2nd of October, 1773, "We were greeted with cries from a huge crowd of men and women, but not one of them had a stick in their hands and they crowded around the launch so densely with cloths and mats etcetera, to trade for nails, that it was some time before we were able to set foot on dry land."

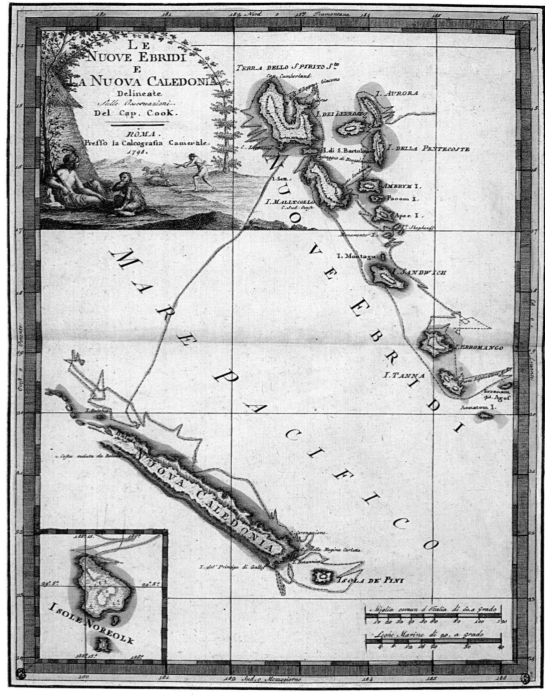

that he was having an adverse effect on the local economy, and with who knows what other concerns in his mind, Cook suddenly decided to leave the island. Three days later the *Resolution* returned to Kelakekua Bay with a broken mast. This time the natives were distinctly hostile: the thefts of equipment escalated to the point where a whaler disappeared. The episode infuriated Cook who landed with a group of armed men determined to take the local chief hostage and to keep him until the boat had been returned. The situation soon got out of hand, and thousands of armed Hawaiians barred the Englishmen's way. Cook's men attempted to breach the barrier by opening fire. The captain's orders were drowned out by the thunder of the final attack in which four sailors and a number of Hawaiians were killed. An eyewitness account relates how Cook was stabbed in the shoulder and fell to the ground. This was on the 14th of February, 1779. In order to exorcise his death, the Hawaiians dismembered Cook's body, stripped the flesh from the bones and burned it. The remains were consigned to the Second in Command, Charles Clerke, who buried them at sea. Clerke guided the ships beyond the Bering Strait but died of consumption during the return voyage to England.

Above: A map of the New Hebrides and New Caledonia, from the Universal Atlas, Rome, 1798. The New Hebrides, on the cultural and ethnic border between Polynesia and Melanesia, were inhabited by people with darker skin and more pronounced features than the Polynesians. The archipelago had already been visited by Quiros in 1606 and by Boungainville in 1766, while New Caledonia was, at that time, completely unknown. Cook painstakingly explored the area, compiling extremely accurate maps of the major islands.

Right: The inhabitants of Erromanga in the New Hebrides violently opposed the landing of the British explorers. Having landed to take on water and food, Cook was reluctantly forced to order a volley of shot and four natives were killed in the struggle.

175

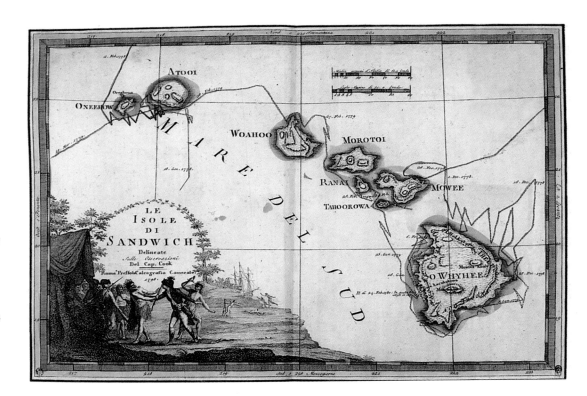

Top and center:
The Sandwich Islands,
today Hawaii, from
the Universal Atlas,
Rome, 1798. The
Hawaiian islands
were Cook's fatal last
destination as he was
killed there during a
battle with the natives
on the 14th of

February, 1779.
On the beach at the
Bay of Kelakekua,
where the tragedy
occurred, a bronze
plaque stands in
memory of the man
who wanted to go
"go further than
any man had ever
gone."

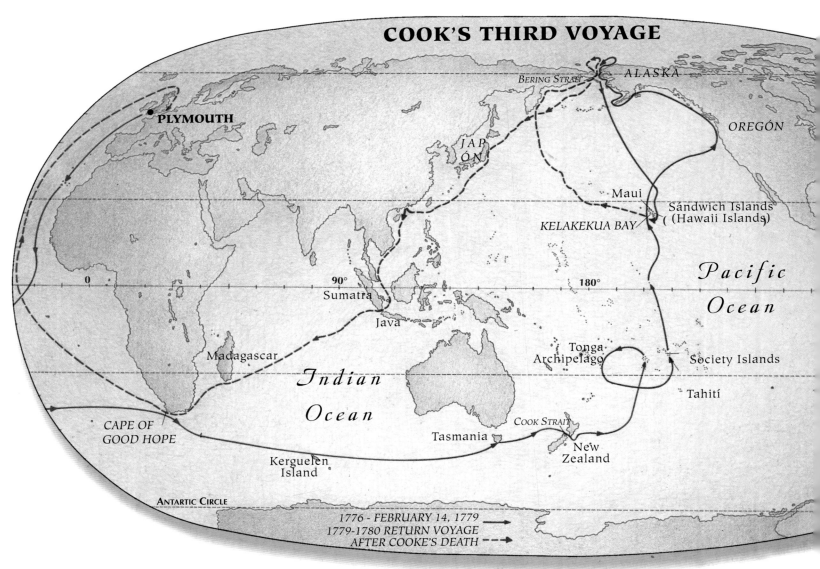

COOK'S THIRD VOYAGE

1776 - FEBRUARY 14, 1779 →
1779-1780 RETURN VOYAGE →
AFTER COOKE'S DEATH - →

Opposite top: An effigy
of Lono, the god of
peace and abundance,
towers above Cook as
he converses with a
number of Hawaiian
leaders. Mistaking his
arrival for the eagerly
awaited appearance of
Lono, the natives
received the British
explorers with great
joy. Cook reached the

Bay of Kelakekua in
the period of
Makahiki, the
celebration of the new
year, arriving from
the correct ritual
direction. Moreover,
the masts and sails of
his ships resembled the
symbols of the god.
From that moment
events took on a fatal
inevitability.

Opposite center: This
Hawaiian native
wears a ritual mask
and helmet made out
of a gourd and
decorated with leaves
and pendants of
beaten cork. This
costume was probably
used during the
celebrations dedicated
to the cult of Lono, the
god of peace and
abundance.

Opposite bottom:
One of the many
versions of the death
of Cook at the Bay of
Kelakekua, painted
by John Webber.
In January, 1779,
on his return from
the Bering Strait,
Cook approached
the Hawaiian Islands
for the second time.
This time the climate
was very different

and the natives did
nothing to disguise
their hostility.
The unwitting victim
of a series of
coincidences, Cook
suddenly found
himself involved in
a battle. Struck in
the back while trying
to organize the retreat
of his men, he fell to
the ground and was
clubbed to death.

Over leaf: In the
"Table of Discoveries"
relating to the
journeys of Cook and
La Pérouse, the
various ethnic groups
of the Pacific islands
have been depicted in
such a way as to leave
ample room for the
imagination.

Cook's arrival in Kelakekua Bay, between December and January, coincided with the period of the makahiki, the solemn festival of the new year. In that period the Hawaiians awaited the return of the god-king Lono whose appearance would bring peace and abundance to the islands. Cook's ships entered the bay from the prescribed direction (anti-clockwise) and the bay itself was considered a sacred site. Moreover, the image of Lono, a kind of draped cross, was echoed in the ships' appearance with their mast and sails. Initially the climate was idyllic and the exchanges of gifts suggested the ritual authority of the king. Cook was revered as a god, and wherever he moved he was preceded by heralds proclaiming his name. Cook's departure from Kelakekua came at the right moment: it was time that Lono left and the island's sovereign reasserted his supremacy over the priests. However, at this point the unexpected came into play: the *Resolution's* foremast broke, and Cook was forced to return. The sudden reappearance of Lono shattered the traditional ritual. The god of war had taken up his place in society once again: Lono was no longer a bringer of peace, and his presence threatened to spark off uncontrollable social tensions. His ritual death became indispensable (following the assassination, the Hawaiian chiefs continued to believe that Cook, as he had promised, would have returned the following year). Perhaps had Cook not decided to recover the lost whaler at all costs things would have turned out differently. The fact remains that the continued provocation and the hostile atmosphere toward the Europeans would in one way or another have created the *casus belli* (justification for the fight). There was something inevitable about the combination of events, as befits the assassination of a god.

JEAN-FRANÇOIS DE GALAUP DE LA PÉROUSE

Count Jean-François de Galaup de La Pérouse was born at Albi in the Languedoc region. He entered the French Navy as a cadet when he was very young, and by the time he was 18 years old, he had embarked with the French fleet involved in the Seven Years War. La Pérouse was wounded and captured by the British, but the incident was not to mar a career that, by all accounts, was fairly spectacular. In 1773 he was assigned the command of a ship: the vast theater of operations of the Seven Years War that stretched from India to North America allowed him to accumulate experience that was to stand him in good stead in the future. La Pérouse was part of that group of young officers on which the defeated French Navy based its recovery. Cook's enterprises had an enormous impact in France, and it was Louis XVI himself who urged that the French Navy took similar initiatives. In the rarefied political and cultural circles of Paris, it was thought that a great voyage of exploration in the Pacific would have conferred political-commercial advantages and national glory. Great importance was given to the scientific side of the expedition: its objective was not only to fill in "the gaps left by Cook" in the geographical field, but also to compile the most accurate census possible of the people of the Pacific, the flora and fauna, the geology, and the environmental conditions. Naturally such an enterprise required massive investments in terms of men and equipment. In the five hundred pages of detailed orders edited personally by the king and by the various scientific academies, nothing was left to chance: they dealt with hygiene, medicine, chemistry, physics, experiments in crop sowing, and the introduction of new species of animals, procedures for the sterilization of the water to render it drinkable, techniques for the conservation of scientific specimens (Diderot and D'Alembert's Encyclopedie had been published in 1751).
The itinerary to be followed had already been established and even the period of the

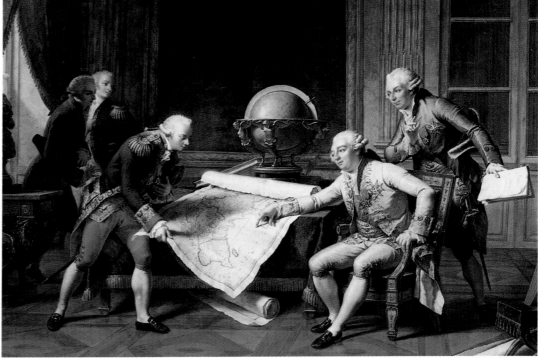

Top: François de Galaup, Count de La Pérouse was born in 1741, in the Languedoc region, La Pérouse entered the French Navy very early. After having taken part in numerous military campaigns, from

India to Canada, he was selected to lead a major expedition to the largely unknown North Pacific. La Pérouse's fleet disappeared in 1788 in still mysterious circumstances close to the Vanikoro atoll in the Solomon Islands.

Above: This painting "Empire and science", N. A. Mansiaux hanging in the Musée de Versailles, shows Jean-François de Galaup de La Pérouse (left, standing) receiving

his orders for his Pacific voyage from the king of France, Louis XVI. Among the tasks set by the king was the search for "all the lands to escape the attention of Cook."

Left: La Pérouse's ships, the Astrolabe and the Boussole, are here depicted anchored off the island of Maui (Hawaii), surrounded by the canoes of the natives. La Pérouse was dazzled by the beauty of the islands and, "in spite of my prejudices against them for the death of Captain Cook," the honesty and gentleness of the inhabitants.

Below: Numerous geographers, physicists, doctors, and illustrators embarked on the Astrolabe and the Boussole. They had the task of scrupulously recording and studying everything they encountered during their long voyage. This illustration shows a blackbird from French Port on the northwest coast of America, drawn by the talented illustrator Duché de Vancy.

return voyage had been fixed: the third week of July, 1789. The command of the expedition was entrusted to La Pérouse: noble birth and education played their part, but more influential was his career record. The French government counted on significant results from the expedition and only a resolute and pragmatic spirit would have the strength to bring it to a successful conclusion. La Pérouse had in the meantime married a young Creole girl that he had met some years earlier at Mauritius, winning a personal battle against the conformism of the era. The two ships selected by the naval ministry, rebaptised for the occasion as the *Astrolabe* and the *Boussole*, were notably capacious and robust: La Pérouse preferred them to faster more prestigious vessels, following the example set by Cook. Rather than speed, a Pacific voyage required large holds and maneuvrability. On La Pérouse's advice the command of the *Boussole* was given to Paul-Antoine de Langle, one of his old companions from the battles in the Canadian seas.

The expedition that left the port of Brest on the 1st of August, 1785, was the best organized (and most expensive) that had ever departed on a voyage of exploration. The scientific instruments that it carried represented the very best that contemporary technology could offer:

181

Top and bottom: These two prints realized by the famous illustrator Duché de Vancy show the dress of two people La Pérouse met during his long journey: the inhabitants of Concepción (top) and those of Manila (bottom). Concepción, in Chile, was founded in 1550 by the Spanish governor Pedro de Valdivia and was subjected to numerous earthquakes in its history. A similar fate awaited Manila, today the capital of the Philippines, which was founded by Miguel Lopez de Legazpi and hit by natural disasters on more than one occasion.

Opposite: This image shows the frontispiece of the atlas published with the four volumes of the first edition of Voyage, in 1798. The atlas contains nautical charts and reproductions of drawings executed by the expedition's artists and naturalists. This precious material escaped the disaster because, having landed at Kamkatka, La Pérouse decided to entrust the most important documents to one of his officers to be taken to France by land, across Siberia and Russia.

ATLAS

DU

VOYAGE

DE

LA PÉROUSE

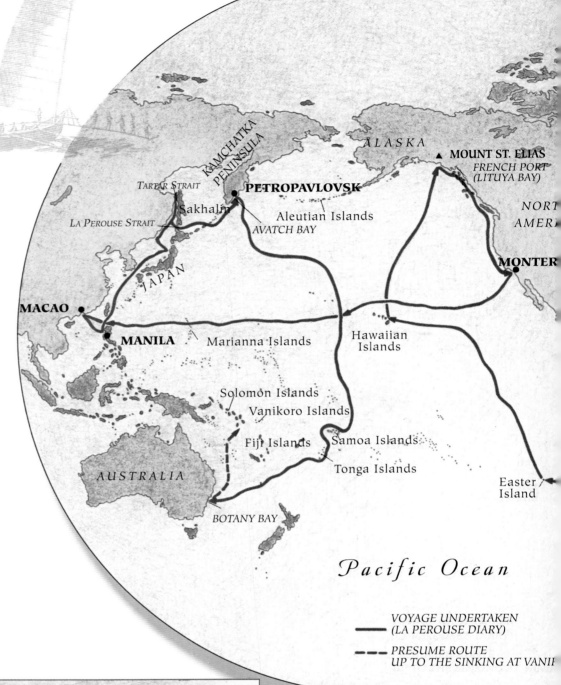

the marine chronometers, built in Switzerland and extensively tested, allowed time to be measured to an accuracy of one and a half seconds a year. Banks, in the name of scientific progress, ensured that La Pérouse was provided with the sophisticated compasses used by Cook, overcoming the political rivalry between France and Britain. The large group of scientists assembled for the mission included noted academics whose specialities covered all branches of human knowledge: among them were the mathematician and astronomer Dagelet, the botanist La Martinière and the geologist Lamanon. Then there were the geographers, the physicists, the physicians, and the illustrators like Duché de Vancy and the two Prévosts (uncle and nephew). Abundant provisions were loaded including 200 hens and several dozen goat, reams of paper for the plant records, sacks of seeds, and the usual baubles destined to be traded with the natives, including plumed hats and a million pins of various sizes. Louis XVI urged La Pérouse to forbid his crews to "use force to obtain from the natives what they would have refused to give voluntarily." In the paradise of the

Pacific Ocean

———— VOYAGE UNDERTAKEN
(LA PEROUSE DIARY)

- - - - PRESUME ROUTE
UP TO THE SINKING AT VANIK

184

Left: This plate executed by the draftsman Blondela, shows the constructional techniques used by the natives builiding pirogues at French Port: the framework of seasoned wood was suitably shaped and then covered with animal skins. While recognizing that the North American Indians had a certain skill in the manual arts, La Pérouse baldly defined them as "as rough and barbaros as their land is rocky and wild."

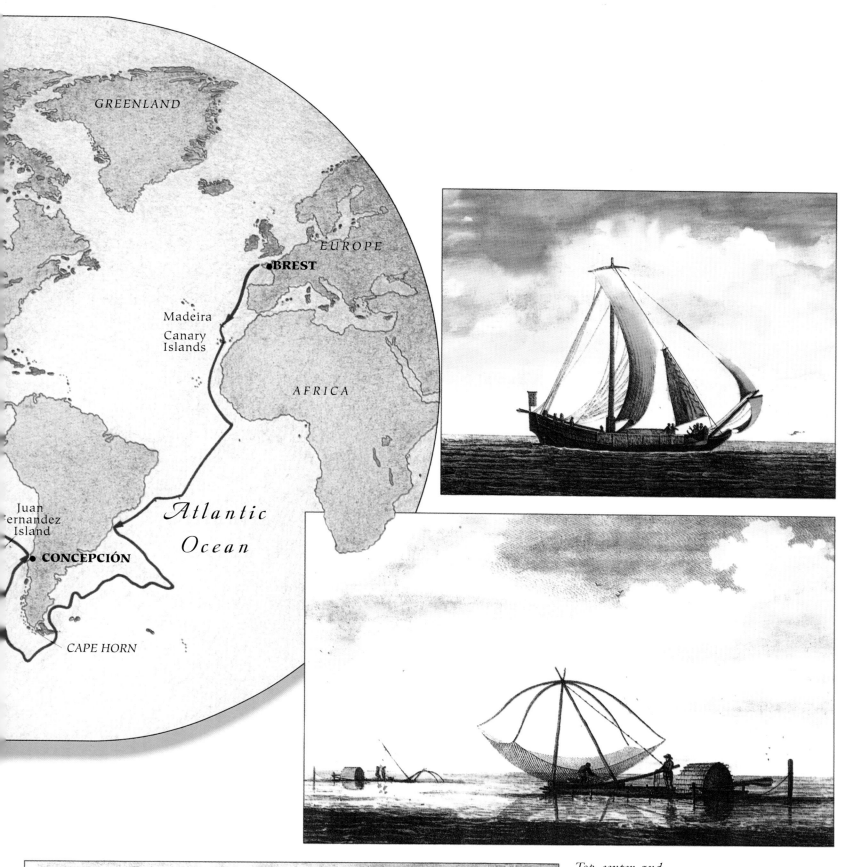

Top, center, and bottom: These plates taken from La Pérouse's atlas show the painstaking work of the scientists aboard the Astrolabe and the Boussole. They took note of every feature — in this case the boats — of the countries they visited, in particular Japan (top and bottom) and Manila (center).

185

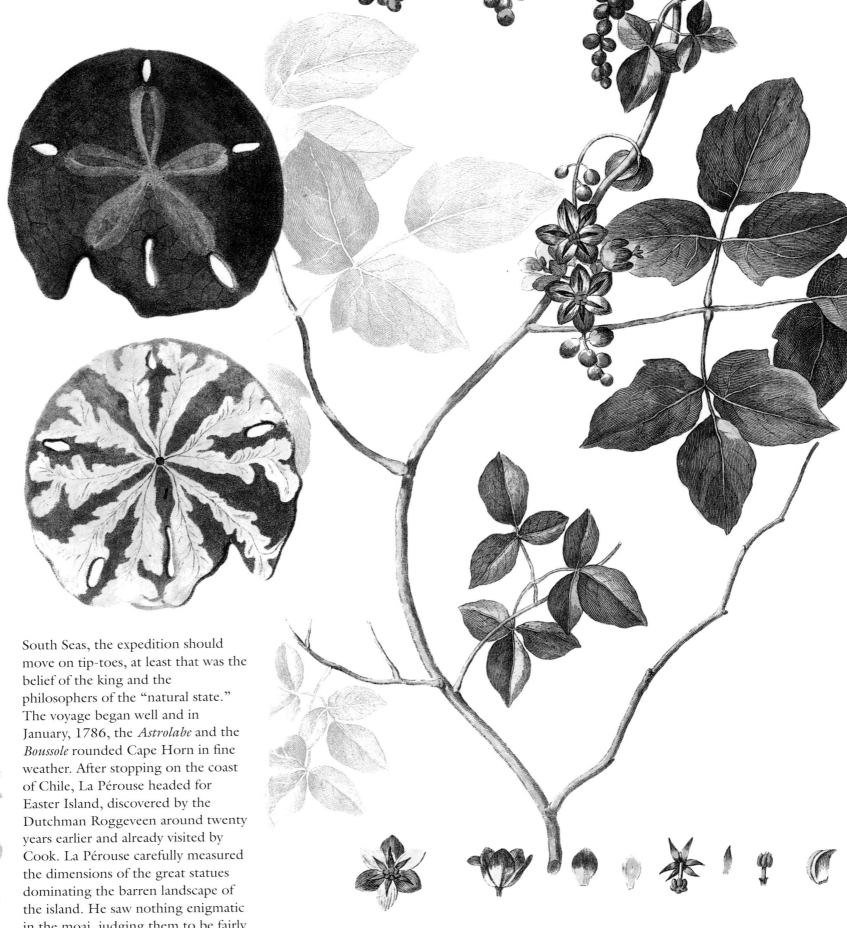

South Seas, the expedition should move on tip-toes, at least that was the belief of the king and the philosophers of the "natural state." The voyage began well and in January, 1786, the *Astrolabe* and the *Boussole* rounded Cape Horn in fine weather. After stopping on the coast of Chile, La Pérouse headed for Easter Island, discovered by the Dutchman Roggeveen around twenty years earlier and already visited by Cook. La Pérouse carefully measured the dimensions of the great statues dominating the barren landscape of the island. He saw nothing enigmatic in the moai, judging them to be fairly crude and of recent manufacture. Not even their erection appeared problematical to La Pérouse in that they were made of "a very light volcanic rock, and that with the aid of levers of five or six toise slipped beneath the stone, as explained by Captain Cook, even heavier weights can be lifted." Irritated by continual thefts, La Pérouse began to doubt that the "savages" were actually as noble as was believed in Europe. Foregoing the recovery of his stolen hat, La Pérouse left the island two days after his arrival. After a brief stop in the Hawaiian Islands, and the calculation of their correct position, the two ships headed northward. Towards mid-June, a clearing

in the fog revealed the coast of Alaska, dominated by the glaciers of Mount Saint Elias. La Pérouse aimed to explore that portion of the American coast ignored by Cook, descending south as far as California. In search of a safe landing spot, the *Astrolabe* and the *Boussole* entered a deep inlet that was baptised French Port (now Lituya Bay), and La Pérouse declared the bay as French property. This was his only act of taking possession in the whole of the voyage as he found the process useless and ridiculous. On the 13th of July, 1786, the unexpected happened: while they were in the middle of making preparations to depart, a group of

Above: These botanical specimens, meticulously reproduced by the Prévosts, two of the naturalists aboard the Astrolabe *and the* Boussoule. *Apart from its precise*

political aims, La Pérouse's expedition was required to collect as much information as possible about the inhabitants, fauna, flora, and geology of the Pacific islands.

187

Left: This magnificent bird of Northern California, drawn by Prévost, is part of the immense corpus of illustrative material produced by the biologists, botanists, and scientists who traveled with La Pérouse; it is called "Promerops de la Californie Septentrionale."

Bottom: These male and female California partridges were drawn by one of the Prévosts (uncle and nephew), specialists in botanical and zoological illustrations.
The Astrolabe *and* the Boussoule *entered the bay of Monterey, California, on the 14th of September, 1786: welcomed by the local political and religious authorities, La Pérouse allowed his crews to rest for around ten days before tackling the long crossing to the Asiatic coast of the Pacific.*

officers and seamen were given permission to land in order to form a hunting party. Only one of the three boats that landed returned to the ships. The others had been engulfed by a particularly violent ebb tide. Nobody was able to explain what exactly happened. Around twenty men perished, and the event left La Pérouse profoundly depressed. He delayed his departure by two weeks in the hope that the search for survivors might be successful. As time grew short the two ships headed south, abandoning the plan to chart that irregular, difficult coastline. The slumbering town of Monterey in California was reached on the 14th of September. Ten days later, La Pérouse set sail once more heading for the Asian coast of the Pacific. After 100 days of sailing in a virtually straight line along the Tropic of Cancer, the *Astrolabe* and the *Boussole* reached the port of Macao. Apart from the odd emergent rock, no island worthy of the name had been spotted by the navigators. La Pérouse was able to expunge the last remaining fantasies from the charts of the Pacific Ocean. The French ships spent a couple of months in Macao and Manila, repairing their well-worn ships and trying to trade the furs they had acquired in North America (La Pérouse judged that particular trade to be rather unprofitable). On the 9th of April, 1787,

PLAN DE L'ÎLE DE PÀQUE

Levé en Avril 1786.

à bord des Frégates Françaises la Boussole et l'Astrolabe.

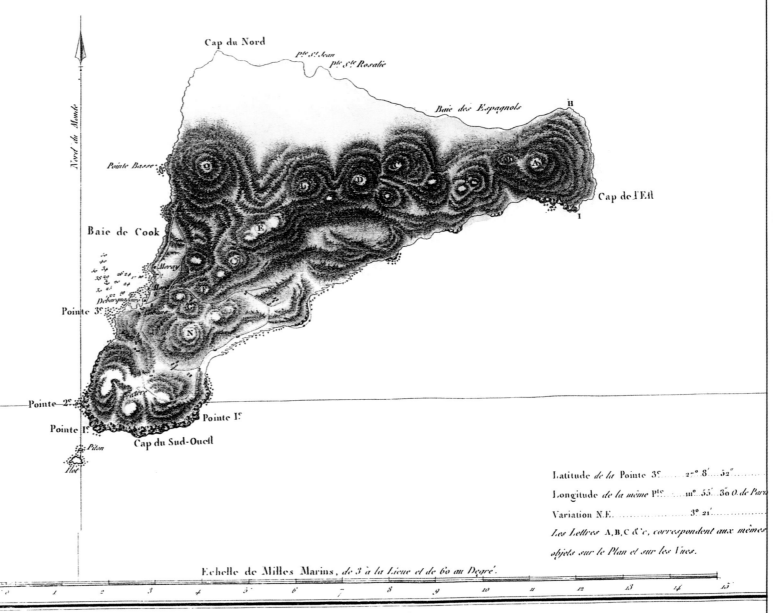

Nord du Monde

Cap du Nord

Pte St Jean
Pte Ste Rosalie

Baie des Espagnols

H

Pointe Basse

O

Baie de Cook

E

Cap de l'Est

I

Mercy

Pointe 3e.

N

Pointe 2e.

Pointe 1e.

Pointe 1e.

Cap du Sud-Ouest

Piton

Îlot

Latitude de la Pointe 3e......2-° 8'.. 52''........

Longitude de la même Pte.......m° 55'. 3o O. de Paris

Variation N.E.....................3° 21'.

Les Lettres A,B,C &e, correspondent aux mêmes

objets sur le Plan et sur les Vues.

Echelle de Milles Marins, de 3 à la Lieue et de 60 au Degré.

1 2 3 4 5 0 1 2 3 4 5 6 7 8 9 10 11 12 13 14 15

VUES DE L'ÎLE DE PÀQUE.

proportionelles entr'elles et sur une Echelle de 2 pouces par lieue, comme le Plan ci dessus.

A   K

I   H

Ie. Vue; A restant à 0 4e. S, distance 4 Lieues; la Pointe V à 0 4e. S O 1° O, et le Cap le plus Nord à 0.1° 3o N. du Compas.

N G F   E   L   D   C   B   A

Cap SO   Cap le l'E.

2e. Vue; le Cap de l'Est, restant au N. distance de 2 Lieues, et le Cap du Sud-Ouest à l'O. 5e. N.

O   A

Pte Basse   Îlot   B   Cap de l'Est
Cap SO

3e. Vue; le Cap de l'Est restant au N. 54° 3o'E; la Pointe Basse au N.18° 3o'E; l'Îlot et Piton au N. 3o°. dist. 1 Lieue.

Cap du Nord

A   Pte St Jean   Cap SO

4e. Vue; le Cap du Nord restant au S. 15° E, distance 13 Lieues; le sommet A au S. 25° E; et le Cap du Sud-Ouest au S. 9° E.

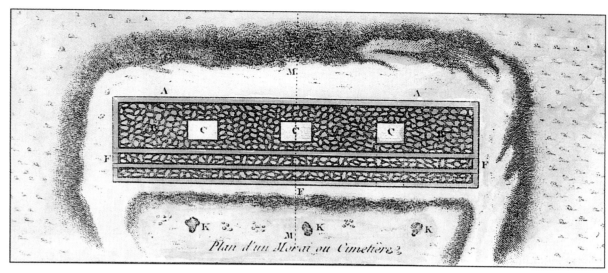

Plan d'un Morai ou Cimetière.

Top and center:
On the 9th of April, 1786, La Pérouse's ships approached Easter Island. Although irritated by the kleptomania of the inhabitants, the Admiral had the opportunity to draw up an exhaustive picture of their way of life and to examine the gigantic stone statues known as moais.

Bottom: The moais of Rapanui are set along the coast and on the slopes of the Ranu Ranaku volcano. All the statues are facing west. Alfred Metraux who studied the statues at length defined them as "the vertigo of the colossal on a minuscule universe with men of extremely limited resources: such is the aesthetic miracle of Easter Island."

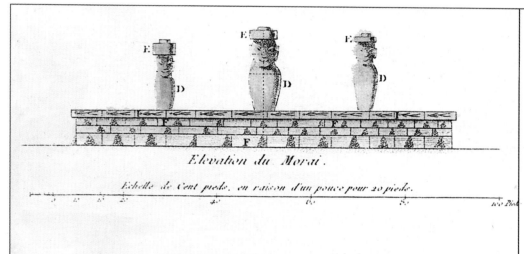

Elevation du Morai.

Echelle de Cent pieds, en raison d'un pouce pour 20 pieds.

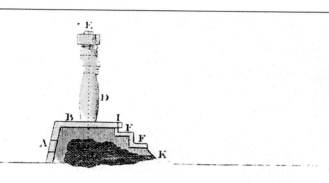

Coupe du Morai, pris sur la ligne M.M.

189

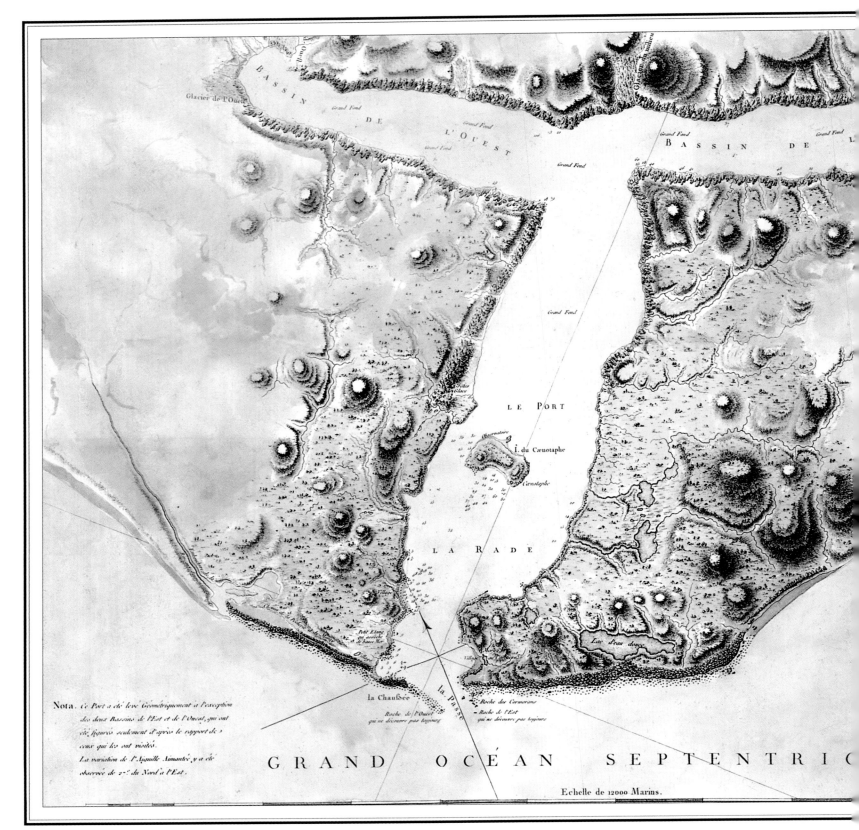

Within the map:

BASSIN DE L'OUEST

BASSIN DE L'...

Glacier de l'Ouest

Grand Fond

Grand Fond

Grand Fond

Grand Fond

Grand Fond

Grand Fond

Grand Fond

LE PORT

I. du Cænotaphe

Cænotaphe

LA RADE

Lac d'eau douce

Petit Etang qui se remplit de haute Mer

la Chaussée

la Passe

Roche des Cormorans

Roche de l'Ouest qui ne découvre pas toujours

Roche de l'Est qui ne découvre pas toujours

Nota. Ce Port a été levé Géométriquement à l'exception des deux Bassins de l'Est et de l'Ouest, qui ont été figurés seulement d'après le rapport de ceux qui les ont visités. La variation de l'Aiguille Aimantée y a été observée de 2°.½ du Nord à l'Est.

GRAND OCÉAN SEPTENTRIO...

Echelle de 12000 Marins.

Above: This map of the "French Port," today Lituya Bay on the northwest coast of America, was drawn up on the basis of the surveys effected by the Boussoule and the Astrolabe. La Pérouse's fleet came within sight of Mount St. Elias at the end of June, 1786. A few days later, the ships anchored in a magnificent bay that La Pérouse named French Port, taking formal possession in the name of the king.

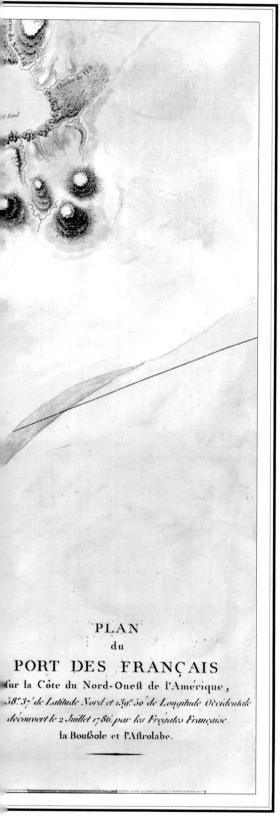

the *Astrolabe* and the *Boussole* set sail for Japan. They navigated the Tshushima Strait close to the Korean coast and set off toward the last great geographical question left unresolved by Cook: the coast of Siberia. At that time it was not known whether Hokkaido was really an island or a promontory of the mainland coast and the position of Sakhalin was equally uncertain. La Pérouse continued sailing northward and entered the strait separating Sakhalin from the mainland: the Ainu natives provided much valuable information and told La Pérouse that a narrow sea channel guaranteed a passage to the north and the Sea of Okhostsk. The French frigates continued to advance along what La Pérouse doubted would prove to be a trap. Fog and unfavorable winds could have made a return voyage impossible. On the 26th of July, the depth of the water was no more than six fathoms, and La Pérouse realized that he was in a dead end and facing a "difficult situation."

On the 7th of September, the expedition reached the coast of Kamchatka. The Russian authorities at Petropavlosk gave the Frenchmen a warm welcome. Escorted by the Cossacks provided by the governor, the scientists and naturalists set to work and the hinterland of the bay was explored as carefully as possible while La Pérouse studied the movement of the tides and the winds. Early in October, 1787, the expedition left Petropavlosk for the south. It was decided to send a young officer across Siberia and Russia to France with the ships' logs and the valuable charts. La Pérouse was a cautious man but he could hardly have foreseen that his fortunate emissary would be the expedition's only survivor. On the 6th of December, after having crossed the equator for the third time, the explorers dropped anchor off a Samoan island. The natives proved to be invasive and hostile, but the ships needed to take on fresh water. Against La Pérouse's

Above right: "A disaster a thousand times more terrible than any disease or other event that may occur during a long voyage." Thus did La Pérouse bitterly describe the tragedy that cost the lives of twenty-odd French seamen and officers in Lituya Bay, when two launches were swamped by a sudden and unexpected tidal surge.

The navigator's calculations revealed a latitude of 51° 44', just a little south of the mouth of the Amur and a stone's throw from the open sea. On the 2nd of August, the *Astrolabe* and the *Boussole* turned back: as the southern tip of Sakhalin was rounded La Pérouse realized that he was sailing along another strait that until then had been unknown and separated Sakhalin from Hokkaido.

wishes, the commander of the *Boussole*, De Langle, insisted on reprovisioning. The squad sent to search for fresh water was attacked as they were returning to their boats, and 12 men were killed, including De Langle, Lamanon, and another officer. Another 20 were seriously wounded. With them died for ever the concept of the "good savage." La Pérouse avoided taking revenge, instead expressing his anger

through his writings: "I am however much more aggrieved with those philosophers who exalt the savages than with the savages themselves. The unfortunate Lamanon, who they massacred, told me on the very eve of his death that those men were worth more than us. In accordance with my orders, I have always treated them with the greatest moderation; but I have to confess that if I were to undertake another similar expedition, I would ask for different orders." There were to be no further expeditions for La Pérouse. After having reached Tonga, he headed toward Australia. At Botany Bay he consigned his charts to the captain of the British ship *Sirius,* who was about to establish the first colony in Australia. The *Astrolabe* and the *Boussole* then disappeared. La Pérouse's last letter is dated 7th of February, 1788. Only forty years later did the Frenchman Dumont d'Urville locate the remains of a wreck on the reef around the coral atoll of Vanikoro in the Solomon Islands. The material recovered from the seabed belonged to the *Astrolabe.* There is something prophetic in La Pérouse's sinking and death. According to the orders he received from his king, he would have returned just in time to witness the storming of the Bastille. And the end of an era.

Top: La Pérouse reached Macau in January, 1787, arriving from California after over three months' sailing. He liked neither the city nor the Chinese: "That population," he wrote, "whose laws are so quoted in Europe, is perhaps the most unhappy, the most vexed and the most arbitrarily governed on Earth." As for trade, he adjudged that China could not offer Europe anything other than tea, silk, a little Malabar pepper, opium, and useless porcelain, a veritable "ballast for ships."

Above: During the voyage from Macau to the Philippines and then on the route north toward Korea and Japan, La Pérouse's fleet encountered a multitude of Chinese and Japanese trading vessels shuttling between the various ports of the eastern Pacific. They were equipped with a single mast, and their fragile structure, according to the French officers, offered little security on the open sea.

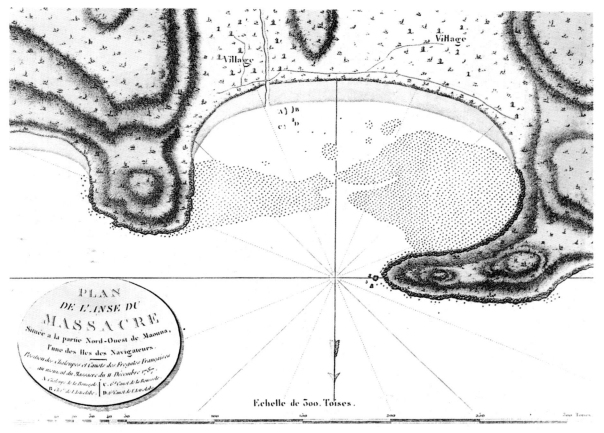

Top: A map of the "Massacre Bay" on Manua (actually Tutuila), one of the Samoan Islands. The position of the French vessels at the moment of the assault is marked. La Pérouse, wracked with pain and anger, compared the bay to "a trap, more deadly than a den of lions and tigers."

Above: The French launches were attacked by the natives of Eastern or American Samoa where La Pérouse had stopped to reprovision with fresh water and food early in December, 1787.

12 men were killed and another 20 seriously injured. La Pérouse avoided reprisals, respecting the orders he had been given, and expressed his bitterness with the pen. "If I should undertake another expedition of this kind, I would ask for different orders" he confessed. Along with the sailors of the Astrolabe and the Boussoule, the myth of the "noble savage" died forever.

193

S purred by an insatiable scientific curiosity and a desire to investigate the existence of a link between the two great fluvial systems of South America, the Amazon and the Orinoco, two young scientists left Europe on one of the most significant private expeditions in history. During their five-year wanderings, from 1799 to 1804, which led them from the forests of the higher Orinoco to the volcanoes of the Andes and Mexico, Alexander von Humboldt and Aimé Bonpland accumulated a remarkable quantity of data and scientific specimens that revealed to Europe for the first time the natural wonders of the New World. This was the second, authentic discovery of America.

HUMBOLDT:
THE TRIUMPH OF SCIENCE

Top: This significant portrait of Humboldt shows some drawings that the German explorer drew during his long journey across South America.

Above: When, in 1850, at the age of 81, Humboldt posed for this portrait, photography was still in its infancy. This is a fitting tribute to a man who was, in all fields, a pioneer and,

who Goethe likened to a "many spouted fountain: all that one must do is place receptacles below them and they will be filled with his refreshing and inexhaustible flow."

"What magnificent vegetation! And the brightness of the birds' plumage and the colour of the fish! Even the crabs are blue and gold! Until now all we have done is run here and there like madmen and, for the first three days, we were incapable of anything useful, such was our enthusiasm as we abandoned one thing for another. Bonpland says that he will go mad if all these wonders do not finish soon..." At the age of thirty, Baron Alexander von Humboldt had finally realized his great dream: some days earlier he had landed on the Caribbean coast of Venezuela and was about to undertake a long journey through the lush vegetation of the New World. At that moment there was nothing more important or more beautiful in the world than the dusty town of Cumanà, slumbering along the banks of the Manzanares. After many contretemps it seemed to good to be true: Humboldt and Bonpland were intoxicated with their new-found freedom. That journey, five years of wandering from the Amazon forests to the Mexican volcanoes, was to bring them fame and maturity. Although today his work is all but forgotten, Humboldt was one of the leading intellectuals of his

Center: This signature by the German scientist appears at the end of a letter sent to Professor Loder at Moscow on the 18th of April, 1824.

Bottom: Humboldt in his study at Berlin, where he spent the last years of his life working on Kosmos, the monumental work in which he put forward an organic view of the diverse natural phenomena. Albeit in contact with all the most brilliant intellectuals and scientists of his time, Humboldt conducted a solitary existence until his death in 1859 at the age of 89.

time. He frequented and had ties of friendship and mutual respect with the most important scientific and political figures of the era: Jefferson, Gay-Lussac, Banks, Cuvier, and Laplace to name but a few. Goethe considered him to be "an extraordinary man." Humboldt lived to the age of ninety and was an enlightened and knowledgeable witness to the events that shook Europe, from the French Revolution to the birth of Marxism. His scientific activity can be described as feverish. He was a pioneer in all of the fields that were to become the modern disciplines, from anthropology to ecology, according to an all-encompassing philosophy: nature was to be studied in its totality, according to a general strategy that linked the various phenomena in an

195

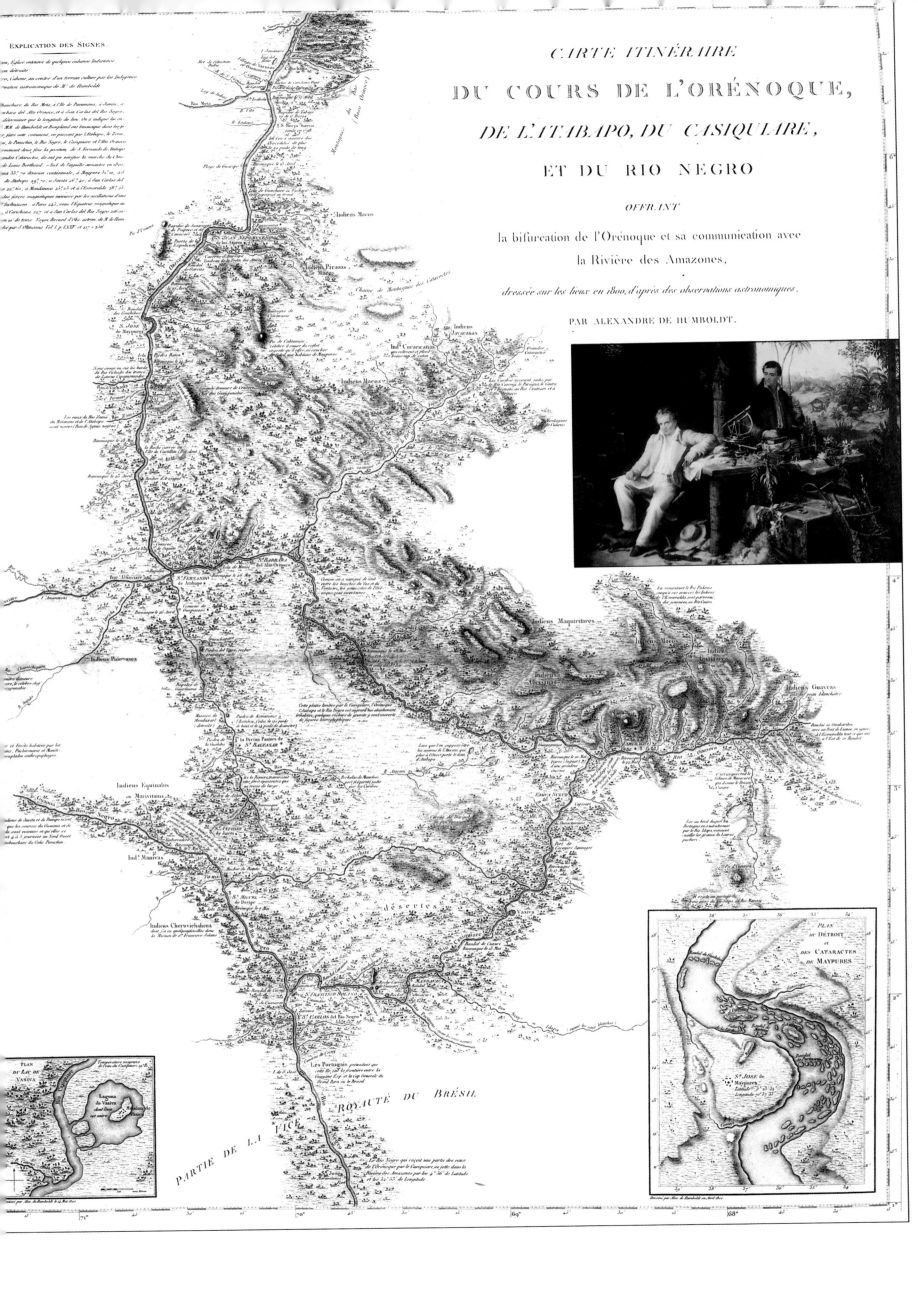

CARTE ITINÉRAIRE

DU COURS DE L'ORÉNOQUE,

DE L'ATABAPO, DU CASIQUIARE,

ET DU RIO NEGRO

OFFRANT

la bifurcation de l'Orénoque et sa communication avec
la Rivière des Amazones,

dressée sur les lieux en 1800, d'après des observations astronomiques.

PAR ALEXANDRE DE HUMBOLDT.

organic vision. Within this complex system of interactions, the discovery of a new botanical species was as important as the survey of an Incan temple or the social structure of an Indian tribe. As far as Humboldt was concerned, an individual fact was of value only when taken in context: in isolation it was of no use. Humboldt was perhaps the last example of the universal genius. At least a thousand places around the globe carry his name: towns and villages in America, forests and rivers throughout the world. The cold current flowing past the Peruvian coast is known as the Humboldt Current. He is even honored in lunar topography (one of the seas is named after

him). Alexander von Humboldt was born in Berlin in 1769 to an aristocratic family. His cold, authoritarian mother wanted him to become a state official and personally took charge of his education. At 22 years of age, his future appeared to be mapped out. Humboldt became a mine inspector for the Prussian government, and his professional performance was beyond reproach. However, he harbored very different ambitions. During his studies at Gottingen he had met Georg Forster, a naturalist who had sailed with Cook in the Pacific, and had been entranced by his stories. He had been carrying out nature research on his own account for some years. In 1797, the death

of his mother radically changed his way of life. Humboldt suddenly found himself rich and independent. One thing was very clear to him – he wanted to travel. The following year he headed to Paris, the intellectual and scientific capital of Europe in that era. His meeting with the twenty-five year old Aimé Bonpland was decisive. Bonpland was a doctor but had a passion for botany. A close friendship was established between the two men based on common interests and aspirations. They decided to depart together. Their first opportunity was to participate in a voyage around the world, but the project was aborted. Humboldt and Bonpland then turned their attention to Egypt: they

197

Top: "This drawing... represents a great balsa raft, a typical vessel of the Peruvian coast and the river Guayaquil. The raft is loaded with equinoctial fruit, pineapples, avocados, Theophrasta longifolia *berries, bunches of bananas shaded... by* Eliconia *and coconut flowers." Having left Venezuela, in the years between 1801 and 1804 Humboldt and Bonpland visited Cuba, Colombia and Ecuador, finally reaching the Pacific coast of Peru.*

Bottom: These illustrations show a Gymnotus electricus *studied by Humboldt in Venezuela and dissected to show the electrical apparatus.*

transferred to Marseille with the intention of joining the group of scientists following Napoleon. However, their plans again came to nothing. Humboldt's passport was full of visas but it appeared that destiny was preventing him from leaving Europe. They then turned to Spain: it was by no means an exotic country, but they felt that it would be good experience for their future journeys. All that was important was to keep moving and to make things happen. Better fortune awaited them at Madrid: the two enthusiastic scientists were taken under the wing of an important figure who introduced them to the court. The king of Spain was favorably impressed by Humboldt's plans and conceded him a special permit to explore the Spanish overseas territories. America beckoned! In over three hundred years, this was the first time that a foreigner had been given permission to visit the Hispano-American lands. Humboldt threw himself into the preparations, and on the 5th of June, 1779, sailed out of the port of La Coruña bound for the New World. "Friedrich Heinrich Alexander, Baron von Humboldt, born at Berlin, age 28, height 1.70 meters, hair light brown, eyes gray, large nose, broad forehead marked by smallpox scars. Traveling for the acquisition of knowledge." Thus

read the French passport that Humboldt had obtained two years earlier at Paris. In America he was to become known simply as Señor Baron. Humboldt and Bonpland spent over four months at Cumanà, collecting examples of plants and fine-tuning their scientific equipment. For the wealthier families of the town whose principal pastime was chattering about the latest fashions of Havana and Caracas, the two young foreigners were a welcome diversion. Their microscope revealed the horrors of lice to more than one young lady. Humboldt consoled them by informing them that there were no less than 37 species of these parasites, and they were not necessarily the same as those that infested the serving classes and that undoubtedly the lice of the wealthy were "aristocrats among lice." In the Cumanà region Humboldt visited the enormous Caripe cavern inhabited by thousands of nocturnal birds. The Indians extracted a kind oil from the abdomens of the guacharos *(Streatornis caripensis)* that they used for cooking and conserving food. Bonpland shot an example, and Humboldt dissected it noting that "the peritoneum is covered with fat, and a fatty panniculus extends from the abdomen to the anus, forming a kind of cushion between the feet of the bird." The name of the cavern, the "Mine of Fat," was highly appropriate. After a further stay at Caracas, the scientists felt themselves to be ready to tackle the arduous journey toward the source of the Orinoco. On horseback, followed by a small caravan of mules, they headed into the Llanos, the immense alluvial plains between the Orinoco and the eastern cordillera of the Andes: travelling across that sun-baked, deserted savannah was an exhausting experience. The temperature frequently exceeded 50°C, and Humboldt was obliged to dress his hat with leaves in an attempt to find relief. Tormented by thirst, the travelers were forced to drink the muddy, malodorous water in the few remaining waterholes. Here Humboldt was able to observe one of the most extraordinary animals of the New World, the South American electric eel or gymnotid. In order to capture a number of live specimens, the Indians drove a number of horses into the water triggering instant pandemonium. Struck by the violent electric shocks the

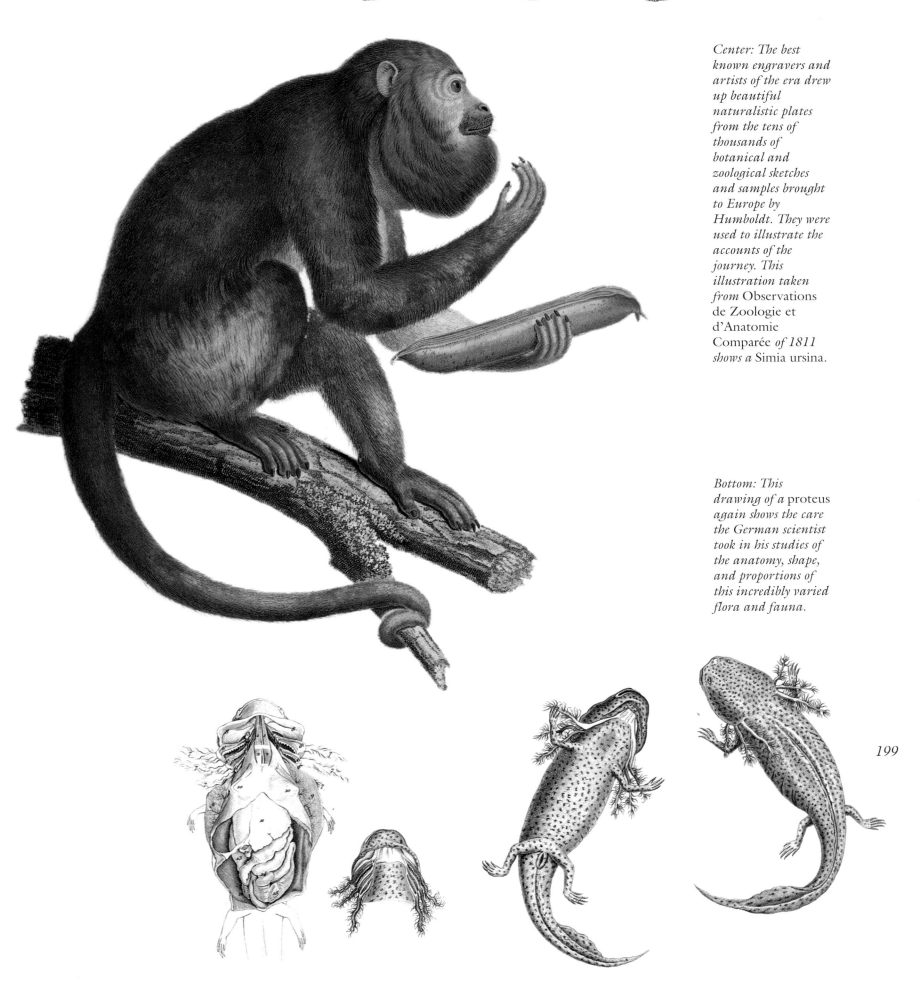

Top: Humboldt had the habit of painstakingly recording everything that took his interest, and during the course of his explorations he produced thousands of sketches of plants and animals, many of which were completely unknown to European science. This plate shows an example of Simia leonina, so called because of its thick mane, that Humboldt had occasion to observe on Andes mountains. The ear of corn highlights the small size of the animal.

Center: The best known engravers and artists of the era drew up beautiful naturalistic plates from the tens of thousands of botanical and zoological sketches and samples brought to Europe by Humboldt. They were used to illustrate the accounts of the journey. This illustration taken from Observations de Zoologie et d'Anatomie Comparée of 1811 shows a Simia ursina.

Bottom: This drawing of a proteus again shows the care the German scientist took in his studies of the anatomy, shape, and proportions of this incredibly varied flora and fauna.

199

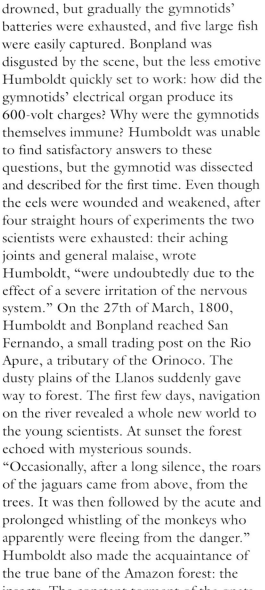

horses attempted to make for the banks but were repelled by the cries and sticks of the Indians. In just a few minutes two horses drowned, but gradually the gymnotids' batteries were exhausted, and five large fish were easily captured. Bonpland was disgusted by the scene, but the less emotive Humboldt quickly set to work: how did the gymnotids' electrical organ produce its 600-volt charges? Why were the gymnotids themselves immune? Humboldt was unable to find satisfactory answers to these questions, but the gymnotid was dissected and described for the first time. Even though the eels were wounded and weakened, after four straight hours of experiments the two scientists were exhausted: their aching joints and general malaise, wrote Humboldt, "were undoubtedly due to the effect of a severe irritation of the nervous system." On the 27th of March, 1800, Humboldt and Bonpland reached San Fernando, a small trading post on the Rio Apure, a tributary of the Orinoco. The dusty plains of the Llanos suddenly gave way to forest. The first few days, navigation on the river revealed a whole new world to the young scientists. At sunset the forest echoed with mysterious sounds. "Occasionally, after a long silence, the roars of the jaguars came from above, from the trees. It was then followed by the acute and prolonged whistling of the monkeys who apparently were fleeing from the danger." Humboldt also made the acquaintance of the true bane of the Amazon forest: the insects. The constant torment of the gnats during the navigation along the river was

Top: The bright colors of the equatorial flora and fauna had a great impact on Humboldt who, at thirty years of age, had finally fulfilled a long-held ambition: to study the luxuriant vegetation of the New World. The image shows the study of some butterflies taken from one of Humboldt's plates.

Center: This romantic oil painting by Georg Friedrich Weitsch from 1809 portrays Humboldt dealing with one of his principal chores during the expedition: arranging the flowers collected during the explorations in the special holders to press and dry them. Humboldt's work was truly important and he collected no less than 60,000 different botanical specimens, many of them belonging to unknown species.

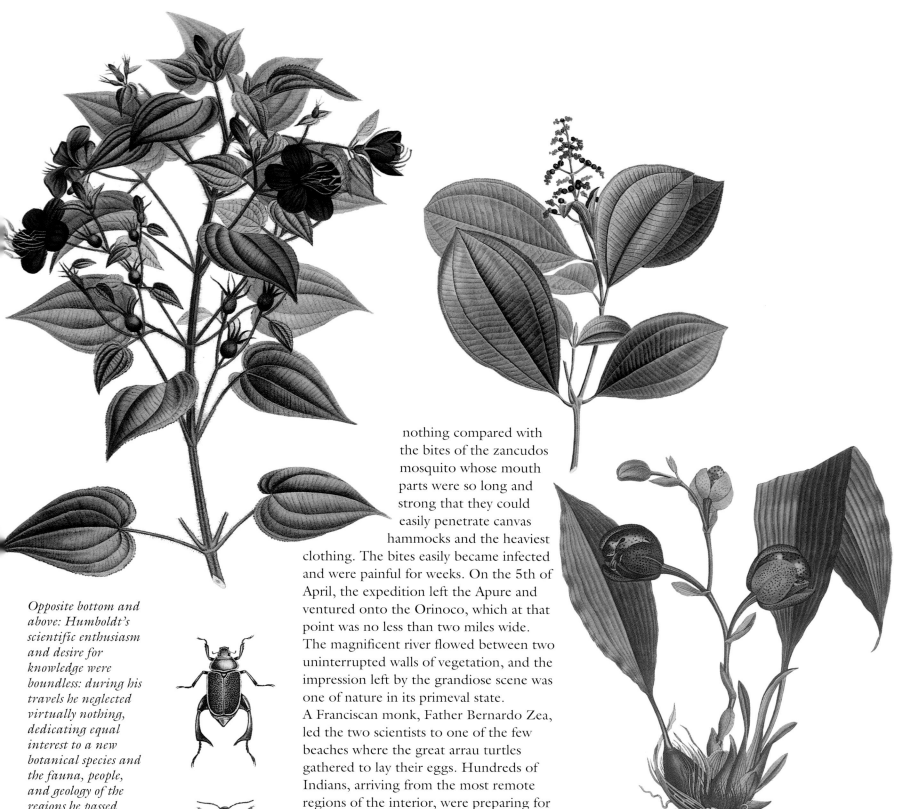

Opposite bottom and above: Humboldt's scientific enthusiasm and desire for knowledge were boundless: during his travels he neglected virtually nothing, dedicating equal interest to a new botanical species and the fauna, people, and geology of the regions he passed through. These illustrations demonstrate the breadth of his enquiries and depict a Melastoma coccinea, *a* Rhexia stricta, *a* Rhexia grandiflora *and a* Melastoma racemosa.

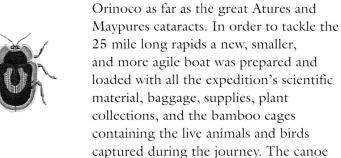

nothing compared with the bites of the zancudos mosquito whose mouth parts were so long and strong that they could easily penetrate canvas hammocks and the heaviest clothing. The bites easily became infected and were painful for weeks. On the 5th of April, the expedition left the Apure and ventured onto the Orinoco, which at that point was no less than two miles wide. The magnificent river flowed between two uninterrupted walls of vegetation, and the impression left by the grandiose scene was one of nature in its primeval state.

A Franciscan monk, Father Bernardo Zea, led the two scientists to one of the few beaches where the great arrau turtles gathered to lay their eggs. Hundreds of Indians, arriving from the most remote regions of the interior, were preparing for the seasonal harvesting of the eggs from which they would extract an edible oil. Humboldt estimated that over 330,000 turtles congregated on that beach each year. Accompanied by the competent guide Father Zea, the expedition moved up the Orinoco as far as the great Atures and Maypures cataracts. In order to tackle the 25 mile long rapids a new, smaller, and more agile boat was prepared and loaded with all the expedition's scientific material, baggage, supplies, plant collections, and the bamboo cages containing the live animals and birds captured during the journey. The canoe was improbably overloaded and extremely

Bottom left: This study of different beetles is taken from a plate from the Observations de Zoologie et d'Anatomia Comparée, *the fruit of the methodical cataloging that Alexander von Humboldt undertook on his return to Europe.*

Bottom right: Humboldt observed this extraordinary orchid (Angulea superba) *on the borders of Ecuador and Peru. The water-color was subsequently rendered by Pierre Jean Francois Turpin, who scrupulously followed the indications of the German scientist.*

201

Above: This oil painting by Friedrich Georg Weitsch from 1810 shows an episode during the voyage of Alexander von Humboldt and Aimé Bonpland, recognizable on the right, when the expedition camped at the foot of the Chimborazo volcano.

Center: The geography of the equinoctial plants. Studying the volcanoes of Ecuador, Humboldt analyzed the distribution of the various botanical species according to altitude. Cross-referencing the data with information relating to the geology, fauna, atmospheric pressure, and temperature, he came to the conclusion that nature, even in its extreme diversity, must be considered a unitary system. The German scientist was the first to know the complex network of interrelations that link organisms to their environment, thus anticipating the basis of modern ecology.

uncomfortable and the insects were more aggressive and numerous than ever. Even the indefatigable Humboldt was obliged to suspend all scientific activities as he was too occupied with day-to-day survival. Beyond that foaming labyrinth extended a practically unknown region, "the land of fables and fantastic visions." Legend had it that on the other side of the mountain lay El Dorado and the lake of Parima. According to the Indians the stars were nothing more than the reflections of stones of silver. Humboldt, however, was not interested in such riches, the mirage of which had led generations of adventurers to lose themselves in the great forest. His plan was to verify whether in fact there existed a link between the basin of the Orinoco and that of the Amazon. La Condamine's journey of around sixty years earlier had revived the debate: the Casiquiare united the Rio Negro with the Orinoco. But at what point of their course? And was it navigable? Humboldt was determined to resolve the matter once and for all. Ascending the course of a confluent of the Orinoco, the Tuamini, the expedition came within 7 miles or so of the Rio Negro. From that point the canoe and all the baggage was transported overland to the great river, the waters of which were pleasantly cool and clear. Within a few days the expedition had descended the Rio Negro as far as the mouth of the Casiquiare, which they then began to ascend. The ten days the group spent navigating the Casiquiare were the worst of the entire journey. The sky was constantly covered by clouds, day and night. The towering, impenetrable forest embraced the river in its oppressive grip: it was impossible to land and, pitch a camp, and Humboldt and Bonpland were forced to spend the nights on the canoe. When the food supplies were exhausted, they attempted to satisfy their hunger by eating raw cocoa beans. The course of the Casiquiare was charted for the first time. On the 21st of May the expedition reached the Orinoco close to the Esmeralda mission: "a terrible, remote place," wrote

Opposite bottom left: In September, 1801, Humboldt and Bonpland left the Rio Magdalena in Colombia in order to climb the Andes. A few months later, they attempted an ascent of Chimborzo, thought to be the highest mountain in the world, but were forced to turn back a few hundred yards from the summit.

Opposite bottom right: The gas vents at Turbaco near Cartagena in Colombia. Humboldt was interested in all forms of volcanic activity and was struck by the strange features of the Turbaco volcanoes: "At the center of a vast plain," he wrote, "18 or 20 small cones rise to a height of not more than 7 or 8 meters. Cones of a blackish clay at the summit of which is an aperture filled with water. Approaching those small craters you can hear, at regular intervals, a dull, fairly loud noise that precedes by about 15-18 seconds the emission of a great quantity of gas... Frequently that phenomenon is accompanied by the spouting of jets of mud."

203

Humboldt, "that gives the traveler the impression having reached the end of the world." Esmeralda, a semi-abandoned village, was the only inhabited place in that vast region. To go on would have been too dangerous: the reputation of the Indians of the Upper Orinoco was sufficient to convince Humboldt to turn back. Before leaving Esmeralda the scientists had the opportunity of seeing the Indians prepare curare, the lethal poison extracted from the bark of the liana Strychnos. On more than one occasion the Poison Master invited Humboldt to taste the deadly substance: "in fact one judges from the more or less bitter taste whether the concentration obtained from the heat is sufficient. There is no danger in this as curare is only effective if it comes into direct contact with the blood." By early June the expedition had overcome the great rapids for the second time and was navigating tranquil waters in the direction of Angostura (now known as Ciudad Boliva). In August, 1880, Humboldt and Bonpland re-entered their beloved Cumanà. However, in spite of the long months spent in the forests of the Orinoco, Humboldt's curiosity was by no means sated. Over the following years, after having visited Cuba, the two scientists returned to the South American mainland. From Cartagena they ascended the Rio Magdalena as far as Bogotà, crossed the Andes and proceeded southward to the Peruvian coastal desert. Working on his accurate survey of the Ecuadorian volcanoes, Humboldt was able to establish the igneous origins of the oldest rocks, revolutionizing the geological theories of the time. From Lima they traveled to Mexico and, after a final sojourn at Washington, eventually set sail for Europe. This was in the summer of 1804. The journey had cost Humboldt a third of his

entire fortune. The botanical collections he brought home contained over 60,000 specimens, many of them belonging to previously unknown species and the quantity of data the pair had gathered was quite remarkable. Humboldt established himself at Paris and began working on the publication of a report of his journey. Bonpland, however, failed to find the necessary dedication for such a project. He felt more at home in the open air of the Royal Gardens, which he superintended until 1814. Later, following an unsuccessful marriage, he once again left for America. In Paraguay he was imprisoned for ten years by a local dictator. He was never to return to Europe and ended his days in a mud-hut on the borders between Uruguay and Brazil in the company of his Brazilian mistress and a horde of children. He died at the age of 85 in the middle of the forests he loved. Humboldt remained in Paris for over twenty years, leaving the city only on brief trips to Italy and Switzerland. He then returned to Berlin, where he entered the service of the king of Prussia. In 1829 he traveled through Russia and Siberia on behalf of the Czar and reached the remote confines of China. He spent the rest of his life hunched over his papers, isolating himself in his modest Berlin apartment crammed with books and scientific specimens: "I am searching for the nutriment for a still unsettled spirit in my work" he wrote to Gay-Lussac in 1837. For a man who received around three thousand letters a year and considered music to be a "social calamity," modern life could not have offered great satisfaction. He died at the age of 89 while he was working on the fifth volume of Kosmos, the work in which he attempted to bring a unitary vision to bear on the immense variety of nature.

Top left: In October, 1801, Humboldt and Bonpland crossed the Andes cordillera via the Quindeo Pass, reaching the valley of the Cauca and Popayan. Humboldt defined it as the "hardest of the Andean passes." The explorers covered part of the route for a dozen days or so, on rudimentary seats of bamboo belted to the shoulders of bearers.

Right: The Vultur gryphus *(condor in the Quechua language) captured Humboldt's imagination, who observed it soaring "almost as high as Chimborazo," that is to say at an altitude of over 19,000 feet. The condor is the largest bird of prey in existence with a wingspan of up to 10 feet. It is found throughout the Andes cordillera.*

No other environment arouses such distinct feelings of inadequacy and solitude in modern man than the rainforests. For the explorers of the last century the rainforest was a "green hell," the hostile environment par excellence, and far more terrible than the deserts in which man is truly a biological misfit. For outsiders the forest is a difficult place: the climate is oppressive, the insects are particularly numerous and aggressive, and the whole environment is so damp that it is often impossible to light a fire. Life is wet in the forest, clothes rot and wounds never heal: you sweat copiously but the absence of evaporation ensures that your body temperature remains constantly high. You drink more in the forest than in the desert. However, not even all the dangers and the difficulties are sufficient to explain that "hostile environment syndrome" that emerges from the diaries of those explorers that penetrated the rainforests.

The problem is partially psychological: the European explorers were accustomed to open or semi-open environments. This implies a broad vision of the territory. The forest, on the other hand, requires close reading: you need to distinguish one tree from another, to distinguish figures against the background. For those accustomed to wide-ranging vistas, an empty plain is more comprehensible (and therefore reassuring) than the enclosed world of the forest, where visibility is restricted to just a few yards. The jungle has no horizons and is apparently uniform and lacking in depth, while your senses are overwhelmed by a mass of incomprehensible stimuli. Everything appears threatening: the environment rejects us and becomes an "enemy." In the case of the forest dweller, whether they are Amazon Indians or Pygmies from the Congo basin, hunters or farmers, the problem is reversed. Kenge was the most famous pygmy in the world and his name appears in all the texts dealing with perceptive psychology. Taken out of the forest, into the open savannah of the Virunga, Kenge saw a herd of buffalo in the distance, a mountain of meat in the eyes of a hunter. Kenge, however, appeared uninterested and asked the anthropologist that accompanied the name of those insects. All attempts at convincing him that the black shapes on the plain were large animals twice as big as the forest buffalo were in vain. Panoramic vision simply had no place in his perceptive sphere: Kenge was incapable of evaluating (as we do automatically) the relationship between the size of an object and its position in space. He had no need to do so in the jungle. As far as Kenge was concerned, the world without trees, the "dry, dirty land" that extended beyond the protective cradle of the forest was an inconceivable environment. And hostile.

Above: Cutting a route through the jungle (in this case an African forest) is still a physically and mentally debilitating procedure in spite of technical advances in clothing and equipment. Strange as it may seem, the damp jungle environment leads one to drink more than in a desert (due to the low rate of evaporation that keeps the body temperature constantly high).

Right: This engraving from the 19th century shows the extraordinary natural world of the Amazonian forest: the Itarnaraty falls near Serra Estrella in Brazil.

Center: An explorer accompanied by a group of porters advances through the twilight of a great equatorial forest: the illustration shows the density of the virgin forest at the source of Lake Dos Patos. The exploration of the Amazon basin was almost exclusively made along the various rivers.

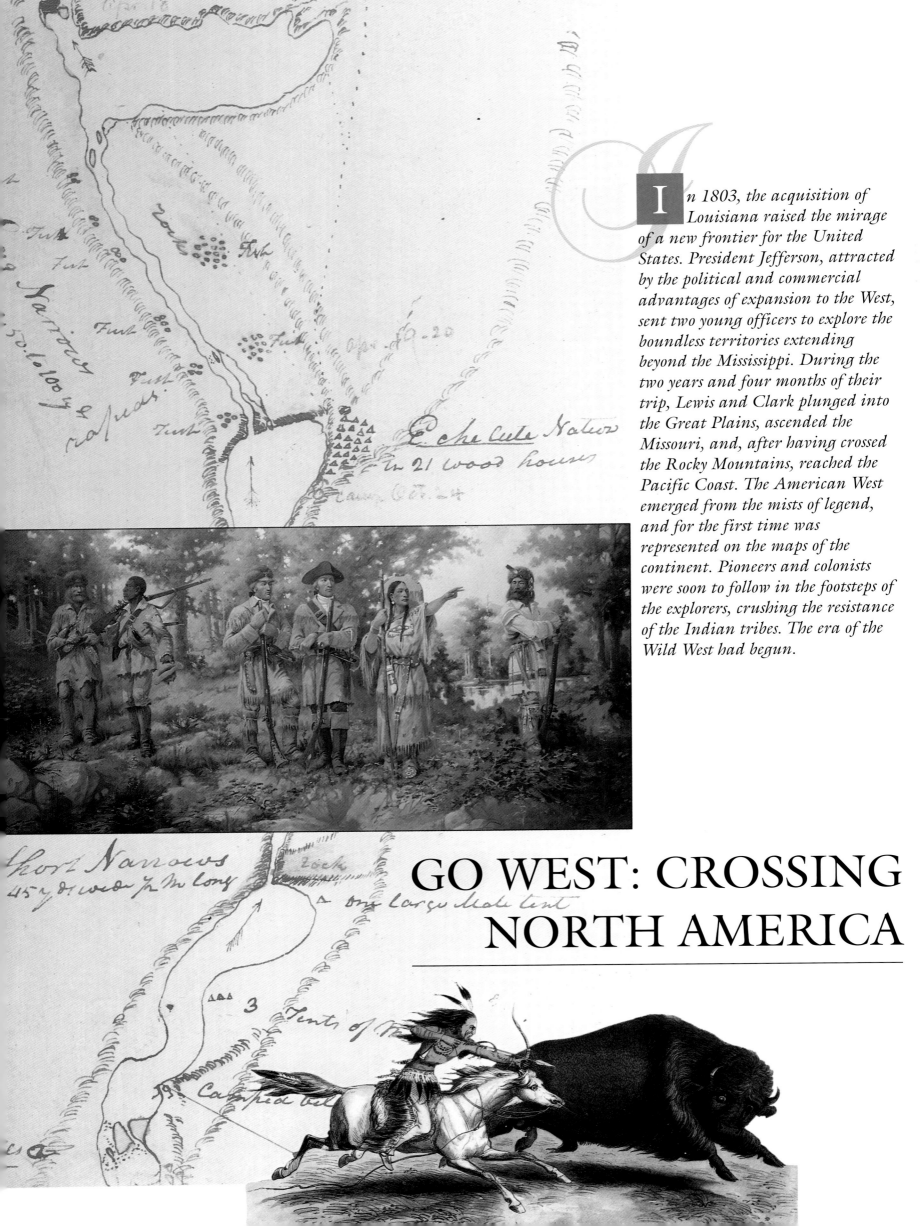

I n 1803, the acquisition of Louisiana raised the mirage of a new frontier for the United States. President Jefferson, attracted by the political and commercial advantages of expansion to the West, sent two young officers to explore the boundless territories extending beyond the Mississippi. During the two years and four months of their trip, Lewis and Clark plunged into the Great Plains, ascended the Missouri, and, after having crossed the Rocky Mountains, reached the Pacific Coast. The American West emerged from the mists of legend, and for the first time was represented on the maps of the continent. Pioneers and colonists were soon to follow in the footsteps of the explorers, crushing the resistance of the Indian tribes. The era of the Wild West had begun.

GO WEST: CROSSING
NORTH AMERICA

"The aim of your mission is to explore the Missouri River and those of its principal tributaries that, by their course and by linking with the Pacific Ocean, may offer the most direct and practicable fluvial communications across this country to commercial ends." The orders issued by Thomas Jefferson to commanders of the great expedition to the West could hardly have been more explicit. The ancient legend of a northern passage to the Pacific and the East once more took center stage, invested with new pragmatism. In 1790, the mouth of the Colombia River had been discovered, after having been overlooked by Cook and La Pérouse. A few years later the Scottish explorer MacKenzie had traversed Canada, reaching the Pacific in the vicinity of Vancouver Island. Jefferson,

Opposite top: Sacajewa, shows the direction to the two American explorers at the Three Forks. Sacajewa, the sister of a Shoshoni Indian chief, was known by the name Bird Woman. The courageous

woman, wife of a French-Canadian guide, Toussaint Charbonneau, had a fundamental role in the Lewis and Clark expedition: she was their interpreter and mediator with the Indian tribes.

Opposite: This painting by George Catlin shows a North American Indian stalking a buffalo.

Left: A portrait of William Clark. Aware of the difficulty of the task facing him, Lewis asked for and was granted permission to share the command of the expedition with his old army colleague William Clark. Of a practical and sociable nature, Clark was well experienced in life in the wild country. His personality complemented perfectly that of Lewis, and the two enjoyed excellent relations.

Center left: A portrait of Meriweather Lewis. A personal friend and secretary of President Jefferson, Lewis was 29 when he was commissioned to organize the great expedition to the West. His qualities as a diplomat and co-ordinator were essential to the success of the enterprise.

Center right: This image shows the camp of Lewis and Clark at the sources of the Columbia River.

elected president of the United States three years earlier, had carefully read MacKenzie's report and had for some time been considering sending an expedition to the lands west of the Mississippi. In 1803 the acquisition of Louisiana from France removed the last hurdles. The United States suddenly found themselves the masters of vast territories two thirds the size of India and almost completely unexplored (over 800,000 square miles of land for 27 million dollars, one of the greatest bargains in history). Louisiana was an immense chunk of America and included the entire course of the Mississippi and the Rocky Mountains. The exploration of the new frontier

became a political necessity. Jefferson moved rapidly and decisively. He soon obtained an initial grant of 2,500 dollars from Congress and commissioned his personal secretary, Meriwether Lewis, to take charge of the organization. Lewis was to assume command of the expedition, the aims and modus operandi of which had been previously established. As well as answering the geographical questions, Lewis had to establish peaceful relations with the Indian tribes on behalf of the new "White Father" in Washington and to collect as much information as possible about the flora, fauna, weather patterns, and resources of the boundless western territories. The explorers were invited to

FORT CLATSOP

RANGE

Columbia

Bitterroot

Marias

Missouri

Clearwater

CASCADE

LEWIS

CLARK

Yellowstone

FORT MANDAN

Pacific Ocean

R O C K Y   M O U N T A I N S

Snake

Mississippi

Platte

ST. LOUI

Colorado

L O U I S I A N A

Mississippi

Rio Grande

LEWIS AND CLARK 1804-1805

LEWIS AND CLARK 1806

keep a detailed diary of their observations and to trace maps that were as accurate as possible. The best cartographers and scientists in the United States coached Lewis in the use of scientific instruments and the principal notions regarding botany, zoology, and natural history. Jefferson expected great results from this expedition and did not want to leave anything to chance. Conscious of the enormity of the task that he had been given, Lewis asked for and received permission to share the command with an old colleague of his, William Clark. Lewis was 29 and Clark 33, both had extensive experience of life in the wild regions and were accustomed to the pressures of command. Lewis insisted that Clark should have responsibilities and decision-making powers equal to his own. The personalities of the two men were complementary: Clark was an extrovert and had the gift of inspiring trust. Lewis on the other hand was quieter and more prudent, and his apparent romanticism concealed great organizational gifts. In the history of exploration, Lewis and Clark made one of the most successful couples: they never had

any serious disagreements and conducted their long and difficult expedition with skill and determination.

In the autumn of 1803, the expedition established its headquarters at St. Louis on the banks of the Mississippi: the future Gateway to the West was at that time little more than a village with a few houses. Lewis and Clark spent the winter assembling their equipment and supplies. Their stocks of food were rather meager: flour, salt, dried meat, and some emergency rations. Lewis intended to obtain most of the group's food en route, trusting the skill of the professional hunters that he had hired. The scientific equipment, the tools, the arms, and the gunpowder were divided into eight large packs. A robust chest continued the medical supplies and surgical instruments. The articles to be traded with the Indians filled fifteen large sacks and chests and included an infinite variety of baubles, braided uniforms, knives, cloth, and mirrors (the expedition's most expensive items). Lewis also carried with him a collapsible canoe formed from a metal frame that could be panelled with

skins of strips of bark and was baptised with the rather appropriate name of *Experiment*. The long period of preparation also served to train the mixed team of civilians and soldiers, and to establish the chains of command and the regulations that would ensure the group functioned smoothly during the exploration. Lewis and Clark knew that discipline would be indispensable to the success of the expedition. On the 14th of May, 1804, the 45 men chosen for the mission embarked on two boats and a large flat-bottomed barge equipped with sails and oars. The first part of the project involved ascending the Missouri as far as its source, an objective that was thought to be thousands of miles from St Louis. In late October the small fleet reached the Mandan territory close to the confluence with the Knife River in modern-day North Dakota: up to that point the Missouri was well known and used by traders and fur trappers. The expedition's navigation of the river was made dangerous by sandbanks and submerged trunks but had been completed without significant

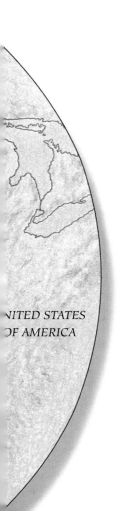

incident. The famed Sioux Indians had proven to be less hostile than anticipated. Mosquitoes aside, the expedition had yet to face any serious problems and now prepared to spend the winter in the Mandan villages. The Indians were friendly and observed the construction of huts and the strange customs of their guests with curiosity. York, Clark's black servant, attracted particular attention and by an overwhelming request, he was obliged to exhibit himself in dances and feats of strength while the most audacious spectators attempted to scrub the black from his skin. Lewis and Clark took on the interpreters and guides that would be indispensable to the expedition's progress. One of these, a French-Canadian named Toussaint Charbonneau, arrived at the camp in the company of his wife Sacajewea, a Shoshoni Indian snatched from her tribe when she was still a child. The Shoshoni lived in the Rocky Mountains region not far from the presumed source of the Missouri. As far as was known the Shoshoni used horses, an essential means of transport for the crossing of the mountain

Opposite: This painting by A. Wahlen from 1843 shows an Indian chief in all his finery. Lewis and Clark had received strict orders from President Thomas Jefferson with regards to the behavior they should adopt with the natives: they were always to prefer mediation to force even at the expense of the success of the expedition. Overcoming the diffidence of the Shoshoni chiefs, thanks largely to the help of Sacajewea, the explorers succeeded in obtaining horses and food as well as useful advice on how to tackle the difficulties of the journey.

Top: This painting, completed according to the information supplied by George Catlin, shows two Indians camouflaged with wolf skins while they stalked a herd of buffalo. In 1830, when Catlin undertook his journey into the Indian territories, the buffalo herd filled the prairies as far as the eye could see. However, from the mid-nineteenth century the massacre began: millions of animals were killed for their skins and in order to claim new pastures. As the prairies emptied, it was the beginning of the end for the Indian tribes. As the genocide began, a way of life and a culture was obliterated.

Center: This painting was also realized on the basis of George Catlin's indications and shows a dramatic moment during a bear hunt. Bears represented just one of the many problems that Lewis and Clark had to tackle during their explorations, together with rattle snakes, rainstorms, hail, and a lack of fresh food.

ranges separating the Missouri and Columbia Rivers. Lewis and Clark realized that the woman could prove to be the key to the success of the mission. Sacajewea gave birth during the winter, and it was decided that the new-born baby would follow the expedition. On the 7th of April the group left their base camp, which they had named Fort Mandan, heading west. The true exploration began at this point. Lewis did not hide his enthusiasm: "I would say this moment of departure is one of the happiest of my life," he wrote in his diary, "we are about to enter a vast region stretching at least 2,000 miles in which civilized man has never set foot." A team of twelve men was sent back to St Louis with the first taste of the West for Jefferson: notes, maps, objects, and scientific specimens, including a live prairie dog and birds. The expedition was now composed of 32 men, aboard 6 canoes and two large

boats. Lewis and Clark alternated sailing with long marches along the river banks. There was abundant game, and everything proceeded smoothly until the 14th of May when a sudden gust of wind caught one of the boats and threatened to sink it with all its cargo. The two commanders were ashore and could only watch helplessly. Fortunately Sacajewea kept her head and was able to save much of the baggage before it disappeared into the muddy waters of the Missouri. The scientific instruments were intact to Lewis's relief. Without his compass, chronometer, and sextant, it would have been impossible to draw up the maps Jefferson was counting on. This incident seemed to mark the beginning of a period of bad luck for the team. The men fell ill one after the other, and a group of hunters only just managed to escape from a wounded bear.

Lewis himself was almost bitten by a rattlesnake. On the 3rd of June, the explorers reached a fork in the river and decided to pitch a camp. They needed to rest as they were all exhausted, and they also had to decide on which branch to follow. At that point an error of judgement could have prejudiced the outcome of the mission. Which was the principal stream of the Missouri? The patrols sent to reconnoiter returned with confusing information. Everything seemed to point to the northern branch being the correct route, but Lewis was anything but convinced: the Indians had spoken of great cascades, a series of impassable cataracts that interrupted the course of the river. He had to find them. A few days later he left with a group of four men to fully explore the southern branch. On the 13th of June, after having

Top left: This painting from the school of George Catlin shows a group of Plains Indians. It was the vastness of the Great Plains and the possibility of limitless expansion beyond the Mississippi that encouraged President Jefferson to send two young officers to explore the region. Prior to their departure, Jefferson brought in the United States' leading scientists so that they could instruct Lewis and Clark in the rudiments of "botany, natural history, mineralogy, and astronomy."

Top left and opposite top: These drawings by Karl Bodmer show the regal dress of two Hidatsa Indians.

Left: This oil painting by Charles M. Russell from 1912 depicts Lewis and Clark with the Indians at Ross's Hole.

climbed a steep hill, he found himself facing "the grandest spectacle" he had ever seen. The Missouri, which at that point was almost 1000 feet wide, plunged downward in a series of foaming rapids almost 10 miles long. It took twelve exhausting days to bypass the falls through a rocky, barren landscape.

The canoes were fitted with wheels and axles and were hauled up the hill by the men. Violent storms battered the explorers, and at one point a flash flood threatened to wash men and materials downstream. After the tempest, Lewis collected a number of hail stones, the largest of which was 7 inches in diameter, more than large enough to kill a man. By mid-June, however, the canoes were once again navigating the tranquil waters of the Missouri. The river was now flowing south, parallel to the foothills of the Rocky Mountains. It was clear that the expedition would

soon have to proceed overland, and they would have to find horses. They were by now traveling through the Shoshoni territory, but the region appeared to be uninhabited. On the 25th of July, the explorers reached the point at which the Missouri splits into three branches. Following Sacajewea's directions they decided to ascend the western branch which they named the Jefferson River. Lewis realized that they had reached the continental watershed: from that point onward all the water ran to the west to eventually drain into the Pacific. It was a crucial moment and Lewis began to worry. The Indians seemed to have disappeared, and without pack animals, they had no hope of being able to cross the snow-covered mountains that obscured the horizon on all sides.

The expedition's first encounter with the Shoshoni occurred midway through August. The Indians were diffident and it took all Lewis's diplomatic skill to convince their chief, Cameahwait, that the white strangers had come in peace. The Shoshoni confirmed the expedition leader's fears – there was no navigable river to the west. As for the horses, the Indians appeared to have no intention of giving them to the explorers. Jefferson's orders were clear: rather than use force, the expedition would have to forego its objectives. The situation appeared to be at an impasse, and only the unexpected could have changed matters. The unexpected duly happened. Sacajewea, called upon to act as an interpreter, "entered the tent and sat down and when she began to translate, she recognized Cameahwait as her brother." By the end of the month, Lewis and Clark had managed to obtain 29 horses and a guide. Crossing the Bitterroot Ranges was extremely arduous. The first snow fell early in September, and the temperature fell rapidly. Men and animals proceeded slowly along the steep and seemingly endless mountain crests.

The expedition diaries contain the barest notes: "we killed a wolf and ate it"; "one of our horses slipped and rolled down the side of a hill." On the 20th of September the expedition descended into the valley of the Clearwater River. The plain was inhabited by the Pierced Nose tribe, and the exhausted men could finally regain their strength with fresh food. The Indians offered to tend the horses, which Lewis intended to use on the return journey. Five new canoes were built, and early in October the explorers took to

Above: Charles M. Russell's painting shows Lewis and Clark on the lower course of the Columbia River. Before reaching the Pacific, the expedition had to overcome a series of waterfalls and wild rapids as the river rushed between sheer rock walls. Moreover, the Chinook Indians were friendly but refused to sell the white men their supplies of dry fish, and the explorers were obliged to survive on the scarse game they were able to catch.

213

the water once again, heading for the Columbia River. The Clearwater flowed into the Snake and the Snake into the Columbia: the expedition's final objective appeared to be within reach. At least in theory. The first rapids and the first problems, immediately occured after the departure. On the 14th of October, three canoes were swept away by the current and hurled against the rocks. Part of their cargo was lost and a number of men risked drowning. The Columbia, which at the confluence with the Snake was more than half a mile wide, narrowed to 132 feet at some points. Almost every day the expedition had to tackle interminable series of rapids and falls, putting the stamina of the men to the severest tests. The river flowed between towering rock walls: it was difficult to land, and suitable camp sites were rare. The Indians that inhabited the Columbia were peaceful, friendly people. Salmon fishing was their principal activity, and in just one camp Lewis and Clark saw stocks of dried fish that must have weighed at least five tons. Nevertheless, given their lack of suitable trading goods, the explorers had to be content with what little game they were able to catch. On the 8th of November, in pouring rain, the expedition reached the river mouth and the Pacific. In the distance, behind an impenetrable curtain of fog, Clark could hear the crashing ocean waves. "What joy!" he wrote in his diary but rather unconvincingly. The expedition had reached it objective, but there was little to cheer about. At that time of the year, the mouth of the Columbia is a hellish place blasted by freezing winds and continual rain. Soaked through and numb with cold, the men wandered along the shores of the bay for weeks in search of a suitable place in which to spend the winter. Lewis knew that the dense fog meant they had no hope of being spotted and picked up by a passing ship. At the end of November, they began to construct their winter lodgings on the south bank of the river. There was nothing further they could do except wait for the better weather of spring. The winter months were long and monotonous. Food was in short supply, and Lewis noted bitterly that there had been only six fine days in the entire period. On the 23rd of March, 1806, the

expedition set off again, heading toward the East. Lewis and Clark initially followed their outward route in reverse until they had crossed the mountains for the second time, at which point they split up. Lewis followed an overland route to the north of the Missouri, exploring the northern basin while Clark descended the entire length of the Yellowstone River. The two groups met up again at Fort Mandan, the first base camp, in mid-August. They eventually reached St. Louis on the 23rd of September, 1806. The returns on the total of 38,000 dollars that the enterprise had cost were more than satisfactory: Lewis and Clark may not have found a practicable river route to the Pacific, but they had discovered five passes across the Rocky Mountains and drawn up the first reliable maps of those vast regions. Their diaries contained not only descriptions of the river systems, mountains, animals, and plants (no less than 122 species and sub-species previously unknown to science), people and natural environments, they also presented America with a new frontier. Thus was born that obsession with the West that was to dominate the imagination and politics of the nation for over a century. The conquest of the Wild West had begun.

Top left: This painting depicts a break during the navigation of the Columbia, in the foreground are Lewis and Clark while seated behind them are Sacajewea and her husband Toussaint Charbonneau. The Indian guide, thanks to her knowledge of the territory and her intelligence, played a significant role in the expedition she followed and sometimes led through to its return to St. Louis.

EXPEDITION DIARIES

Broadly speaking, from 1700 onward one can distinguish two kinds of explorer, corresponding to different ways of compiling their expedition diaries. The first category comprised those explorers working for third parties with political or scientific interests (a government or a geographical society). The others take their place within that broad group motivated by direct contact with their public. In the first case (for example Lewis and Clark) the explorers were asked not only for a chronological account of events, but also for answers to a series of questions regarding the climate, inhabitants, soil composition, longitude and latitude, flora and fauna, and so on, of the places through which they had traveled. Ever since the Renaissance there had been treatises that defined the various areas of investigation: a German author writing in 1789 codified 37 fields of enquiry, subdivided into 2,443 specific questions. The expedition diary in this case became a list of data. The required style was concise and dry with an impersonal point of view.

In the second case the explorer was simply recounting his story and the form was that of reportage. Until the advent of the mass media, firstly national newspapers and then radio and television, expedition diaries were the only means of diffusing news of distant lands that were inaccessible to the vast majority of people. It was no coincidence that many explorers were also journalists (Stanley being the classic example). The traveler's tale thus had to satisfy the tastes of the public, with the sensational taking pride of place: strange customs and more or less revolting habits, cannibalism, and hostile tribes. The authors knew their accounts could never be verified: their expedition diaries were their own personal vision of reality, based on the comparison of the savage and the civilized, the hostile and the friendly, good and bad, beautiful and ugly. The photographic diaries compiled in the most remote corners of the globe by modern tourists are to some extent a continuation of this tradition.

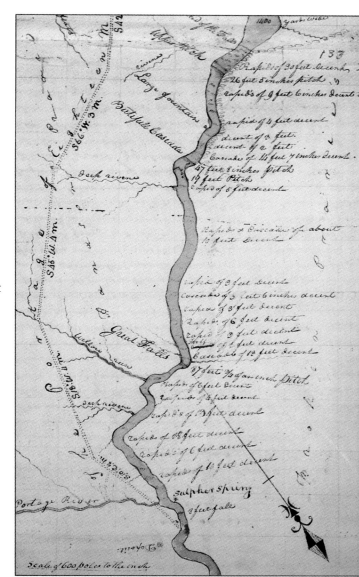

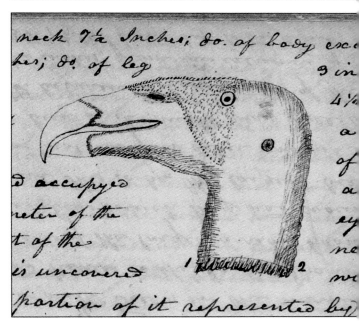

Above center: This sketch, rich in information and notes, taken from the diaries of Lewis and Clark, shows the great rapids on the Colombia River. President Jefferson's explicit orders invited each member of the expedition to compile a detailed diary, noting all they felt to be significant. At least seven men, as well as Lewis and Clark, followed these orders.

Right: The expedition diary compiled by the two leaders was written on special water-resistant birch paper. The illustration at the top shows a page from Lewis's journal, probably from the 4th of July, 1805, showing his survey of the course of the Missouri and in particular the great cascades region. The lower illustration shows a vulture sketched on the 17th of February, 1806.

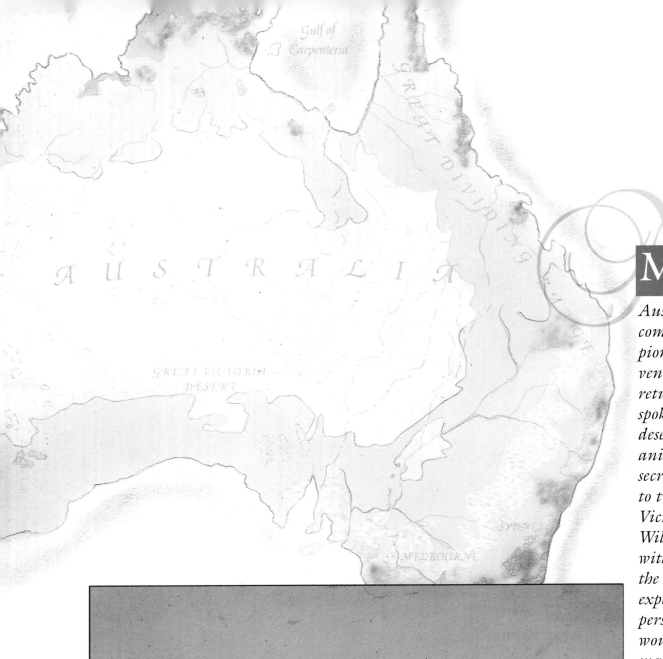

idway through the last century, the heart of the Australian continent was still completely unknown. The few pioneers and explorers who had ventured into the outback had all returned defeated: their accounts spoke of Stone Age tribes, endless deserts, and strange plants and animals. The task of revealing the secrets of the interior eventually fell to two young immigrants from the Victoria colony. In 1860, Burke and Wills left Melbourne heading north with the ambitious plan of reaching the Gulf of Carpentaria. Lacking experience, badly organized, and persecuted by bad luck, the two would-be explorers nevertheless managed to reach the north coast. Their great mission had been accomplished, but Burke and Wills died on their return journey, and the entire expedition ended in disaster. In a blend of farce and tragedy, Australia had for the first time been crossed from South to North.

THE EMPTY CONTINENT

ROBERT O'HARA BURKE AND WILLIAM JOHN WILLS

Top: A portrait of William John Wills, the expedition's topographer. Reserved, quiet, and rather shy, Wills was just 26 when he joined the expedition. His personality was diametrically opposed to that of Burke, but the relations between the two were always excellent, and Wills was perhaps the only expedition member never to doubt Burke's frequently reckless decisions.

Dream-Time. The totemic ancestors left their subterranean domain and sang the features of the world into existence. The reality created during the Dream-Time was a primordial land, an endless desert. The Aborigines have lived there for thousands of years: as far as they are concerned the arid heart of Australia is by no means empty. It is criss-crossed by a dense network of mythical lines and symbols. Clinging to the coastline, the first Europeans to colonize the country saw the interior of the new continent as nothing more than a desolate land to be feared. It was as inaccessible and unknown as the surface of another planet. The discovery of gold in 1851 led to a rapid change in attitudes: within just a few months tens of thousands of men flooded into Victoria in search of their fortune. Melbourne was transformed from a village into a thriving town. A contemporary reporter pulled no punches in describing it as crowded with "thugs, gamblers, and drunks" and full of infamous bars and prostitutes: anything but a sacred topography. Pioneers and golddiggers set up shop along the Murray and Darling Rivers a few hundred miles inland, but nobody had yet ventured beyond Menindee, the last outpost of civilization. Charles Sturt penetrated as far as the Simpson Desert, and a German immigrant, Leichhardt had followed the northwest coast from Brisbane to the Gulf of Carpentaria. Leichhardt departed again in 1848, determined to cross the country from east to west, but his expedition disappeared creating a great sensation. The geographical center of Australia appeared to be inviolable, and the accounts of survivors referred to the horrors of the heat, thirst, and hostile natives, while the belief spread that the interior of the continent concealed an inland sea. Seas apart, thought some, the interior territories might offer good grazing land for sheep and who knows what other riches. Moreover, a North-South route to the Gulf of Carpentaria would allow Melbourne to be directly linked to the telegraph lines that had already reached Southeast Asia, thus overcoming the colony's isolation. It was just such a blend of pragmatism that persuaded the new-born Victoria Philosophical Institute to get involved in a continental exploration.

Opposite top: This drawing by Ludwig Becler, the expedition's naturalist shows the caravan with Burke portrayed between the two wings, in the saddle of his favorite horse.

Opposite bottom: This bas-relief by Charles Rudd depicts the caravan setting out on the conquest of the Australian desert.

Above: A portrait of Robert O'Hara Burke. Selected by the Royal Society of Victoria to lead the great expedition to the interior of the continent, Burke was an ex-policeman of Irish descent, with no experience of traveling in the bush. His brusque and irascible character contributed to the differences of opinion among the expedition members.

A wave of enthusiasm led to the collection of the sum of 9,000 pounds and an organizational structure was prepared, at least on paper. All that remained was to find the right man to lead the expedition. The exploration committee interviewed many candidates and eventually chose, for reasons that are difficult to understand, a police superintendent named Robert O'Hara Burke. Burke was then 39 years old, boasted an honorable police career, but had no experience of exploration. In contrast with his public image, Burke's private life was rather unstable: tempestuous love affairs, gambling debts, and extravagant habits. Unmarried and penniless, Burke was above all a soldier and would run the expedition as such. A fist of steel, a notion for self-sacrifice, and a dash of romanticism were the qualities the committee felt indispensable for success. In reality, the bush proved a far more subtle adversary than had been expected. The euphoria of the moment had now gripped the protagonists, however, and the urgency of the preparations soon overwhelmed any lingering doubts. Burke selected around fifteen men: a couple of naturalists, a topographer (John Wills), a group of assistants (including John King and William Brahe) with a variety of talents, and a shady character called James Landells, who acted as the second in command of the ill-assorted group. The only certainty known about Landells was his love of money: he actually succeeded in obtaining a higher salary than his leader and was sent to distant Afghanistan to acquire 25 camels. What with the travel and shipping expenses, these animals cost over half of the sum allocated to the expedition. Landells also brought three Indians back to Australia with him: along with King, whom he had met en route, they were to have handle the camels. Nobody thought to question how four men could have been expected to cope with all those animals, loading them, and allowing them to graze without losing them. The caravan was completed with 27 horses and two covered wagons. The carnival atmosphere reached its climax when Landells, dressed in Eastern costume, made his grand entrance to Melbourne amidst cheering crowds. The expedition's supplies and equipment (all 21 tons of it) included tents, camp-beds, farrier's tools,

217

clothing for occasions, a small library, surgical instruments, a veritable armory, and enough food for an eighteen-month trip. Apart from dried meat, biscuits, jam and flour, the provisions included numerous demijohns of lemon juice as protection against scurvy and 5 gallons of brandy. Even the camels' presumed preferences had been taken into consideration: Landells claimed that there was no better cure for a sick animal than rum, and consequently 70 gallons were taken along. The orders given by the

expedition committee were rather vague: an itinerary was suggested, but if the route proved to be impracticables the explorers were free to head west, or east, or in any other possible direction. Still, it has to be said that nothing was known about the outback, except that according to Sturt there was always water at Cooper Creek. It was decided to establish a base camp there as a point of departure for the final advance. The expedition left Melbourne's Royal Park on the 20th of August, 1860, in "picturesque confusion," saluted by

thousands of people and with Burke leading the interminable caravan on horseback. The first problems came to light immediately. The early rains had reduced the roads to muddy furrows that slowed the progress of the wagons, and the camels were overloaded. Burke soon came to the conclusion that they would not get far under those conditions.

On the 6th of September, the caravan reached Swan Hill, a village on the Murray River. During the halt, Burke decided to auction off part of the provisions, including the lemon juice and some sugar. It is difficult to understand the reasoning behind his decision, but this was certainly the first in an interminable series of errors: lemon juice, as Cook had demonstrated a century earlier, was an indispensable remedy for scurvy; and sugar was important for providing emergency energy. Burke, however, had no hesitation in dispensing with these supplies. In the meantime the relations between the members of the group were degenerating: six men abandoned the expedition, and Burke enrolled another two including an unemployed ex-sailor named Charles Gray. Early in October, the expedition reached Menindee, the last inhabited outpost before the great emptiness. At Menindee the incompatibility between Burke and Landells exploded into open conflict: Burke accused his lieutenant of being incompetent and a liar, while in Landells's eyes, Burke was simply insane. They had nothing more to say to each other and Landells returned to Melbourne. The caravan was in a pitiful state. Many animals were sick and the men were divided. The heavy wagons caused exhausting delays, and the expenses were spiralling out of control. The news that another expedition, led by Sturt, was being equipped to cross the continent acted as a catalyst. Burke was now in a hurry and decided to restructure the caravan, dividing it into two groups. On the 19th of October, Burke, Wills, Gray, Brahe, King, and another 3 men, 16 camels and 15 of the best horses left Menindee heading for Cooper Creek, 372 miles to the north.

Top: John King, the only survivor of the Burke and Wills expedition to the Gulf of Carpentaria, together with the more the ambiguous figure of James Landells, who was responsible for the camels.

Right: Charles Gray, an unemployed sailor, was enrolled by Burke following the considerable differences of opinion that led six men to leave the expedition.

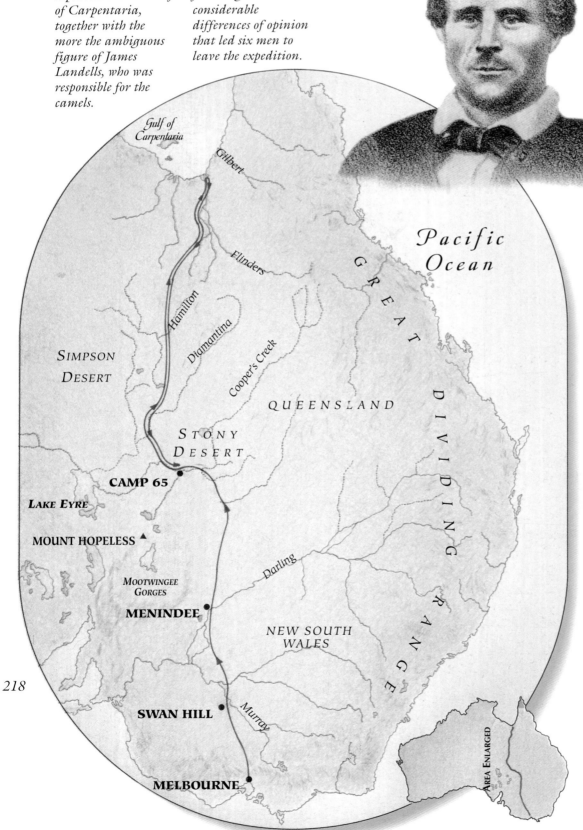

The rest of the caravan had orders to remain at the camp until the exhausted animals were able to depart and then reach the advance party at the Cooper Creek base camp. The command of the second group was entrusted to William Wright, a former sheep farmer that Burke had met during the march. Wright knew the region, and although he was hardly the most brilliant of figures, Burke trusted him. Events were to transform him into an unwitting but decisive element in the destiny of the expedition. The light, self-contained advance party moved swiftly across the plain extending beyond the Darling River. Wright was well acquainted with the area, and with his help the group soon reached the Mootwingee gorges, a sacred site for the Wilyakali Aborigines. Wills was struck by the sinister solemnity of the place, but none of the men noticed the pictures decorating the walls of the caves in the mountainside. As far as the explorers were concerned, the Aborigines were barely human: they had nothing to learn from those "vile and despicable" savages, and each evening Burke prepared his camp as if to defend it from attack. Wright returned to Menindee on the 29th of October while the advance party headed on through increasingly desert-like terrain. They were fortunate in that there was always abundant supplies of water. On the 11th of November, the expedition reached the deep pools of Cooper Creek. The first part of the journey had been completed without incident and, as Wills wrote, it had been nothing more than a "simple country walk." Burke and his men had covered the 372 miles from Menindee to Cooper Creek in less than 25 days. The organizational problems appeared to have been resolved and the objective to be within their grasp. The group now had to establish a permanent camp in that area rich in water. Burke intended to divide the group once again and to march with a few men and light packs to the Gulf of Carpentaria. There was no need to wait for Wright who was due to arrive shortly. Brahe was to remain at the camp, the 65th camp since Melbourne, with three men and the bulk of the supplies. Burke, Wills, Gray, and King with six camels and a horse were to proceed north. Burke was optimistic, and he trusted in the logistical agility of a small group of determined men. According to his calculations, twelve weeks would be sufficient to reach the coast and return rapidly to the base camp. The list of rations destined to feed four men was short: 374 pounds of flour, 198 pounds of dried and salted meat, 50 pounds of rice, a few pounds of biscuits, a little over 4 pounds of salt, 11 pounds of tea, a few cans of vegetables, and a ridiculous quantity of sugar (just 50 pounds, less than 2.5 ances per day for each man). Burke judged that tents were superfluous. His agreement with Brahe was rather vague: the German was to have waited for the group for around three months after which period he was free to decide what to do. In any case Burke left no written instructions. The small group of men disappeared over the horizon on the morning of the 16th of December: facing them were 744 miles of unknown territory. It was now high summer. Judging by the laconic diary kept by Burke, the group forced the pace, and by Christmas they had reached the borders of the Stony Desert

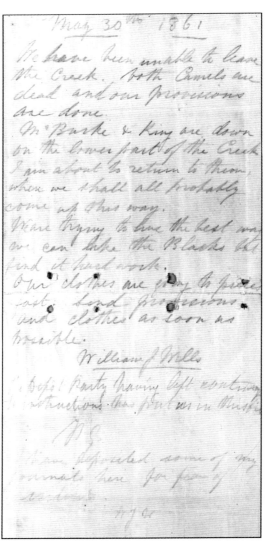

which they crossed without difficulty. On the 1st of January, Burke wrote just one word in his diary: "water." On the 2nd of January "Marched nine and a half hours. Desert." On the 4th, "Twelve hours traveling." Each morning King had to recover the camels that had wandered off in search of pasture, an exhausting task that could take him hours. Burke spared neither men nor animals, and he avoided any contact with the Aborigines: his sole preoccupation in this respect was to keep them at a distance. By the end of January, 1861, the expedition had entered the tropical region of Queensland: the bush became denser and taller, and the heat was oppressive. When the rains began, heavy downfalls transformed the dust into mud, and the march soon became a nightmare. The camels got bogged down in continuation, and it was decided to abandon them. Burke and Wills headed on alone, leaving King and Gray to take care of the animals: the sea was just 31 miles away. Under streaming rain and tormented by mosquitoes, Burke and Wills forced a way through the labyrinth of pools and streams. A week later, in a state of exhaustion, they reached the mangrove swamps. The Gulf of Carpentaria was but a short distance away, but this last great hurdle obstructed the explorers. It was only the rising tide that proved that they had actually reached the coast. Burke and Wills retraced their steps, their mission accomplished, but they now had to tackle the return journey. With the obligation to advance at all costs having been removed, Wills was able to take stock and realized that they were facing problems: "It has taken us two months to reach this place from Cooper Creek, but we are left with provisions for just one month. It is not an attractive proposition." They had paid dearly in fatigue to traverse Australia and had not even had the satisfaction of seeing the sea thanks to the mangrove swamps. Wills had perhaps begun to harbor doubts as to the expedition's success, but he could hardly have predicted the imminent disaster. The rains showed no mercy, making the march more difficult day by day, and the nights spent in the open were horrific.

Exhausted, the four men headed south, their only hope being to reach Cooper Creek as soon as possible. Little is known of that return journey. Burke and Wills's diaries contain very few notes and the entries become briefer with each passing day. Gray's condition worsened early in March. His companions ignored his complaints, and he decided to look out for himself by stealing the remaining food supplies. Burke was furious when he caught him and struck him with all his remaining strength. This was on the 25th of March, 40 days after they had left the Gulf of Carpentaria. The group was only half way to Cooper Creek and the rations had to be further restricted. By the 10th of April, only two camels survived and a week later Gray died. In the meantime Brahe was having problems of his own at the base camp. For over three months he had been scanning the horizon as he awaited the return of his companions, and he now began to wonder what he should do. Wright should have reached the camp just a few days after Burke's departure but nothing had been seen of him. What was the use in planning meetings if nobody turned up? How long, and for whom, should he wait? The days passed slowly. The men were being brutalized by the way of life at the camp and some of them had fallen ill. The rains then began, and the camp was infested with rats and mosquitoes. After a four-month wait Cooper Creek had become insufferable and Brahe decided to leave on the 21st of April.

At 10:30 in the morning, the caravan moved out heading for Menindee. While Brahme was making his last preparations for the departure, Burke, Wills, and King were camping 31 miles away from Cooper Creek: they ate their remaining rations and prepared to spend yet another freezing night in the open. The following day required one last effort, and they would have made it. In a remarkable demonstration of stamina for men in their condition, they reached the base camp at 7:30 in the evening. There was no light, and no sign of movement. Perhaps Brahe had moved to higher ground? The horrible truth slowly sank into Burke's fatigue-dulled mind. There was no one there and no one would ever return to Cooper Creek. They were doomed. Wills then noticed an inscription in the bark of a eucalyptus tree. By moonlight he read the following words: "Dig three feet northwest. 21st April 1861." They found a buried a supply of food and a message from Brahe describing his planned itinerary and the reasons for his departure. A deathly silence reigned over the abandoned camp: after four months traveling Burke and his companions had missed the rendezvous by a matter of hours. Stunned by the atrocious irony of their situation, they ate some of the rations before falling into a deep sleep. The reality of their situation became clear the following day. They were alone and trapped within the Cooper valley. They had rations sufficient for a number of days; perhaps they could still make it. They had to answer the fundamental question of where they should go. Should they try to catch up with Brahe, or head toward the settlements near Mount Hopeless 155 miles away? Burke decided on the second option. He could hardly have imagined that Brahe (who in the meantime had met up with Wright on his way to Cooper Creek) would have returned to the camp to search for them. At this point there is an air of inevitability about the events that follow. Wright's story was farcical: he remained penniless at Menindee for over three months. When he received funds from Melbourne, he tried to organize the support expedition, but incapable of managing a complex structure such as a caravan, he soon found himself in difficulties. There was nobody capable of driving the camels and half of the men fell seriously ill with scurvy. The caravan advanced with exasperating slowness and apathy was added to the expedition's technical errors. When Wright and Brahe arrived back at the base camp, Burke and his companions had already left in the opposite direction, and the two men failed even to notice the signs of their passing. If they had dug at the foot of the same eucalyptus tree they would have found a message from Wills. They failed to do so. The rest of the story is a chronicle of tragedy: trapped within the Cooper Creek valley lacking food and camels, the three survivors tried to keep alive with the aid of the Aborigines. They learned to gather nardoo seeds (*Marsilea quadrifolia*) and obtain an edible flour. However, it was too late: they no longer had the strength and lucidity to deal with the situation. All of the paths leading away from the river petered out in the desert. On the 30th of May, Wills left a last message at base camp: "All the camels are dead and the supplies exhausted. We are trying to survive as best we can, like the natives do, but it is difficult. Our clothes are falling to pieces. Send supplies and clothing as soon as possible." Burke died on the 30th of June, Wills a couple of days later. King, found moribund by the Aborigines, was picked up by a rescue expedition on the 15th of September. The tragedy of Cooper Creek was only the closing verse in a litany of woes. Death, disease, defection, and argument: the entire expedition disappeared, crushed by a chain of events that for the most part could have been avoided. Just a few weeks after the departure from Melbourne, the expeditions organization was falling apart at the seams, and it was clear that a dramatic finale was looming. Burke had no experience as an explorer, and none of those involved in the expedition (promoters included) appeared to have the faintest idea how to go about things. The entire enterprise was based on individual initiative, as if brute force and extrovert personalities would inevitably get the better of the environment. There is more to exploration than reaching an objective: you also need to get back home alive (survival being an essential criteria in judging the success of an expedition). The caravan is an artificial structure, that allows the explorer to cross territories in which he is a biological outcast. It is an organism to be managed with skill if disaster is to be avoided. Burke was not simply unfortunate: 1860 was a favorable year, and the expedition found water everywhere. He had all the necessary means with which to lead the expedition to a successful conclusion. His errors were due to inexperience and poor organization. Burke erred in his selection of companions (firstly Landells and then Wright), in the packing of equipment and food supplies and in not keeping a proper diary and not leaving written instructions for Brahe. None of the men knew how to work with camels, and the animals were overloaded and treated badly. A camel can go for long periods without drinking but must eat regularly. However, there was never sufficient time to allow the animals to graze, firstly because of the hurry to reach the coast, and then because of the need to return to base camp as soon as possible. The greatest error committed by Burke and his companions was in their attitude toward the Aborigines and their absolute refusal to establish relations. The unknown is unknown for those exploring, not for those who live there: with the help of the locals, the group could have learned to extract the resources they so desperately needed from the environment. By the time the survivors eventually realized that the Aborigines were their only hope, it was too late. The tragedy had run its course.

Above: This oil painting of 1911 by Strutt depicts the burial of Burke. The death of Burke and Wills aroused great scandal in Australia. A commission of enquiry was established to ascertain the degree of responsibility of Brahe and Wright, but the case was dismissed, and the blame was attached to Burke. As a last affront, the committee that had backed the expedition refused to pay his gambling debt of £18.

Right: The tragic destiny of Burke and Wills caught the imagination of the Australian public, and the press devoted ample space to the story of the two explorers, as shown by this engraving published in the Illustrated Melbourne Post on the 1st of January, 1863, which depicts the funeral procession.

Even though Europe had already explored most of the rest of the world, Africa, just the other side of the Mediterranean, remained an inaccessible mystery. Harborless coastlines, rivers interrupted by rapids, rugged coastal mountains: the very physical conformation of the continent appeared to be designed to prevent penetration of the interior. An immense Terra Incognita in which no white man had ever set foot stretched from Timbuktu to the Orange River. At the beginning of the last century, Africa was a single, immense geographical enigma. Even the source of the Nile, the waters of which had given life and vigor to the ancient Egyptian civilization had yet to be discovered. This was the reality facing the pioneer explorers: over the following few decades their journeys were to fill the vacuum with names, mountains, plateaus, and river systems. A new continent and its people were about to enter European history. At the end of the century, the discovery of Lake Turkana, the last of the legendary inland seas, filled in the remaining blank space on the maps and concluded the heroic phase of African exploration.

AFRICA:
THE LAST GREAT ENIGMA

RENÉ CAILLÉ

"Nothing is to be seen in any direction except immense plains of sand, of a white that merges into yellow and of an extreme aridity. The sky is a pale red on the horizon. There is an infinite sadness in the nature; a total silence reigns; not a bird is heard to sing. Nevertheless there is something striking that I find difficult to explain in such a large city built in the middle of the sands, and you cannot but admire the audacity of its founders." This was how, on the 20th of April, 1828, René Caillé described his arrival in Timbuktu, the legendary city on the Niger and his lifetime's ambition, that he had reached after a year's traveling and unspeakable suffering.

Caillé was the prototype of the self-made man: of humble origins (his father had died in jail when he was just seven years old), lacking influential friends, education, and means, he strove after his objectives with extraordinary tenacity, finally succeeding where many before him had failed. It was perhaps in the slumbering village of Mauzé, in the French province of Poitou, not far from the Atlantic coast, that the young shoemaker was possessed by his African vision. The travel books that he devoured were no longer sufficient to satisfy his hunger: Africa had become an obsession, and Caillé grasped the first opportunity that came his way to embark as a cabin boy on a ship heading for Senegal. He was then sixteen years old and had a little less than 60 francs to his name. His first attempts to penetrate the interior of the continent were all unqualified disasters, but failure did nothing but strengthen his determination. When, in 1826, Caillé reappeared on the coast of Senegal for the third time, he had a precise objective in mind: to reach Timbuktu at all costs. The destinies of the previous expeditions inland were hardly encouraging: apart from the unpleasant climate and the geographical obstacles, the exploration of West Africa was made difficult by the hostility of the native peoples, the majority of whom had been converted to Islam. It was clear that no Christian was welcome in the unknown domains of Islam, of which Timbuktu, a center of wealth and knowledge, was the beating heart. All that was then known in Europe about the

mysterious city was based on the accounts of the ancient Arab travelers, and those few and fragmentary reports supplied by merchant adventurers of dubious reliability. Even the precise geographical location of Timbuktu was unknown to the Europeans, and the broad white spaces on the maps left ample room for the imagination. In the summer of 1826, a British explorer, Alexander Gordon Laing, had actually succeeded in entering the city, crossing the Sahara along the interminable caravan trails that, ever since most remote of ages, had connected the Niger and the Mediterranean. Laing never returned to Europe, however: on his return journey he was assassinated by members of his own caravan. His tragic end convinced Caillé that there was only one way of surviving the enterprise: he would have to renounce his own identity, and exchange his European clothes for those of the Muslim pilgrims. It was more than simple camouflage: even the most careful of disguises would not have fooled the Moors. It was therefore vital that Caillé immersed himself in his new personality, learning the dictates of the Koran and to

speak Arabic. Caillé's true journey, or rather its prologue, commenced in September, 1824: having left Saint-Louis on the Sengal estuary (then a French possession), he headed for the Maure tribes along the left bank of the river. There, the guest of the Emir of Brakna, he stayed for over a year, studying Arabic and immersing himself in the customs and etiquette of Islam. The first important step of his new career had been taken. Now Caillé needed money. He appealed to the governor of Saint-Louis for help but without success: he then found work as a guardian, but soon realized that his miserable salary would never have allowed him to save sufficient funds to finance his projects. Renouncing his national pride, he thus transferred to Sierra Leone, hoping that the British authorities would prove to be more generous, but was again to be disappointed. However, at Freetown, the capital of the colony, he found a job with the local administration that paid a decent salary. In the meantime, he had invented a story and had taken care to make it known to the city's native traders who would undoubtedly have spread it to the four

223

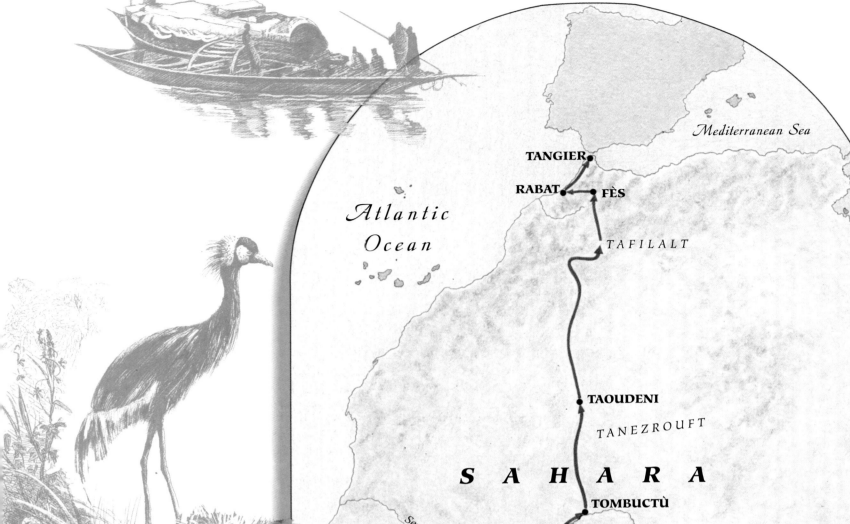

Atlantic
Ocean

Mediterranean Sea

TANGIER

RABAT   FÈS

TAFILALT

TAOUDENI

TANEZROUFT

S A H A R A

TOMBUCTÙ

Senegal

SENEGAL

Niger

DJENNÉ

Río Nunez

KOUROUSSA

KANKAN

TIÉMÉ

FREETOWN

Gulf of Guinea

winds during their travels through the interior: his real name, he revealed, was Abd-allahi, he was born in Egypt and had been kidnapped as a child by French soldiers under Napoleon and taken to Senegal. The one desire of Caillé-Abd-allahi was to return to the land of his fathers in search of what remained of his family. At the end of March, 1827, having converted all his savings (2,000 Francs) into gold, silver, and goods to trade, he dressed in Arab clothing, and set sail from Freetown for the mouth of the Rio Nunez (near the present day Boké in Guinea). His great adventure was finally underway. After a few days waiting, Caillé joined up with a caravan of Mandingo traders who, with their cargo of salt, aimed to reach the

mountains of Fouta Djallon and the markets of the upper Niger. The first few weeks of the march were tiring but pleasant: the country was rich and well cultivated, and the natives were friendly. Even though he was obliged to repeat his rather suspect story countless times, Caillé was well received wherever he went, and every evening when the sun set he retired into the privacy of the dense forest to write up his notes. As often happens in Africa to solitary travelers without a precise social status, the foreigner was soon attributed with the powers of a healer: he had no medical knowledge whatsoever but, in recompense, he was highly inventive and immediately inspired faith in his improvised patients. On the 11th of June,

the caravan reached Kouroussa on the Niger and proceeded toward Kankan, at that time an important commercial town and a communications center between the coastal region of the Gulf of Guinea and the internal countries. Just four days' march northwest of Kankan, noted Caillé in his diary, lay the legendary country of Bouré, the source of the gold that lay at the roots of the great Sudanese empires of the past and the hub of trans-Saharan commerce. The mines of Bouré had made the fortune of the cities along the Niger and of Timbuktu itself. The mysterious metropolis was perhaps beyond those impenetrable forests, but where? How many weeks, or months, of traveling before he reached his objective? Caillé had no idea, and was unable to pick up any reliable information. In the last few weeks the heat had become unbearable, an unmistakable sign of the arrival of the rainy season. On the 3rd of August, seriously ill and weak, the explorer reached the village of Tiémé, in Bambara territory on the borders between the modern-day states of Mali and the Ivory Coast. This was the starting point for the caravans heading for Djenné, the market town on the internal delta of the Niger and an obligatory staging post on the route to Timbuktu. Caillé realized that he could go no further: prostrated by frequent bouts of fever and lamed by a severe infection of one leg, he decided to stop at Tiémé. Then came the incessant, torrential rains. Rather than improve, his condition worsened.

Early in November, he was struck by atrocious pains in his jaw, the first unequivocal symptom of scurvy: "I soon experienced all the horrors of that terrible illness," he wrote, "Strips of flesh hung off my palate, together with fragments of bone, while my teeth seemed about to fall from their sockets... I was soon reduced to

a skeleton... Only one thought ran through my mind, that of death. I desired it and implored the Lord to grant me a rapid passage." By the end of December the storms were less frequent and less violent and Caillé regained hope. For five long months he had survived lying on the damp floor of a hut with no other help than that provided by the family that had taken him in, alone and isolated in the heart of an unknown country. He had frequently approached the threshold of desperation and madness, but had finally pulled through. As he gradually regained his strength, his thoughts returned once more to his journey. At last, on the 9th of January, 1828, he left Tiémé with a caravan heading to Djenné, arriving two months later. The local Sultan benevolently accepted his story, offering him his protection. On the 23rd of March, armed with a precious letter of introduction for the notables of Timbuktu, Caillé abandoned the crowded port of Djenné aboard a cargo boat heading north. The navigation of the Niger through the monotonous flood plains of the internal

Below: An image of Timbuktu taken from the diaries of René Caillé, the first European to visit the mysterious city that he described as squalid and already ruined. Twenty-five years later, Barth gained a different impression: Timbuktu, albeit far from its celebrated medieval splendors, appeared to him to be a lively and crowded market, the prosperity of which was based on the trade in gold, salt, and cola nuts (Cola acuminata, a mild stimulant). Caillé's account, he pointed out, was guilty of "grave inaccuracy."

delta, was slow and tiring. After three weeks' sailing, the villages began to become less frequent, and the first yellow sand dunes appeared on the left bank of the river. As it flowed out of Lake Debo, the Niger turned northwest, entering the desert, the undisputed domain of the Tuareg nomads. During the hours of daylight, Caillé was now obliged to remain hidden in a poky cabin below decks. Had the Tuaregs discovered an Arab on board they would have demanded greater tributes than those they punctually collected each evening. Not until the 19th of April could the explorer emerge from his uncomfortable hiding place, once the boat had reached Kabara, the river port of Timbuktu, just a few hours walk from the city walls. Timbuktu presented itself before his eyes at twilight: the minarets of its three mosques were silhouetted against the sky on the horizon of a barren desert. Was this then the fabulous city for which he had suffered so much? The irrepressible joy of discovery was overwhelmed by disappointment: Timbuktu was nothing more than a huddle of mud-colored houses. An atmosphere of tedium and

indolence pervaded the silent streets and squares. Not only was there no gold or wealth, but even the most common of goods, even firewood, were rarities. The following day Caillé was received by the local sheikh: he was assigned a house, right in front of the one that had been inhabited two years earlier by the unfortunate Laing, and was free to wander the city as he pleased. Timbuktu, he observed, had around 12,000 inhabitants whose survival depended absolutely on the caravan and river trade, and who lived under the tacit and continual threat of the Tuareg bandits who could at any time cut the supply lines and reduce the city to starvation.
Caillé had seen enough: the city that had been his lifetime's dream was no longer of any interest to him. Other matters now preoccupied him. For how long, he asked himself, would he be able to maintain his cover? Were he to be unmasked his fate would certainly be no better than that of Laing. If he managed to avoid death then slavery would await him. Reluctantly, the sheikh, who had taken to Caillé, authorized his departure for the 4th of May, together with a caravan of camels

heading toward the distant oasis of southern Morocco. Crossing the Sahara was uniquely arduous: for almost three months the caravan of over 1,400 animals loaded with ivory, gold, ostrich feathers, textiles, and luxury goods from the Sudan, advanced across the seemingly endless Tanezrouft plain that Caillé judged to be similar to "a dry ocean floor." The heat was atrocious and the men were constantly tormented by thirst: hundreds of miles separated one well from the next, and the slightest error of navigation or miscalculation of the caravan's resources could be fatal. "I thought of nothing but water," the explorer confessed in his notes, "rivers, streams, and brooks were all that came into my mind in that burning delirium." After the Taoudeni salt pans, an uninhabitable hell at the heart of the Sahara, the watering holes became more frequent and the march easier. At the end of the third week in July; the oasis of Tafilalt in the extreme south of Morocco appeared on the horizon. The great desert had been conquered, and the terrible thirst was a thing of the past. Caillé's trials were not over, however. Having reached Fès on the 12th of August, the Frenchman realized that his false identity was in danger: in that cosmopolitan city, crowded with merchants and travelers it would be difficult to remain incognito. Moving with extreme caution, Caillé set off toward the Atlantic coast, in search of a French representative to whom he could reveal his secret. Given the cold shoulder at Rabat, he proceeded on to Tangier where, after repeated attempts, he succeeded in persuading the consul (who had mistaken him for a beggar) to repatriate him. On the 27th of September, having abandoned his disguise for ever, Caillé set sail from Tangier heading for Toulon. The lone explorer soon became one of the most celebrated figures in France: he was invested as a knight in the Legion of Honor and was granted a generous pension. However, his story failed to convince every one, both at home and abroad. There were those who suggested that Caillé was a braggart and that he had never seen Timbuktu but that having got hold of Laing's diaries, he had used them to his own ends. The argument found fertile ground in the growing colonial rivalry between France and Britain: the question of the discovery became a political and diplomatic affair. Embittered by the continual attacks on his integrity, Caillé sought refuge at Mauzé where he died around ten years later, a virtually forgotten man.

Above: Caillé, disguised as an Arab, writing up his notes (a plate from the first edition of Voyage à Tembouctou et à Jenné, *published in 1830). Each evening, with the excuse of meditating on the verses of the Koran, Caillé withdrew, away from suspicious eyes, and compiled his diary. In spite of the constant risk of being unmasked, the explorer kept a painstaking record of his adventures.*

227

HEINRICH BARTH

From 1828, when Renè Caillè reached the legendary Timbuktu for the first time, dozens of European explorers ventured onto the desert trails. Many of them were never to return, killed by the Tuaregs or overcome by adversity and disease. The accounts of the survivors (less than a third of those who set out) added little to Europe's knowledge of the Sahara, the southern regions of which were still wreathed in mystery. In 1846, an Englishman, Richardson, penetrated the Libyan desert following a slave caravan. His reports of the atrocities he witnessed in the region convinced Britain to organize an expedition with aims that were at once humanitarian, scientific, and commercial. Richardson's project called for the crossing of the Sahara to Lake Chad, and then the exploration of the eastern regions of the continent through to Zanzibar. Via the intervention of the Prussian embassy in London, two German scientists were invited to take part in the mission: Overweg, a geologist, and Heinrich Barth, a historian and geographer. Barth's curriculum described him as a "33 year old man, with a classical education including the modern languages, who speaks French, Spanish, and Italian as well as English and Arabic, and who has completed at his own expense a scientific expedition lasting some months along the coasts of the Mediterranean." Barth, a large man over six feet tall, had recently broken off his engagement and could hardly wait to depart. He immediately plunged into a study of all the available texts on West Africa and began a rigorous physical training program.

Top: This image shows an accurate portrait of Barth. Born at Hamburg in 1821, Heinrich Barth was a man of culture, blessed with an uncommon spirit of observation: historian, geographer, archaeologist, and ethnographer, he enthusiastically undertook the long and difficult journey that was to lead him as far afield as Timbuktu and Lake Chad. His diaries, edited with meticulous care and assiduousness, are still today a precious mine of information for travelers and academics interested in the Sahara and Sudanese Africa.

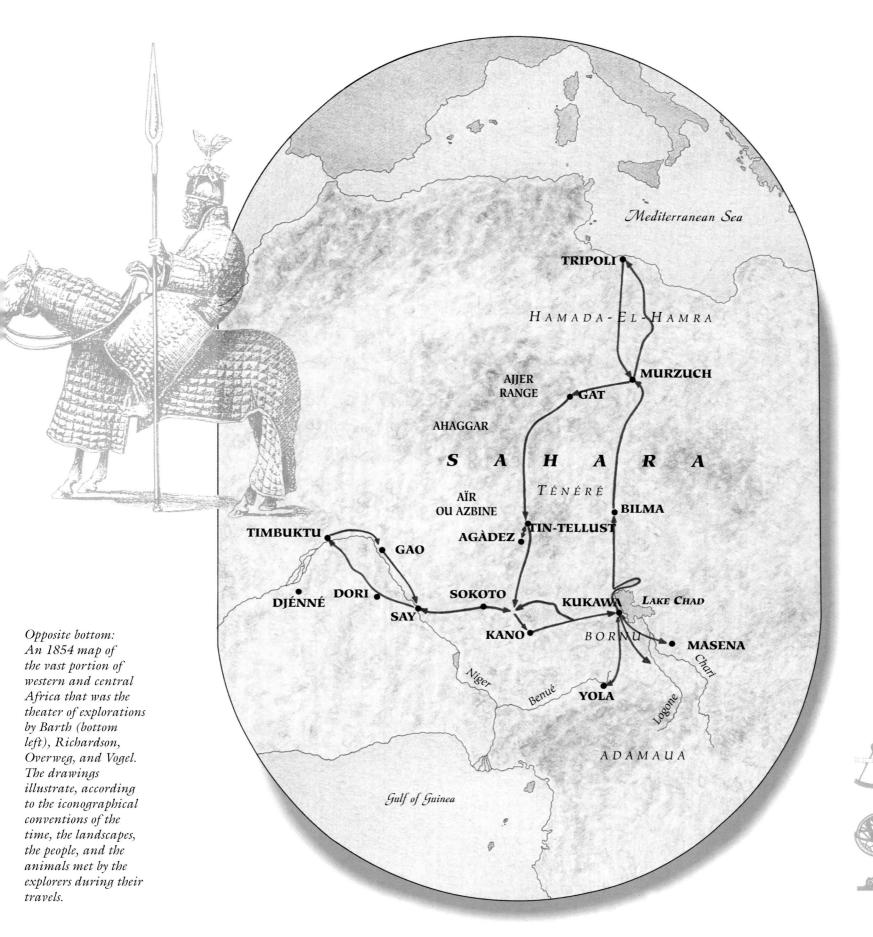

229

Opposite bottom:
An 1854 map of
the vast portion of
western and central
Africa that was the
theater of explorations
by Barth (bottom
left), Richardson,
Overweg, and Vogel.
The drawings
illustrate, according
to the iconographical
conventions of the
time, the landscapes,
the people, and the
animals met by the
explorers during their
travels.

At the end of 1849, the trio left London bound for Tripoli, the terminus of the caravan trail to Lake Chad. No expense had been spared, and the expedition was very well organized. The team acquired around twenty camels on which to load their supplies and equipment: tents, goods to barter with, foodstuffs, and a collapsible boat divided into four sections destined for navigation on Lake Chad. The caravan left Tripoli in March, 1850: the first objective was the oasis of Murzuch, beyond the immense stony desert of El-Hamra where no European had ever set foot. The relationship between Richardson and Barth

deteriorated immediately: during the arduous crossing, the caravan split into two groups. Richardson and the English sailor in charge of the boat to one side, and Barth and Overweg to the other. In the evenings the men even pitched separate camps. The oasis was reached after a month's march. In order to cross the bandit-infested no-man's land between Murzuch and Ghat, the two groups joined up again, escorted by a group of Tuaregs. The slopes of the Iniden, a mountain that the nomads believed to be inhabited by spirits, rose not far from Ghat. Barth decided to explore the area even though

none of the locals was prepared to act as his guide. The labyrinth of gorges and turrets seemed to suggest an easy access route to the heart of the massif, but after just a few hours march Barth realized that he had lost his way and was in serious trouble: he had finished his water some time earlier, and he began to be tormented by thirst. He repeatedly fired his pistol into the air to indicate his position, but apart from the distant echo of his own shots, had no reply. By now delirious, he opened a vein and drank his own blood. He was on the point of exhaustion and collapsed under the patchy shade of an acacia. He fired another couple of rounds before slipping into the state of semi-consciousness that precedes death. The following morning he was found by chance by a solitary nomad who, after having given him something to drink, put him on his camel and carried him to his camp a few miles away. Barth learned his lesson well and was never again to take chances with the Sahara. The expedition proceeded towards the eastern spurs of the Ahaggar range. The rocky walls were covered with paintings and incisions which the explorer faithfully copied into his diary (the frescos at Tassili n'Ajjer were only to be rediscovered in the following century). The last of the sandstone ridges soon disappeared beyond the horizon, and the caravan entered the interminable gravel plains of the Ténéré, an absolute desert through which even today it is still difficult to travel. By early September the caravan had come within sight of the Aïr mountains in modern-day Niger: after some initial difficulties the Kel-Oui Tuaregs accepted the presence of the foreigners, and the Sultan of Tin-Telloust offered them his hospitality. While his companions rested, Barth decided to reach Agadez, the trading and caravan center of the region. At one time the city had up to 50,000 inhabitants but was now in decline: "on the walls, which were falling into disrepair, perched ravenous vultures waiting for the chance to pounce on any discarded scraps," wrote Barth in his diary before returning to the base camp. At Tin-Telloust the caravan split up definitively, with each group making their own way to Kukawa, the capital of the kingdom of Bornu. Barth reached the banks of Lake Chad on the 2nd of April, 1851. He found no one there waiting for him: Richardson had died of fevers along the way, and Overweg arrived a month later in poor health. Barth, on the other hand, felt fit and strong and, leaving his companion at Kukawa, set out once again to explore the area around Lake Chad and the upper reaches of the Benue River. The two men spent 15 months in the region, but Overweg died in September, 1852, at the age of 29. Barth now found himself master of his own destiny and decided to continue the journey on his own, but with a new objective, Timbuktu on the Niger. The indefatigable German left Bornu in late November and, after a ten-month march, reached the walls of the

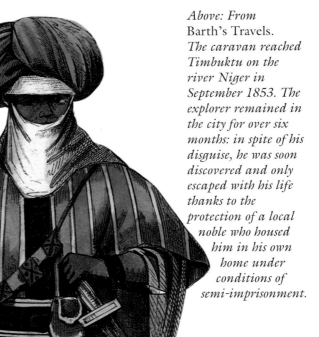

Above: From Barth's Travels. The caravan reached Timbuktu on the river Niger in September 1853. The explorer remained in the city for over six months: in spite of his disguise, he was soon discovered and only escaped with his life thanks to the protection of a local noble who housed him in his own home under conditions of semi-imprisonment.

Below: A Tuareg warrior as depicted in 1843 in a treatise on the habits and customs of the African people. Barth and his companions, like their predecessors, frequently had to overcome the hostility of the desert nomads, who considered robbery to be simply the exercizing of a natural right.

mysterious city. Timbuktu had a bad reputation: of all the Europeans who had attempted to reach it only Caillè had returned to tell the tale. Barth disguised himself as an Arab, but realized that he would not be able to maintain the deception for long. When he judged that his life was in danger, he chose to reveal his true identity to Sheik El Bakay, a local nobleman. He asked for and obtained protection, but paid for it with a partial loss of his liberty. The six months he spent at Timbuktu were a nightmare. It was not until mid-May, 1854 that the sheik decided that Barth could set out on his journey

once again: with an escort he descended the Niger as far as Say and then headed to Kukawa, anxious to return to Europe. After a brief stop in Bornu, he set out once again for Murzuch. At the end of August, 1855 he reached Tripoli. His journey, lasting five and a half years, produced the first reliable picture of West Africa. His report ran to five weighty volumes and contained a mine of information on the history, languages, and people of that immense region. Barth offered a global overview of African civilization, a vision in "space and time" based on an understanding and a sincere respect for a vastly different culture.

His work was an act of science and friendship. Back in Europe, Barth was not to encounter similar success. His brusque, strong-willed character made life difficult for himself. He was never to return to Africa, but nor was he able to resign himself to its absence. "I am accustomed to the desert," he wrote, "to the infinite spaces where I have no need to worry about the trivial affairs of men. It is painful to find myself here in chains." Heinrich Barth, known to the Africans as Abd El Karim, "The Compassionate One," died ten years after his return, misunderstood and forgotten.

Left: This plate taken from Journeys in Search of Africa *by Heinrich Barth, shows a panoramic view of the Ashenoumma region. Barth, polyglot, geographer, historian, and enthusiastic explorer compiled an accurate report of his long journey through western Africa, the first window opened onto the reality of the continent.*

Below: This plate was also taken from the book Travels and Discoveries *by Heinrich Barth shows a large herd of elephants drinking on the shores of Lake Chad. The German explorer reached the lake in 1851, and throughout his journey he studied the history and idioms of the people he encountered.*

RICHARD BURTON AND JOHN HANNING SPEKE

"At last I was on the banks of the Nile; it was a magnificent spectacle, matchless! It was a perfect example of the effect one might hope to achieve in a grandiose park: a splendid river, 600 or 700 meters wide, punctuated by small islands and rocks." Bombay, the African leading the caravan, declined the white man's offer: to shave his head and immerse him in the sacred river. Speke was rapt in mystical exaltation: he was the first European since the time of Herodotus to see the source of the Nile. Years earlier Speke had seen Lake Victoria, and ever since that moment he had been certain that that was the true source of the Nile. Now he had the proof. On his return journey, Speke sent a telegram to England. The message ended with the phrase "the Nile is solved." However, the reality was far different: the age-old question of the source of the Nile was anything but resolved. The true battle would take place in Europe and would be more tragic than any of the attempts at exploration. No other place on Earth has remained a mystery for so long. From a rational point of view the Nile is a hydraulic miracle, thanks to which the equatorial rains are carried to the Mediterranean, passing through the greatest desert in the world. For thousands of years, the river's periodic floods that inundated Egypt during the driest season were an inexplicable phenomenon. Where did all that water come from? Herodotus and the Greek geographers claimed that the Nile rose in the Mountains of the Moon, peaks as high as the sky and covered with snow, a fabulous country with fantastical creatures. At the

232

Top: John Hannig Speke, in a portrait painted by James W. Wilson in 1871. During his second journey, accompanied by James A. Grant, he reached the source of the Nile at Lake Victoria (depicted in the background), but was unable to provide scientific proof of his discovery. He died in a mysterious hunting accident (or perhaps committed suicide) just before he was due to take part in a public debate with Burton organized by the Royal Geographical Society.

beginning of the last century, the heart of Africa was about as familiar as the deepest ocean abyss or interplanetary space. Then, in 1848, incredible news reached Europe: a German missionary claimed to have seen a towering mountain with a sparkling cap of ice. He was dismissed as a visionary but was proved right (the mountain was Kilimanjaro). The rumors were sufficient to spark off a wave of interest in African exploration similar to that which in earlier centuries had sent Spanish and Portuguese caravels as far as China, the Americas, and Australia. The principal objective of this exploration fever was central Africa and above all, the source of the Nile. In 1856, the Royal Geographical Society in London decided to send two men to Africa with orders to uncover the secret of the Nile: both had already completed long expeditions providing them with solid experience and were blessed with exceptional constitutions. Richard Burton, disguised as an Arab, had visited the forbidden cities of Harer and Mecca. He was fluent in 30 languages and had a taste for the dramatic. His companion, John Haning Speke, was a sportsman with little time for the sophisticated way of life: he was 30 years old, six years younger than Burton, but had

Left: A portrait of Richard Burton in Eastern costume. In 1853 Burton penetrated the prohibited city of Mecca disguised as an Afghan pilgrim. When he left with Speke in search of the sources of the Nile, he was 36 years old and could boast an adventurous past. Brilliant, extroverted and irascible, he spoke 30 languages and was a connoisseur of erotica. Bottom: A map of Africa from the 15th century, based on the data of Ptolomeic geography. Ptolomy, an Egyptian cosmographer of the second century AD, believed that the source of the Nile was in very high mountains with a perpetual snow cover, the Mountains of the Moon, of which he actually provided the exact latitude and longitude.

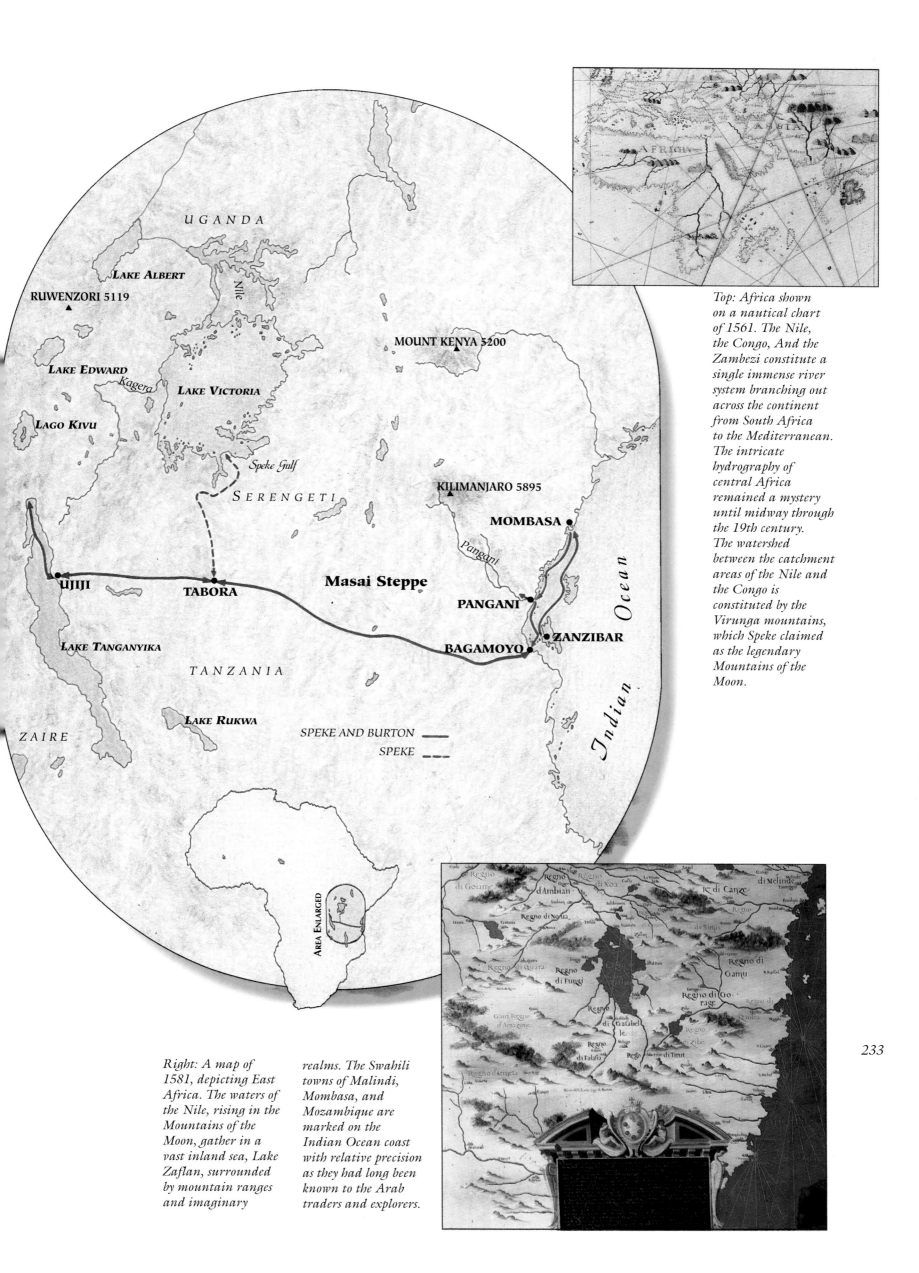

UGANDA

LAKE ALBERT

RUWENZORI 5119 ▲

Nile

LAKE EDWARD

Kagera

LAGO KIVU

LAKE VICTORIA

MOUNT KENYA 5200 ▲

Speke Gulf

S E R E N G E T I

KILIMANJARO 5895 ▲

MOMBASA ●

Pangani

Masai Steppe

UJIJI ●

TABORA ●

PANGANI ●

ZANZIBAR

LAKE TANGANYIKA

BAGAMOYO ●

T A N Z A N I A

Indian Ocean

LAKE RUKWA

ZAIRE

SPEKE AND BURTON ————
SPEKE – – – –

AREA ENLARGED

Top: Africa shown
on a nautical chart
of 1561. The Nile,
the Congo, And the
Zambezi constitute a
single immense river
system branching out
across the continent
from South Africa
to the Mediterranean.
The intricate
hydrography of
central Africa
remained a mystery
until midway through
the 19th century.
The watershed
between the catchment
areas of the Nile and
the Congo is
constituted by the
Virunga mountains,
which Speke claimed
as the legendary
Mountains of the
Moon.

233

Right: A map of
1581, depicting East
Africa. The waters of
the Nile, rising in the
Mountains of the
Moon, gather in a
vast inland sea, Lake
Zaflan, surrounded
by mountain ranges
and imaginary

realms. The Swahili
towns of Malindi,
Mombasa, and
Mozambique are
marked on the
Indian Ocean coast
with relative precision
as they had long been
known to the Arab
traders and explorers.

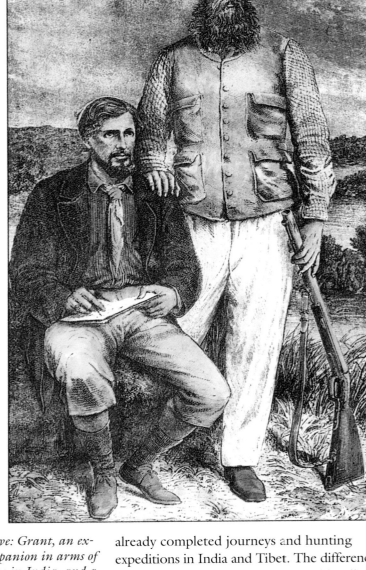

Above: Grant, an ex-companion in arms of Speke in India, and a good friend, proved to be an ideal traveling companion. A quiet, shy man, he was happy with a marginal role in the expedition, leaving the glory for the discovery to the more extroverted Speke, "not a hint of jealousy, distrust or irritation ever fell between us."

Above center: The Nile flowing out of Lake Victoria as seen by Speke on the 28th of July, 1862. "A spectacle that could enchant for hours... the waters roared, thousands of fish leaped against the current with all their strength... the hippopotami and the crocodiles wallowed lazily in the water." Speke named the falls after Ripon, the president of the Royal Geographical Society.

already completed journeys and hunting expeditions in India and Tibet. The difference in character between the two could hardly have been greater. The caravan left Zanzibar heading west on the 16th of June, 1857, following the precarious Arab trading route leading to the outpost of Kazeh (now Tabora in Tanzania). From the very first days, Burton and Speke had realized that managing an expedition in Equatorial Africa was very complex: the climate was unhealthy, the insects ravenous, and the porters deserted as soon as they could taking their packs with them. The pack animals died one by one, victims of sleeping sickness. "Each morning," wrote Burke, "brings with it new torments, each day that passes makes me think that tomorrow will be even worse." Sudden storms hit the caravan and the porters sank up to their knees in mud. The explorers were struck by malaria, and only after 134 days did they reach Kazeh. The Arab merchants in the town received them warmly. For Burton, who spoke Arabic and respected the Muslims as much as he despised the native Africans, the halt was a blessed breath of civilization in the midst of a hostile world. A month later, when Speke had recovered his strength, the caravan set out towards Lake Tanganyika. On the 13th of February, they reached Ujiji. Burton was suffering from an abscess and could hardly talk, while Speke was blinded

by an eye infection. The expedition was falling apart, but the first objective had been reached. No European before them had ever set eyes upon the great lake. Burton was convinced that the Tanganyika was the reservoir that fed the Nile, and it was with bitterness that he discovered that there was no river that drained to the North. Having returned to Kazeh, the two explorers split up: Burton, a guest of the Arabs, remained at the base camp in order to reorganize the caravan. Speke decided to continue the march to the north where, the according to the usual vague rumors there ought to be another great lake. On the 3rd of August, he came within sight of an immense stretch of water. An intuition struck him like a thunderbolt: he had found the source of the Nile. Even though he had no proof, he was sure that he was right. He baptised the lake with the name Victoria, and just three days later set off back to Kazeh. The revelation failed to excite the pragmatic mind of Burton who found Speke's hypothesis "weak and inconsistent." During their journey to the coast, the relationship between the two deteriorated beyond repair. Speke was the first to reach England and, without waiting for Burton, he reported his discovery to the Royal Geographical Society and immediately obtained financing for a new expedition. When Burton arrived the matter had already been decided: Speke was to depart

Opposite top: Speke and Grant's caravan departing from Bagamoyo on the coast of present-day Tanzania in front of the island of Zanzibar. The typical African expedition of the Victorian era was a vast and inevitably slow moving affair. Porters (often hundreds of them) were recruited on Zanzibar and at Bagamoyo, and goods for bartering were acquired. These trinkets were then exchanged for rights of passage from the tribal chieftains of the interior. The confidence and order depicted in this illustration lasted at most for a few days' march before things began to fall apart.

234

Grant voyageant du Karagoué à l'Ouganda.

with a new companion, Captain James Grant. Speke and Grant reached Lake Victoria in 1862: before their eyes, the Nile gushed from the lake in a foaming cascade. However, Speke's triumph was short-lived. On his return, Burton was waiting for him, cool and implacable. Where was the proof that the river they had seen was the Nile? Was Lake Victoria the same lake that Speke had seen from the south? Speke had not circumnavigated it and could not be sure. The situation became more confusing with each passing day, and the Geographical Society decided to bring and end to the polemics with a public debate, Speke against Burton. Speke was never able to defend his position because he died a few hours before the debate in a hunting accident. In a classic mystery atmosphere suicide was debated but the facts were never confirmed. A few years later, at the spot where Speke had halted, a tablet was erected with the inscription "Speke discovered this source of the Nile on the 28th of July, 1862." The search went ahead without success. The Nile was about to sink back into legend: a map of 1873 showed five lakes in place of Lake Victoria. It was Stanley who was to resolve the question: in 1875, he circumnavigated the immense basin and identified the course of the Kagera, its principal tributary. Speke's hypothesis had been proved: the Nile rose from Lake Victoria.

Center: Grant, forced to travel on a stretcher, leaving the Karagwe region on the west bank of Lake Victoria. Suffering from a serious infection in his leg, Grant was unable to keep up with his companion's forced march toward the source of the Nile. Speke, anxious to reach his objective, freed himself of the burden by entrusting Grant with secondary logistical duties.

Bottom: Frequently, in the absence of other available resources, the feeding of a caravan depended almost exclusively on the hunting skills of its leader. At that time the bush and savannah of East Africa were swarming with large game: a true paradise for Speke who, in contrast with Burton, had an almost maniacal passion for hunting.

235

"I heard a roar. I turned round with a start and saw a lion ready to pounce. I was on a small embankment, the beast savaged my shoulder and we fell to the ground together. Growling ferociously in my ear, it shook me like a terrier shakes a rat. The shock sent me into a kind of stupor... There was neither pain nor fear, and yet I was perfectly aware of what was happening." One of his companions shot the lion and Livingstone was miraculously saved, although the incident rendered him an invalid for the rest of his life. At that time, he was 36 years of age and had been in Africa for five years. Livingstone was born at Blantyre in Scotland, in 1813. His was not a wealthy family: the young David was soon introduced to the delights of the Industrial Revolution. At the age of ten, he was employed in a cotton mill from six o'clock in the morning until 8 o'clock in the evening. It was perhaps during those years of back-breaking labor that the dominant traits in Livingstone's character were formed: tenacity, enduring faith, and a clear-cut individualism. At the age of 25, having completed his medical studies, he became a member of the London Missionary Society and was sent to southern Africa. At that time, apart from a few coastal settlements, the continent was wild and unknown, an immense mystery from the Cape to the Mediterranean. Livingstone reached the mission of Kuruman, on the edge of the Kalahari, in 1841. The evangelical work was proceeding slowly and had yet to produce any significant results: Livingstone soon realized that he was not cut out to be a missionary. Beyond Kuruman extended an unexplored region, virgin land for the propagation of the Christian faith, but above all, for his insatiable curiosity. This was how David Livingstone's incredible career began, with an uninterrupted series of journeys across the inhospitable bush of the Kalahari. In 1849, he reached Lake Nag in the northern territory of what is now Botswana. Beyond the desert once more lay the unknown: the natives spoke of a great river whose waters

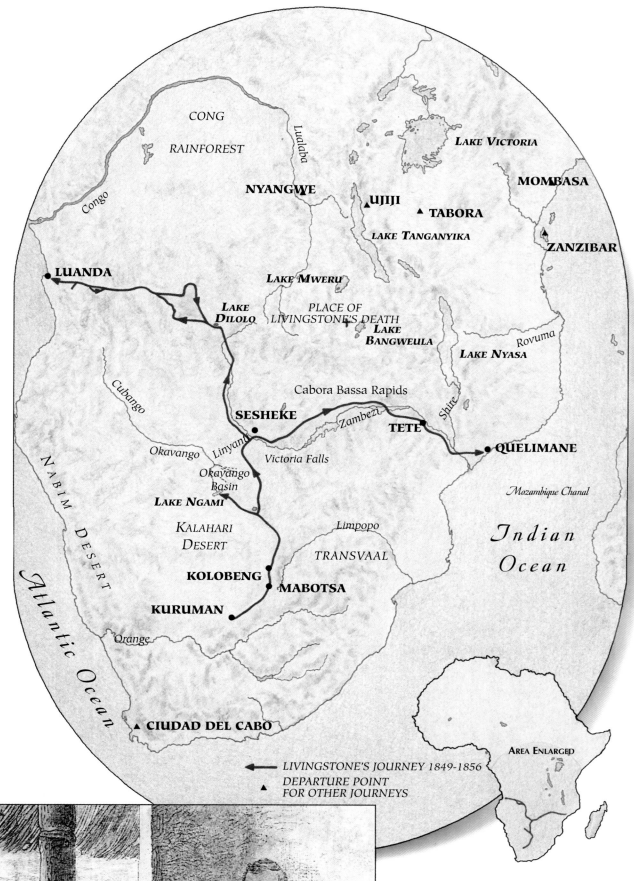

CONG
RAINFOREST

Lualaba

LAKE VICTORIA

MOMBASA

NYANGWE

▪UJIJI

▪ TABORA

LAKE TANGANYIKA

ZANZIBAR

Congo

LUANDA

LAKE MWERU

PLACE OF
LIVINGSTONE'S DEATH

LAKE
DILOLO

LAKE
BANGWEULA

Rovuma

LAKE NYASA

Cabora Bassa Rapids

Cubango

SESHEKE

Zambezi

Shire

TETE

QUELIMANE

Okavango

Linyant

Victoria Falls

NABIM DESERT

Okavango
Basin

Mozambique Chanal

LAKE NGAMI

Indian
Ocean

KALAHARI
DESERT

Limpopo

Atlantic Ocean

TRANSVAAL

KOLOBENG

MABOTSA

KURUMAN

Orange

AREA ENLARGED

▪ CIUDAD DEL CABO

→ LIVINGSTONE'S JOURNEY 1849-1856
▪ DEPARTURE POINT
   FOR OTHER JOURNEYS

*Opposite:
The frontispiece
of a contemporary
biography dedicated
to the life and
exploration of David
Livingstone. Born into
a poor Scottish family,
Livingstone arrived in
southern Africa in
1840 as an envoy of
the London Missionary
Society. When his
extraordinary career
as an explorer drew to
a close 30 years later,
he had covered at least
25,000 miles on foot
across the continent.*

*Left: Livingstone
arranging his notes
in his quarters at
Ujiji on Lake
Tanganyika. Perhaps
no other explorer
wrote such detailed
accounts of his
travels, collecting all
sorts of information
about the flora,
fauna, geography,
and the customs of
the inhabitants of the
areas through which
he moved.
Livingstone wrote*

*every day, even in
the most trying of
conditions, using any
kind of paper and
ink he extracted
himself from certain
plants. His work was
collected into three
weighty tomes
containing almost
a million words
(according to the
estimate of one of his
biographers)
describing 33 years
of wandering
throughout Africa.*

237

Above: In 1843, at the Mabotsa mission in the western Transvaal, Livingstone was attacked by a large male lion. One of his companions shot the beast just in time to save his life. "There was neither pain nor fear," he later wrote in his diary, but only a strange sensation of partial unconsciousness "similar to that experienced by patients under anaesthesia who witness all the details of the operation, but do not feel the scalpels."

Below: In the August of 1849, Livingstone and his family reached Lake Ngami in the northern Kalahari. In the absence of the tse-tse fly, the exploration of southern Africa was generally completed with carts drawn by oxen. Livingstone stated that "traveling with carts in Africa is like taking a long walk, excellent for the health and pleasant for those who love the open air."

irrigated fertile lands in the distant north. Taking his family with him (he had married in the meantime) and ignoring all discomforts, Livingstone reached the Zambezi two years later, close to the confluence of the Linyanti: this was his first real discovery, the light on the way to Damascus. A great navigable river would have represented a direct route to the heart of Africa, the expansion of faith and commerce, and the development of civilization. The exploration of the Zambezi basin was occupy the following twelve years of his life. Livingstone accompanied his family back to the Cape before heading north once again: he had now severed his links with the outside world, and nothing and no one could obstruct his plans. In 1853, with no equipment and the help of 27 improvised porters, he ascended the river almost as far as its source and then headed west through the bush of Angola, finally reaching Luanda and the Atlantic Ocean. During the journey, almost all of his men died of fever, and Livingstone himself fell seriously ill. He rested at Luanda and organized a caravan before, driven by his obsession, he retraced his steps and followed the Zambezi to its delta on the Indian Ocean. On the 17th of November, 1855, Livingstone found himself facing the grandiose falls that he named after Queen Victoria. The natives knew the falls as simply "the smoke that roars," due to the cloud of water vapour visible for dozens of miles. The Zambezi's dramatic plunge across a lip 5,610 feet broad and around a hundred high, should have been the definitive proof that the river was not navigable. Not for the Livingstone, however,

Top: In 1858
Livingstone attempted
to ascend the great
river with a steam-
powered boat, brought
from England in
dismantled sections
and baptised Ma
Robert in honour of
his wife Mary. The
vessel was, however,
finally defeated by the
rapids at Cabora
Bassa. The sole result
of the expedition, that
had begun under poor
auspices and had been
badly organized, was
the rediscovery of Lake
Nyasa, once known to
the Portuguese but
which had subsequently
disappeared from the
maps.

stubbornly convinced that he had been right all along. In 1858, he ascended the Zambezi once again: this time his boat was halted by the Cabora Bassa rapids, fifty kilometers of insuperable cataracts. At this point the explorer attempted to ascend a tributary, the Shire, but without success. The expedition's one positive result was the discovery of Lake Nyasa earlier described by the Portuguese, but which then disappeared from the maps. The region was disease-ridden and devastated by slave-hunters. Failure did nothing to obscure Livingstone's fame, and the Royal Geographical Society contented itself, in the absence of concrete results, with an impassioned report about the curse of slavery. In that period, the press and the public were engrossed by the "Nile Question": the story of Speke and Burton, together with a thesis presented by Baker, had aroused intense arguments between the various factions. Who could have resolved the age-old enigma of the source of the Nile if not Doctor Livingstone? The proposal for a new expedition to Africa caught the explorer by surprise: geographical mysteries were not what concerned him, and he was more interested in abolishing the slave trade. A compromise was reached, and Livingstone departed for Zanzibar on the 13th of August, 1865. Another river, the father of all rivers, had become part of his destiny. The expedition proposed to follow the course of the Ruvuma, now the natural border between Tanzania and Mozambique, to reach Lake Nyasa and then penetrate the region to the south of Lake Tanganyika. There Livingstone hoped to find the first clues to the whereabouts of the source of

Center: Livingstone discovered the waterfall on the Zambezi in 1855 during his return from Angola. The explorer reached the island of Kazeruka on the edge of the drop aboard a canoe: lying prostrate he peered into the chasm and saw "a great gorge between one bank and the other of the Zambezi: a sheet of water 1,000 meters wide fell from 33 meters and funnelled into an aperture 7 to 10 meters wide. The most beautiful spectacle I had ever seen in Africa."

Bottom: A caravan of slaves marching toward the coast. This trade, the absolute monopoly of the Arabian "dogs of war," was strenuously opposed by Livingstone. His furious reports on the atrocities and massacres perpetrated by the slave drivers aroused a potent wave of indignation among British and European public opinion. In 1873, the sultan of Zanzibar was forced to sign a treaty that obliged him to abolish the trade and to close down the slave markets on the island.

239

the Nile. For three years he combed the equatorial lakes region, investigating the continent's most complex hydrographical system: Lakes Mweru, Bangweula, and the Tanganyika were not in fact tributaries of the Nile but rather the Congo. Livingstone was searching for a river that did not exist. His porters deserted him, his pack animals were decimated by the tse-tse fly, and it was only thanks to the help of the despised slave traders that the explorer managed to reached Ujiji, the Arab trading outpost on the shores of Lake Tanganyika. He was a devastated man: "I am so weak that I can hardly speak," he wrote in his diary. Nevertheless, he set out again in search of the phantasmal Nile: once again he came across the Lualaba (the upper reaches of the Congo) and halted at the borders of the rainforest. Twenty days after his return to Ujiji, he was told that a large caravan led by a white man was about to reach the shore of Lake Tanganyika. His "saviour" was named Henry Morton Stanley, a correspondent with an American newspaper.

The historic encounter ("Doctor Livingstone I presume?") was for Stanley

Top: "Doctor Livingstone, I presume?" One of the numerous illustrations of the historic meeting between Stanley and Livingstone on the 30th of October, 1871, at Ujiji on the banks of Lake Tanganyika. Stanley, in Africa as a correspondent for an American newspaper, was thus presented with the biggest scoop of his career. Livingstone, however, wearied by years of privation and illness, had no intention of being "rescued" and simply desired to continue his wanderings in search of the source of the Nile, an obsession that had taken on mystical proportions. The supplies brought to him by Stanley allowed him to leave Ujiji on his last expedition.

the greatest scoop of all time and the beginning of a brilliant career. For Livingstone, who was by no means lost in the heart of Africa, the supplies brought by the American were a breath of fresh air. He could now set out again and carry his folly through to its conclusion. Livingstone and Stanley explored vast areas of the lake (excursions which Livingstone called picnics), and then they separated. In April,

Above: The only trip that Stanley and Livingstone made together was to the northern extremity of Lake Tanganyika. On that occasion Livingstone discovered that the river Rusizi supplied the lake (rather than drained it as Burton thought), and this increased his conviction that the Lualaba was actually the Nile. In reality lake Tanganyika forms part of the Congo basin and the Lualaba is actually the upper course of the great river.

1873, Livingstone was caught by the rains in the Lake Bangweulu region. The ground soaked up water like a sponge, and flooding rivers and streams transformed the region into an endless swamp. Livingstone intuited that he would never make his way out of the trap alive. On the 13th of April, he wrote in his diary "The fishing eagle screams its characteristic cry. It is a falsetto voice, very old as if the bird is calling some one in the next world. When you hear it, that cry does not seem to be of this world, you cannot forget it. It remains with you all your life." The words have a premonitory air. Livingstone died twenty days later. Legend has it that he was found kneeling as if in prayer. This was on the 1st of May, 1873. His most trusted men embalmed the body and carried it to Zanzibar. The autopsy carried out left no room for doubt: the wound he had received almost thirty years earlier from the lion had left an unequivocal mark. What is more difficult to establish is the explorer's true spiritual identity and where Livingstone stands in relation to the history of Africa. Was he a philanthropist, a man in search of glory or simply restless? His journeys did not resolve the great geographical questions, nor did they make a serious contribution to the abolition of slavery or open up new trading routes. Perhaps Doctor Livingstone would have recognised himself in the confession of Joseph Thomson his fellow countryman and explorer: "I am destined to be a nomad. I am not a founder of empires, nor a missionary nor a true scientist. I just want to return to Africa to continue my wanderings."

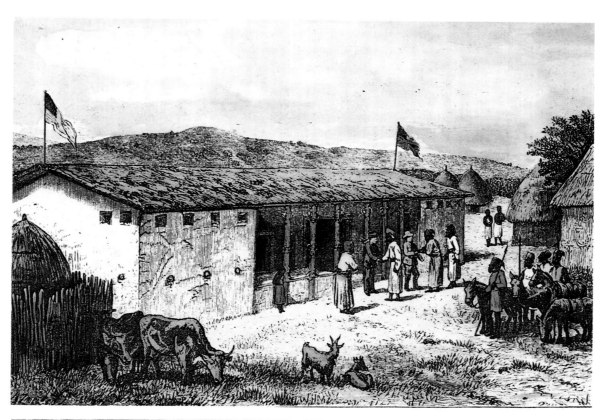

Top: The tembe *at Kwihara, close to present-day Tabora in Tanzania, that was home to Livingstone in the first half of 1872. Tabora was then an obligatory staging post for travelers heading for the interior along the Arab trading route that linked the Indian Ocean coast with the great equatorial lakes region. The* tembe *was a simple flat-roofed construction with a floor of beaten earth, a large courtyard and a few rooms for guests and their servants; this was what passed for luxury in East Africa at that time.*

Center: At the end of April, 1873, Livingstone's caravan was surprised by the rains on the plain surrounding Lake Bangweulu in northern Zambia. The entire region was reduced to an endless marsh. Unable to walk or ride, the explorer had to be carried by his companions.

Bottom: "The last mile," by Livingstone. From his diary (10th of April): "... it is absolutely impossible now to see where the land ends and the lake begins: everything is water, water everywhere... I am pale, anaemic and weak from the haemorrhaging, abundant since the 31st of March..." 12th of April: "I dragged myself for around two hours and then collapsed exhausted... I did not want to be carried, but when pressed I allowed the men to help me in rotation." 17th of April: "... I can only just lift the pencil." There follow only dates and brief notes about the duration of the marches. Livingstone died on the 1st of May, 1873, at the village of Chitambo in silence and solitude.

WILLIAM BURCHELL

Early in 1808, a young scientist was wandering the stony footpaths of the island of St Helena in search of plants and grasses to classify. William Burchell was at that time little more than a brilliant student involved in his field work. A couple of years earlier he had been entrusted with the task of conducting a census of the flora of the isolated Atlantic Island, one of the few stop-overs on the routes from Europe to Cape Town. While on St Helena, he visited one of the many passing ships and met a group of naturalists returning from a journey through the distant southern Africa. At the time he had expressed his desire to visit those regions, the descriptions of which had fascinated him, but it was nothing more than

a dream. He was now awaiting the arrival of his fiancée who was due to reach him from England in just a few weeks. He could hardly have imagined that the girl would have fallen in love with the captain of the ship on which she was traveling and that the two would have married. As far as Burchell was concerned, the failure of one marriage before it, which had even been celebrated, was more than enough: he remained celibate for the rest of his life. Two years later, he left St Helena for Cape Town, landing in November, 1810. William Burchell was then 30 years of age: his small frame concealed an incredible tenacity and extraordinary stamina. Even though he lacked any experience of traveling in wild country, he was determined

to penetrate the interior of the continent. Early in that century much of southern Africa was still unexplored, and the plateaus extending beyond the coastal scarp were still a formidable barrier to be overcome. The last expedition that ventured beyond the Orange River had disappeared without a trace, massacred, it was said, by unknown tribes from the interior. During the four months he spent at Cape Town, Burchell set to work organizing all that he felt necessary for the expedition: he acquired a robust covered wagon, tools and provisions, tents, medical supplies, and firearms. Finding men prepared to accompany him on his trip was rather more difficult: the Hottentots and the mixed-bloods of the Cape were afraid of

Opposite: William Burchell, born in London in 1782, was one of the first explorer naturalists to visit the unknown lands to the north of the Cape Colony. In spite of his fragile constitution, Burchell tackled the privations of the journey with great determination, enthusiastically dedicating himself to his scientific work. Between 1811 and 1815, he collected and cataloged over 63,000 items concerning "every branch of natural history." Among these items were 40,000 botanical samples, 120 skins of quadrupeds, and 265 species of birds, most of them previously unknown to science.

Top: During the crossing of the Roggeveldt, the mountain barrier, which at that time delimited the confines of the Cape Colony, the rear axle of one of the carts broke away from the chassis, and the vehicle risked overturning. Burchell and his men were obliged to completely empty it, repair the fault, and replace the load: the whole operation was completed in a couple of hours.

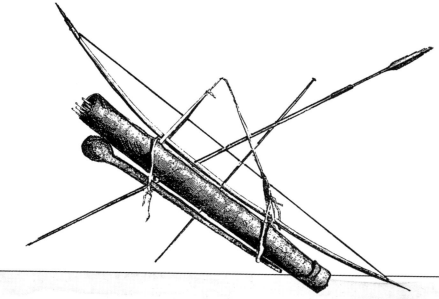

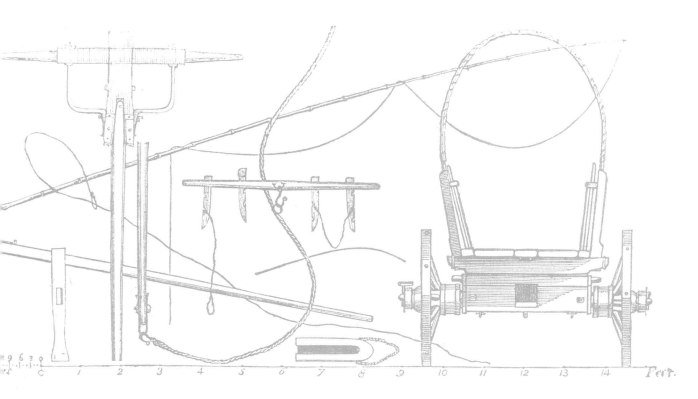

Bottom: The covered wagon, the favored means of transport for the explorers and pioneers of South Africa, was noted for its robustness, versatility, and loading capacity. 13 or 16 feet long, they were hauled by a dozen (or more) oxen yoked in pairs and could, if necessary, be transformed into a rudimentary raft. Burchell drew a sectional view and the constructional principles with notable technical accuracy.

243

Top: *During his journey toward the Graaf-Reinet, in search of new recruits for his expedition, Burchell crossed an arid and sparsely inhabited area infested with bands of brigands. It was with great relief that the caravan reached in* *mid-March, 1812, the vague confines of the Colony, identified by a typically flat-topped rise similar to the Table Mountain that dominates Cape Town, that the explorer faithfully reproduced in one of his sketches.*

Center: *On the 23rd of June, 1811, a few days after leaving Cape Town, the expedition reached the banks of the Berg River, one of the torrents that descend from the mountains* *of the Cape hinterland. The small caravan, a wagon hauled by eight oxen, and seven men (including Burchell himself) were ferried to the other side without difficulty.*

Atlantic Ocean

finishing up like their colleagues who departed with the previous white man's expedition and were never seen again. Their knowledge of the territory and experience of life in the bush was indispensable to the success of the enterprise. At last, after having combed all the most sordid hovels of the town, Burchell succeed in enrolling a small group of men. The expedition left Cape Town on the 18th of June, 1811. Eight days later Burchell was forced to acquire a second wagon to carry part of the heavy load. The crossing of the Great Karoo, the immense plateau extending from the coastal mountains to the Orange River was arduous. For two weeks, rain, freezing winds, and snow made the going very tough. The trail would disappear suddenly in seas of mud, or would thread its way through interminable fields of stones. Tired and cold and with his bones aching from the jolting wagon, Burchell methodically continued with his work: unknown or rare plants, insects, birds, and mammals soon filled the empty cases brought along to house just such a collection. As they moved further north, the landscape became increasingly arid and water was the

244 most pressing problem. On the 15th of September, the muddy waters of the Orange River barred the way to the wagons. Beyond the river, a few days march away, was the village of Klaarwater (now Griquatown), a few huts, and a Protestant mission. Burchell intended to head toward the Kalahari Desert and Angola, his ultimate objective, as soon as possible, but once more he was unable to find a team of volunteers willing

Bottom and opposite top: Burchell did not restrict himself to observing, cataloging and collecting the plant species of South Africa, but also investigated the use of each plant by the local people and the beliefs linked to them.

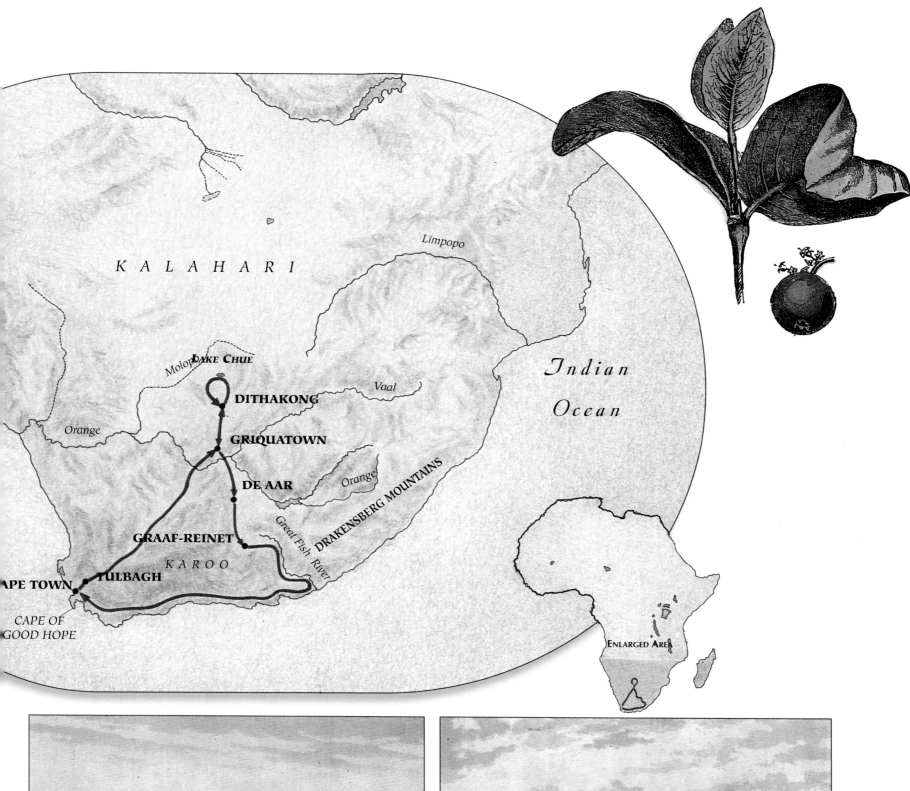

KALAHARI

Limpopo

Indian
Ocean

Molopo **LAKE CHUE**

DITHAKONG

Vaal

Orange

GRIQUATOWN

DE AAR

Orange

DRAKENSBERG MOUNTAINS

GRAAF-REINET

Great Fish River

K A R O O

CAPE TOWN **TULBAGH**

CAPE OF
GOOD HOPE

ENLARGED AREA

Bottom left:
Dithakong
(or Litakun), the
capital of the Tlhaping,
as it appeared to
Burchell early in July,
1812. His relations with
the natives were initially
good, but suddenly took a
turn for the worse when
Burchell refused their
request for firearms.

Bottom right:
Burchell was
impressed by the
remote majesty of the
Snow Mountains that
belted the Graaf-
Reinet region to the
north: "The rough
and powerful
appearance of the
wild nature, and the
sublime beauty of the

landscape," he noted
in his diary, "carried
not the slightest trace
of human
intervention; only the
beaten trail snaking
below our feet
signalled to the
traveler that those
barren valleys were
occasionally
frequented by men."

245

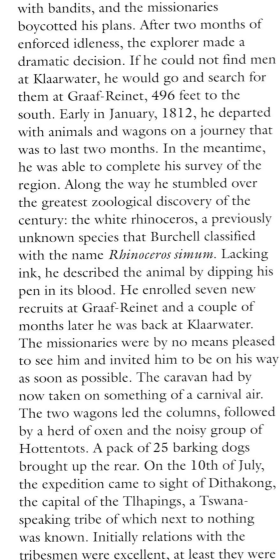

to accompany him. The region was overrun with bandits, and the missionaries boycotted his plans. After two months of enforced idleness, the explorer made a dramatic decision. If he could not find men at Klaarwater, he would go and search for them at Graaf-Reinet, 496 feet to the south. Early in January, 1812, he departed with animals and wagons on a journey that was to last two months. In the meantime, he was able to complete his survey of the region. Along the way he stumbled over the greatest zoological discovery of the century: the white rhinoceros, a previously unknown species that Burchell classified with the name *Rhinoceros simum*. Lacking ink, he described the animal by dipping his pen in its blood. He enrolled seven new recruits at Graaf-Reinet and a couple of months later he was back at Klaarwater. The missionaries were by no means pleased to see him and invited him to be on his way as soon as possible. The caravan had by now taken on something of a carnival air. The two wagons led the columns, followed by a herd of oxen and the noisy group of Hottentots. A pack of 25 barking dogs brought up the rear. On the 10th of July, the expedition came to sight of Dithakong, the capital of the Tlhapings, a Tswana-speaking tribe of which next to nothing was known. Initially relations with the tribesmen were excellent, at least they were until the local chief decided that Burchell should present him with a gift of firearms. Burchell's refusal overturned the situation and the Tlhaping became more hostile. In that heated climate the men feared for their lives and Burchell had to draw his pistol to quell a mutiny. In the end the chief was given his gun and the expedition left Dithakong heading north.

The environment became more desert-like as each day passed: the first red dunes of the Kalahari rolled on towards a distant horizon. There was no trace of water. A month later, the explorers reached a salt lake which Burchell named Chue. The group was exhausted, and the desert seemed endless. Early in August, Burchell realized that in those conditions they would never reach Angola and decided to turn back. His return journey was to last another two and a half years. Long halts were called as Burchell continued with his accurate census of the South African flora and fauna. On his return to Cape Town, on the 13th of April, 1915, Burchell carried with him a priceless treasure: over 60,000 scientific specimens, many of them completely unknown to European science. Apart from a spell in Brazil, Burchell spent the rest of his life cataloging and classifying the immense quantity of material collected during his travels. At the age of 82 he committed suicide.

Left: Halfway through September, 1811, continuing his march northward, Burchell finally reached the banks of the Orange River, where he visited a "genuine Hottentot village. The techniques used in the construction of the huts corresponded perfectly to the demands of the nomadic life-style: in less than an hour the building could be dismantled, loaded onto a pair of oxen."

Right: Burchell sketched this portrait of a Tlhaping girl, "a notable example of the local beauty" at the end of July, 1812. The girl was wearing the ornaments typical of the women of her tribe: a cloak sewn from the skins of various small mammals, a necklace of acacia bark, and pair of copper pendants in her left ear.

Bottom left: "A portrait of Speelman, a Hottentot," one of Burchell's trusted traveling companions. "I drew his portrait," wrote the explorer, "in September, 1814, when he left my service."

Center: The Tlhaping tribe, in Burchell's opinion, was generally of a good character. During his stay at Dithakong, the explorer wrote "true politeness and gentility are natural qualities and not acquired."

Top right: Burchell saw himself as one of those travelers who, through the study of different peoples, try to "better understand themselves, and learning from the comparison, try to form an objective idea of the society in which they live and to which they belong." This illustration shows a portrait of a Tlhaping woman.

Center right: On the 8th of September, 1811, Burchell, searching for water and led from the Bushmen, camped close to one of the rare springs in the region shown in this delicate watercolor.

Bottom right: When Burchell undertook his journey, the Bushmen had inhabited most of the interior of South Africa ever since the remotest times. Today no more than a few hundred, if not a few dozen, survive in the less accessible areas of the Kalahari, living according to the ancient traditions of hunting and gathering.

SAMUEL TELEKI VON SZÈK

A discussion was in progress on a luxurious yacht anchored of an island on the Dalmatian coast: Count Teleki von Szèk was giving a detailed exposition of his latest project, a hunting expedition in Africa, to Rudolf the crown prince of the Austro-Hungarian empire. Teleki's planned destination was the Lake Tanganyika region. A third figure, the naval officer Ludwig von Höhnel, was listening to the conversation with interest: a trip to Africa was his greatest dream, one frustrated by a lack of money. The count, on the other hand, was indecently rich. Perhaps if he asked Prince Rudolf to bring his authority to bear... Von Höhnel was a geographer and an experienced traveler. Thanks to his protector's efforts he not only took part in the enterprise, but was able to divert the Count's attention away from hunting in favor of exploration.

There was still a vast white space on the maps of Africa, an area where no Europeans had ever set foot, to the south of the Ethiopian mountains. The caravans coming from the interior brought with them heavily embroidered tales: it was said that apart from Lake Baringo, discovered by the Scotsman Thomson some years earlier, there was a great inland sea that the natives called Basso Narok (Black Water in the Maa language). Teleki raised the necessary funds for the expedition by selling one of his properties and a famous diamond that had belonged to his ancestors. Von Höhnel traveled to Zanzibar ahead of the count in order to organize the expedition and to hire guides and porters. Their provisions, equipment, and bartering goods were so abundant that they had to enroll 650 men: the expedition that left Zanzibar on the 2nd of January, 1887, was one of the most expensive and best equipped that had ever ventured into the African interior. At the end of March, the caravan reached the outpost of Taveta at the foot of Kilimanjaro and, after a long halt, proceeded through the Kikuyu territories as far as the Aberdares massif and Mount Kenya. Ten months later, Teleki camped on the shores of Lake Baringo: the region was noted for its abundant supply of food and it was thought that Baringo would

Top: A portrait of Samuel Teleki from the English edition of the expedition diary diligently compiled by Ludwig von Höhnel. Initially Teleki simply intended to undertake a hunting trip in equatorial Africa. It was von Höhnel who redirected his attention to more ambitious questions of exploration.

Bottom: Teleki, who at the outset was rather well-built (and thus nick-named Bwana Tumbo or Master Belly), was obliged to tackle the inevitable problems faced by a large caravan: the supplying of food for hundreds of men and the systematic desertion of the porters. The discovery of Lake Turkana cost the enterprising Habsburg nobleman a year's labor and 70 pounds in weight.

Top left: The camp on the southern shore of Lake Turkana, seen from the saddle of the Teleki volcano. "There was a little vegetation but the most frightening aspect of the landscape was a chaos of sand and rocky detritus, uprooted trees, and bushes" wrote von Höhnel. The water of the lake was undrinkable being bitter and purgative) and the constant East wind gave no respite, making sleeping, lighting a fire, and cooking difficult.

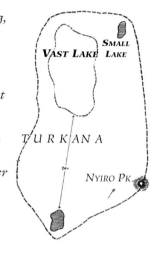

Right: This drawing, published in Teleki's diary, shows the outline of Lake Turkana. This was the only map, at that time, of the area, and it had been drawn following the indications of Thomson, an explorer who had reached Lake Baringo a few years before Teleki's expedition.

provide the last opportunity for provisioning the caravan before tackling the true exploration of the unknown areas. The count could hardly have known that in that period the area was afflicted by severe shortages and that the local people were starving and had no food to trade. Teleki and von Höhnel were obliged to send an armed group to negotiate with the hostile Kikuyu for the acquisition of rations. It was nevertheless apparent that the reserves would be sufficient for no more than two weeks. They nevertheless decided to try their luck. The further the expedition advanced into the northern region, the landscape became increasingly bare and arid. The spiny bush gradually transformed into a desert. The region surrounding Lake Turkana is still today a squalid, remote area. Soon the search for water became the explorers' dominant concern, forcing the caravan to make long diversions towards the mountains on the horizon. There were no traces of trails or human settlements, and the surrounding landscape was hostile and depressing. The porters had to search for a way through the enormous blocks of solidified lava, masses of razor-sharp detritus, and deep

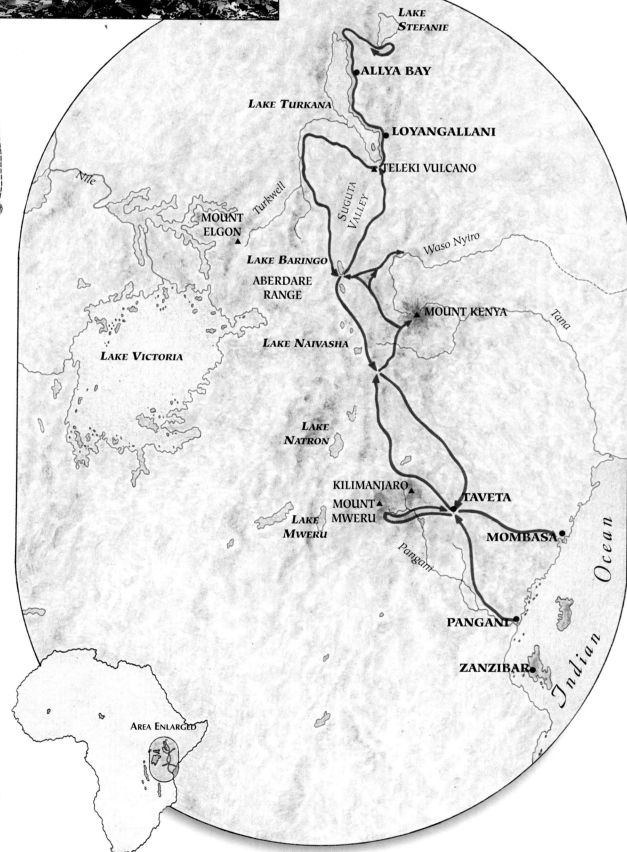

trenches filled with soft sand. A surreal silence reigned over the area. The lake appeared before Teleki as if in a vision, behind a last hill of black gravel. "Suddenly the emptiness in front of us was filled, as by magic, with picturesque reliefs forming a perfect frame to the sparkling expanse of the dark green lake stretching before our eyes to the horizon." It was an incredible discovery, an immense sheet of water in the very heart of a barren desert. The count solemnly baptised the lake Rudolf in honor of His Highness the Crown Prince of Austria and Hungary on the 6th of March 1888. A single day's march separated the caravan from the supply of water. During the long approach march, thirst had been a constant problem: such a large expedition was unsuited to travel through arid areas with very few permanent waterholes. At times, the water in the wells rose so slowly that by the time the last man had drunk the first was already thirsty again. They were now but

a stone's throw away from the lake, and all their suffering appeared to be over. They were, however, to be bitterly disappointed: the cool, clear water was so rich in sodium carbonate that it proved undrinkable. Not a blade of grass grew on the shore, and there were no animals to be seen. The terrible cross wind that blows constantly over the Turkana was so strong as to tear the packs away from the heads of the porters. It was difficult to light a fire, cook or rest, even mere survival was a struggle. The supplies of food were running out and even though the lake was full of fish, they were unable to catch any at all. Teleki felt that he must be the victim of a curse. During those difficult days von Höhnel's notes reflected the desperation he shared with the rest of the men: in the midst of that desolate scenario, even his pragmatic mind wavered. The words refused to flow, and his diary is full of agitated topographical notes, almost as if the explorers were trying to fill the

Above: Coronated grub (Balearica pavonina). *The naturalistic and ethnographic collections (thousands of items) assembled by von Höhnel during the expedition were donated to the museums of Vienna and Budapest? Teleki, the expedition's financier, much preferred hunting to scientific investigation and left the demands and rewards of worldly glory to his lieutenant.*

Bottom: The crossing of a rain-swollen river in the Lake Naivasha region. The caravan of 200 porters, 55 asses, 25 oxen, and 300 sheep and goats took less *than an hour to reach the opposite bank, in spite of the violent current. "Normally," observed Teleki, "it would have taken an entire day, but we were* *returning from our long and arduous journey and the men, anxious to get back to their wives and children, worked with zeal and enthusiasm."*

vacuum with reassuring symbols: the name of a mountain, the profile of a stretch of coastline, a height. Where should they go? There were days of doubts and uncertainties before Teleki decided to advance along the east shore. It marked a change in their fortunes: four days later the men were able to slake their thirst at the Loyangallani springs, the only ones worthy of the name in the whole region. As the caravan moved north, the environmental conditions gradually improved: the desert gave way to the yellow grass of the savannah, and once again there were numerous animals. Elephants, rhinoceroses, and antelopes transformed into mountains of meat allowed variations in the monotonous diet based on the fish bought from the El Molo fishermen after lengthy negotiations.

Refreshed and encouraged, the explorers reached the northern extremity of the lake (on the border between modern-day

Top: Midway through March, 1888, the caravan reached Allia Bay at the northern tip of the lake (today the world's most important anthropological park, the "cradle" in which humanity evolved). The region was less arid, and the savannah vegetation sustained a large number of herbivores. Teleki immediately wanted to dedicate himself to his favorite pastime of hunting, not that he was a great shot in reality. In an attempt to finish off a wounded elephant that had sought refuge in the shallows of the bay, the count sent a party of hunters to deliver the coup de grâce. The episode had an unexpected ending as the elephant furiously charged its persecutors, destroyed the precious portable canvas boat, and slowly disappeared out of sight "as if the bullets that it had in its body did not concern it."

Bottom: Teleki was the first European to attempt to climb the mountain (17,127 ft), coming within hundreds of feet of the summit. The expedition crossed the dense, marshy forest of bamboo that covers the base of the mountain, and the men were forced to cut their way through with machetes, according to the count, "the most arduous and exhausting task imaginable."

Kenya and Ethiopia) and then headed east toward a second basin, which they named Lake Stephania. The return journey was less gruelling: the location of the wells was now known and the trail already marked. Crossing the territory of the Turkana people, the global immorality of whom disgusted the count, the expedition returned to Baringo. On the 26th of October, 1888, after a journey lasting a year and nine months, Teleki and von Höhnel reached Mombassa on the Indian Ocean. The count, rather fleshy when they set out, and therefore nicknamed *Bwana tumbo* or Master Belly by the porters, lost 70 pounds during the trip. The sacrifice was well worth it: Teleki's expedition revealed the continent's last geographical secret and concluded the classic era of African exploration.

Bottom: While he was wandering in the bush hunting guinea-fowl, the count found himself face to face with a leopard, a rather more demanding quarry. He shot two rounds, missing the animal which melted away like a shadow among the greenery. "The incident," wrote a rather shocked Teleki, "really brought it home to me that I was in Africa."

Top: "A two-pronged attack." While tackling a wounded elephant, Teleki was surprised by a charging black rhinoceros: the "unpleasant dilemma" was resolved with the death of both animals. Elephants and the rhinoceroses (Teleki alone killed around 80 examples of both the black and white species) have not been seen in the Lake Turkana region for some time.

Bottom: A conflict with the Kikuyu "savages." At the end of August, 1887, the Teleki's caravan entered the territory of the Kikuyu, a Bantu-speaking tribe living in the fertile region between Mount Kenya and the Aberdares in Kenya. The natives proved to be hostile and on more than one occasion Teleki was obliged to use force to continue his march.

253

T he 24th of April, 1879, was a public holiday in Stockholm: Nordenskjöld had returned from his triumphant expedition to the Arctic seas and was acclaimed by a cheering crowd. A boy of 15 watched the scene. His name was Sven Hedin, and from that moment his driving ambitions were travel and glory. Between 1893 and 1935, the Swedish explorer journeyed through Central Asia using all the means at his disposal, covering tens of thousands of miles across deserts and mountains which were for the most part unexplored. At the turn of the century Hedin departed on the most important journey of his life. Lhasa was not just a city forbidden to the Europeans, but also a sentimental destination. Lhasa was exploration's last romantic legend, and Hedin, the last romantic explorer, missed it by a whisker. A few years later, the British troops entered the city of the Dalai Lama, and Tibet emerged from legend and took its place in the history of the world.

THE HOLY CITY: THE LAST ROMANTIC LEGEND

Above: A portrait of Hedin. A complex and controversial figure, Hedin can rightly be considered one of the greatest explorers of Central Asia.

Top: "Fortunate is he who, from boyhood, discovers his vocation in life. At the age of 20 my objective was already well defined. My dearest friends were Fennimore Cooper and Jules Verne, Livingstone and Stanley, Franklin, Payer and Nordenskjold, and in particular that numerous group of heroes and martyrs of polar exploration." Thus did Hedin (portrayed here in Tibetan costume) describe the motivations behind his exploring in his autobiography. The Swede never went to the Arctic himself: his own great obsessions were the forbidden city of Lhasa and Lop Nor, the mysterious "wandering" lake.

"For a whole year long I have not smiled because of you/ because you lied to me/ I have never known joy from you/ My tears have flowed like a river/ God has not wanted us to be friends/ How beautiful are your eyes and your long lashes." The monotonous melody accompanied by the tinkling of the dutar (a local stringed instrument), had been hummed for over a century by the inhabitants of Lop Nor, the errant lake lost in the heart of Asia. Sven Hedin, or He-Dani as the nomads of the Sin Kiang called him, transcribed it accurately into his expedition diary. This was on the 11th of June, 1900, when the brief continental summer provided warm nights and clear skies. Hedin had left Sweden a year earlier on his second expedition to Central Asia. He now felt ready to delve into the continent's last secrets; where many had failed he was sure he would succeed. He would reach Tibet and the forbidden city of Lhasa, classical exploration's last remaining legend. At all costs. Hedin, born at Stockholm in 1865, grew up in the comfort and security of a wealthy family dominated by his mother and elder sisters. They were to be the only female influences in his life: they supported him in his ambitions and helped him in every way, supplying him with the necessary funds for his interminable journeys. His family was his sole support in the moments of depression to which his unstable character was subject. Hedin never married and never had any true friends. His career was marked by an almost mystical sense of purpose: his every act was aimed at preparing his mind and body for the vocation of the professional explorer. From when he was very young, he trained himself to bear cold and suffering. He learned to plot maps and to draw. He studied Russian, Persian, and the idioms of Central Asia. He also studied under famous geographers in Germany. Hedin's early journeys through Russia and the Middle East revealed his taste for audacious feats bordering on the insane: while traveling with a Swedish delegation in Persia, in order to satisfy the bad taste of a colleague, he stole a number of skulls from the Towers of Silence, where the Parsis abandoned their dead to the vultures. A prank that could have cost him his life. Traveling, as far as Hedin was concerned, was a challenge, an exercise of the will to overcome each and every obstacle on the way to the final objective. Once accepted, this challenge had to be carried through at all costs: the reward would be glory. In the years between 1893 and 1897, the Swedish explorer traveled uninterruptedly through the vast open spaces of eastern Turkestan:

Bottom: Sven Hedin (photographed here in 1905 riding a camel in the direction of Belucistan) undertook his first Asian journey at the age of 21: in 1886 he departed from Baku and, crossing the Caspian Sea, reached Persia and then the coast of the Persian Gulf. From there he headed to Bassora, visiting Baghdad and the Tigris regions and then proceeding towards Teheran. This three-month journey was just the beginning of an extraordinary career as a traveler.

255

Left: Linguist, cartographer and talented painter, Hedin spent much of his life traveling in the remotest regions of Tibet and Chinese Turkestan. His support for Nazism was severely condemned in his home country and abroad. He died at Stockholm in 1952, lonely and forgotten.

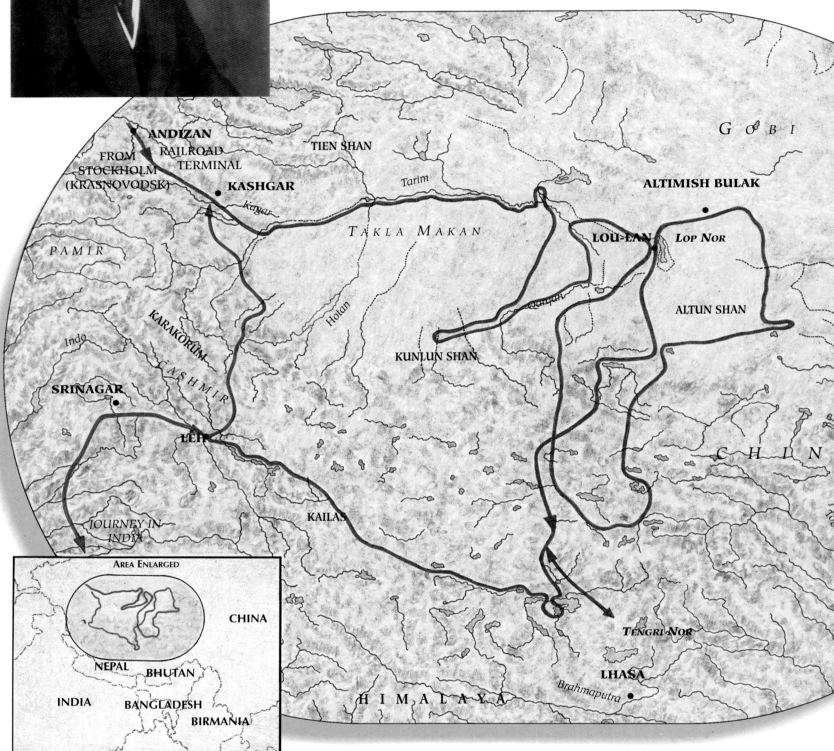

GOBI

ANDIZAN
FROM STOCKHOLM (KRASNOVODSK)
RAILROAD TERMINAL

TIEN SHAN

Tarim

ALTIMISH BULAK

KASHGAR

Kagar

TAKLA MAKAN

LOU-LAN

LOP NOR

PAMIR

Hotan

ALTUN SHAN

KARAKORUM

KUNLUN SHAN

CASHMIR

Indo

SRINAGAR

LEH

CHIN

KAILAS

JOURNEY IN INDIA

TENGRI NOR

AREA ENLARGED

CHINA

NEPAL

BHUTAN

INDIA

BANGLADESH

BIRMANIA

HIMALAYA

LHASA

Brahmaputra

256

Above: Hedin, who from a very early age had been a talented draughtsman, executed this watercolor showing the entrance to the tomb of the fifth Dalai Lama at Tashi-Lunpo.

Top: Hedin was struck by the solemn dignity of the tombs of the high priests. In Tasci-Lunpo he painted a series of fine watercolors: the one in this illustration shows the Namgjal-Lhakang with the likeness of Tsongkapa.

Above and bottom left: Sven Hedin, well aware of his vocation as a traveler, was an attentive and curious observer. The meticulous captions, precise notes, and careful watercolors

reveal the true spirit of the modern explorer. His images depict the elaborate hair styles and precious jewellery of the three Tibetan women of Kjangrang in the Himalayas.

flying in the face of logic he tackled the Tien Shan mountains in mid-winter, and early in the summer he ventured into the Takla Makan, the immense sandy desert extending for thousands of kilometers from the Tarim River to the Tibetan highlands. The crossing of the Takla Makan was the most terrible experience of his life: almost all of his men and camels died of thirst and Hedin himself only survived by a miracle when, already delirious, he stumbled by chance over a well.

He remained for a further year in the region, exploring the Tarim basin on the northern margins of the desert. He then headed east, following the caravan trails to China. In May, 1897, after a long trip on the Trans-Siberian railway, he re-entered Stockholm. To his great disappointment he found not the celebrating crowds he had dreamed of, but just the members of his own family. It was in Britain that Hedin's merits as an explorer were most fully recognized. He was received at court and met Stanley on his return from the forests of the Congo. The Royal Geographical Society presented him with medals and honors. It was not yet the true fame he craved, but at least Europe was beginning to notice the name of Sven Hedin. Soon he would be acclaimed as the greatest traveler of all time, as soon as he returned from Lhasa. Mindful of the previous disaster, Hedin concentrated all his energy on the preparation of the most important expedition of his career. "For this journey my equipment was incomparably more comprehensive than on any previous occasion. It weighed no less than a ton and filled two dozen chests, many of which were specially constructed to be carried on horseback."

His equipment included dozens of scientific instruments, firearms and ammunition, a collapsible canoe, gifts for local leaders, a small library, canned food, and no less than 58 pairs of ice glasses. Furthermore, Hedin carried with him a series of cameras and lenses and all the necessary material for developing and printing his photographs. The Russian government guaranteed him free transport as far as the last station in eastern Turkestan. Hedin left Sweden in the summer of 1899, and a few months later

257

was navigating the tranquil waters of the Tarim heading toward the Lop Nor region. After having spent over a year roaming the immense territory between Tibet and the Takla Makan, the Swedish explorer found himself celebrating his 36th birthday, the happiest of his life, in an unexplored region of the Gobi desert. Over the previous few days, a violent sandstorm had erased the faint trail followed by the caravan. The men were exhausted and were wandering in search of a spring hidden in an unmarked spot in the deadly sea of sand. Within a day or two the camels would start to die one after the other. Hedin inevitably cast his mind back to the tragic adventure in the Takla Makan some years earlier. On that occasion, he had been fortunate. Would he be so again? All around them were endless, barren dunes. The tracks of the wild camels then reappeared and became increasingly numerous. The water had to be close, but the slightest undulation of the ground, one dune slightly higher than another might be enough to conceal it from view. Suddenly the spring appeared before their eyes: a frozen pool a few yards in diameter.

This took place on the 19th of February, 1901, and there could hardly have been a more welcome birthday present. They were safe. They drank and distributed the cracked ice among the camels "whose eyes shone with contentment." Their thirst slaked, the men dug large pits, which they filled with glowing embers and covered with sand. lying on the warm ground they were able sleep for a few hours during the freezing night when the temperature could drop as far as 20°C below zero.

The oasis of Altimish-bulak was now just over a dozen miles away, but Hedin decided to turn to the south, toward the ancient dry basin of Lop Nor. Some months earlier, during his wanderings through the area, he had chanced upon the ruins of an ancient settlement. Marco Polo himself had probably ventured along that same caravan road almost six hundred years earlier. In the past, the Lop Nor region must have been a flourishing commercial center and perhaps those weathered fragments of sculpted wood and the copper coins he had discovered were testimony to the existence of a town, the ancient Loulan on the banks of what was once a lake. The excavations up to that point had turned up a few decorated columns, pieces of cloth, and terracotta vases. Nothing decisive. Stubbornly Hedin decided to continue with his search until on the 8th of March, 1901, he discovered over 200 manuscripts and 42 wooden panels covered with Chinese characters hidden in a clay container buried at a depth of 24 inches. Those tattered pieces of paper not only proved the existence of Loulan, a major center for the distribution of grain and other goods in the region, but also contained an explanation of the mystery of Lop Nor: the ruins of Loulan were surrounded by the desert, but in the past the city had stood on the shore of the lake. The archaeological remains confirmed Hedin's theory that the Lop Nor "migrated" over the course of the historic epochs. He made an accurate survey of the area and found it to be

Below: Hedin working on an improvised desk aboard his raft anchored on the banks of the Tarim in the autumn of 1899. The flat-bottomed vessel specially constructed for navigation in the shallow river waters was around 36 feet long and 8 feet. The navigation of the Tarim was a pleasant interlude before tackling the desert expanse of the Takla Makan.

Opposite bottom left: Hedin took great care over his disguise: everything he had with him was of Chinese or Mongol manufacture except for a compass and a set of notebooks in which to write his diary, a map of Tibet and a few other objects. His clothing was specially bought in Mongolia and comprised a long, dark red coat, a cap with ear-flaps and a pair of soft leather boots. In order to remember his true identity, he wrote, he had to "look long and hard into the mirror."

perfectly flat: over a distance of 20 miles there was a rise of just 4 inches. Continuing with the exploration, the expedition soon found itself in a watery labyrinth. In just one week an enormous lake had formed through infiltration virtually in front of the explorers very eyes. At certain points the water spouted up to a meter high, propelled by large air bubbles. Hedin noted that the basin was slowly shifting toward the north: on one side the shore extended in deposits of mud, sand, and organic detritus, on the other the strong wind sculpted the dry land, preparing a new bed for the lake. It must always have been so: the vegetation, the animals, and the inhabitants followed the Lop Nor in its periodic movements. "In the future," wrote Hedin, "it will be possible to determine the length of the period of these oscillations; at the moment we only know that in the year 265, the last in the reign of the Emperor Yuan Tis, the Lop Nor was to be found in the northern part of the desert." The wandering lake's parting gift was a violent sandstorm and Hedin was forced to remain in his yurt, the comfortable Mongol tent he had adopted as his living quarters, for two days. By the flickering light of a lantern he updated his diary and planned his attempt to reach the Tibetan borders and Lhasa. By the orders of the Dalai Lama, no foreigner was permitted to enter the holy city: over the previous fifty years, at least a dozen travelers had attempted to violate this taboo, but without success. Hedin planned to out-wit the controls of the Tibetan militia by disguising himself as a Mongol pilgrim. Then, as soon as an opportunity presented itself, he intended to leave the caravan and to ride hard for Lhasa. Perhaps in this way he would manage to confuse the efficient Tibetan spy system. In great secrecy he began preparations for his departure. Sheber, a true Lama, born in Urga, had agreed to take part in the journey and to teach Hedin the basics of the Mongol language. At the head of a caravan of 30 men and 150 pack animals, the Swede left the Lop Nor region on the 17th of May, 1901. After having climbed the northern slopes of Altin Tagh, the caravan halted close to the Kum-kol lake at an altitude of 13,200 feet. The march

was heavy going: the mountain ranges succeeded one another with monotonous regularity from east to west, obliging the expedition to make continual ascents and descents of the valleys as they headed the mountain passes. The region was completely uninhabited and the driving rain made the trek even more unpleasant. At the end of July, Hedin halted no more than 186 miles from Lhasa: he felt that it would not be wise to proceed further under those conditions and prepared to put the final part of his plan into action. He shaved off his hair and mustache, blackened up his face with a mixture of grease and earth, and dressed in the costume of a pilgrim. With two companions, five mules, and four horses he set off in the direction of Lhasa, fifteen days' march away. There was no respite from the rain. Three days after their departure, a patrol of three horsemen appeared as if in a vision on the brow of a hill. They observed the strangers for a few minutes before melting away again. Hedin realized that the Tibetan frontier guards were aware of his presence. The following

day the bogus pilgrims met a caravan of nomads with hundreds of yaks loaded with tea heading toward the Brahamaputra valley. While Sheber spoke with their chief, exchanging courtesies and information on the condition of the trails leading to the capital, Hedin distinctly heard an old man pointing toward him and identifying him as a "Peling," a European. His suspicions were confirmed: his true identity was known. What had happened? Who had betrayed his secret? He thought he had taken every possible precaution to maintain his anonymity. Perhaps Sheber had been right: the Dalai Lama really was omniscient and knew everything about them, where they were going, and even what they spoke about each day. There was nothing to be done. On the 8th of August, Hedin was halted by a platoon of armed Tibetan soldiers. Their orders were explicit: "Not a single step closer to Lhasa." The foreigners were to be escorted back to their base camp. Hedin was forced to accept that his mission had failed. He had had enough of Tibet and its hellish climate. Linking up again with his caravan, he decided to

Above: Between 1906 and 1908, with his interest in Lhasa having been diminished by the British occupation of a few years earlier, Hedin devoted all his energy to the exploration of the remotest areas of the Tibetan uplands. His maps and sketches (the illustration shows Ter-Namtso and Poru-tso, two lakes to the North of the Himalayas) made a great contribution to geographical knowledge of the region.

Opposite bottom: This watercolor by Hedin depicts a lama of Tscoktuschu.

Bottom: The spirituality of the people of Tibet profoundly affected Hedin who produced numerous sketches and watercolors of the pilgrims he encountered on his journey toward Lhasa. In the illustration on the right can be seen two monks from Mendong, the image on the bottom depicts some Tibetan soldiers.

Top: This sketch by Sven Hedin depicts Tikse-gumpa, a monastery built on a rocky outcrop in Ladak.

Bottom: This drawing also reveals the artistic talent of the Swedish explorer. It shows a religious dispute in the games courtyard at Tashi-Lunpo.

Opposite top: A map of the Himalayas, the location of the sources of the Indus, the Brahmaputra and the Sutlej, compiled in 1909 and based on the observations of Sven Hedin. Having lost interest in Lhasa after it was occupied by the British, Hedin devoted his third expedition (1906-1908) to the exploration of the western regions of the Tibetan uplands.

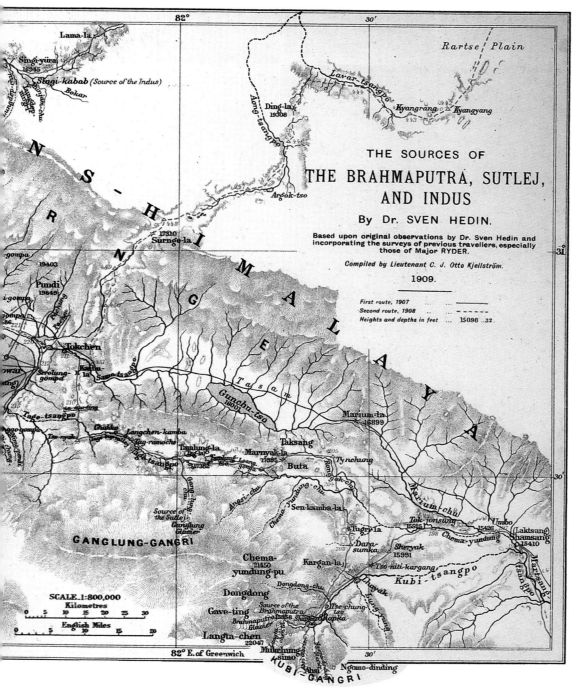

THE SOURCES OF
THE BRAHMAPUTRA, SUTLEJ, AND INDUS

By Dr. SVEN HEDIN.

Based upon original observations by Dr. Sven Hedin and incorporating the surveys of previous travellers, especially those of Major RYDER.

Compiled by Lieutenant C. J. Otto Kjellström.

1909.

First route, 1907 ...
Second route, 1908 ...
Heights and depths in feet ... 15098 .32.

SCALE 1:800,000
Kilometres
English Miles

82° E. of Greenwich

retreat to Ladakh to the west. The march away from the Tibetan authorities was long and difficult. Many of the men died en route together with most of the animals. Four months later, the exhausted survivors left the inhospitable mountains of Tibet and entered the city of Leh where at last they were warmly welcomed. Even for the indefatigable Swede, prepared to support all kinds of privations, the crossing of the vast plateau had been a gruelling experience. Hedin was not the kind of man to indulge in regrets and yet, "when, toward sunset, the sky begins to darken in the East," he wrote in his diary, "it seems, to me as if the night wants to draw its veil over the land of the Dalai Lama and protect the mysteries therein with its shadows." Tibet was not to remain isolated for much longer, however: in 1904 British troops entered Lhasa, forcing the Dalai Lama to flee. The violated holy city lost all its attraction for Hedin, and he was to dedicate his next journey to the exploration of the western part of the plateau, researching another geographical mystery: the sacred mountain of Kailas and the source of the Indus.

After visiting India, he returned to Leh and from there led his caravan across the high passes of the Karakorum as far as Kashgar, the capital of eastern Turkistan. He returned to Sweden in June, 1902. In three years and three days of traveling he had traced a web of routes across the deserts and mountains of Central Asia. A journey which, to use his own words, had been "no bed of roses."

Right: Mount Kailas, in a sketch by Hedin. The Swedish explorer was the first European to penetrate the Kailas region, the sacred mountain par excellence and the navel of the world according to Buddhist and Hindu mythology. Hedin stayed in the area for some time and was struck by the profound beliefs of the Tibetans, who each year arrived in the thousands for the ritual pilgrimage around the mountain.

I n 1884, the wreckage of a ship lost off Siberia was found on the coast of Greenland, on the other side of the Arctic Ocean. What was the route followed by the currents that carried it over 3,000 miles? What lay beneath the pack-ice? Open sea or dry land? Virtually nothing was known of the extreme Arctic regions. Ten years later, Fridtjof Nansen, a Norwegian explorer, allowed his ship to drift with the pack so as trace the currents and to explore the unknown Polar deserts. His attempt to reach the Pole was unsuccessful, but from that moment, the race was on. The North Pole, an imaginary geographical point, became the most sought after prize in global exploration, an activity transformed into a contest of speed and efficiency. In 1909 an American, Robert Peary, finally reached the objective, inaugurating a new mode of Arctic travel. However, his glory was short-lived as another explorer, Frederick Cook claimed the merit for the discovery. Their feats, both extraordinary, were overshadowed by interminable petty wrangling: who was the true conqueror of the North Pole?

THE NORTH POLE

FRIDTJOF NANSEN

In the November of 1884, wreckage from a ship was found on the south coast of Greenland. There was nothing strange in this; many ships had sunk in the Arctic seas. However, this particular wreckage came from the *Jeannette*, a vessel that had disappeared three years earlier off the coast of Siberia over 3,000 miles away. What lay behind this mystery? Fridtjof Nansen had no doubts: only a strong ocean current could have carried the wreckage to the opposite side of the Arctic Ocean. A current that, according to his calculations, moved at a velocity of 2.6 nautical miles a day and should pass close to the North Pole. In 1889, Nansen had recently returned from an expedition to Greenland which he had crossed from coast to coast on skis. That enterprise had made him famous in his home country of Norway, and he had been acclaimed as a national hero. Nansen was then 28 years old and had already accumulated a wealth of experience and had a solid scientific background: it was the right moment to exploit his success by obtaining the necessary financing for a new exploration project. In 1890 he presented his plans to the Geographical Society in Oslo: he intended to allow his ship to be imprisoned in the pack-ice and to drift with it to the North Pole. Just as the *Jeannette* had done. His ship, however, would not be crushed by the pack. The secret, according to Nansen, lay not so much with the robustness of the hull as no ship could withstand the tremendous pressures exerted by the moving ice floes by strength alone, what counted was the shape of the hull. The perfect exploration vessel had to be capable of escaping the grip of the pack, lifting itself above the sheets of ice and "slipping eel-like" from their deadly embrace. Nansen personally designed each and every detail of his ship: "Prow, stern and keel; everything was rounded so that the ice could not take a hold at any point." Two years later, with the help of a skilled boat builder, the *Fram* (Forward in Norwegian) was ready. She was forty meters long, a dozen wide, and could carry

Above: Nansen personally designed the ship on which he was to approach the North Pole. A heroic mission that was very nearly completed and led to important scientific discoveries.

Left: In the summer of 1888, Nansen (here portrayed in an imaginary Arctic landscape in the company of his dogs) crossed the Greenland ice-cap on skis. Dissatisfied with the available equipment he personally designed for the occasion new types of sleeping bags, stoves and light sleds, revolutionising the techniques of Polar exploration.

Left: During the
interminable days
spent drifting among
the ice floes, the crew
of the Fram devoted
themselves to the most
diverse occupations.
During the summer
days, when the
climate was milder,
the deck of the ship
was transformed into
a veritable workshop:
the worn equipment
was repaired and
ropes, shoes, and
tools of all kinds
were made. "Our
days," wrote
Nansen, "were
always very
busy."

NOR

SWED

a crew of thirteen. Her cabins were lined with cork, felt, and linoleum so as to completely isolate the interior from the cold and damp. Nansen predicted that his voyage would be lengthy (from two to five years), and it was therefore vital that ship was comfortable. Ignoring those skeptics who judged his project to be "an illogical plan for self-destruction," he left Norway on the 24th of June, 1893. The *Fram* followed the Nordenskjöld's route along the Siberian coast turning her prow northward, as she approached the New Siberian Islands. Early in September, the first ice floes began to form: the Polar winter was on its way, and Nansen would soon know whether his theories were correct. It was a question of days before the sea would be completely frozen, trapping the ship. While they were waiting the crew proceeded with a program of scientific analyses: each day they measured the temperature of the water, its salinity, and the strength of the current on which the outcome of the expedition depended. Samples were taken from the seabed and it was to Nansen's great surprise that the shot-line revealed a depth of 4,723 feet, a discovery that definitively destroyed the belief that the Arctic Ocean was shallow. On the 9th of October, the *Fram* was subjected to the pack's first assault: the air was suddenly rent by a deafening crack and enormous sheets of ice squeezed around the ship's flanks, lifting her by several feet.

Above: On the evening of the 20th of November, 1894, Nansen called together the crew of the Fram *to put forward his plans. "There was no reason not to depart on an expedition to the Pole, and the scientific benefits that could* result from such an exploration obliged us to make the attempt," he wrote in his diary. Captain Sverdrup, whose duty was to take the Fram *safely back to Norway, having been excluded, Nansen's choice of companion was Johanssen.*

Opposite left: A box of matches used by Fridtjof Nansen during his Arctic exploration aboard the Fram. *The ship was built to resist the elements. The cabins were insulated with cork, felt, and linoleum but the explorer had to abandon her to proceed toward his objective with dog sleds.*

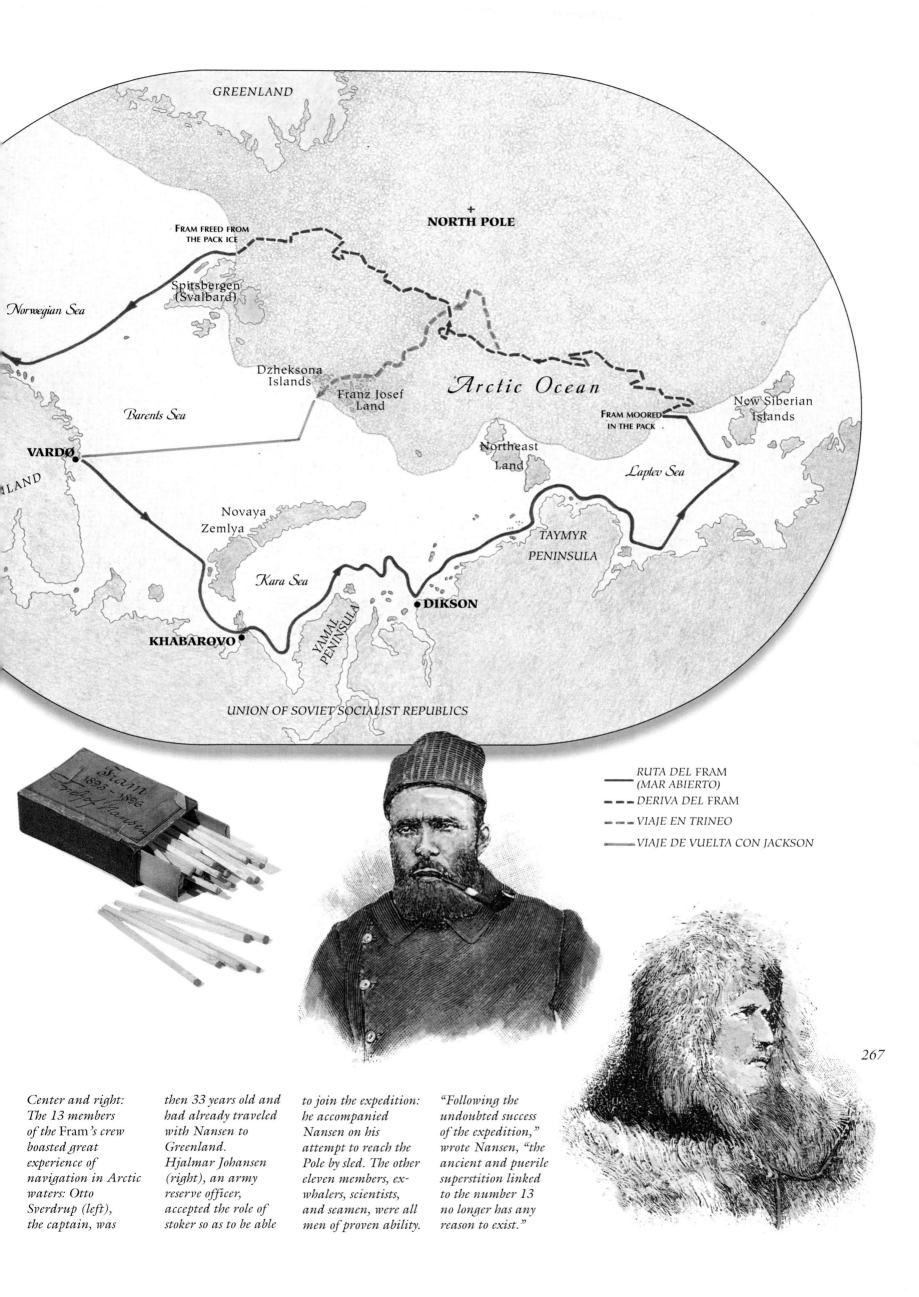

GREENLAND

NORTH POLE

FRAM FREED FROM THE PACK ICE

Spitsbergen (Svalbard)

Norwegian Sea

Arctic Ocean

Dzheksona Islands

Franz Josef Land

FRAM MOORED IN THE PACK

New Siberian Islands

Barents Sea

Northeast Land

VARDØ

Laptev Sea

NLAND

Novaya Zemlya

TAYMYR PENINSULA

Kara Sea

DIKSON

YAMAL PENINSULA

KHABAROVO

UNION OF SOVIET SOCIALIST REPUBLICS

——— RUTA DEL FRAM (MAR ABIERTO)
- - - - DERIVA DEL FRAM
– · – · VIAJE EN TRINEO
——— VIAJE DE VUELTA CON JACKSON

267

Center and right: The 13 members of the *Fram*'s crew boasted great experience of navigation in Arctic waters: Otto Sverdrup (left), the captain, was then 33 years old and had already traveled with Nansen to Greenland. Hjalmar Johansen (right), an army reserve officer, accepted the role of stoker so as to be able to join the expedition: he accompanied Nansen on his attempt to reach the Pole by sled. The other eleven members, ex-whalers, scientists, and seamen, were all men of proven ability. "Following the undoubted success of the expedition," wrote Nansen, "the ancient and puerile superstition linked to the number 13 no longer has any reason to exist."

It was, wrote Nansen, an unimaginable noise, similar to that "produced by the simultaneous sounding of all the pipes of an organ." The *Fram* was undamaged and, little by little, the apprehensions of the crew disappeared, giving way to the monotony of their daily routine. The days passed slowly in an eerie silence: Nansen began to note that the drifting of the pack was not as constant as he had hoped. The *Fram* followed a capricious, irregular route first to the north and then to the south. Summer arrived followed by a second winter without anything happening. Nansen began to be frustrated by that wait at the mercy of forces beyond his control: "Ah! The very soul turns to ice," he wrote, "What I would not give for a single day's struggle, even for a moment of danger." His wishes were soon to be granted. His yearning to abandon the ship and reach the pole by sled grew stronger every day. It was now clear that as far as could be calculated the winds and current were dragging the *Fram* to the west, away from the objective. The winter was very harsh, and the thermometer fell to 58°C below zero. On the 14th of March, 1895, as spring approached, Nansen departed with a companion, Frederick Johansen, three sleds drawn by dogs and all the equipment necessary for the decisive assault on the North Pole. He carried rations for three months: dried meat and fish, 86 pounds of butter, an oil stove, firearms, ammunition, and two kayaks constructed in canvas and bamboo. From that moment the two men were on their own. Should they get into difficulties they had no means of contacting, the *Fram* as she continued her westward drift. Nansen hoped to cover the 403 miles separating him from the Pole rapidly, and then head south to reach Franz Josef Land. However, after the first few days

Center: "It all began with a slight creak, almost a squeal, around the flanks of the ship. Then the noise gradually increased little by little; it transformed into an acute lament that became a grumble and then a roar. The tumult redoubled and thundered like the simultaneous blasting of all the pipes of an organ." Thus did Nansen describe the first, serious assault made by the pack-ice that in mid-October locked in around the Fram: the ship came through the trial undamaged.

Bottom: During the Arctic summer, broad channels of open water opened around the hull of the Fram, *revealing a surprising concentration of algae and diatoms: Nansen dedicated long days to the collection and study of the micro-organisms present in the freezing waters of the Arctic Ocean, an activity that he defined as "of extreme interest and secure success." The windmill seen on the deck of the* Fram *was connected to a dynamo and guaranteed a constant supply of electricity.*

Left: The observation of a solar eclipse. Early in October, 1893 the Fram *was imprisoned in the pack-ice and began her interminable drift toward the northwest. Any event that interrupted the monotony of the daily routine was enthusiastically welcomed by the crew: the predicted solar eclipse of the 6th of April, 1894 was described by Nansen in his diary as "a great event" and provided an opportunity to verify the efficiency of the scientific instruments.*

Bottom left: The reading of the deep water thermometers, repeated for five consecutive days during the August of 1894, revealed the unexpected presence of a layer of relatively warm water at a depth of between 264 and 1,485 feet, sandwiched between two layers of cold water. Nansen subsequently observed that such temperature differences remained constant throughout the different seasons.

Bottom right: The daily calculations of latitude revealed the capricious nature of the drifting pack-ice pushed by the wind and ocean currents in a slow rotation around the Pole. On the 8th of September, 1894, the discouraged explorer noted that the Fram *was located at 78° 35' North "half a degree lost in nine days."*

the flat uniformity of the pack was disrupted by a labyrinth of crests and turrets that were desperately difficult to overcome. Men and dogs advanced extremely slowly through that tormented landscape, hauling and lifting the heavy sleds over the icy buttresses. Exhausted and with their frozen clothes imprisoning them as if in "a crystalline carapace," Nansen and Johansen realized that they were never going to make it. On the 8th of April, Nansen recorded their position in his diary: "Latitude 86° 10', Longitude 95° East of Greenwich. Temperature at 8 o'clock in the morning -32°C." In front of them extended a chaotic stretch of ice. There were still 248 miles to the Pole and they simply did not have the strength to cover them. They had to turn back before it was too late. The long retreat south was appalling. The spring thaw had opened great crevasses in the ice which the two men were forced to detour around. Their food supplies were virtually exhausted, and one after the other the dogs were shot and eaten. At last, on the 24th of July, on their last legs and with all hope gone, they spotted a dark line on the horizon: it was the northernmost island of Franz Josef Land. However, it took another fifteen days of superhuman effort before they reached the open sea and were able to launch their kayaks. They wandered the deserted archipelago until September, when the first flocks of migratory birds appeared in the sky. It was time to commence their preparations for surviving the endless Arctic winter, the third since they left Norway. They built a shelter using the materials they had on hand, stones, bones and walrus skins, and procured sufficient supplies of bear meat. On the 19th of May, 1896, they set out once again with their kayaks: perhaps, with a bit of luck, they might have reached Spitzbergen and encountered one of the seal hunting ships that cruised the area. Then on the 17th of June, the completely unexpected happened: During a momentary period of

Top left: Amundsen Hendriksen, Mogstad Blessing, and Sverdrup pose for photographs during the expedition to the North Pole (September 1894). The enterprise was obstructed by the sheets of ice that trapped the Fram.

Top right: In June, 1896, Nansen and Johanssen, in excellent physical condition, reached the British base at Cape Flora in Franz Josef Land. During the third and last Arctic winter they had lived like Eskimos, holed up with stones, bones, and skins, eating bear and walrus meat and sewing the clothes they wore themselves.

Opposite center:
On the 14th of March, 1895, Nansen and Johansen left the Fram *and, with 3 sleds and supplies for 3 months, struck out for the North Pole. The bad weather conditions and the mutating pack-ice made the trip a torment. Four weeks later, their strength was running out. The explorers realized that they were never going to make it to the Pole and decided to turn back.*

Opposite bottom:
During the monotonous days passed in the pack-ice Nansen and his crew dedicated themselves to systematic scientific observations. Sounding the sea bed, Nansen measured depths varying from 10,890 to 12,870 feet, definitively disproving the theory of a shallow Arctic Ocean.

fine weather Nansen climbed a hill not far from their camp. The fog had cleared revealing a monochrome landscape. In the midst of that solitude he suddenly seemed to hear a dog barking. Surely it was impossible! Perhaps the long confinement on the ice had begun to affect his mind. He set out to reconnoiter, heard further barks and then the unmistakable timbre of a human voice. In the distance he made out the shape of a sled and a man coming toward him. He was clean shaven, smelled of soap and introduced himself as Frederick Jackson, a member of a British expedition to the Franz Josef Islands. His camp was close by. A ship carrying supplies, said Jackson, would be arriving within a few weeks. They were safe. On the 7th of August, Nansen and Johansen embarked for Norway.

In the meantime the *Fram*, after having reached Spitzbergen, had freed itself from the ice and returned home without problems. The Pole had not been reached, but the expedition could be said to have been a success all the same. For months on end Nansen and his companion had lived like Eskimos, eating bear and walrus meat and using the skins to keep warm. Not only had they survived in extreme environmental conditions, but they had even put on weight. From a scientific point of view the exploration had been extremely profitable. The rest was of no importance: "My trip's only goal," wrote Nansen in his report, "was the study of these deserts. As I see it the search for a mathematical point that identifies the Pole is not of the slightest interest." Robert Edwin Peary, an ex-officer in the United States Navy, thought differently.

Top: Navigation in the fragile kayaks was made even more dangerous by the presence of walruses. Usually when threatened, the explorers sought refuge on one of the many sheets of floating ice while they waited for the animals to depart. But on the 15th of June, 1896, an "old monster" succeeded in sinking Nansen's kayak and he risked losing boat, equipment, and supplies.

Center: Nansen's arrival in the port of Oslo aboard the Christiana *on the 9th of September, 1896.*

Bottom: A 1928 photo of Fridtjof Nansen. "The only aim of my journey," he wrote on his return from the epic expedition to the North Pole, "has been the study of these deserts."

271

ROBERT PEARY

On the 1st of April, 1909, the last support group left the advanced camp at 97° 47' latitude to return to the base on Ellesmere Island. Peary was left with his black friend and assistant Matthew Henson and four Eskimos. The following day they were to leave on their final assault with five sleds drawn by dogs. Their objective, the North Pole, was now just 155 miles away. Robert Peary was then 52 years old and had considerable Polar experience. His career as an explorer had begun 23 years earlier in Greenland. For almost ten years from 1886 onward he had roamed the great island's ice cap for thousands of miles, pushing on as far as the remote northern coastline gripped by the pack-ice. He made contact with the Eskimos and studied their age-old methods of Arctic survival. From then on, all his efforts were dedicated to the conquest of the Pole. His previous attempt in 1906 had failed around 200 miles from the objective. Peary had learned from

that defeat and, over time, he had come to a number of conclusions. The most favorable season in the Polar regions lasted a just a few months: the key to the success of an expedition to the Pole was therefore rapidity. In order to advance quickly and return before the thaw, it was vital to travel with light packs, and to waste as little time as possible pitching and striking camps. No tents, therefore, as they were bulky and subject to freezing, but rather solid igloos constructed in situ, in which the necessary supplies of food could be stored safe from hungry bears. Step by step, Peary developed his system of advanced camps: special teams were used as trail blazers and to set up permanent deposits of food and equipment before returning to base. Just a small group of selected men in peak condition would then go on to reach the Pole. The labors of many contributing to the success of a few: Peary was convinced that with this method he would succeed in raising the Stars and Stripes over the Pole. In April, 1908, the

Left: When he left for the Pole on the 6th of April, 1909, Peary was 53 years old: his physical condition, was excellent, but he realized that this was his last chance to reach his objective. On his return, intoxicated by his success, he wrote in his diary, "My task is finished. That which from the outset I had decided to do, that which I believed I could do , and that which I wanted to do, I have done. The North Pole is mine, after 23 years of effort, hard work, disappointments, privations, sufferings great and small, and a certain degree of risk."

Right: Peary personally took care of every aspect of the organization of the expedition, paying particular attention to clothing. The experience accumulated during his earlier trips to Greenland had convinced him to adopt the clothes used by the Eskimos rather than wool as they were without doubt better suited to the severe Arctic conditions: trousers and parkas made of bear and fox skins, fur gloves, and boots in warm, waterproof sealskin.

Roosevelt, a ship specially designed for navigation in the ice fields, dropped anchor near Cape Sheridan, in the narrow strait separating Greenland from the Canadian archipelago. Peary had the provisions and equipment unloaded and organized their transportation by sled to Cape Columbia, the extreme northern tip of Ellesmere Island. There he settled in to spend the long Arctic night, preparing the last details of the expedition. Early in the spring, as soon as the temperature was a little milder, the great adventure got under way: on the 1st of March, 1909, the long caravan of 19 sleds, 133 dogs and 24 men, including 18 Eskimos from Greenland, set off to the north. Exactly a month later, the first phase of Peary's project had been completed, and permanent camps had been established along two thirds of the route along the 70th parallel to the Pole. In spite of the delays and difficulties caused by the pressure ridges and broad channels of open water created by the continual movement of the ice floes, the mechanism had worked perfectly. Now, with the support group's work completed, Peary had to rely on his own energies. The dogs and the men were well rested and in good health, and the equipment was in perfect condition: success beckoned. If everything went to plan, the run to the Pole would be completed in a matter of days. After a few hours rest, on the 2nd of April, 1909, Peary gave the order to depart. The sleds advanced rapidly on the flat expanse of ice: there were no unexpected incidents, and none of the feared channels that could open in the ice from one moment to the next appeared to upset the team's rhythm. They maintained an average speed of 30 miles a day. During a halt on the 6th of April, Peary calculated their position as 89° 57' latitude, just over three miles from the Pole. They had done it! To make quite sure, the explorers continued along their route well beyond the point indicated by the instruments. They did not want to run the risk of missing their objective, that imaginary

Bottom: In the September of 1909, the Italian Sunday newspaper, the Domenica del Corriere, *dedicated its cover page to Frederick Cook, portrayed in the act of planting the American flag at the North Pole. The controversy between Peary and Cook inflamed public opinion; the press threw itself eagerly into the debate and the polemic dragged on for years with no real winners or losers being declared. Both pretenders probably reached their objective, but neither was able to provide convincing proof of his exploit.*

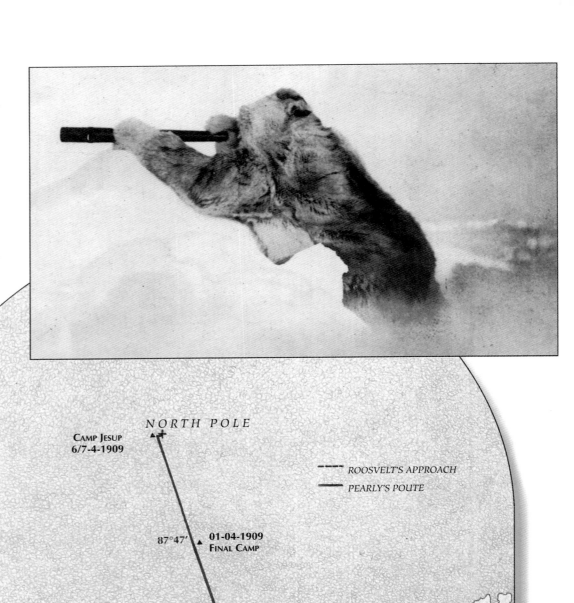

Top: The surveying instruments available to Peary, here photographed while scrutinizing the horizon through a telescope, essentially comprised a compass, a series of chronometers, and a so-called "artificial horizon" (a vessel filled with mercury that allowed the true position of the horizon to be established even when it was hidden behind the ice masses). The measurements made by the explorer were not, however, sufficient to prove his success: only recently has research, promoted by the American National Geographical Society, confirmed that Peary actually reached the Pole.

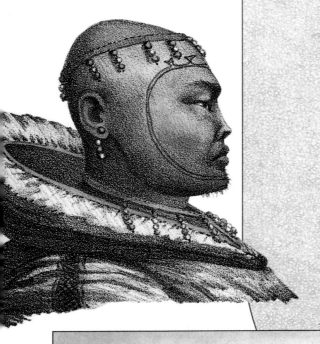

NORTH POLE

CAMP JESUP
6/7-4-1909

- - - - ROOSVELT'S APPROACH
———— PEARLY'S POUTE

87°47'   01-04-1909
            FINAL CAMP

Arctic Ocean

BASE CAMP

ROOSEVELT ANCHORS
FOR THE WINTER   1905-1906
                      1908-1909

CAPE COLUMBIA   CAPE SHERIDAN
DEPATURE 01-03-1909

                        GREENLAND
                        (DENMARK)

FLOAT DRIFT

CANADA
(ELLESMERE)

Center: Frequently the Arctic explorers owed their success and survival to the help received from the Eskimos (this illustration shows an inhabitant of St. Lawrence Island, taken from von Kotzebue's "Voyage"). Today the traditional culture of the Eskimos, threatened by the encroachment of modern civilization, is in rapid decline.

Bottom left: The Arctic pack is composed of an endless expanse of floating ice in continuous movement due to the action of the winds and marine currents. Peary's expedition was obliged to make its way through great masses of ice (the so-called pressure dams) formed by the random collisions of the drifting ice masses.

Top: Peary's success was essentially based on his meticulous logistical preparations and system of advanced camps: special teams traced the route and established a series of food and equipment dumps before returning to base. Only a small group of well rested men with the best dogs would have made the final assault on the Pole. Captain Bartlett's group (in the photo) was the last to return to Ellesmere Island on the 1st of April, 1909: from that moment onward Peary had to rely on his own resources.

point where all the lines of longitude intersected. Up there the usual geographical coordinates lost all meaning: "East, West and North had disappeared," noted Peary, "there remained only one direction, and that was South." The expedition stayed at the Pole for thirty hours, the time needed to complete the necessary calculations and to raise a forest of flags, dominated of course by that of the United States. The return trip was completed smoothly and two weeks later, on the 23rd of April, Peary was back at the base camp on Ellesmere Island. As soon as the Roosevelt reached the first inhabited center of any size, Peary rushed to the Post Office, anxious to communicate his remarkable news to the world. He was the first human being to return from the northern tip of the globe. Overcome by emotion he wrote: "The pole, at last! The reward for three centuries of effort, my dream and my objective for twenty years. Mine at last!" However, his joy was short-lived. Once he returned home, Peary discovered that Frederick Cook, his old exploring companion in Greenland, claimed to have beaten him to the Pole. Cook stated that he had reached the Pole a year earlier, on the 21st of April, 1908. On the return journey, he had been forced to spend the winter on a deserted island which was what delayed his report. In reality, neither Peary, nor Cook had sufficient evidence to support their claims: the testimony of the Eskimos did not count, nor did that of Henson, given the unsuitable color of his skin. Bitter arguments were to follow. The press and the public fell hungrily upon the story, transforming it into a matter of national importance: to whom should the merit for the "conquest" be given? The two adversaries did all they could to discredit each other, and the controversy dragged on for years without any concrete verdict being reach. By then the world's attention had been attracted by the far more tragic Polar adventure that was underway in Antarctica.

Bottom: Robert Edwin Peary, portrayed here about a year after his return from the Pole, was born in 1856 in Pennsylvania. At the age of 30, he discovered his vocation for Arctic exploration. He organized numerous expeditions to Greenland and in 1893 he made his first attempt to reach the North Pole "the last of the great geographical objectives" (conveniently ignoring Antarctica) and his lifetime's ambition. He died in Maine in 1920.

UMBERTO NOBILE:
TO THE POLE IN A DIRIGIBLE

Top: Umberto Nobile, born in the province of Avellino, in Italy, on the 21st of January, 1885, was the designer of the new semi-rigid dirigibles and one of the pioneers of aeronautical engineering. The Italia *expedition, he wrote, "was intended to be the first aerial scientific expedition in the Arctic regions." On his return home, he became the victim of a ruinous campaign of defamation and had to defend himself against accusations of having saved himself, abandoning the crew of the* Italia *to their fate. He died in Italy in 1978.*

Umberto Nobile was sure that he was right: his dirigibles were safer and more reliable than airplanes. His adventure with the *Norge* had proved it. Nobile and Amundsen had left Spitsbergen on the 10th of May, 1926 and had crossed the Arctic Ocean to Alaska, flying over the Pole, in just 72 hours in spite of adverse weather conditions. Nobile decided to set out again two years later. This time the aims of the expedition would be principally scientific. And the glory would be wholly Italian. The new dirigible, the *Italia*, contained 22,800 square yards of hydrogen and was equipped with powerful engines, which allowed it to achieve a maximum speed

of 62 mph. The *Italia* left the base at Spitsbergen and reached the Pole without problems on the 23rd of May, 1928. On the return leg, the dirigible was struck by strong cross winds and snowstorms. For motives that are still unclear, she began to lose height, crashing onto the pack. The impact was violent, and nine men were thrown from the cabin. Another six remained trapped within the dirigible and perished as the wreckage was dragged away by the wind. Many of the survivors were injured, and Nobile himself had a broken leg and arm. Fortunately, sufficient material had been recovered to permit their immediate survival: a few cases of food, a tent, blankets, scientific instruments, and, most importantly, a two-way radio. They could establish their position and call for help. But, strangely, no one received the regular S.O.S. messages anxiously transmitted from the

Center: The Norge *took just 16 hours and 40 minutes to reach the geographical pole: the dirigible then descended to 660 feet above the surface of the pack so that Nobile and Amundsen could launch the Italian and Norwegian flags with precision. In spite of their reciprocal respect, the relationship between the two men was never good, but this did not prevent Amundsen from taking part in the search for the survivors of the* Italia *disaster. He was killed during this search.*

Bottom: Roald Amundsen was almost 53 years old when he embarked on the Norge *for the first flight over the North Pole. The previous year the Norwegian explorer had attempted to reach the objective in a seaplane but had been forced down just 140 miles from the Pole by an engine failure.*

276

Top: The crew of the Norge: seated in the first row, from the left, the three protagonists of the expedition, Roald Amundsen, Lincoln Ellsworth, and the Italian Umberto Nobile. Ellsworth, an American millionaire personally interested in polar exploration, supplied the 75,000 dollars needed to acquire the dirigible from the Italian government.

Bottom: The Norge left Kingsbay in the Spitsbergen archipelago on the 10th of May, 1926, reaching the coast of Alaska, 2,480 miles away, just 72 hours later. Aboard, apart from Amundsen and the American Lincoln Ellsworth, was the designer of the airship, the Italian Umberto Nobile. The Norge's feat opened the way for the aerial exploration of the Arctic.

pack. On the 1st of June, three men in the grip of panic decided to attempt to walk to the nearest land, about 60 miles away. Finally, ten days after the disaster, an amateur radio enthusiast heard the weak distress signal. Rescue operations were immediately organized. Various international expeditions involving a total of 1,500 men, 18 ships, and 22 airplanes left to search for Nobile and his companions. On the 24th of June, a Swedish plane succeeded in landing on the ice, not far from the tent which the survivors had painted in red to make it more visible from above: there was only room for one passenger on board and, for reasons to do with loading, the pilot insisted on taking Nobile in spite of the explorer's protests. The subsequent rescue attempts came to nothing. In the meantime the weather conditions were worsening and the five remaining men's

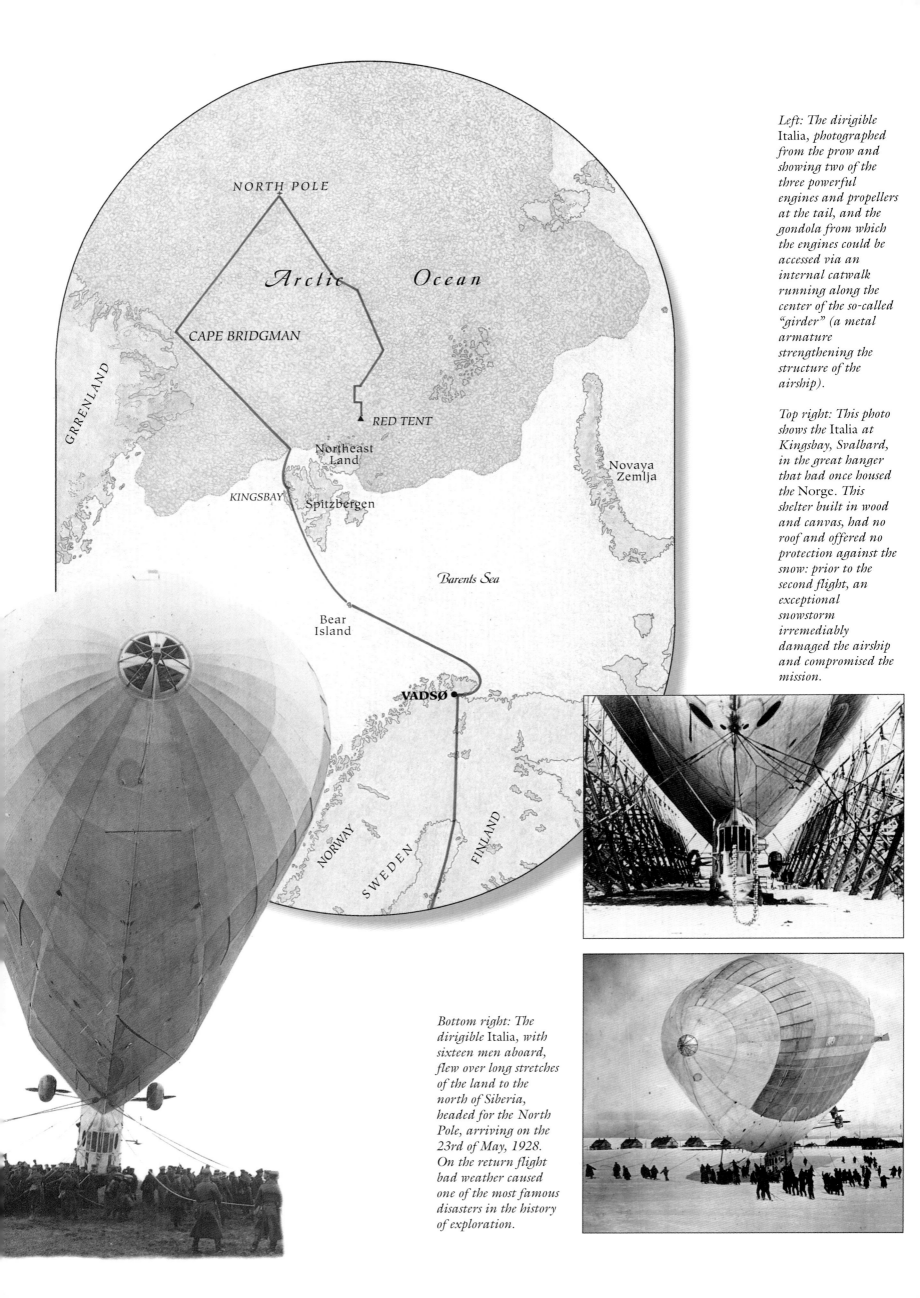

Left: The dirigible Italia, photographed from the prow and showing two of the three powerful engines and propellers at the tail, and the gondola from which the engines could be accessed via an internal catwalk running along the center of the so-called "girder" (a metal armature strengthening the structure of the airship).

Top right: This photo shows the Italia at Kingsbay, Svalbard, in the great hanger that had once housed the Norge. This shelter built in wood and canvas, had no roof and offered no protection against the snow: prior to the second flight, an exceptional snowstorm irremediably damaged the airship and compromised the mission.

Bottom right: The dirigible Italia, with sixteen men aboard, flew over long stretches of the land to the north of Siberia, headed for the North Pole, arriving on the 23rd of May, 1928. On the return flight bad weather caused one of the most famous disasters in the history of exploration.

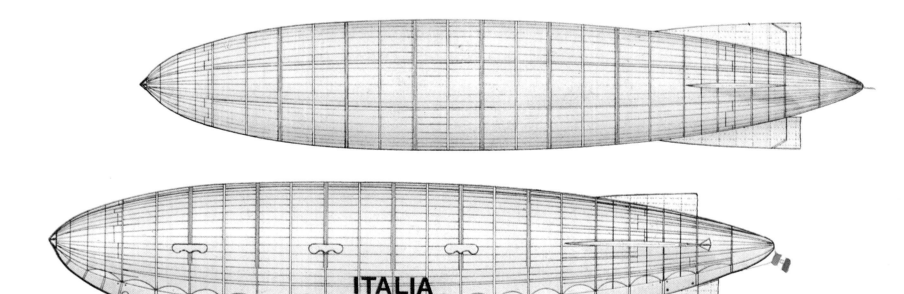

ITALIA

Top: The Italia *was composed of a huge tapering envelope containing 24,000 square yards of gas, reinforced longitudinally with a metal skeleton. The crew of 16 men, including many scientists, was housed in a spacious gondola slung below the envelope. The* Italia, *powered by three engines with propellers, and equipped with large rudders, could reach a speed of 62 mph.*

Above: This photo shows a number of the crew members relaxing: all of the participants in the expedition were Italian with the exception of the Swedish meteorologist Malgren, and Behounek, a Czech professor of physics from the University of Prague. Eight men died in the disaster.

Right: The tragedy of the Italia, *which crashed on the pack-ice during its return flight from the Pole, cost the lives of 8 men. The survivors fortunately succeeded in salvaging a two-way radio set: the repeated SOS messages were only picked up two days after the disaster by a Russian radio fan, who immediately notified the rescue organizations. The crew of the* Italia *was rescued by the icebreaker* Krassin *on the 11th of July, 1928, after almost two months' anxious wait on the pack.*

situation was increasingly critical.

It was not until the 10th of July that the Russian icebreaker *Krassin* succeeded in reaching the red tent and taking off the survivors of the *Italia*. A few hours earlier the Russians had collected two of the men who had left the tent forty days earlier from an ice floe: they were in desperate condition, and in the arguments that followed, one of them was accused of cannibalism.

Nobile himself, accused of abandoning his men, was crushed by the criticism he received at home and abroad. Among the rescuers, there was an illustrious victim: Roald Amundsen crashed into the Barents Sea with his seaplane while trying to reach the pack-ice.

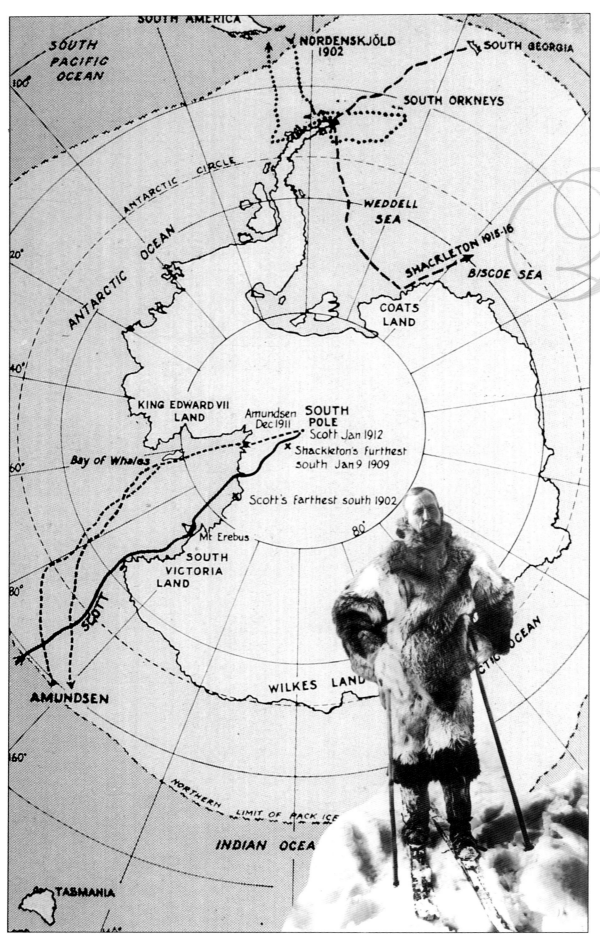

Early in 1910 two expeditions faced each other across the Ross Ice Shelf, the immense frozen sea that permits access to the heart of Antarctica. Both of the men commanding the two parties were figures of exceptional temperament who were striving toward the same objective: planting their national flag on the South Pole, the last great challenge in global exploration. They had similar background experience, but the methods they intended to use to achieve their goal were diametrically opposed. Roald Amundsen was a great believer in sled dogs and their extraordinary stamina. Robert Falcon Scott placed his faith in Siberian ponies and human strength of will. The two explorers found themselves, against their wishes, involved in a competition, a race against time in which they would be either winners or losers. In front of them stretched the Earth's most formidable frozen desert, frighteningly cold and swept by merciless winds. Amundsen reached the Pole on the 14th of December, 1911, while Scott, betrayed to last by ill fortune, was to perish with his companions on their return journey. With this tragedy, the heroic era of polar exploration drew to a definitive close.

THE SOUTH POLE

ROBERT FALCON SCOTT AND ROALD AMUNDSEN

Opposite top: Rather than heavy woollen clothing that was likely to freeze solid, Amundsen (portrayed here in full polar gear) preferred to adopt the Eskimo style of dress. The careful study of the lifestyle of the inhabitants of the Arctic regions, technical innovations and above all, complete faith in dogs as the motive power for the sleds, were the decisive elements in his stunning success.

Opposite bottom: On his return from the South Pole, Amundsen was received personally by the king and queen of Norway. The fame he achieved with his triumphant Antarctic expedition allowed the explorer to repay numerous debts and devote himself to the preparation of a new Arctic expedition. The plan was to repeat Nansen's attempt on the Pole but the project failed.

"Dear Captain Scott, you will probably be the first to read these words... ." Amundsen's letter was dated the 16th of December, 1911. The wind was buffeting the desolate Antarctic plateau and the signs of fatigue and disappointment were carved into the faces of Scott and his four companions. This was on the 17th of January, 1912: after two and a half months of effort and suffering, the British team had finally reached the South Pole, only to find that Amundsen had got there before them. All around the tent, on which flew the Norwegian flag, there were the tracks of men and dogs. It was clear that Amundsen had combed the area so as to be sure that he found the right spot and to carry out all the calculations necessary to establish the exact position of the Pole. There would be no argument as to his victory as had happened between Peary and Cook. The conquest of the South Pole had been transformed into a race and the British team had lost. That was all there was to be said. Scott raised the Union Flag and took the ritual photo. The team now faced the return journey to their base camp no less than 806 miles away. Considering their physical condition, this promised to be a gruelling trek. There was little hope of clemency from the weather, but with a little good fortune Scott felt that they could make it. Just a little good fortune.

The story had begun many years earlier. Scott had first set foot in Antarctica in 1903, when he was a thirty-five year old Lieutenant in the Royal Navy and full of enthusiasm. The expedition he led penetrated as far as 82° South latitude with their sleds: it was no more than a sample for what was to come, but sufficient to underline the immense difficulties posed by the environment. Antarctica was a truly

Above: After having reached the Pole and camped close to the tent abandoned by Amundsen, Scott and his companions faced up to the difficult return journey: "Thus we now turn our backs on the objective of our ambitions and affront 1,280 kilometers across which we must drag our heavy burden at the price of arduous labors. Farewell to our greatest dream!"

Left: Ill fortune and a series of questionable logistical decisions played determinant roles in the tragic failure of Scott's expedition. Scott is portrayed here in full polar gear by the photographer Herbert Pointing.

281

hellish place: inaccessible, unbelievably cold, and ceaselessly battered by violent winds that raised fearful blizzards sweeping across the plateau at speeds of over 186 mph. Nevertheless, another Briton, Sir Ernest Shackleton, had demonstrated in 1909 that the conquest of the Pole was feasible, coming within 124 miles of his objective. Scott's new expedition, which landed on the coast of Ross Island in June, 1910, appeared to have all the necessary ingredients for success. The meticulous organization of the expedition was based around the use of the Siberian ponies Scott preferred to dogs. Scott also had a number of motorized sleds, but these broke down almost immediately. Everything proceeded smoothly and it appeared that the South Pole, the last great challenge in global exploration, would be yet another British conquest. Then, out of nowhere, appeared Amundsen. The Norwegian had, in fact, been preparing an expedition to the North Pole, but having received the news of Peary's success, his enthusiasm for the project had evaporated. Amundsen then turned his attention to the extreme south

Top left: Roald Amundsen in a photograph taken at the Bay of Whales on his return from the South Pole. Amundsen's name is linked to some of the most audacious episodes in polar exploration: between

1903 and 1906 he navigated the Northwest Passage, and fifteen years later, he flew over the North Pole in a dirigible. He died in 1928 in an aircraft accident while flying to the aid of the Nobile expedition.

Top right: The Norwegian flag flying at the South Pole. Amundsen stayed in the area for four days, carrying out all the necessary calculations and completing a vast circle around the pole by sled, thus ensuring

that nobody could subsequently contest the success of the expedition.

Below: This illustration shows the Siberian ponies employed by Scott on his Polar expedition.

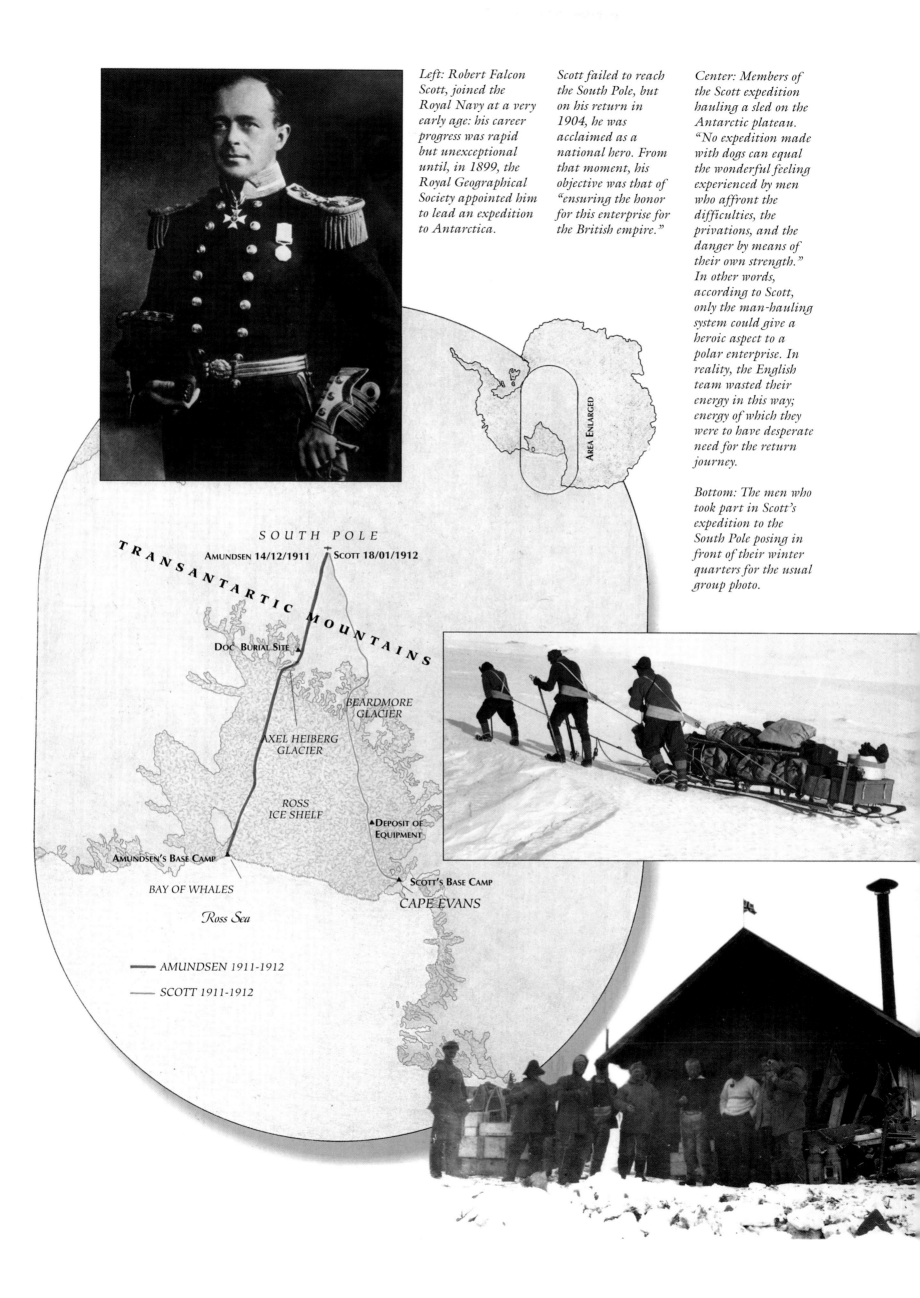

Left: Robert Falcon Scott, joined the Royal Navy at a very early age: his career progress was rapid but unexceptional until, in 1899, the Royal Geographical Society appointed him to lead an expedition to Antarctica.

Scott failed to reach the South Pole, but on his return in 1904, he was acclaimed as a national hero. From that moment, his objective was that of "ensuring the honor for this enterprise for the British empire."

Center: Members of the Scott expedition hauling a sled on the Antarctic plateau. "No expedition made with dogs can equal the wonderful feeling experienced by men who affront the difficulties, the privations, and the danger by means of their own strength." In other words, according to Scott, only the man-hauling system could give a heroic aspect to a polar enterprise. In reality, the English team wasted their energy in this way; energy of which they were to have desperate need for the return journey.

Bottom: The men who took part in Scott's expedition to the South Pole posing in front of their winter quarters for the usual group photo.

AREA ENLARGED

SOUTH POLE

AMUNDSEN 14/12/1911 · SCOTT 18/01/1912

TRANSANTARTIC MOUNTAINS

DOG BURIAL SITE

BEARDMORE GLACIER

AXEL HEIBERG GLACIER

ROSS ICE SHELF

▲Deposit of Equipment

AMUNDSEN'S BASE CAMP

BAY OF WHALES

▲SCOTT'S BASE CAMP

CAPE EVANS

Ross Sea

——— AMUNDSEN 1911-1912

——— SCOTT 1911-1912

and the opposite Pole. He maintained strict secrecy regarding his plans, and it was not until he reached Madeira and his project had been set irreversibly in motion, that he informed Scott of his true intentions through a laconic telegram. The two expeditions reached the Ross Ice Shelf almost contemporaneously: competition was inevitable. Amundsen moored his ship, the famous *Fram* already used by Nansen in the Bay of Whales. Before the onset of the southern winter, he would have already established a series of supply dumps and marked the route that would lead him to the Pole. The Bay of Whales was around a hundred kilometers closer to the Pole, but the Norwegians were faced with unknown terrain. Scott, on the other hand, could follow the route already charted by Shackleton. The advantages and disadvantages were therefore more or less equally divided. The polar winter fell like a leaden cloak over the two camps, and the challenge was postponed until the following spring. As soon as the temperature was acceptable, on the 19th of October, 1911, Amundsen headed south with four men and 52 of his best dogs. The sleds carrying just the indispensable equipment, progressed rapidly across the Ice Shelf until they reached the slopes of the Transantarctic Mountains. Climbing the imposing Axel Heiberg glacier with its deep crevasses was extremely arduous, but completed without significant problems. On the 21st of November, the expedition reached the edge of the plateau, at an altitude of around 1000 feet. There

Amundsen slaughtered many of his dogs, as at that point they were of no further use, and buried their bodies in the snow: they represented a precious stock of fresh meat for the return journey. The worst was now over, and in front of the Norwegians, extended a smooth, gently rising plain. The Pole was reached relatively easily on the 14th of December. Little more than a month later, Amundsen was back at his base camp. Men and dogs were in perfect health and his system of advance camps had functioned perfectly, even allowing the Norwegians the luxury of by-passing some of the food dumps intended for the return journey. Helped by excellent weather conditions, the team had covered 1,848 miles in 99 days, maintaining an extremely high average speed. Amundsen's faith in his dogs had been amply rewarded. While the Norwegian team was leaving the Pole, the British expedition were struggling through the exhausting crevasses of the Beardmore glacier. Their ponies had been

Above: The Framheim, the winter quarters Amundsen built on the Ross Ice Shelf at the Bay of Whales in just over a week of feverish work. It housed eight men and over a hundred dogs.

Left: The first depot established by Amundsen on the Ross Ice Shelf, at 80° South latitude (almost a ton and a half of provisions and equipment were stored there). The Norwegians, enjoying excellent physical health and favored by the weather conditions, needed less than a month to return to their base camp from the Pole; they were even able to permit themselves the luxury of missing out on a number of intermediate depots established along the route.

Bottom left: Amundsen and his team posing for the ritual photo at the South Pole, in front of the tent on which the Norwegian flag was raised.
"The Arctic regions," wrote the explorer, *"and obviously the North Pole itself, had attracted me ever since my youth, and now I found myself at the South Pole. Can you imagine possibly imagine, a greater contrast?"*

Bottom right: Amundsen, favored with excellent weather conditions, reached the South Pole on the 14th of December, 1911, with eleven dogs and four companions. In this *photo, one of the expedition members is posing alongside the Norwegian flag: although exhausted, men and dogs were in excellent health. Early in March, 1912 the international press* *lent great importance to the news. During the same period, Scott and his gallant team were struggling across the Ross Ice Shelf in their desperate attempt to reach their base camp.*

put down a few days earlier as they were too weak to continue the trek, and the men were obliged to haul their heavy sleds themselves. On the 22nd of December, Scott wrote in his diary "Forty-third camp. Altitude around 2,130 meters. Temperature -18.3°. The third part of our journey promises well." The last support group returned to the base camp a couple of weeks later. The Pole was just 149 miles away. The men chosen by Scott for the final assault, Wilson, Oates, Bowers, and Evans, were strong and well prepared, and the objective appeared to be within their grasp. Other depots were laid along the route, reducing the load carried on the sleds. Nevertheless, the fatigue suffered by the five men was greater each day. On the 15th of January, the temperature descended to 15° below zero and the men were exhausted. "Only two days' march separates us from the Pole," wrote Scott, "our success is now assured, and just a single fear assails us; that the Norwegian team may have preceded us." The following day Bowers noticed a dark smudge in the distance. A hillock of ice? No, that would

Center: Scott working on the winter quarters at Cape Evans in October, 1911; photo by Herbert G. Pointing. The hut built by the British team at the foot of Mount Erebus was around fifteen meters long and seven and a half wide. According to Scott, it was "the most comfortable home one could imagine."

Top left: The sailing ship Terra Nova *took the British explorer Robert Falcon Scott to Antarctica to attempt the conquest of the South Pole in open competition with the Norwegian Roald Amundsen. Having reached the Polar ice-cap, Scott's team intended to proceed on sleds hauled by Siberian ponies.*

Top right: The monotony of winter life at Cape Evans was occasionally interrupted by parties. Scott's birthday menu on the 6th of June, 1911, included seal soup, roast mutton, asparagus, chocolate and an "immense cake," all washed down with cider and liqueurs. Scott is seated at the head of the table.

Left: In this photograph, taken aboard the sailing ship Terra Nova, one can see a number of the expedition members exercizing the Siberian ponies. The ponies were confined in narrow stalls and suffered from the rolling of the ship and the privations of the long sea voyage. By the time they reached Antarctica they were already in poor condition.

Opposite bottom: This photo taken by Pointing on the 26th of November, 1910, aboard the Terra Nova, shows Captain Lawrence Oates inspecting the ponies. The animals, confined in narrow stalls, suffered from the rolling of the ship on the long sea voyage and reached, Antarctica in poor condition. The frostbitten Oates deliberately disappeared into a blizzard so as not to hinder his companions during the return from the Pole.

Right: A cave within an iceberg: the surreal profile of the opening frames of Scott's ship Terra Nova, anchored in the frozen sea; photo by Herbert G. Pointing, taken in January, 1911. Pointing, a professional photographer and traveler, spent just a single season in Antarctica. Considering the prohibitive conditions in which he had to work, his photographs are of exceptional technical and aesthetic quality. He also made a documentary film, among the best ever shot in Antarctica.

be impossible. The Britons' suspicions were confirmed when, an hour later, they found the remains of an abandoned camp. Amundsen! All their efforts had been in vain. For a moment Scott was overcome by the inhuman monotony of the landscape. The Pole was nothing more than "a horrible place, and the thought of having struggled so to reach it without even the boast of priority is frightening!" Perhaps had Scott known of Amundsen's success, he would not have risked his life and those of his companions. In their depression the men began to feel the weakness accumulated over the previous long weeks. They had to move quickly: the brief southern summer was about to finish. The first days of the return march were relatively easy: the wind blew from over their shoulders, pushing the sleds rigged with improvised sails. Then the weather suddenly changed, and a violent storm engulfed the expedition. Scott decided to pitch camp. Oates and Evans began to suffer the first symptoms of frostbite. Scott's diary recorded increasingly brief marches. The reduced visibility obliged the men to make prolonged stops and made it difficult to navigate from one depot to the next. It was becoming colder and colder as each day passed, and food supplies were running short. The meager rations were no longer sufficient to replace the body heat lost due to the incessant windchill, and the men's woollen clothing proved unsuited to the extreme conditions as it froze solid. At the end of January, Wilson strained a tendon during a fall, and a few days later Scott himself slipped on the ice and injured his back. "We'll laugh about this if we make it back alive." he wrote, "Wilson's leg is much better, but the slightest strain

could compromise his convalescence; as for Evans' fingers." At last the explorers reached the Beardmore Glacier. After seven terrible weeks they left the plateau and Scott began to nurture some hope once again. The cold was now less intense and Wilson took advantage to collect a number of fossils. The respite did not last long: Sunday, the 11th of February was "a disastrous day." Confused by the dazzling reflections off the snow, Scott found himself trapped in a deep labyrinth of crevasses that were only overcome at the price of unheard of labors. A week later Evans fell into a semi-conscious state: he was found kneeling on the ice, his eyes dull, and his hands exposed and frozen. He died a few hours later. The survivors continued their march across the Ice Shelf, hampered by the powdery snow and ever close to complete exhaustion. Early in March the temperature dropped to -40°: the dreaded Antarctic winter was setting in. On the 17th of February, Oates left the tent in the middle of a snowstorm saying "I'm just going out for a while." They all knew he was gone forever. Wilson, Bowers, and Scott made another attempt to advance: the next depot was just over a dozen miles away. On the 21st of March, they were brought to a halt by an appalling storm.

It was no longer possible to go on, and there was no hope of a rapid improvement in the weather. In their small tent, with no fuel with which to warm themselves, the men lay in their sleeping bags and waited to die. There they were found, eight months later, by an expedition sent to search for them. The last page in Scott's diary was dated 29th March: "The storm is worsening... each day we prepare to march toward the depot just 11 miles away, but outside the tent, the conditions remain terrible. We no longer have any hope; we will resist to the end, but I realize that we are becoming ever weaker and death cannot be far away. It is painful, but I do not think I can write anything else."

Left: Scott and his companions taking advantage of a pause to refresh themselves. In this photo, taken by Oates, Evans, Bowers, Wilson, and Scott (from the left) can be recognized.

Bottom: The expedition's advance party posing in front of one of the three motorized sleds used by the British explorers. Scott took this photograph on the 22nd of October, 1911. The motorized sleds broke down a few days later, even though they had been tested in the Alps.

Left: The winter quarters of the British expedition were described by Scott in enthusiastic terms: apart from the personal bunks and the meeting room, the base housed a well equipped darkroom, a meteorological station, and physics, and biology laboratories. The suitably restored hut is now a historical monument.

Center: Music was a pleasant diversion for Scott's men during the interminable wait at the base camp. In this photo, one of the perplexed sled dogs approaches the gramophone.

Bottom: A familiar scene of polar exploration, the repose of the exhausted sled dogs at one of the temporary camps. The British expedition took along 30 dogs and 17 ponies acquired specially in Siberia.

289

Top: The discovery they had been beaten to the Pole by Amundsen was a severe blow to Scott and his team, here posing for the ritual photo at the Pole on the 18th of January, 1912. The return journey was a torment for the exhausted British team: the first to fall by the wayside was Evans, followed by Oates. The tragedy was completed on the 29th of March: the lifeless bodies of Scott and his companions were only found eight months later by a rescue team, just a few hours march from the nearest food dump.

Center: Scott's team photographed while hauling a sled loaded with equipment and provisions across the desolate surface of the Antarctic plateau: each man hauled around 176 lbs. The prolonged efforts in adverse weather conditions eventually proved fatal.

Bottom left: This photo illustrates the special polar clothing used by Scott's team. The British explorer himself is seen here.

Bottom right: "If we had survived," wrote Scott in his last message, "the story of the suffering, the energy and the courage demonstrated by my companions would have warmed the heart of every Englishman. These rough notes and our remains will speak for us, but surely a great and wealthy nation like our own will take care of those who were dear to us and will provide for them."

Dogs and Horses

Ill fortune undoubtedly played a part in the tragedy of the British expedition. Scott had no help from Lady Luck: both on the outward and the return journeys, his progress was obstructed by dreadful weather conditions. The intense cold and blizzards slowed the group drastically, to the point where they were eventually brought to a halt just a few kilometers from the depot that may have saved them. This, however, is not enough to explain Amundsen's triumph. In reality the crucial factor, the difference between success and failure, was the choice of their respective means of transport. Amundsen believed in his dogs, while Scott relied on Siberian ponies even though they had not been successful on previous expeditions. The ponies proved to be unable to bear the gelid Antarctic temperatures and the furious blizzards. Even before the expedition had reached the Antarctic plateau, while they were still on the Ross Ice Shelf, the ponies had begun to die one by one. The survivors were slaughtered to alleviate their distress just 434 miles from the point of departure. From that moment Scott and his companions were obliged to haul their sleds themselves, depleting reserves of energy of which they were subsequently to be in desperate need. Moreover, the horses had to be fed on hay, with all the inherent logistical complications, while the dogs could be fed on the meat of their companions slaughtered during the march. As if this were not enough, a pony is far heavier than a dog and is exposed to a greater risk of sinking into the snow: the pressure per square centimeter imposed by the hooves of a pony (around 2 pounds) is four times greater than that imposed by a sled dog. There were moments in which Scott had to adapt the men's snowshoes to the ponies' feet in order to cross the icy crust of the Ice Shelf. Undoubtedly the British team would have disapproved of the cruel strategy of slaughtering the dogs as soon as they had served their purpose, but they inevitably had to put down their own ponies. There was also another factor, however. Scott firmly believed in the strength of the human will: he saw the fact that they hauled their sleds themselves as a heroic that increased the moral quality of the enterprise. In his words, "no raid

completed with dogs can match the wonderful sentiment experienced by men overcoming difficulties, suffering, and danger by virtue of their own strength." This philosophy, applied to the endless Antarctic desert, cost him his life. Amundsen was much less romantic: Nansen and Peary's journeys had demonstrated that a successful polar expedition was based on two fundamental factors: the use of survival techniques and sled dogs. Before departing, he acquired around a hundred of the best dogs, bringing them from Greenland and concerned himself personally with their well-being. He had special kennels constructed on the *Fram* that protected the animals from the equatorial temperatures to which they were not accustomed and insisted that their rations should be of the best quality. The dogs ate like the men, or vice versa. Thanks to such precautions, the animals reached the Bay of Whales in excellent condition, and Amundsen rapidly succeeded in establishing a closely spaced line of depots. During the journey to the pole, the dogs allowed him to maintain an extremely high average speed — over 18 miles per day — and to return to base in good health and before the onset of the bad weather. His was undoubtedly the winning choice.

Top: In spite of the fact that for over half a century dogs had been the most popular means of hauling sleds on polar expeditions, Scott had no faith in their abilities. The British team brought only a few teams to Antarctica, and only used dog sleds for secondary logistical duties and brief excursions close to the base.

Above: The Siberian ponies proved unsuited to the severe Antarctic temperatures, and the difficulties of the terrain. The last of the exhausted animals were put down just 434 miles from the point of departure.

Everest, the world's highest mountain, rises dramatically on the border between Nepal and Tibet. In the years following the First World War, no less than 13 expeditions attempted to reach the summit from the Tibetan side, but without success. Everest became an obsession for British climbers, and its conquest a question of national pride. In 1949, Nepal opened its frontiers to Europeans, and the following year a French party reached the summit of Annapurna, breaking the psychological 26,400 feet barrier. In 1953, a British expedition led by John Hunt established a camp at the foot of Everest: thanks to the help of oxygen and backed up by a massive operation, Edmund Hillary and the Sherpa Tenzing Norgay conquered the summit. Their victory concluded 32 years of incessant attempts. A few months later, a German team planted their flag on the summit of Nanga Parbat, and in 1954 an Italian team climbed K2. Within just a few years all the major Himalayan peaks had succumbed to the assaults of the Europeans Mountain climbing, which began as a form of exploration, was then transformed into a sport.

ON TOP OF THE WORLD: HILLARY AND EVEREST

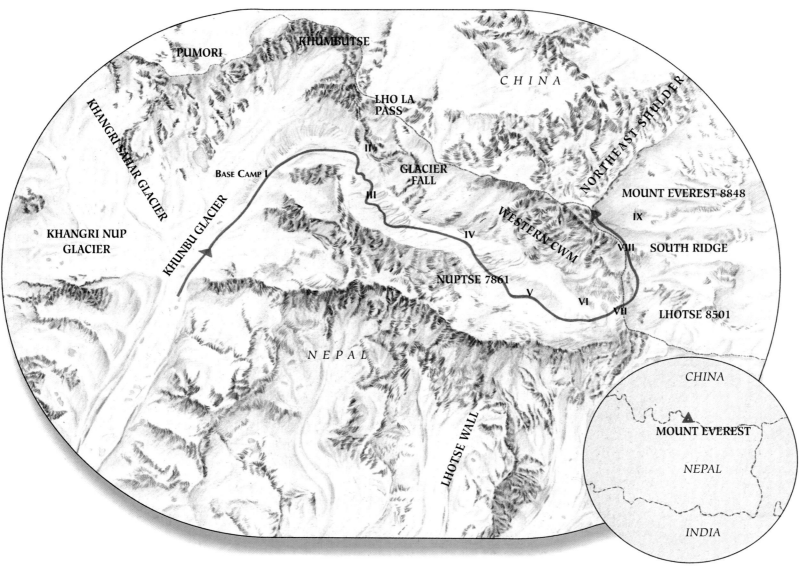

"Sir, I have discovered the highest mountain in the world!" The excited claim made by the Bengalese employee failed to disturb the poise of Andrew Waugh, the director of the geodetic Survey of India: the trigonometric survey of the Himalayas had been going on for some years, in spite of the logistical difficulties and the distance separating the Indian plains from the remote northern frontier of Nepal. In 1852, successive triangulations established the height of peak IV as it was called in the topographical index, as 29,172 feet. Waugh wanted to baptise the mountain with the name of Sir George Everest, his illustrious predecessor: the local name Chomolunga (Goddess Mother of the Land) referred to the entire massif rather than that particular peak. Thus, Everest appeared on the maps of Asia, taking over from Chimborazo as the "roof of the world."
The mountain is found in the heart of the Himalayas, a region closed to Europeans and inaccessible for over half a century. In 1904, British troops invaded Tibet, and for the

first time, Everest attracted the attention of the Royal Geographical Society and the Alpine Club: mountain climbing, when motivated by scientific aims, was a form of exploration in its own right, a noble activity worthy of public support. In 1919, an Everest committee was formed, and under its aegis no less than 11 expeditions attempted to climb the mountain from the Tibetan side over the next three decades. Everest proved to be a tough nut to crack. Its summit appeared unapproachable, and the mountain itself appeared to have something of the infernal about it: interminable walls of ice, precipitous slopes exposed to howling winds, and blizzards were the order of the day. Beyond a certain altitude every step was an immense effort and climbers' minds became less lucid. The first victims were claimed by the mountain in 1924: Mallory and Irvine reached 28,050 feet before being engulfed by a furious storm. They were never to be seen again and their bodies were never found. The tragedy

failed to dent the determination of the British climbers, who stubbornly continued to make attempts on the summit. Everest was the British climbers' mountain, just as Nanga Parbat was the Germans' and K2 the Italians'. When Nepal opened up its borders to Europeans in 1949, hopes of a successful ascent were revived. The South Face appeared more practicable, less windy, and was illuminated by the sun from very early in the morning. This last factor allowed very early departures from the camps. The following year, a French expedition conquered the summit of Annapurna I, breaking the psychological barrier of the 26,400 foot peaks. The Everest Committee set to work with renewed energy, and in 1951, Eric Shipton identified a possible route to the summit across the unexplored Western Cwm, a deep channel that climbed from the Khumbu glacier up to the base of the Lhotse wall. Shipton considered that from there it would be relatively easy to reach the South Col separating the Lhotse from the Everest pyramid. Everything depended on the successful negotiation of the 1,980 feet high "ice-cascade": a labyrinth of serracs and crevasses in continual movement, the only access route to the Western Cwm. The expedition organized in 1953 had but a single objective: to take at least two men to the summit of Everest. The organization was entrusted to John Hunt, an army officer, who prepared the assault on the mountain as if it were a military exercise. His work consisted of meticulous pyramidal planning whereby collective effort would transport tons of rations and equipment ever higher up to the last camp directly on the South Crest at an altitude of 28,050 feet. The expedition's equipment included specially designed boots, two kinds of tent, extendible aluminium ladders, warm but lightweight

clothing, radio gear, and even a 2 in. mortar to clear the slopes of potential avalanches. In particular, Hunt decided to use oxygen respirators "on a far wider scale than before, a decision which proved to be one of the keys to the success of the expedition." The selection of the climbers depended largely on nationality: the primary requirement, apart from the climbing expertise, was possession of a British passport. It was only later that it was decided to open the expedition to participants from the Commonwealth countries and the Nepalese Tenzing Norgay, who in previous years, had accompanied a Swiss expedition to within 1000 feet of the summit. Tenzing was a Sherpa, and was accustomed to high altitudes. He was 39 years old and an experienced mountaineer. He was joined in

that a route had to be found and roped across the serracs of the "ice cascade." Working in shifts, the teams of Sherpas (34 men) then transferred all the necessary material up to Camp IV at an altitude of over 19,800 feet. After three weeks' hard work, the first phase of Hunt's program had been completed, in spite of the technical difficulties posed by the terrain and the almost daily snowfalls. In the meantime, other groups had been sent to scout ahead as far as the 3,960-foot high and very steep Lhotse wall. The high altitude began to take its toll, making every effort that much more fatiguing: many men fell ill, and those few still in good health were obliged to forego their rest periods. Time was short as Hunt wanted everything ready for the middle of May so as to take full advantage

Left: This photo shows Hillary and Tenzing pausing for refreshment. The preparations and the approach march toward the summit were extremely arduous. In three weeks of incessant labor and in spite of the virtually daily snowfalls, 34 Sherpas transferred three tons of material from base camp to an altitude of over 19.800 feet.

Right: Tenzing and Hillary checking their equipment before heading for the South Col at 26,334 feet. Hillary, born in 1919 at Auckland in New Zealand, was 34 years old when he reached the summit of Everest. In 1958, he completed the first crossing of the Antarctic from the McMurdo Strait (near the Ross Ice Shelf) to the Weddell Sea. He returned to Nepal in the seventies to take part in a nature conservation program in close collaboration with the local people.

the group by two New Zealanders, George Lowe and Edmund Hillary. The latter had already accompanied Eric Shipton on his reconnaissance trip to the Western Cwm, giving proof of his "demonic energy" and notable technical expertise. His file described him in a few words: "a tall, thin professional beekeeper from Auckland." The average age of the group was around thirty, with Hunt being the only member over forty. All except two of the group had already climbed in the Himalayas. Backed up by 350 porters, the expedition left Katmandu on the 10th of March, 1953: the approach march through the Nepalese hills was slow but pleasant. Fifteen days later, the column reached the Buddhist monastery of Thyangboche at an altitude of 11,880 feet on a rocky spur dominating the valley of the Dudh Kosi, the "River of Milk" that drains the Everest massif. After a brief period of acclimatization, Hunt had the base camp established on the Khumbu glacier at 18,150 feet. The expedition's bulky baggage (all three tons of it) had to be transported up to the entrance to the Western Cwm, which meant

of the brief season of good weather between the last of the winter storms and the beginning of the monsoon in early June. Without the aid of oxygen, Lowe spent ten days on the Lhotse wall, cutting steps into the ice and setting up fixed ropes to provide a safe access route to the South Ridge. Thanks to his remarkable stamina, everything was ready by the 20th of May, right on schedule. Two groups were to attempt the final assault from Camp VIII on the desolate saddle of ice between the Lhotse and the Everest pyramid. The first, composed of Evans and Bourdillon, had in reality an explorative mandate: only in the case of favorable atmospheric conditions would they have proceeded to the summit. In the case of failure, Hillary and Tenzing, making use of an intermediate camp, would have left on the second attempt. On the 22nd of May, the last team of Sherpas reached the South Ridge with 660 pounds of equipment, mostly oxygen bottles. Three days later, Evans and Bourdillon set off. During the first afternoon, they reached Everest's South Peak at 28,275 feet: in front of them rose the profile of the rib leading to the summit, three hours of difficult climbing on ice and rock. The two men were exhausted and their supply of oxygen was running very low. They realized that they would not be able to make the summit and decided to turn back. Hunt listened to their report with apprehension: the South Crest appeared to be full of difficulties and the summit was perhaps not quite as close as they had hoped. That same day, a violent gust of wind battered the camp. Hillary and Tenzing, locked into their tent, had to delay their departure by 24 hours. At last, on the morning of the 28th of May, the weather turned fine again and the two men, preceded by Lowe and a pair of Sherpas, set off along the rib leading to the South Peak. Having reached the established spot at 28,182 feet, the support group turned

steeply on either side, "impressive and rather frightening". All was now dependent on the condition of the snow. Had it have been friable there would have been little hope of success. Hillary mechanically cut the first step and was relieved to find that the snow held. They could now proceed slowly but surely, and the weather conditions continued to stay fine. The last obstacle, a buttress of solid rock several feet high, was cleared without problems, and from there on it was a case of cutting step after exhausting step. Then, suddenly, Hillary realized that the crest ended brusquely in a rounded cap of snow. Before his eyes, the mountains of Nepal and Tibet stretched away to the horizon. They had reached the summit of Everest. "My first reaction was one of relief," wrote Hillary, "relief at not having

Left: Hillary and Tenzing about to leave the South Col to establish Camp IX at 28,182 feet. From there they launched their final assault on the summit. During the last stage of the climb, the two men used oxygen gear weighing 29 pounds.

back, and Tenzing and Hillary pitched their tent on a narrow, snow-covered ledge. That night Hillary slept fitfully. What awaited them beyond the South Peak? Would the weather have been favorable? When they emerged from their tent at 6:30 the next morning, the sky was clear and the wind that had blown up to a few hours earlier had died down. The oxygen they had consumed during the night had allowed the two men to recuperate, and they felt fit and ready. In silence, they began climbing the razor sharp frozen crest. Far away, 16,170 feet below them, they could make out the Thyangboche monastery and the lower valleys sparkling in the rarefied air. The snow was powdery: the men sank knee-deep, and Hillary realized that their lives were hanging by a thread. An accidental fall, a banal slip and everything would be over in a split second. At a certain point he asked Tenzing whether it was worth continuing in those conditions: "As you like" was the Sherpa's terse response. By 9 o'clock they had reached the South Peak, the point where Evans and Bourdillon had turned back. The ridge dropped away

any more steps to cut, crests to cross, drops to clear." No photograph could possibly do justice to the emotion of the moment: Hillary was the first man to gaze upon that surreal landscape, the only European to have reached the highest point on the Earth. It was 11:30 on the 29th of May, 1953. Tenzing dug a hole in the snow, burying his offerings to the spirit of Chomolungma. Perhaps the Goddess Mother of the Land would have enjoyed the chocolate. The climbers remained on the summit for a quarter of an hour before carefully beginning their descent. Everest had finally been conquered, but the victory left an ambiguous taste. The expedition had resolved no geographical problems, nor had it carried out any scientific research. What was it then that had pushed the British team to the summit of the world's highest mountain? Hunt's response was much the same as Mallory's laconic comment before he lost his life on the mountain thirty years earlier, "because it's there."

Right: Sherpa Tenzing Norgay on the summit of Everest, posing for the ritual photograph with the flags of Great Britain, the United Nations, Nepal, and India. Tenzing was then 39 years of age and had a remarkable breadth of high altitude climbing experience: the previous year, with a Swiss expedition, he had come within just 825 feet of the summit of Everest.

The conquest of the North and South Poles early in the twentieth century could be said to be the symbolic end to the discovery of the Earth. Europe had exported its model of civilization throughout the planet, from the remotest Pacific islands to the vast continental expanses of Africa and America. Certain regions, the most isolated and uninhabitable, were perhaps still relatively unexplored, but none were completely unknown.

The world's last secrets appeared to have been revealed. More recently, however, extraordinary technological developments have opened new horizons. Rather ironically, it was from rational thought that the new epic explorations were to derive. Ever more sophisticated and highly developed machinery reawakened interest in objectives that, until that moment, had been relegated to the status of impractical dreams: the submarine abysses, outerspace, and the very bowels of the Earth.

MODERN EXPLORATION

Above and right: Pannemaker's illustrations for Verne's From the Earth to the Moon *show the "projectile" forerunner of the modern spaceship. The novel forms part of the monumental series of* Voyages extraordinaires *across the known and unknown worlds that anticipated for a century, the most remarkable conquests of science and technology.*

In 1930, when William Beebe and Otis Barton designed their bathysphere, virtually nothing was known of the submarine world. Diving beyond a certain depth presented a series of apparently insoluble problems linked to the lack of oxygen and the extreme variations in pressure lethal for human beings. The bathysphere, a metal shell no more than a meter and a half in diameter, had walls thirty-eight centimeters thick and, suspended from a steel cable, could be lowered into the sea from a support ship. In 1934, Beebe and Barton descended into the waters off Bermuda, reaching a depth of 906 meters. Their enterprise marked the beginning of the systematic exploration of the oceans. In 1953, a Swiss scientist, Auguste Piccard, invented the bathyscaph, based on an ingenious system of floodable tanks and ballasts, which allowed the craft to move independently. Seven years later, the suitably perfected bathyscaph touched the

Top: In the over sixty volumes of the Voyages extraordinaires, *Jules Verne conjured up infinite stories inspired by progress, giving rise to a literary genre that still enjoys great success, science fiction. This illustration is taken from a contemporary edition of "Around the Moon."*

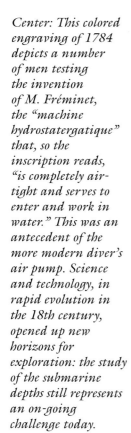

Center: This colored engraving of 1784 depicts a number of men testing the invention of M. Fréminet, the "machine hydrostatergatique" that, so the inscription reads, "is completely air-tight and serves to enter and work in water." This was an antecedent of the more modern diver's air pump. Science and technology, in rapid evolution in the 18th century, opened up new horizons for exploration: the study of the submarine depths still represents an on-going challenge today.

298

Bottom: The first submersibles, constructed in wood and equipped with rudimentary hand-powered propellers, like the one in this illustration, were conceived during the Italian Renaissance. It was not until the late 18th century that the designs had practical applications as warships: the submarine built in 1776 by the American David Bushnell was equipped to lay mines below the keels of enemy ships.

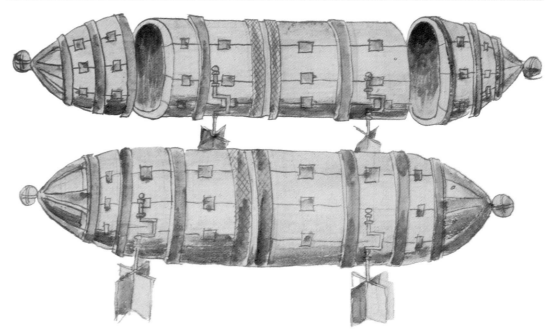

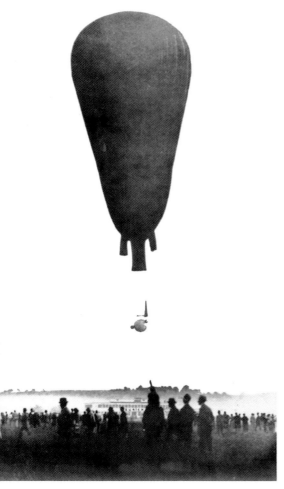

Above: Within the ambit of his studies on cosmic rays and the ionized strata of the atmosphere, Auguste Piccard designed a balloon with a pressurized cabin that contained a laboratory for the observation of the stratosphere. In the photo, a flight in August, 1932.

Bottom left: The image shows the delicate moment when the bathyscaph Trieste *enters into the water. In 1960, the bathyscaph touched bottom in the Mariana Trench, a depth of 35,970 feet.*

Top right: After the stratosphere, the submarine depths: Auguste and Jacques Piccard in the bathyscaph Trieste *at Castellammare di Stabia, Italy, in 1953.*

Bottom right: In this picture taken in the interior of the vessel, Jacques Piccard and Don Walsh can be seen shortly before the historic dive that was made possible by a system of floodable tanks and ballasts.

bottom of the Mariana Trench in the Pacific, 35,970 feet below the surface. From then on progress has been constant and oceanographic research has benefited from ever more sophisticated technology: modern submersibles are equipped with mechanical arms capable of taking samples of the seabed, electronic analysis systems, and powerful searchlights. The latest technology has also made a significant contribution to archaeology, and the theory of plate tectonics, which suggested the process of continental drift and has been backed up by scientific proof. Many of the oceans' mysteries have been solved, and veritable underwater laboratories are executing fascinating research programs studying the geology and the flora and fauna of the depths. Serious obstacles still have to be overcome, however, and the achievement of future objectives is more than ever dependent on the development of new technology.

The most important exploration of the present century has taken place in outerspace. On the 20th of July, 1969, an American astronaut was the first man to set foot on the Moon, thus realizing one of the wildest fantasies of the writer Jules Verne, who over a hundred years earlier, had described with remarkable precision a similar trip. The American space program had been inaugurated around a decade earlier, somewhat behind that of the Russians. As early as 1957, the Soviet

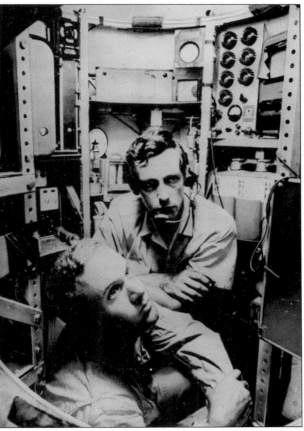

Top: The Swiss physicist and engineer Auguste Piccard working, together with his son Jacques; the two scientists are checking the drawings for the bathyscaph Trieste.

Center: This photo shows the bathyscaph Trieste *flying the US and Swiss flags as she re-enters the port of San Diego in California after a dive. Piccard's oceanographical research led to a series of discoveries that have revolutionized modern science.*

Bottom: This photograph taken in London in 1972 shows a reunion of some of the most important figures in modern exploration. In the center is Jacques Piccard, the designer of the bathyscaph Trieste *that descended to the bottom of Challenger Deep in the Mariana Trench, a depth of 35,970 feet. On the left is the Norwegian Thor Heyerdahl who in 1947, sailed his balsa raft* Kon-Tiki *across the Pacific ocean from Peru to* Polynesia *and in 1970 left Morocco aboard* Ra II, *a boat constructed of bound papyrus reeds, landing on the American coast two months later. His voyages demonstrated the extraordinary capacity for exploration of the ancient civilizations, offering interesting new hypotheses for historical research. On the right is the astronaut Neil Armstrong, the first man to set foot on the surface of the moon in July, 1969.*

Left: The submersible Ben Franklin designed by Jacques Piccard in 1968 for the Grumman Aerospace Corporation, has allowed numerous oceanographic research projects to be carried out. It can house six persons for six weeks. In this photo, a triumphant arrival in New York.

Right: Jacques Piccard aboard the small submersible F. A.-Forel. Launched on the 8th of January, 1979, this vessel is equipped with electronically controlled arms for the taking of samples and the manipulation of various accessories. She can house 3 persons for a maximum of 3 days.

scientists had launched an artificial satellite, and four years later Yuri Gagarin, aboard a Vostock spaceship, successfully completed the first orbit around the Earth. The enterprise had an enormous impact on public opinion, giving a great boost to the image of the Soviet Union. Stimulated by the Cold War, the space race, with the conquest of the moon as the final goal, was well and truly underway. In 1962, NASA also launched a man into space, John Glenn. While the Russians were working on the creation of satellites specially designed for lunar exploration, the Americans launched their Apollo program. After numerous preliminary missions, on the 16th of July, 1969, the Saturn 5 rocket, 281 feet high and weighing 3,000 tons, lifted off from Cape Kennedy in Florida, heading for the moon. The Apollo 11 spacecraft carrying the lunar module (known as the LEM) housed Neil Armstrong, Edwin Aldrin, and Michael Collins, all three technical experts and experienced astronauts. The Saturn 5 completed all the various phases of the outward journey without incident, and on Saturday, the 19th of July, the Apollo

Above: The whole world was able to watch, thanks to live television coverage, the Apollo 11 adventure, the first in a series of six moon landing missions. Apart from demonstrating the *extraordinary technical capabilities of the US space agency compared with that of the Soviet Union — it should not be forgotten that in 1969 the two super powers were locked into the Cold War —* *the trips to the moon were opportunities for countless scientific experiments. The astronauts collected geological samples, took photographs, and performed field tests. Today the results obtained are usually* *considered to be out of proportion with the expense of the program. This does nothing to alter the fact that almost thirty years on, the lunar landing is an event that we all still know about or remember.*

command module entered lunar orbit.
A few hours later, the LEM crewed by two
men, left the Apollo and began its descent
towards the Sea of Tranquillity, the site
chosen for the first lunar landing. The
LEM touched down softly on the dusty
surface of the moon. Earlier than planned,
Armstrong opened the hatch and ventured
outside. He slowly descended the ladder to
the lowest rung and paused for a few
seconds: that last small step was in his
words "one giant leap for mankind."
The thirty-eight year old Neil Armstrong
was the first human being to set foot on
another planet. The TV images were
transmitted throughout the world, vastly
amplifying the impact of the event.
The Americans sent another five missions
to the moon, accumulating an enormous
quantity of data on the geological
structure and physical characteristics
of the Earth's satellite. The exploration
of space is proceeding with increasingly
ambitious objectives: in 1982 two Russian
astronauts spent no less than 211 days
aboard the *Salyut 7* orbital space station.
Space flights have gradually become
routine procedures.

*Above: The Stars
and Stripes, "flying"
above the surface of
the Sea of
Tranquillity. This
was the* Apollo 11
*mission: the lunar
module* Eagle *can be
seen on the left, while
the astronaut is
Edwin Aldrin,
photographed by Neil
Armstrong. Below the
flag are clearly visible
footprints left by the
first explorers to land
on the satellite.*

*Bottom: The Earth as
seen beyond the lunar
horizon. In the
foreground is the*
Apollo 11 *lunar
module carrying
Aldrin and
Armstrong.*

Top: On the 3rd of November, 1994, the space shuttle Atlantis *took off carrying five American astronauts and a European scientist, Jean-François Clarvoy. The shuttle contained a complete laboratory for scientific experiments. Man now has infinite new methods of studying the world and exploring the unknown.*

Bottom left: The space shuttles have represented a revolution in aerospace technology: for the first time, an "aircraft" could be launched into orbit like a rocket and then complete a normal landing so that it could be reused for further missions. This photo shows the Challenger *in July, 1983 with its cargo-hold doors open.*

Bottom right: This photo shows an episode during the Challenger's *mission on the 19th of June, 1983. During this mission, a number of satellite systems were set up, and this photograph taken during the operation shows part of the American shuttle's cargo hold.*

In 1977 NASA sent two probes, Voyager 1 and Voyager 2, toward the outer limits of the solar system. Two years later Voyager 1 came within 483,600 miles of Jupiter. The analysis of the data sent back to Earth confirmed the existence of a dense gaseous atmosphere and revealed the nature of some of its mysterious satellites. Voyager 2 approached the rings of Saturn formed from myriad fragments of ice, before heading on towards Uranus and Neptune. The appearance of the two most distant planets in the solar system of which virtually nothing was known reserved significant surprises for the scientists: one of the satellites of Uranus, Miranda, revealed unusual features such as deep valleys, high mountains, and curious zig-zag incisions, the signs of mysterious geological phenomena which are still unexplained. The new space programs have entered what was once the realm of science fiction and there are those who believe that we are only at the beginning of inter-planetary travel.

Top: This spectacular photo shows the astronaut Bruce McCandless Jr. on mission 41-B set against the vastness of the blue ocean while working outside the shuttle. The astronaut is attached to the shuttle via the anchorage of the mechanical arm.

Bottom: The astronauts Bruce McCandless Jr. (left) and Robert L. Stewart working within the cargo hold of the space shuttle Challenger as she orbits the Earth during mission 41-B.

INDEX

BIBLIOGRAPHY

Introduction - Eric J. Leed, *The mind of the traveler: from Gilgamesh to global tourism*, Basic Books, United States of America, 1991

Chapter 1 - Salza A., *Ominidi; uomini e ambienti 3 milioni di anni fa*, Giunti, Florence, 1989
- Richard E. Leakey, *The Making of Mankind*, The Rainbird Publishing Group Lts, London, 1981

Chapter 2 - Ferro G., Caraci I., *Ai confini dell'orizzonte*, Mursia, Milan, 1979
- AAVV (edited by G. Mokhta), *Storia generale dell'Africa*; vol. 2: *L'Africa antica*, Editoriale Jaca Book spa, Milan, 1988. Translation by Ada Ceruti from "Historie générale de l'Afrique: vol. 2: Afrique ancienne", UNESCO, 1980
- R. Carpenter, *Beyond the Pillars of Hercules*, Universal-Tandem Publishing Co, 1986
- R. Burgard, *L'expedition d'Alexandre et la conquête de l'Asie*, Gallimard, Paris, 1937
- Finzi C., *Ai confini del mondo*, Newton Compton Editori s.r.l. per la Casa del Libro F.lli Melita, Rome, 1982

Chapter 3 - A. t'Serstevens, *Les précurseurs de Marco Polo*, Arthaus, Paris, 1959
- N. Ohler, *Reisen im Mittelalter*, Artemis Verlag, München un Zürich, 1986
- Polo M., *Il Milione*, introduction and notes by M. Ciccuto, including an essay by A. Burgess, Rizzoli, Milan, 1981
- Zorzi A., *Vita di Marco Polo veneziano*, Rusconi, Milan, 1982
- G. di Rubruck, *Voyage dans l'empire mongol*, Payot, Paris, 1985
- J.-P. Drège, *Marco Polo et la Route de la Soie*, Gallimard, Paris, 1989

Chapter 4 - Ferro G., *I navigatori portoghesi sulla via delle Indie*, Mursia, Milan, 1974
- John H. Parry, *The Age of Reconnaissance*, World, London, 1963
- John H. Parry, *The Discovery of the Sea*, Dial Press, London, 1974
- E. Axelson, *Dias and his successors*, Saayman & Weber, Cape Town, 1988
- E.G. Ravenstein, *A Journal of the First Voyage of Vasco da Gama*, Hakluyt Society, London, 1898
- B. Landstrom, *La via delle Indie*, Martello, Milan, 1964
- R. Humble, *The Seafarers-The Explorers*, Time-Life Books Inc., United States, 1978

Chapter 5 - T. Todorov, *La conquête de l'Amerique. La question de l'autre*, Editions du Seuil, Paris, 1982
- S.E. Morison, *The European Discovery of America. The Southern Voyages*, Oxford University Press, New York, 1974
- AAVV (edited by P. Collo e P.L. Crovetto), *Nuovo Mondo. Gli italiani 1492-1565*, Einaudi, Turin, 1991
- M. Lequenne, *Christophe Colomb admiral de la mer Océane*, Gallimard, Paris, 1991

Chapter 6 - A.P. Newton, *Travel and Travellers of the Middle Ages*, Kegan Paul, trench, Trubner & Co., London, 1926
- I. Battuta, *Voyages* (introduction et notes de Stéphane Yerasimos) 3 vol., Maspero, Paris, 1982
- Foccardi G., *I viaggiatori del Regno di Mezzo*, Einaudi, Turin, 1992
- J. Neddham, *Science and Civilisation in China*. Vol. 4, Cambridge U. Press, Cambridge, 1971

Chapter 7 - O.H.K. Spate, *The Spanish Lake*, University of Minnesota Press, Minnesota, 1979
- Pigafetta A., *Il primo viaggio intorno al mondo*, (edited by C. Manfroni), Istituto Editoriale Italiano, 1956
- E. Roditi, *Magellan of the Pacific*, McGraw-Hill, 1972

Chapter 8 - R. Wright, *Continenti rubati*, Casa Editrice Corbaccio, Milan, 1993
- William H. Prescott, *History of the Conquest of Mexico and History of the Conquest of Peru*, New York, Random house, Modern Library, 1843; 1847
- B. de Las Casas, *Historia de las Indias*, 3 voll., Fondo de Cultura Economica, México, 1951
- B. Diaz del Castillo, *Historia vertadera de la conquista de la Nueva España*, 2 voll., Porrúa, Mexico, 1955
- G. P. Hammon and Agapito Rey, *Narratives of the Coronado Expedition*, New Mexico Press, 1940
- C.W. Ceram, *Der erste Amerikaner. Das Rätsel des vor-kolumbischen Indianers*, Rowohlt Verlag GmbH, Reinbek bei Hamburg, 1972
- K. Romoli, *Balboa of Darien*, Doubleday & Co., 1953

Chapter 9 - R. Collinson, *The Three Voyages of Martin Frobisher*, Hakluyt Society, 1867
- Barbieri G., *I viaggi di Giovanni e Sebastiano Caboto*, Cassa di Risparmio di Verona, Vicenza, Belluno and Ancona, Verona, 1989
- B. Lehane, *The Seafarers-The Northwest Passage*, Time-Life Books Inc., United States, 1981
- S.E. Morrison, *The European Discovery of America: The Northern Voyages*, Oxford University Press, 1971
- A.E. Nordenskjöld, *La Vega; viaggio di scoperta del Passaggio Nord-Est tra l'Asia e l'Europa*, F.lli Treves, Milan, 1882

Chapter 10 - J.C. Beaglehole, *The Journals of Captain James Cook on his Voyages of Discovery*, voll. 1,2,3, Cambridge University Press, 1955
- A. Villiers, *Captain James Cook*, Charles Scribner's Sons, 1967
- M. Sahlinsn, *Islands of History*, The University Chicago Press, Chicago, 1985
- G. Forster (edited by Nicolao Merker), *Viaggio Intorno al mondo*, Laterza, Bari, 1991
- J. François de Lapérouse, *Viaggio intorno al mondo sull'Astrolabe e la Boussole*, Rizzoli, Milan 1982
- O.H.K. Spate, *Paradise Found and Lost*, Pergamon Book Ltd., England, 1988
- Oliver E. Allen, *The Seafarers-The Pacific Navigators*, Time-Life Book Inc., United States, 1980

Chapter 11 - Victor W. Von Hagen, *South America, The Green World of the Naturalists*, Eyre and Spottiswoode, 1951
- A. von Humboldt, *Viaggio alle Regioni Equinoziali del Nuovo Continente*, 3 vol., (edited by Fabienne O. Vallino), Fratelli Palombi Editori, Rome, 1986
- A.e T. Seppilli, *L'esplorazione dell'Amazzonia*, UTET, Turin, 1964

Chapter 12 - J. Bakeless, *The Journals of Lewis and Clark*, New York, 1964
- Harold P. Howard, *Sacajavea*, University of Oklahoma Press, Norman, Publishing Division of the University, 1971
- E. Coues, *History of the Expedition under Lewis and Clark*, Dover Publication Inc., 1965

Chapter 13 - K. Fitzpatrick, *Australian Explorers, A selection from Their Writings*, Oxford University Press, 1958
- C.T. Madigan, *Crossing the Dead Heart*, Rigby, 1946
- W. Joy, *The explorers, Angus & Robertson*, 1974
- F. Clune, *Dig, Angus & Robertson*, 1944
- A. Moorehead, *Cooper's Creek, Harper & Row*, 1963

Chapter 14 - Migliorini E., *L'esplorazione del Sahara*, UTET, Turin, 1961
- E. Barth, *Travels and Discoveries in North and Central Africa*, Centenary edition in three volumes, Frank Cass & Co. Ltd., London, 1965
- P. Forbath, *The River Congo*, Newsweek Inc., 1977
- Robert I. Rotberg, *Africa and Its Explorers, Motives, Methods, and Impact*, Harvard University Press, Cambridge, Massachusetts; 1970
- T. Jeal, *Livingsone*, Pimlico, London, 1993
- R. Hall, *Stanley: an Adventurer Explored*, Collins, Glascow, 1974
- F. Galton, *Art of Travel*; a reprint of *The Art of Travel, or, Shifts and Contrivances Available in Wild Countries* (1872), David & Charles Ltd., Newton Abbot, Devon, 1971
- L. von Höhnel, *Discovery of Lakes Rudolf and Stefanie* (reprint 1894), 2 volumes, Frank Cass & Co. Ltd. London, 1968
- M. Brown, *Where Giants Trod*, Quiller Press, London, 1989
- Surdich F. (edited by), *L'esplorazione italiana dell'Africa*, Il Saggiatore, Milan, 1982
- William J. Burchell, *Travels in the Interior of Southern Africa* (reprint from the original edition of 1822-24), The Bathcworth, London, 1953

Chapter 15 - G. Sandberg, *The exploration of Tibet*, Cosmo Publications, Delhi, 1987
- C. Allen, *A Mountain in Tibet*, Futura Publications, London, 1983
- L. Miller, *On the Top of the World; Five Women Explorers in Tibet*, The Mountaineers, Seattle, 1984
- S. Hedin (edited by Pier Paolo Faggi), *Il lago errante*, Cierre Edizioni, Verona, 1994
- S. Hedin, *Central Asia and Tibet*, 2 volumes, Tiwari's Pilgrims Book House, Kathmandu, 1991 (first edition 1903)

Chapter 16 - Dainelli G., *La gara verso il Polo Nord*, UTET, Turin, 1960
- E.E. Reynolds, *Nansen*, Penguin Books, Great Britain, 1949
- H. Johansen, *With Nansen in the North*, London, 1899
- Robert E. Peary, *The North Pole*, Frederick A. Stockes & Co., 1910
- P. Emile Victor, *Chiens de traineaux*, Flammarion, Paris, 1974
- Umberto Nobile, *La tenda rossa*, Mondadori, Milan 1970

Chapter 17 - R. Falcon Scott, *Scott's Last Expedtion*, John Murray, London, 1923
- Hugh R. Mills, *The Siege of the South Pole*, Alston Rivers, London, 1905
- Zavatti S., *L'esplorazione dell'Antartide*, Mursia, Milan, 1974
- R. Amudsen, *La conquista del Polo Sud*, Treves, Milan, 1913
- L.P. Kirwan, *A History of Polar Exploration*, N.W. Norton, 1960

Chapter 18 - J. Hunt, *The Ascent of Everest*, Hodder & Stoughton, 1953
- T. Hagen, *Mount Everest*, Oxford University Press, 1963
- I Cameron, *Mountains of The Goods*, Time Books International, New Delhi, 1987
- Reginald H. Phillimore, *Historical Records of the Survey of India*, Dhera Dun, India, 1945

Chapter 19 - O. Barton, *The Word Beneath the Sea*, Longmans Green & Co., 1953
- R. Lewis, *Appointment on the Moon*, The Viking Press, 1969

General works
- AAVV, *Great Adventure that Changed our World*, The Reader's Digest Association Inc., 1978
- AAVV (General Editor M. Gavet-Imbert), *Explorers and Exploration*, Guinnes Publishing Ltd., Enfield, Middlesex, 1991
- Dainelli G., *La conquista della Terra*, UTET, Turin, 1954
- H. Wright & S. Rapport, *The Great Explorers*, Harper & Brothers, New York, 1957
- Daniel J. Boorstin, *The Discoverers*, London, 1984
- R.A. Skelton, *Explorers' Maps*, London, 1958
- R. Burton, R. Cavendish, B. Stonehouse, *Journeys of the Great Explorers*, The Automobile Association, Great Britain, 1992
- Zavatti S., *Dizionario degli esploratori*, Feltrinelli, Milan, 1967

ILLUSTRATION CREDITS

All the maps showing the routes followed by the explorers were compiled by Giancarlo Gellona.

1 Giovanni Sacrobosco. C. P.
2 top, left, Cristopher Columbus, Maritime Museum, Madrid. © Giovanni Dagli Orti.
2 top, center Details of the Map of South America in the Hydrographical Atlas by Fernan Vaz Dourado from 1571, Torre de Tombo Archive, Lisbon. © G. Dagli Orti.
2 top right, top Red-tailed parrot by Sidney Parkinson. © N.H.M.
2 top right center *Cicholospermum gilliurali* by Sidney Parkinson. © N.H.M.
2 top right bottom, *Simia ursina* in *Observations de Zoologie et d'Anatomie Comparée* by Alexander von Humboldt. © R.G.S.
2 center left, One of Columbus's caravels, Castello di Albertia, Genoa. P.C.
2 center right Naturalistic drawings in *Atlas du Voyage de La Pérouse.* P.C.
2 bottom left James Cook, portrait by Nathaniel Dance. © N.M.M.
2 bottom right The meeting between Cook's men and the inhabitants of Tahiti, Decorative Arts Library, Paris. © G. Dagli Orti.
3 top left Boat in *Atlas du Voyage de La Pérouse.* P.C.
3 top right Marco Polo, engraving from 1857. © F.S.N.
3 bottom left Explorer in the forest, engraving by J.B. Debret, 1834, Museum of African and Oceanic Arts, Paris. © G. Dagli Orti.
3 bottom right Magellano, Civic Museum, Seville. © Giancarlo Costa/Agenzia Stradella.
5 Portuguese navigator, Maritime Museum, Lisbon. © G. Dagli Orti.
7 top left Omphalos of Delphi, Museo of Delphi. © Agenzia Ricciarini.
7 top right Laetoli footprints, Tanzania. © John Reader/Science Photo Library/Grazia Neri.
7 bottom Footprint on the Moon. © NASA.
8 top Projection of the Earth by Giovanni Sacrobosco. P.C.
8 bottom Map of the World, in *Geographia* by Claudius Ptolemy, Marciana Library, Venice. © G. Dagli Orti.
9 Frontispiece of Gerard Mercator's *Atlas*, Biblioteca Alessandrina, Rome. © A. Ricciarini.
10 *Antorcha de la mer* by Nicolas Jansz Voogt, Amsterdam 1700, N.M.M. © A. Ricciarini.
10-11 Universal Hydrographcal Map by Hydrographical Waldseemüller in *Geographia.* P.C.
11 bottom Rhinoceros in *Storia degli animali* by Ulisse Alorovandi. © Agenzia Ricciarini.
12 Cranium Knm-er 1470. © Rim Campell/Bruce Coleman.
13 Cranium Knm-er 3733. © Camerapix.
15 top Arrow, El Fayum. © A. Ricciarini.
15 center Laetoli footsteps, Tanzania. © John Reader/Science Photo Library/Grazia Neri.
16 Viking ship, Oslo. © G. Veggi/A. White Star.
17 Hatshepsut, Museum of Cairo. © Jurgen Liepe.
18 top The queen of Punt, Museum of Cairo. © G. Dagli Orti.
18 bottom Hatshepsut, Dayr al-Bahari. © Alberto Siliotti.
19 top Relief from the temple of Hatshepsut, Dayr al-Bahari. © M. Bertinetti/A. White Star.
19 center left Relief from the Temple of Hatshepsut, Dayr al-Bahari. © Giulio Veggi/Archivio White Star.
19 center right Relief from the Temple of Hatshepsut, Dayr al-Bahari. © M. Bertinetti/Archivio White Star.
19 bottom Relief from the Temple of Hatshepsut, Dayr al Balah. © Idem.
20 top The Tarso boat, Archaeological Museum, Beirut. © G. Dagli Orti.
20 bottom Phoenician necklace in vitreous paste, Archaeological Museum, Cagliari. © A. Scala.
21 Punic fictile mask, Bardo Museum, Tunis. © Agenzia Ricciarini.
22 Ships arriving in the port of Santorini, National Archaeology Museum, Athens. © G. Dagli Orti.
23 Map of the North Atlantic, 15th century, C. Ptolemy, Plut. 30.3. © Biblioteca Medicea Laurenziana, Florence. Photographs courtesy of the Ministery of Cultural and environmental Resources.
24 top Bust of Alexander the Great, Acropolis Museum, Athens. © Archivio Scala.
24 bottom Mosaic of the battle of Issus, National Museum, Naples. © Araldo De Luca.
25 top The fleet of Alexander the Great along the Indus, Municipal Library, Reims. © A. Ricciarini.
25 bottom Alexander the Great riding an elephant, Limoges enamel, 16th century, Galdiano Museum, Madrid. © Agenzia Ricciarini.
26 top left Alexander the Great and his horse Bucephalos in *Cosmografia* by Julius Solinus. © G. Costa/Agenzia Stradella.
26 top right, Monsters, idem.
26 bottom Alexander the Great fighting against the turtles, in *Hagiography of Alexander the Great*, Royal Library, Brussels. © Idem.
27 Alexander the Great fighting against the six-handed men, idem.
27 bottom, Alexander the Great fighting against the men with animals' heads, idem.
28 top Alexander the Great passes the Tigris and the Euphrates in *De Rebus Gestis Alexandri Magni* by Curzio Rufo Quinto. Municipal Library, Reims. © Agenzia Ricciarini.
28 bottom Alexander in the Siwa oasis, in *De Rebus Gestis Alexandri Magni*, B.N.P. © F.S.N.
28-29 Alexander the Great's fleet after the high tide. Fr. 22547 Fol. 242. © B.N.P.
29 bottom left Alexander the Great exploring the undersea world, Fr. 9342 Fol. 182. © B.N.P.
29 bottom right Alexander fighting against the King of Poro, Fr. 22547 Fol. 219. © B.N.P.
30 top, Viking ship, Maritime Museum, Oslo. © Giulio Veggi/Archivio White Star.
30 center Viking vessel, Maritime Museum, Madrid. © G. Dagli Orti.
30 bottom Bas-relief with Viking ship, Historical Museum, Stockholm. © Idem.
31 Miniature with Viking ship. © F.S.N.
32 Map of the world by Fra Mauro Camaldolese, Biblioteca Marciana, Venice. © A. Ricciarini.
32 center Mappa Mundi, in the *Book of Psalms*, Ms-Add 28681. © B.L.
33 top Prester John and his court. © F.S.N.
33 bottom The death of Prester John, Fr. 2810 Fol. 27. © B.N.P.
34 left Giovanni da Pian del Carpine, engraving. © Jean Loup Charmet.
34 right The cynophaluses in the *Livre des Merveilles*, Fr. 2810 Fol. 188V°. © B.N.P.
35 left William of Rubruk. © Jean Loup Charmet.
35 right Franciscan monks gathering herbs, Biblioteca Augustea, Perouse. © G. Dagli Orti.
36 top Marco Polo, engraving, 1857. © F.S.N.
36 bottom right Piazza San Marco in Venice, miniature, 15th century, Condé Museum, Chantilly. © Agenzia Ricciarini.
36 bottom right Map of Asia and North America, Palazzo dei Dogi, Sala delle Mappe, Venice. © AKG Photo.
37 top Marco Polo's departure from Venice, in *Roman d'Alexadre* Ms. Bodl. 264 Fol. 218r. © Bodleian Library, Oxford.
37 bottom left Sugar merchant, in *Tractatus de Erbis*, Biblioteca Estense, Modena. © G. Dagli Orti.
37 bottom right Incense merchant, idem.
38 top Catalan Map, 1375. © B.N.P.
38 bottom The Polo brothers receiving the Tablets of Gold from Kublai Kahn, in the *Livre des Merveilles*, Fr. 2810 Fol. 3V°. © B.N.P.
39 bottom left Marco Polo in Tatar costume, Museo Correr, Venice. © G. Dagli Orti.
40 bottom The Chinsai Road, in the *Livre des Merveilles*, Fr. 2810 Fol. 67. © B.N.P.
40-41 Boat with exotic goods, in the *Livre des Merveilles*, Fr. 2810 Fol. 4. © B.N.P.
41 bottom left The men of the Great Khan conquer Cipangu. © Jean Laup Charmet.
41 bottom right The Great Khan involved in a commercial transaction, in the *Livre des Merveilles*, Fr. 2810 Fol. 29. © B.N.P.
42 top Fox hunters, B.N.P. © F.S.N.
42 center The inhabitants of the lands of the East, in the *Livre des Merveilles*, Fr. 2810 Fol. 14. © B.N.P.
42 bottom Pepper harvest, in the *Livre des Merveilles*, Fr. 2810 Fol.84. © B.N.P.
43 top Marco Polo departing for China, in the *Livre des Merveilles*, Fr. 2810 Fol. 86 V°. © B.N.P.
43 bottom The departure of Marco Polo, in the *Livre des Merveilles*, Fr. 2810 Fol. 76 V°. © B.N.P.
44 top The frontespiece of *Il Milione*, Spanish edition, 1503, Biblioteca Braidense, Milan. © G. Costa/Agenzia Stradella.
44 bottom Frontispiece of the first edition of *Il Milione*, National Library, Paris. © F.S.N.
45 top left Marco Polo on horseback, miniature, XV century, B.N.P. © A. Ricciarini.
45 right The oldest Portuguese edition of *Il Milione*, B.N.P. © G. Costa/Agenzia Stradella.
46 center The Portuguese fleet, miniature, 1513, Archivio della Torre de Tombo. © G. Dagli Orti.
47 top Detail from the Cantino map, Biblioteca Estense, Modena. © Archivio Scala.
47 bottom Henry the Navigator, Museum of Ancient Art, Lisbon. © G. Dagli Orti.
48 top Portuguese ship, Maritime Museum, Lisbon. © Idem.
48 bottom Portuguese ambassadors received by the King of Congo. © Jean Loup Charmet.
49 top Map of the African coast, Archivio della Torre de Tombo. © G. Dagli Orti.
49 bottom Cantino Map, B.M. © AKG Photo.
50 top Portuguese traders, Indian miniature, 16th-17th century. © Jean Loup Charmet.
50 bottom the port of Lisbon, engraving by Theodore de Bry. © AKG Photo.
51 Bartolomeo Dias, Maritime Museum, Lisbon. © G. Dagli Orti.
52 bottom Sea serpent, in *Icones animalium aquatilium* by Konrad von Gesner. © AKG Photo.
52-53 The Cape of Good Hope, in *Description de l'Afrique* by Olfert Dapper. © AKG Photo.
54 top left The departure of Vasco da Gama, The Academy of Science, Lisbon. © G. Dagli Orti.
54 top right Vasco da Gama, Museum of Ancient Art, Lisbon. © G. Dagli Orti.
55 left One of Vasco da Gama's ships, engraving, 1800. © AKG Photo.
55 right Vasco da Gama. © Agenzia Ricciarini.
56 Vasco da Gama's arrival at Calicut, Museum of Flemish Tapestries, Tournai. © G. Dagli Orti.
57 top View of Goa. © Portuguese National Photographic Archive Institute, Lisbon.
57 bottom Vasco da Gama with gifts for the king of Calicut, engraving, 1890. © AKG Photo.
58 top view of Macao, engraving by Theodore de Bry. © New York Public Library.
58 top right The port of Aden, Archivio Torre de Tombo. © G. Dagli Orti.
59 top Cabral at Porto Seguro, National History Museum, Rio de Janeiro. © G. Dagli Orti.
59 bottom Cabral in Brazil in *Livro das Armadas*, The Academy of Science, Lisbon. © Idem.
60 top The portolan of B. Agnese. © Fotoflash.
60 center Map of Africa *Tabula Terra Novae.* P.C.
60 The Portuguese conquest of Brazil, engraving by Theodore de Bry. © G. Dagli Orti.
61 The Portuguese in China, in *The travels of Fernão Andrae in China.* © Jean Laup Charmet.
61 bottom The port of Bantam. © Idem.
62 Portuguese trading ships in Japan, Museum Port Soares dos Reis. © A. Ricciarini.
63 top Pharmacist's shop, Castello d'Issogne, Valle d'Aosta. © G. Dagli Orti.
63 center, Nutmeg seller, Biblioteca Estense, Modena. © Idem.
63 bottom Cinnamon seller, Biblioteca Estense, Modena. © Idem.
64-65 Flying fish at sea, in *America Pars Quarta* by Theodore de Bry. © AKG Photo.
66 bottom left Christopher Columbus. © Civica Raccolta Stampe A. Bertarelli, Castello Sforzesco, Milan.
66 bottom right Christopher Columbus. © Idem.
67 top Columbus by Ghirlandaio, Pegli Maritime Museum, Genova. © G. Costa/A. Stradella.
67 center Request for money signed by Christopher Columbus. © Civica Raccolta stampe A. Bertarelli, Castello Sforzesco, Milan.
67 bottom Columbus, Civic Museum, Como. © F.S.N.
68 top Columbus's caravels, Maritime Museum, Madrid. © G. Dagli Orti.
68 bottom Columbus with Garcia Fernandez, Monastero della Rabida, Palos. © Idem.
69 top Columbus with the Franciscan monks at Granada, idem.
69 center Gold coin bearing effigies of the Spanish monarchs, National Archaeology Museum, Naples. © BIP Agenzia Ricciarini.
69 bottom Naval hourglass, Maritime Museum, Madrid. © Agenzia Ricciarini.
70 top Columbus' caravels, Castello di Albertia, Genoa. P.C.
70 bottom The departure of Columbus, engraving by Theodore de Bry. © AKG Photo.
70-71 Route of Columbus' first voyage, Monastero della Rabida, Palos. © G. Dagli Orti.
71 right Mutiny on the Santa Maria, engraving by Amati, 1890. © AKG Photo.
71 bottom Departure of the caravels, Monastero della Rabida. © G. Dagli Orti.
72 top The arrival of Columbus at Hispaniola, in *De Insulis Indie Inventis*, 1493. © AKG Photo.
72 bottom The arrival of Columbus in the Bahamas, engraving by Theodore de Bry. © Idem.
73 top Columbus' landfall at Guahani, engraving by Dioscoro T. de la Puebla Tolin. © Idem.
73 bottom The first Mass celebrated in America, Blanchard, Fine Arts Museum, Dijon, France. © G. Dagli Orti.
74 top The coastline of Hispaniola drawn by Columbus. © AKG Photo.
74 center Toscanelli's planisphere, National Library, Florence. © F.S.N.
74 bottom The Navidad colony on Hispaniola, in *De Insulis Indie Inventis*, 1493. P.C.
75 top Map of Hispaniola, in *Isolario* by B. Bordone, 1528. © G. Costa/Agenzia Stradella.
75 bottom Mappa Mundi, Martime Museum, Madrid. © F.S.N.
76 top The coat of arms of Columbus, in the *Book of Privileges*, Archive of the Indies, Seville. © G. Dagli Orti.
76 right Frontispiece of the *Book of Privileges*, Maritime Museum, Pegli. © Idem.
77 top Colombus before the Spanish monarchs painted by R.Balaca, 1874, National History Museum Buenos Aires. © Idem.
77 bottom left The Santa Maria, in *De Insulis Indie Inventis*, 1493. © AKG Photo.
77 bottom right One of Columbus's caravels in *De Insulis Indie Inventis.* P.C.
78 top left The arrest of Columbus, by Theodore de Bry. © G. Costa/A. Stradella.
78-79 top The death of Columbus, by B. Rementeira, The Columbus House-Museum, Valladolid. © G. Dagli Orti.
78-79 bottom Map drawn by Bartolomeo Colombo in 1505. © Civica Raccolta Stampe A Bertarelli, Castello Sforzesco, Milan.
79 top Autograph letter by Columbus to his son, Indies Archive, Seville. © G. Dagli Orti.
80 top The first encounter between Columbus and the Indians, by D.K. Bonatti. © AKG Photo
80 center top Caribbean warriors in *De Insulis Indie Inventis.* © Idem.
80 center bottom Tupinamba cannibalism, by Theodore de Bry. © Idem.
80 bottom Tupinamba cannibalism, engraving by Theodore de Bry. © Idem.
81 The discovery of America, by Cesare dell'Acqua Castello di Miramare, Trieste. © G. Dagli Orti.
82 Arab globe, History of Science Museum, Florence. © Emilio F. Simion/A. Ricciarini.
83 top Ibn Battutah. P.C.
83 bottom Map of the Mediterranean by al-Istakhri, National Library, Cairo. © G. Dagli Orti
85 left top Ottoman pilgrims on route to Mecca, miniature from Ottoman manuscript, Topkapi Palace library, Istanbul. © Idem.
85 bottom Map of the Red Sea and the Holy City by al-Idrisi, National Library, Cairo. © Idem
85 right Arab astrolabe, History of Science Museum, Florence. © Emilio F. Simion/Agenzia Ricciarini.
86-87 Islamic traveler, Ottoman miniature, Topkapi Library, Istanbul. © G. Dagli Orti.
87 top Astronomers in the Galata tower, 15th, University Library, Istanbul. © Idem.
87 bottom left Arab astrolabe, The History of Science Museum, Florence. © A. Ricciarini.
87 bottom right Caravan of Arab merchants, by al-Idrisi, 1237, Arabe 5847 Fol. 31. © B.N.P
88 top A Chinese cartographer, engraving, 1660. © The Bettmann Archive.
88 bottom Chinese compasses. © Jean Loup Charmet.
89 Chinese junks, 13th century. © The Bettmann Archive.
90-91 Planisphere by Giulio Alemi. P.C.
90 bottom Canton, K Top 116.23. © B.L.
91 top Chinese junk. © B.N.P.
91 center top Chinese junk. © G. Costa/Agenzia Stradella.
91 center bottom Chinese boat. © A. Ricciarini
91 bottom Enormous junk, B.M. © F.S.N.
92 The Victoria. © AKG Photo.
93 top Magellan, Civic Museum, Seville. © G. Costa/Agenzia Stradella.
93 bottom Charles V, by Bernard Van Orley, Musée de l'Ain, Bourg Eu Bresse. © G. Dagli Orti
94 top Tabula Magellanica, 17th. © Civica Raccolta stampe A. Bertarelli, Castello Sforzesco, Milan.
94 bottom Magellan's fleet off the Spice Islands, B.M. © F.S.N.
95 bottom World map by B. Agnese, 1538. P.C
96 top left The Strait of Magellan from the diaries of Pigafetta. © G. Costa/A. Stradella.
96 top right Map of South America, in *Atlante Idrografico* by Fernan Vaz Dourado Fol 13, Archivio Torre de Tombo, Lisbon. © G. Dagli Orti.
96 bottom The passage of Magellan through the strait, by Jan ven der Straet. © AKG Photo.
97 top Magellan sailing through the strait, engraving from 1880. © Idem.
97 bottom The astrolabe of Alphonse the Wise 13th century, Maritime Museum, Madrid. © A. Ricciarini.
98 and 99 Watercolors by Debeauchense, Nava History Service, Vincennes. © G. Dagli Orti.
100 top The Moluccas from the diaries of Pigafetta, Fr. 5650 Fol. 8210. © B.N.P.
100 bottom The Ladrone ISLANDs from the diaries of Pigafetta. © G. Costa/A. Stradella.
101 top left Magellan raising the cross in the Philippines. © The Bettmann Archive.
101 top right The Islands of Cebu and Maclan from Pigafetta's diaries. © G. Costa/A. Stradella
101 bottom The death of Magellan, engraving

from the 19th. © F.S.N.
102 bottom Gold boat, Muisca civilization, Museum of Gold, Bogotà. © G. Dagli Orti.
103 top Vasco Nuñez de Balboa, engraving, 16th century. © G. Costa/Agenzia Stradella.
104 top The Indians of the Darièn consigning gold to Balboa, by Theodore de Bry. © AKG Photo.
104 center The Balboa expedition's dogs, by Theodore de Bry. © Idem.
104 bottom Gold breastplate, Museum of Gold, Bogotà. © G. Dagli Orti.
105 top left Gold breastplate, Calima civilization, idem.
105 top right Gold breastplate, Tierradentro civilization, idem.
105 bottom Bartolomeo de Las Casas, Indies Archive, Seville. © Idem.
106 top Hernan Cortés, National Library, Madrid. © Agenzia Ricciarini.
106 bottom Gold breastplate, Regional Museum, Oaxaca. © G. Dagli Orti.
107 top Aztec mask in jade, Museo degli Argenti, Florence. © Archivio Scala.
107 bottom Montezuma, Museo degli Argenti, Florence. © Nimatallah/A. Ricciarini.
108 bottom The arrival of Cortés' ships in the Yucatan, in *Historia de la Indias* by Diego Duran, National Library, Madrid. © G. Dagli Orti.
109 top The meeting between Cortés and Montezuma, painted on copper by A. Solis from the 16th century, Museum of the Americas, Madrid. © Idem.
109 bottom Cortés with Diego Velazquez, idem.
110 top Cortés meeting the Tlaxcala Indians, in *Historia de la Indias*, National Library, Madrid. © Idem.
110 bottom The battle of Tepeaca, painted on copper by A. Solis, Museum of the Americas, Madrid. © Idem.
110-111 Map of Tenochtitlan, second letter by Cortés to Charles V, Museo de la Ciudad, Mexico City. © Idem.
111 bottom Map of Tenochtitlan, in *Civitates Orbis Terrarum* by Georgius Braun, 1594, National Library, Madrid. © Idem.
112 top left An Aztec prince, in *Historia de la Indias* by Diego Duran, National Library, Madrid. © Idem.
112 top right Feather fan from the treasure of Montezuma, Museum für Volkerkunde, Vienna. © Idem.
112 center Feather headress, idem.
112 bottom Exchange of jewels between Cortés and Montezuma, painted on copper by A. Solis, XVI century, National Library, Madrid. © Idem.
113 Cortés receiving tributes from Montezuma, idem.
114 Statue of Xochipilli, National Anthropology Museum, Mexico City. © Idem.
115 top left Statue of Coalticua, idem.
115 top right Statue of a warrior, idem.
115 bottom Aztec mask, Tempio di Mayor, Mexico. © Idem.
116-117 Aztec divinities and scenes of life, in *Historia de las Cosas de Nueva España* by Bernardino de Shagun, Biblioteca Medicea Laurenziana.
118 Montezuma taken prisoner, painted by A. Solis, Museum of the Americas, Madrid. © G. Dagli Orti.
119 left The Aztecs attacking Montezuma's palace, Museum of the Americas, Madrid. © F.S.N.
119 right Don Pedro Alvarado, Colonial Museum of Antigua. © G. Dagli Orti.
120 top left Francisco Pizarro, Versailles. © Idem.
120 top right Ritual knife, Chimù civilization, The Gold Museum, Lima. © Idem.
121 top Funerary mask, idem.
121 bottom left The "Pact" for the discovery of Peru, engraving by Theodore de Bry, 1596. © G. Costa/Agenzia Stradella.
121 bottom right Atahualpa. © G. Dagli Orti.
122 Atahualpa taken prisoner by by Pizarro, engraving by Theodore de Bry, 1596. © Idem.
123 top Atahualpa taken prisoner by Pizarro in the *Atlante dell'America del Sud* by G. Ferrario, 1827, Ajuda Library, Lisbon. © Ajuda Library.
123 bottom left Diego de Almagro seeking his fortune, by T. de Bry. © G. Costa/A. Stradella.
123 bottom right The killing of Atahualpa in *The History of the Spanish Conquests* by G. Poma de Ayala, 1587. © G. Dagli Orti.
124 top Gold and turquoise earring, Mochica civilisation, Mujica Gallo Foundation. © Idem.
124 bottom Female figure in gold, Tolita civilisation, Bruning-Lambaeyque Museum, Perù. © Idem.
125 top Gold vase, Chimù civilization. Museum of Gold, Lima. © Idem.
125 bottom Gold crown, idem.
126 top The conquest of Cuzco, engraving by Theodore de Bry, 1596. © Idem.
126 bottom Gold cat, Chimù civilization, Bruning, Lambaeyque Museum. © Idem.
126-127 View of Cuzco, engraving by Braun-et-Hogenberg, Biblioteca Marciana, Venice. © Idem.
128-129 Funerary mask, Chimù civilization, Museum of Gold, Lima. © Idem.
130 top Francisco Vasquez de Coronado, by Peter Hurd. © Roswell Museum and Art Center.
130 bottom The Spaniards attacking a Zuñi pueblo, by Jan Mostaert, XVI century. © Tom Haartsen - Frans Hals Museum.
131 top Map of South America, in *Atlante Idrografico*. A. Torre de Tombo. © G. Dagli Orti.
131 bottom Coronado at the head of his armada, by Charles M. Russell. © Amon Carter Museum.
132 *Septentrionalum Terrarum*, in Mercator's *Atlas*, 1599. P.C.
133 top Giovanni Caboto, portrait by Manescardi, Palazzo Ducale, Venice. © G. Dagli Orti.
133 bottom Sebastiano Caboto. © AKG Photo.
134 top Jacques Cartier. © G. Costa/A. Stradella.
134 center Cartier ascending the St. Lawrence, Decorative Arts Library, Paris. © G. Dagli Orti.
134 bottom Cartier and his men in Canada, map by Pierre Descaliers, B.M. © AKG Photo.
135 top Martin Frobisher, by Cornelius Ketel. P.C.
135 bottom Frobisher's expedition in the Hudson Strait. © The Bettman Archive.
136 top Henry Hudson aboard the Half Moon, 19th century. © AKG Photo.
136 bottom Henry Hudson with the son of Collier. © The Tate Gallery Publications.
137 top left John Ross. © R.G.S.
137 top right Eskimos by David Havell in *The voyage of Sir John Ross*, Naval History Service, Vincennes. © G. Dagli Orti.
137 center Ross' team with the inhabitants of the Artic by John Sackheouse, idem.
137 bottom The pink ice, drawing by John Ross. © AKG Photo.
138 top William Parry by S. Reynolds. © R.G.S.
138 center left Eskimo sunglasses used by Parry. © Idem.
138 center right Vitus Bering. © The Bettman Archive.
138 bottom John Franklin, portrait by William Derby, N.M.M. © AKG Photo.
139 top The Arctic Council by Stephen Pearce. © National Portrait Gallery, London.
139 center left The tragedy of the Franklin expedition by W. T. Smith, N.M.M. © AKG Photo.
139 center right Franklin's last message. © Agenzia Ricciarini.
139 bottom The MacClintock expedition finds Franklin's mound. © F.S.N.
140 McClure's ship in the pack-ice, by Creswell. © R.G.S.
141 top left McClure in polar gear, photograph by Captain Inglefiel. © G. Costa/A. Stradella.
141 top right Roald Amundsen. © Canterbury Museum, Christchurch.
141 center Amundsen with a number of his crew members. © Norsk Polar Institute.
141 bottom The Gjöa arriving in Alaska. © Idem.
142 top The crew of the Vega, in *The Vega, Journey of Discovery of the Northeast passage between Asia and Europe*. P.C.
142-143 The Vega and the Lena, idem.
143 bottom left Below decks on the Vega, idem.
143 bottom right Officers' saloon aboard the Vega, idem.
144 left View of Wardoe from 1594, idem.
144 right The winter clothing worn by the crew of the Vega, idem.
145 left The Vega, idem.
145 right Portrait of Nils Nordenskjöld. P.C.
146 center Walruses, in *The Vega, Journey of Discovery of the Northeast Passage between Asia and Europe*. P.C.
146 bottom Crab, idem.
146-147 Portraits of the Ciuktci, idem.
147 bottom left The Ciuktci fishing, idem.
147 bottom right Engraved bone, idem.
148 top Barents and Rijp in *The Third Voyage of the Dutchmen* by Gerrit de Veer. P.C.
148 center Willem Barents. P.C.
149 Polar Chart by Barents in *Waerachtighe Beschrijvinghe van die Seylagien*. © AKG Photo.
150-151 Barent's men carrying timber, idem.
150 bottom The shelter constructed by Barents, idem.
151 top Barent's men skinning a bear, idem.
151 center Preparing for the departure, idem.
151 bottom Barent's men cutting a passage through the ice, idem.
152 top The clothing of the first polar explorers. © Freddie Markham/R.G.S.
152 center Sailors hauling a boat across the polar icecap. © A.H. Markham/R.G.S.
152 bottom A ship hauled through a channel in the ice. © Agenzia Ricciarini.
153 top An Anglo-American expedition on the ice, 19th. © Frank Hurley/R.G.S.
153 bottom Ernst Shakleton and Frank Hurley sitting in front of their tent. © R.G.S.
154 top A wooden octant made in Britain in 1750, L'Antiquaire de Marine, Paris. © G. Dagli Orti.
154 bottom Dutch ships in the Pacific, map from 1622 by H. Gerritsz, B.N.P. © A. IGDA.
155 top Abel Tasman with his family, painted by Jacob Gerritsz Cuyp, Rex Nan Kivell Collection NK3. © National Library of Australia.
155 bottom Tasman's fleet at Tonga. © Algemeen Rijksarchief, The Hague.
156 top Map of the eastern Pacific. © A. IGDA.
156 bottom left The meeting with the Maoris, from Tasman's diary. © Algemeen Rijksarchief.
156 bottom right, Tasman receiving the Tongan notables. © Idem.
157 bottom The port of Batavia, Tropen Museum, Amsterdam. © L. Lange/Koninklijk Instituut voor de Tropen.
158 top James Cook, N. Dance. © N.M.M.
158 bottom James Cook with the people of the Pacific by E. Philips Fox, N.M.M. © A. Ricciarini.
159 top left Map of the New Discoveries made in *Altante Zatta*, 1776, Venice. © M. Bertinetti/Archivio White Star.
159 top right Harrison's chronometer n.4. © N.M.M.
159 bottom Navigational instrument by Harrison. © N.M.M.
160 top The forging of an anchor, plate from the *Encyclopédie*. P.C.
160 bottom Plans of the Endeavour. © G. Costa/Agenzia Stradella.
161 The *Endeavour* in Table Bay. © G. Costa/Agenzia Stradella.
162 top left Sidney Parkinson. © N.H.M.
162 top right *Cicholospermum gilliurali* by Sidney Parkinson. © Idem
162 bottom The camp at Botany Bay, watercolor by T. Gosse from 1770. © N.M.M.
163 top Red-tailed parrot by Parkinson. © N.H.M.
163 center Coprifoglio della Nuova Zelanda di Sidney Parkinson. © Idem.
163 bottom left Scorpion fish, idem.
163 bottom center Grouper, idem.
163 bottom right Scorpion fish, idem.
164 top The Society Islands in *Atlante Universale*. © Civica Raccolta Stampe A. Bertarelli, Castello Sforzesco, Milan.
164-165 The Island of Tahiti, idem.
165 top The breadfruit tree by Parkinson. © N.H.M.
165 bottom The inhabitants of Tahiti, Library of Decorative Arts, Paris. © G. Dagli Orti.
166 Tahitian dancers in *A Voyage to the Pacific Ocean* by James Cook. © di G. Costa/A. Stradella.
167 top Preparations for a human sacrifice, from a sketch by John Webber. © Agenzia Stradella.
167 center left Ataongo. © Idem.
167 center right Otoo, by W. Hoolges. © Idem.
167 bottom A moai in Oreihi in the *Galleria Universale di Tutti i Popoli del Mondo*, 1841, Venice. © F.S.N.
168 Map of New Zealand in the *Atlante Universale*. © Civica Raccolta Stampe A. Bertarelli, Castello Sforzesco, Milan.
168 top right The inhabitants of New Zealand in ancient and modern costume by Giulio Ferrario. © M. Bertinetti/Archivio White Star.
169 top Maori fortress, idem.
169 bottom Conflict betwen natives and Cook's men, drawing by Bernati. © Idem.
170 Map of New Holland in the *Atlante Universale*. © Civica Raccolta Stampe A. Bertarelli, Castello Sforzesco, Milan.
170 bottom Aboriginal family in the *Galleria Universale di Tutti i Popoli del Mondo*. © F.S.N.
171 top The animals observed by Cook, by Biasioli. © M. Bertinetti/Archivio White Star.
171 center Military and hunting weapons. © idem.
171 bottom A warrior and a woman of New Zealand in the *Galleria Universale di Tutti Popoli del Mondo*. © F.S.N.
172 top Cook's ships taking on water. © G. Costa/Agenzia Stradella.
172 bottom The *Resolution* and the *Adventure* in Matavai Bay, painted by William Hodges, N.M.M. © G. Costa/Agenzia Stradella.
173 War canoes at Tahiti, painted by William Hodges. © M. Bertinetti/Archivio White Star.
174 top Map of the Friendly Islands, in the *Atlante Universale*. © Civica Raccolta Stampe A. Bertarelli, Castello Sforzesco, Milan.
174 bottom Cook's landfall at Middleburg Eua, Library of Decorative Arts, Paris. © G. Dagli Orti.
175 top Map of the New Hebrides and New Caledonia, in the *Atlante Universale*. © Civica Raccolta Stampe A. Bertarelli, Castello Sforzesco, Milan.
175 bottom Conflict with the inhabitants of Erromaga, N.M.M. © G. Costa/A. Stradella.
176 Map of the Sandwich Islands, in *Atlante Universale*. © Civica Raccolta Stampe A. Bertarelli, Castello Sforzesco, Milan .
177 top Cook conversing with the native chiefs. © M. Bertinetti/Archivio White Star.
177 center Masked native, in *A Voyage to the Pacific Ocean*. © G. Costa/A. Stradella.
177 bottom The death of Cook, by John Webber. © G. Dagli Orti.
178-179 Table of the discoveries of Cook and La Pérouse, engraving by Grasset De St. Sauveur. © Idem.
180 top Jean François de Galaup de La Pérouse, in *Atlas du Voyage de La Pérouse*, 1798. P.C.
180 bottom La Pérouse receiving his orders from Louis XVI, by Nicolas Mansiaux, Museum of Versailles. © G. Dagli Orti.
180-181 The Astrolabe and the Boussole Mowee Bay, in *Atlas du Voyage de La Pérouse*. P.C.
181 bottom Blackbird from French Port, by Duché de Vancy, idem.
182 top The inhabitants of Concepción, idem.
182 bottom The inhabitants of Manila, idem.
183 Frontispiece of the Atlas, idem.
184 Pirogue at French Port, idem.
185 top Japanese vessel, idem.
185 center Fishing boat at Manila, idem.
185 bottom Japanese vessel, idem.
186 and 187 top left Botanical specimens drawn by the Prévosts, idem.
187 top A bird of northern California drawn by the Prévosts, idem.
187 bottom Californian partridges, idem.
188 Map of Easter Island, idem.
189 top and center Survey of the moai, idem.
189 bottom The academics measuring a moai, idem.
190-191 Map of French Port, idem.
191 The boats swamped by the ebb tide at French Port, idem.
192 top La Pérouse arriving at Macao, idem.
192 bottom Chinese ferry, idem.
193 top Map of Massacre Bay on the Island of Manoua, idem.
193 bottom The attack on the boats by the inhabitants of Western Samoa, idem.
194 top Alexander von Humboldt at 81 years of age. © AKG Photo.
194 center *Rhexia speciosa* in *Voyage aux Regions Equinoziales* by Humboldt. © N.H.M.
194 center right and left Butterflies in *Observations de Zoologie et d'Anatomie Comparée* by Humboldt. © N.H.M.
194 bottom *Simia melanocephala*, idem.
195 top Humboldt at 34 years of age, Museo de la Ciudad, Mexico City. © G. Dagli Orti.
195 center Humboldt's signature on a letter to Professor Loper. © AKG Photo.
195 bottom Humboldt in his Berlin studio, by Edward Hildebrandt, 1856. © R.G.S.
196 Map of the Orinoco, Casiquiare and Rio Negro in *Atlas Geographique et Physique du Nouveau Continent*, 1814. © N.H.M.
196 center Humboldt and Aimé Bonpland in the Venezuelan jungle, by E. Ender, Akademie der Wissenschaften, Berlino. © AKG Photo.
197 Humboldt and Bonpland ascending the Orinoco by Ferdinand Keller, 1877. © AKG Photo.
198 top A balsa on the Guayaquil, from a sketch by Humboldt, in *Vue des Cordilleres*. © AKG Photo.
198 bottom *Gymnotus electricus* drawing by Humboldt, in *Receuil d'Observations de Zoologie*, 1911. © AKG Photo.
199 top *Simia leonina* in *Observations de Zoologie et d'Anatomie Comparée* by Humboldt. © N.H.M.
199 center *Simia ursina*, idem.
199 bottom Proteus or mexican salamander, idem.
200 top Butterflies, idem.
200 center Humboldt in a painting by Georg Friedrich Weitsch of 1809.
200 bottom left Beetles, in *Observations de Zoologie et d'Anatomie Comparée*. © N.H.M.
200 bottom and 201 top *Melastoma coccinea, Rhexia stricta, Rhexia grandiflora, Melastoma racemosa*, idem.
201 bottom right *Augulea superba*, water-colour by Pierre Jean François Turpin in *Voyage aux Regions Equinoziales* by Humboldt. © AKG Photo.
202 left Humboldt and Bonpland at the foot of Chimborazo, by Friedrich Georg, 1810, Staatliche Schösser und Gärten, Berlino. © Idem.
202-203 Topographical map of the Andes in *Geographie des Plantes Equinoxiales*, Paris. © Idem.
203 bottom left Chimborazo seen from Riobamba. © G. Costa/Agenzia Stradella.
203 bottom right The volcanoes of Turbaco seen from Cartagena, Naval History Service, Vincennes. © G. Dagli Orti.
204 top Rope bridge at Penipe, aquatint by Marquois Bouquet in *Vue des Cordilliéres*, Paris. © AKG Photo.
204-205 Humboldt and Bonpland close to the Cajambé volcano, Naval History Service, Vincennes. © G. Dagli Orti.

LEGEND

B.L.	British Library
B.M.	British Museum
B.N.P.	Biblioteque Nationale, Paris
P.C.	Private collection
F.S.N.	Fototeca Storica Nazionale
N.H.M.	Natural History Museum
N.M.M.	National Maritime Museum
R.G.S.	Royal Geographical Society